Stephani

SPANISH ENGLISH

POCKET DICTIONARY

SPANISH ENGLISH

POCKET DICTIONARY

Houghton Mifflin Company

Boston New York

Printed in the United States of America

CONTENTS

A SHORT GUIDE TO SPANISH GRAMMAR

Stress

The two fundamental rules of stressing are:

1. Words ending in a *vowel*, in *n* or in *s*, are stressed on the next to the last syllable, e.g. *Pedro, Rosita, examen, Carlos.*

2. Words ending in *any other consonant* are stressed on the last syllable, e.g. *señor, Madrid, nacional.*

If a word does not conform with these two rules, an acute accent (') is written over the vowel of the stressed syllable, e.g. *médico, capitán, inglés.*

In some words a written accent serves only to distinquish words which are pronounced alike, but have a different meaning, e.g. *si* (if), *sí* (yes); *te* (you), *té* (tea), *¿dónde?* (where?) *donde* (where).

Syllables

The vowels *i* and *u* may occur unstressed before or after another vowel, in which case they do not form a separate syllable and are pronounced like English *y* and *w* respectively: *muy bien* (very well), *bueno* (good), *automóvil* (automobile); cf. *continuo* (continuous), *continúo* (I continue), *continuó* (he or she continued).

A single consonant, two letters representing a single sound (like *ch, ll, qu, rr*), or a consonant followed by *l* or *r*, belong to the next syllable: *na-cio-nal, mu-cha-cho, ca-rro, do-ble, Ma-drid.*

Sounds and Spelling

Spanish Letter Sounds	Their pronunciation, like English
a	*a* in father: *Málaga*
b	1. *b*, at the beginning of group or after *m* or *n: bomba* 2. *v*, between two vowels: *estaba*
c	1. *c* in cat, before *a, o, u* or a consonant: *café, clima* 2. *th* in thin, before *e* and *i: Cervantes, nación*
ch	*ch* in child: *muchacha*
d	1. *d* in dog: *dan* 2. softer than 1., like *th* in with: *nada* 3. at end of word softer than 2., or even omitted: *hablad*
e	*e* in they or *e* in bed (if a consonant follows in the same syllable: *enero, negro, respuesta*
f	*f: África*
g	1. *g* in go, before *a, o, u* or a consonant: *Congo, grande* 2. *h* in host, before *e* or *i: Argentina, página*
h	is silent, only written: *La Habana*
i	*i* in machine, each: *China*
j	*h* in host: *José*
k	*k* (=qu): *kilómetro*
l	*l: Irlanda*
ll	*lli* in billiard: *Antillas*
m	*m: Méjico*
n	*n: banana*
ñ	*ni* in onion: *España*
o	*o* in or (very short): *Bogotá*
p	*p: Pepito*
qu	*k* in king: *química*

r 1. *r* in road (trilled *r*): *sombrero*
2. at end, weak: *cantar*
3. at beginning trilled like *rr*: *río*

rr *r* (doubled): *perro*

s *s* in so: *sistema*

t *t*: *patata*

u *oo* in boot: *uno*
(it is silent in the syllables *que, gui*): *Miguel, guía*

v 1. *b*: *Valencia*
2. *v*, (like Spanish *b*, see there): *uvas*

x 1. *x*: *taxi*
2. *s* in so, before a consonant: *extra*

y *y* in yes: *mayo*
i in been, in the word: *y (and)*

z *th* in thin: *zoólogo*

The Articles

1. *The Definite Article*

Before a masculine noun
s. **el** *muchacho* the boy
p. **los** *muchachos* the boys
Before a feminine noun*
s. **la** *muchacha* the girl
p. **las** *muchachas* the girls
Before adjectives with abstract meaning
s. **lo** *hermoso* the beautiful
s. **lo** *útil* all that is useful

2. *The Indefinite Article*

Before a masculine noun
s. **un** *libro* a book
p. **unos** *libros* some books
Before a feminine noun
s. **una** *mesa* a table
p. **unas** *mesas* some tables

*The form *el*, *un* is used before a feminine noun beginning with the stressed sound *a (ha)*; *el agua fresca* the fresh water; *un hacha afilada* a sharp axe.

The Noun

Gender

Nouns belong either to the masculine or the feminine gender.

Nouns ending in *-o* are masculine: *el libro*, the book
Exceptions: *la mano*, the hand; *la (el) radio*, the radio; *la foto*, the photo

Nouns ending in *-a*, *-d*, *-ez* are feminine: *la ventana*, the window; *la ciudad*, the town; *la nuez*, the nut
Exceptions: *el día*, the day; *el tranvía*, the tram; and nouns of Greek origin ending in *-ma;* e.g. *el problema*, the problem; *el sistema*, the system

No special rules for nouns ending otherwise: *m. el cohete*, the rocket; *el lápiz*, the pencil; *el papel*, the paper. *f. la clase*, the class; *la crisis*, the crisis; *la imagen*, the image

The natural gender is maintained in nouns like:
el amigo friend
la amiga (girl)friend
el inglés Englishman
la inglesa Englishwoman
el pianista pianist
la pianista pianist (woman)
el guía guide
la guía guide (woman)
el hermano brother
la hermana sister
(*los hermanos* brothers and sisters; *los padres* the parents; *los abuelos* the grandparents)

The Plural of Nouns

The plural of nouns is formed by adding

—S

to nouns ending in unstressed vowel or stressed -é: *el libro* the book, *los libros* the books; *el poeta* the poet, *los poetas* the poets; *el café* the coffee, *los cafés* the coffee (-houses)

—ES

to nouns ending in a consonant: *el tren* the train, *los trenes* the trains; *la edad* the age, *las edades* the ages

Nouns ending in *-es*, and family names remain unchanged: *el lunes* Monday, *los lunes* on (every) Monday; *el análisis* analysis, *los análisis* the analyses; *López, los López* the family López

Note: The letter *c* is replaced by *qu*, and *z* by c, before *-es*: *el frac: los fraques* (dress-coat); *el lápiz: los lápices* (pencil).

The Declension of Nouns

The single cases are formed by prepositions.

The Accusative. Nouns denoting persons form the accusative with *a*; *veo a mi amigo* I see my friend; *no vemos al profesor* we don't see the professor (al = a + el). — Nouns denoting inanimate objects have the same form in the nominative and the accusative: *pongo el libro en la mesa* I put the book on the table.

The Genitive. It is formed by *de*: *el cuarto de las señoritas* the room of the girls; *el sombrero del médico* the doctor's hat (del = de + el).

The Dative is formed by the preposition *a*; *doy una manzana al muchacho* I give the boy an apple; *escriben muchas cartas a los padres* they write many letters to their parents.

The Adjective

The attributive as well as the predicate adjectives agree with their nouns. Adjectives and nouns are inflected alike; e.g. *he comido una naranja muy bonita* I've eaten a very good orange; *estas naranjas son muy bonitas* these oranges are very good.

Adjectives ending in *-o*, *-án*, *-or* have a special form in *-a* for the feminine*: *largo, larga* long; *largos, largas* *holgazán, holgazana* lazy; *holgazanes, holgazanas* *madrugador, -a* early riser; *madrugadores -as* *mejor* better, *mejores* better.

Most other adjectives have the same forms for both genders: *verde* green, *verdes; fácil* easy, *fáciles*

But the adjectives denoting a nationality have the form in *-a* for the feminine: *alemán, alemana; alemanes, alemanas – francés, francesa; franceses, francesas – español, española; españoles, españolas*

Note: *el inglés* the Englishman *or* the English language; *la inglesa* the Englishwoman; *los ingleses* the English (men); *las inglesas* the English women.

Adjectives generally follow their noun: *la corbata azul* the blue tie.

Some adjectives standing before a masculine singular noun lose their final vowel or syllable:

bueno: un buen vino, a good wine

malo: mal tiempo, bad weather

grande: un gran palacio, a big palace

Santo: San Pedro, Saint Peter

primero: en el primer piso, on the first floor

*Except the irregular comparatives.

tercero: el tercer hombre, the third man

ciento: cien pesetas, a hundred pesetas

Comparison of Adjectives

Positive	Comparative	Superlative I (relative)	Superlative II (absolute)
largo long *larga*	*más largo* *más larga* longer	*el más largo* *la más larga* the longest	*larguísimo* very long
bueno good	*mejor* better	*el mejor* the best	*óptimo* very good, excellent
malo bad	*peor* worse	*el peor* the worst	*pésimo* very bad
grande great	*mayor* greater	*el mayor* the greatest	*máximo* very big or great
pequeño little, small	*menor* less smaller	*el menor* the least, the smallest	*mínimo* very little
alto high	*superior* higher	*el superior* the highest	*supremo* very high
bajo low	*inferior* lower	*el inferior* the lowest	*ínfimo* very very low
mucho much, many	*más* more	*lo más* the most	*muchísimo* very much
poco little	*menos* less	*lo menos* the least	*poquísimo* very little

Diminutives and augmentatives

Spanish nouns and adjectives may receive diminutive and augmentative suffixes.

The suffixes *-ito*, *-illo*, *-cito*, *-cillo* imply small size or affectionate interest: *Pedrito* little Peter; *chiquillo* kid; *mujercita* dear little wife; *camisas bonitas* nice and good shirts.

The more frequent augmentative suffixes are *-ón*, *-ote*, *-azo*, *-acho*, which give the meaning of large size or contempt: *la sala: el salón* hall; *la palabra: la palabrota* term of abuse; *grandote* very large; *la manaza* huge hand; *ricacha*, *ricachona* a (very) rich woman.

Pronouns

Personal Pronouns

The Nominative is used only when stressed: *Tú te quedarás, pero yo me iré*. You'll remain, but I'm going away.—*Como*. I eat, I'm eating.—*Llegarán mañana*. They'll arrive tomorrow.

Tú (plural: *vosotros*) is used only between relatives, intimate friends and in addressing children, servants and animals.

The word *usted* (plural: *ustedes*) is used when speaking to somebody, and takes a verb in the third person: *Es usted muy amable*. You're very kind. —*¿Qué desean ustedes?* What do you want? (An inverted question-mark or an inverted exclamation mark is put at the beginning of an interrogative or exclamatory sentence respectively, in written Spanish.)

The conjunctive pronouns can be used only with verbs. These pronouns precede the verb: *Te espero*. I'm waiting for you.— But they are placed after the verb and written together with it after an infinitive, a gerund and an imperative: *Quiero verlo*. I want to see it.— *Viéndome me saludó*. On seeing me he greeted me.—*Démelo*. Give it to me.

The disjunctive pronouns can be used apart from verbs: *¿A quién doy la llave?* To whom am I to give the key? *A mí*. — All prepositions have after them the disjunctive forms: *con él* with him (but *conmigo* with me, *contigo* with you, *consigo* with himself, with herself); *para mí* for me; *sin ti* without you etc.

Accusative

Nominative		Conjunctive	Disjunctive
yo	I	*me*	*a mí*
tú	you	*te*	*a ti*
él	he	*le,lo*	*a él*
ella	she	*la*	*a ella*
ello	it	*lo*	*a ello*
usted	you	*le,la*	*a usted*
nosotros	we	*nos*	*a nosotros*
nosotras			*a nosotras*
vosotros	you	*os*	*a vosotros*
vosotras			*a vosotras*
ellos	they	*les,los*	*a ellos*
ellas	they	*las*	*a ellas*
ustedes	you	*los,las*	*a ustedes*

Dative

	Conjunctive	Disjunctive	
me	*me*	*a mí*	to me
you	*te*	*a ti*	to you
him	*le*	*a él*	to him
her	*le*	*a ella*	to her
it	*le*	*a ello*	to it
you	*le*	*a usted*	to you
us	*nos*	*a nosotros*	to us
		a nosotras	
you	*os*	*a vosotros*	to you
		a vosotras	
them	*les*	*a ellos*	to them
them	*les*	*a ellas*	to them
you	*les*	*a ustedes*	to you

Reflexive pronouns

The reflexive pronouns differ only in the third person from the personal pronouns. They are chiefly used with the reflexive verbs, e.g. *lavar* to wash; *lavarse* to wash oneself:

me lavo	I wash (myself)
te lavas	you wash (yourself)
se lava	he washes (himself) she washes (herself)
nos lavamos	we wash (ourselves)
os laváis	you wash (yourselves)
se lavan	they wash (themselves)

Disjunctive forms: *a sí (mismo), a sí (misma)*: *Las muchachas se compran las medias para sí mismas.* The girls buy the stockings for themselves.

The form *se* is used impersonally with the 3rd pers. sing. of the verb, cf. Fr. *on*, Ger. *man; se dice* it is said; *no se sabe nunca* you never can tell.

Demonstrative pronouns

The "*neuter*" forms are:
esto this (here);
eso that (near you);
aquello that (over there).

E.g. *¿Qué es eso?* What's that? —*¿Esto? Es una revista inglesa.* This? It's an English magazine.

The "personal" forms are:

m.: *éste, éstos*
ése, ésos
aquél, aquéllos

f.: *ésta, éstas*
ésa, ésas
aquélla, aquéllas

E.g. *Mi libro es éste.* My book is this one. — *Tus lápices son ésos.* Your pencils are those — *Sus hermanas son aquéllas.* His or her or their sisters are those there.

The demonstrative adjectives are the same as the demonstrative pronouns but do not bear a written accent and precede the noun:

Este libro es de él. This book belongs to him.

No puede escribir con esa pluma. He can't write with that pen.

¿Por qué están abiertas aquellas ventanas? Why are those windows open?

Possessive adjectives and pronouns

mi libro my book
Este libro es mío. This book is mine.

tu libro your book
Este libro es tuyo. This book is yours.

su libro his (her) book
Este libro es suyo. This book is his (hers).

nuestro libro our book
Este libro es nuestro. This book is ours.

vuestro libro your book
Este libro es vuestro. This book is yours.

su libro their (your) book
Este libro es suyo. This book is theirs (or) yours.

mi carta my letter
Esa carta es mía. That letter is mine.

tu carta your letter
Esa carta es tuya. That letter is yours.

su carta his (her) letter
Esa carta es suya. That letter is his (hers).

nuestra carta our letter
Esa carta es nuestra. That letter is ours.

vuestra carta your letter

Esa carta es vuestra. That letter is yours.
su carta their (your) letter
Esa carta es suya. That letter is theirs (or) yours.

In the plural: *mis libros* my books; *estos libros son nuestros* these books are ours; *sus cartas* his (her, their, your) letters; *esas cartas son suyas* those letters are his (hers, theirs, yours).

In case of ambiguity instead of *su, suyo* a paraphrase is used:
su carta; la carta de él (de ella, de usted, de ellos, de ellas, de ustedes).
esas cartas son suyas; esas cartas son de él (de ella, de usted, de ellos, de ellas, de ustedes).

Interrogative and relative pronouns

All interrogative adjectives and pronouns bear a written accent mark to distinguish them from the corresponding relative:
¿quién? who?
Interrogative
¿quién? who?
R: quien who
¿quiénes? who? (plural)
R: quienes who (plural)
¿qué? what?
R: que that, which, who
¿cuál? which one?
R: el cual, la cual he who, that which
¿cuáles? which ones?
R: los cuales, las cuales they who, those which
¿cuánto? how much?
R: cuanto all that, as much as
¿cuántos? how many?
R: cuantos all that, as many as
¿cómo? how?
R: como how, as, like
¿cuándo? when?
R: cuando when(ever)

The Adverb

Adverbs are formed from adjectives by adding the suffix *-mente* (to the feminine form): *claro* clear, *claramente* clearly *fácil* easy, *fácilmente* easily *cortés* polite, *cortésmente* politely

If there are more adverbs only the last receives this suffix: *habla clara y distintamente* he speaks clearly and distinctly.

Some adjectives and participles may be used as adverbs: *hable usted más alto* speak up; *se fue contento* he went happily away.

The Verb

According to the way in which they are conjugated Spanish verbs fall into three conjugations:

I. Verbs ending in —AR: *hablar* to speak, *trabajar* to work;
II. Verbs ending in —ER: *comer* to eat, *beber* to drink;
III. Verbs ending in —IR: *vivir* to live, *escribir* to write.

All verbal terminations are added to the radical which you get by omitting the ending *-ar, -er, -ir* respectively: *habl-, trabaj-, com-, beb-, viv-, escrib-.*

Regular Verbs

A) Simple tenses

1. *Indicative Mood*

	I. (-ar)	II. (-er)	III. (-ir
Present tense	-o	-o	-o

	-as	-es	-es
	-a	-e	-e
	-amos	-emos	-imos
	-áis	-éis	-ís
	-an	-en	-en
Future tense	-aré	-eré	-iré
	-arás	-erás	-irás
	-ará	-erá	-irá
	-aremos	-eremos	-iremos
	-aréis	-eréis	-iréis
	-arán	-erán	-irán
Past tense	-é	-í	-í
	-aste	-iste	-iste
	-ó	-ió	-ió
	-amos	-imos	-imos
	-asteis	-isteis	-isteis
	-aron	-ieron	-ieron
Imperfect tense	-aba	-ía	-ía
	-abas	-ías	-ías
	-aba	-ía	-ía
	-ábamos	-íamos	-íamos
	-ábais	-íais	-íais
	-aban	-ían	-ían

2. *Conditional*

Present tense	-aría	-ería	-iría
	-arías	-erías	-irías
	-aría	-ería	-iría
	-aríamos	-eríamos	-iríamos
	-aríais	-eríais	-iríais
	-arían	-erían	-irían

3. *Subjunctive mood*

Present tense	-e	-a	-a
	-es	-as	-as
	-e	-a	-a
	-emos	-amos	-amos
	-éis	-áis	-áis
	-en	-an	-an

Past tense		I.		II. and III.
	-ase or	-ara	-iese or	-iera
	-ases	-aras	-ieses	-ieras
	-ase	-ara	-iese	-iera
	-ásemos	-áramos	-iésemos	-iéramos
	-aseis	-arais	-ieseis	-ierais
	-asen	-aran	-iesen	-ieran

4. *Imperative Mood*

Present tense	-a	-e	-e
	-ad	-ed	-id

5. *Non-finite forms*

Present Infinitive	-ar	-er	-ir
Gerund	-ando	-iendo	-iendo
Past Participle	-ado	-ido	-ido

B) Compound tenses

They are formed by means of the corresponding tense of the auxiliary verb *haber* (see List of Irregular Verbs) and the past participle of the verb.

1. *Indicative Mood*

Present Perfect Tense
I have spoken (eaten, lived) etc.
he hablado (comido, vivido)
has hablado (comido, vivido)
ha hablado (comido, vivido)
hemos hablado (comido, vivido)
habéis hablado (comido, vivido)
han hablado (comido, vivido)
Past Perfect Tense
habia hablado *I had spoken*

2. *Conditional*

Past Tense
habría hablado
I should have spoken

3. *Subjunctive Mood*

Present Perfect Tense
haya hablado
that I have spoken
Past Perfect Tense
hubiese or *hubiera hablado*
(if) I had spoken

4. *Non-finite forms*

Past Infinitive
haber hablado to have spoken
Past Gerund
habiendo hablado having spoken

Use of the single Tenses

The *present* tense of the *Indicative* refers to the present but it is often used instead of the future tense: *Mañana salgo para Londres.* Tomorrow I'll leave for London.

The *future* tense refers not only to action in future time but also to probability: *¿Qué hora es? Serán las diez.* What time is it? It may be ten o'clock.

The *past* tense refers to action at a specific point in past time: *Llegué ayer.* I arrived yesterday.

The *imperfect* tense refers to past action that was going on at the same time as some other action or that was habitual: *Mientras yo leía él jugaba.* While I was reading he was playing. — *Me levantaba siempre temprano.* I used to get up early.

The *present perfect* tense refers to a past action which continues in the present: *He venido para verle a usted.* I have come to see you.

The *imperative* is used to give commands; the courteous form of the imperative is expressed by the *present subjunctive; coma usted más* eat more; *vengan ustedes a verme* come to see me; *escríbame una carta* write me a letter (in negative sentençes: *no me escriba cartas* don't write me any letters).

The *conditional* is used as in English: *desearía una habitación en el primer piso* I should like to have a room on the first floor; *habríamos ido con ustedes* we should have gone with you. — In subordinate clauses the *subjunctive* is used: *Me ale-*

graría si me escribiese (or *escribiera*). I'd be glad if he wrote me; — *Me habría alegrado si me hubiese* (or *hubiera*) *escrito*. I'd have been glad if he had written me.

Irregular Verbs

I. *Radical-changing verbs* are such as have the regular endings of the conjugation to which they belong, but have certain changes in the vowel of the last syllable of the root. There are two main types of radical-changing verbs:

a) The root-vowel is changed into a diphthong (*e* into *ie* and *o* into *ue*) when it is stressed:

pensar to think
pienso I think
piensas you think
piensa he thinks
pensamos we think
pensáis you think
piensan they think

contar to count
cuento I count
cuentas you count
cuenta he counts
contamos we count
contáis you count
cuentan they count

The same occurs in the present subjunctive and in the imperative (piense, cuente, etc.). Some verbs ending in *-ir* change the root-vowel in other tenses too; so, for instance, the root-vowel *e* is changed into *i*, and *o* into *u*, wherever the root is unstressed but followed by *a*, *ie*, or *ió*:

sentir to feel
sentí I felt
sentiste you felt
sintió he felt
sentimos we felt
sentisteis you felt
sintieron they felt
sintiese or *sintiera* if I felt
sintiendo feeling

dormir to sleep
dormí I slept
dormiste you slept
durmió he slept
dormimos we slept
dormisteis you slept
durmieron they slept
durmiese or *durmiera* if I slept
durmiendo sleeping

b) The root-vowel *e* is changed into *i* both in forms where the last syllable of the root is stressed and where the root is unstressed but followed by *a*, *ie*, or *ió:*

pedir to ask
pido I ask
pides you ask
pide he asks
pedimos we ask
pedís you ask
piden they ask
pidió he asked
pidiese or *pidiera* if he asked
pidiendo asking

A

a, un *m.*, una *f.*
abandon, *v. a.* abandonar.
abbey, *s.* abadía *f.*
abbot, *s.* abad *m.*
abbreviate, *v. a.* abreviar.
abbreviation, *s.* abreviación *f.*
abdicate, *v. a.* & *n.* abdicar.
abhor, *v. a.* detestar, aborrecer.
abide, *v. n.* permanecer.
ability, *s.* habilidad *f.*, capacidad *f.*
able, *adj.* hábil, capaz.
aboard, *adv.* a bordo.
abolish, *v. a.* abolir.
abolition, *s.* abolición *f.*
abominable, *adj.* abominable.
abound, *v. n.* abundar.
about, *adv.* alrededor; *prep.* sobre, de; hacia, a eso de; *be ~ to* prepararse a.
above, *adv.* en alto, arriba; *prep.* sobre, encima de.
abroad, *adv.* en el extranjero.
absence, *s.* ausencia.
absent, *adj.* ausente.
absolute, *adj.* absoluto.
absolutely, *adv.* absolutamente.
absolve, *v. a.* absolver.
absorb, *v. a.* absorber.
abstain, *v. n.* abstenerse.
abstract, *adj.* abstracto; — *s.* extracto *m.*, resumen *m.*
absurd, *adj.* absurdo.
abundance, *s.* abundancia *f.*
abundant, *adj.* abundante.
abusive, *adj.* abusivo; injurioso.
academic, *adj.* académico.
academy, *s.* academia *f.*
accent, *s.* acento *m.*; —*v. a.* acentuar.
accept, *v. a.* aceptar.
access, *s.* acceso *m.*
accessible, *adj.* accesible.
accessory, *s.* & *adj.* accesorio *(m.)*.
accident, *s.* accidente *m.*
accidental, *adj.* accidental.
accommodate, *v. a.* acomodar; *~ oneself to* acomodarse a.
accommodation, *s.* acomodamiento *m.*; alojamiento *m.*
accompany, *v. a.* acompañar.
accomplish, *v. a.* acabar, terminar.
accord, *s.* acuerdo *m.*; — *v. n.* concordar; *v. a.* conceder.
according: *~ to prep.* según, de acuerdo con.
account, *s.* cuenta *f.*; —*v.n.* dar cuenta de; *on ~ of* con motivo de; *on no ~* de ningún modo.
accuracy, *s.* exactitud *f.*
accusation, *s.* acusación *f.*
accuse, *v. a.* acusar.
accustom, *v. a.* acostumbrar.
ache, *s.* dolor *m.*; — *v. n.* *my head ~s* tengo dolor de cabeza, me duele la cabeza.
achieve, *v. a.* ejecutar, realizar; conseguir.
acknowledge, *v. a.* reconocer.
acquaint, *v. a.* hacer conocer; informar.
acquaintance, *s.* conocimiento *m.*; conocido *m.*
acquire, *v. a.* adquirir.

acquisition, *s.* adquisición *f.*, compra *f.*
across, *prep.* a través de.
act, *s.* acción *f.; (law)* ley *f.; (theatre)* acto *m.* — *v. n.* actuar.
action, *s.* acción *f.*, acto *m.*
active, *adj.* activo, ágil.
activity, *s.* actividad *f.*
actor, *s.* actor *m.*
actress, *s.* actriz *f.*
actual, *adj.* actual.
adapt, *v. a.* adaptar.
add, *v. a.* añadir; sumar.
addition, *s.* añadidura *f.*; suma *f.*, adición *f.; in* ~ *to* por añadidura. además de.
additional, *adj.* adicional.
address, *s.* dirección *f.*, señas *f. pl.*;—*v. a.* dirigir a.
adjoining, *adj.* lindante, contiguo.
adjust, *v. a.* ajustar, arreglar.
administration, *s.* administración *f.*
administrative, *adj.* administrativo.
admirable, *adj.* admirable.
admiral, *s.* almirante *m.*
admiration, *s.* admiración *f.*
admire, *v. a.* admirar.
admission, *s.* admisión *f.*; entrada *f.*; concesión *f.*
admit, *v. a.* admitir.
adore, *v. a.* adorar.
adult, *adj. &s.* adulto *(m.).*
advance, *v. n.* avanzar, adelantarse.
advantage, *s.* ventaja *f.*
adventure, *s.* aventura *f.*
adversary, *s.* adversario *m.*
adverse, *adj.* adverso.
adversity, *s.* contrariedad *f.*
advertise, *v. a.* anunciar, avisar.
advertisement, *s.* anuncio *m.*, aviso *m.*
advice, *s.* consejo *m.*; aviso *m.*
advise, *v. a.* aconsejar.
aerodrome, *s.* aeródromo *m.*
aeroplane, *s.* avión *m*, aeroplano *m.*
affair, *s.* negocio *m*; asunto *m.*
affect, *v. a.* interesar, tocar; afectar.
affection, *s.* afecto *m.*; cariño *m.*
affectionate, *adj.* afectuoso, carinoso.
affirm, *v. a.* afirmar.
affirmative, *adj.* afirmativo; — *s.* afirmativa *f.*
afford, *v. a.* dar, conferir; *can* ~ permitirse.
afraid, *adj.* inquieto; *be* ~ tener miedo de.
African, *adj. & s.* africano.
after, *adv.* luego; — *prep.* después de.
afternoon, *s.* tarde *f.*
afterwards, *adv.* luego; más tarde, después.
again, *adv.* de nuevo, nuevamente, otra vez.
against, *prep.* contra.
age, *s.* edad *f.*
aged, *adj.* anciano, viejo.
agency, *s.* agencia *f.*; actividad *f.*
agent, *s.* agente *m.*, representante *m.*
aggression, *s.* agresión *f.*
ago, *adv.* hace, *a week* ~ hace una semana.
agree, *v. n.* concordar; estar de acuerdo; ~ *on* concordarse; ~ *to* consentir a; ~ *with* estar de acuerdo con.
agreeable, *adj.* agradable.
agreement, *s.* concordancia *f.*, acuerdo *m.*
agricultural, *adj.* agrí-

cola.
agriculture, *s.* agricultura *f.*
ahead, *adv.* adelante.
aid, *s.* ayuda *f.*, socorro *m.* – *v. a.* ayudar.
aim, *s.* fin *m.*; propósito *m.*; – *v. n.* tender (a); *v. a.* apuntar.
air, *s.* aire *m.*
air-line *s.* línea *(f.)* aérea.
air-mail, *s.* correo *(m.)* aéreo.
airport, *s.* aeropuerto *m.*, aeródromo *m.*
alarm, *v. a.* alarmar; — *s.* alarma *f.*
alcoholic, *adj.* alcohólico.
ale, *s.* cerveza *f.*
alike, *adj.* igual; — *adv.* igualmente.
alive, *adj.* vivo.
all, *adj.* todo; *s.* todos *m. pl.*; *adv.* del todo; *not at* ~ de ningún modo.
alley, *s.* avenida *f.*; paseo *m.*, callejón *m.*
all ed, *adj.* aliado.
allow, *v. a.* permitir, conceder; ~ *for* tomar en consideración.
ally, *s.* aliado *m.*; – *v. a.* unir; *v. n.* aliarse.
almost, *adv.* casi.
alms, *s. pl.* limosna *f.*
alone, *adj.* solo; — *adv.* sólo.
along, *prep.* a lo largo de.
aloud, *adv.* en voz alta.
already, *adv.* ya.
also, *adv.* también.
alter, *v. a.* & *n.* cambiar, mudar.
although, *conj.* aunque.
altitude, *s.* altitud *f.*
altogether, *adv.* enteramente.
always, *adv.* siempre.
amaze, *v. a.* asombrar.
amazing, *adj.* asombroso.
ambassador, *s.* embajador *m.*
ambition, *s.* ambición *f.*
ambitious, *adj.* ambicioso.
ambulance, *s.* ambulancia *f.*
amend, *v. a.* corregir, rectificar.
American, *adj.* & *s.* americano *(m.)*.
amid(st), *prep.* en medio de.
among, *prep.* entre.
amount, *s.* importe *m.*; cantidad *f.*; importancia *f.*; – *v. n.* elevarse a, importar.
ample, *adj.* amplio.
amuse, *v. a.* divertir.
amusement, *s.* divertimiento *m.*
an, *see* **a.**
anatomy, *s.* anatomía *f.*
ancestor, *s.* abuelo *m.*, antepasado *m.*
anchor, *s.* ancla *f.*; *v. a.* & *n.* anclar.
ancient, *adj.* antiguo.
and, *conj.* y.
anecdote, *s.* anécdota *f.*
angel, *s.* ángel *m.*
anger, *s.* cólera *f.*, ira *f.*, enojo *m.*; *v. a.* enojar.
angle[1], *s.* ángulo *m.*; punto *(m.)* de vista.
angle[2], *v. n.* pescar con el anzuelo.
Anglican, *adj.* anglicano.
angry, *adj.* iracundo, enojado, enfadado.
animal, *adj.* & *s.* animal *(m.)*.
ankle, *s.* tobillo *m.*
annex, *s.* anejo *m.*, anexo *m.*; dependencia *f.*; — *v. a.* anexar.
anniversary, *s.* aniversario *m.*
announce, *v. a.* anunciar, avisar.
announcement, *s.* anuncio

m., aviso m.
announcer, s. locutor m., anunciante m.
annoy, v. a. enfadar, molestar; *be ~ed at* estar enfadado con.
annoying, adj. enojoso, molesto.
annual, adj. anual.
annul, v. a. anular.
another, adj. otro.
answer, s. respuesta f., contestación f.; v. a. & n. responder, contestar.
antibiotic, s. antibiótico m.
anticipate, v. a. anticipar.
antipathy, s. antipatía f
antiquity, s. antigüedad f
antiseptic, adj. & s. m. antiséptico (m.).
anxiety, s. angustia f., congoja f.; inquietud f.
anxious, adj. angustioso; inquieto; *be ~ to* querer (hacer algo).
any, pron. algún m., alguna f.; *not ~* ninguno.
anybody, pron. alguien; *(at all)* cualquiera.
anyhow, adv. de cualquier modo.
anyone, *see* **anybody.**
anything, pron. algo;todo; *(at all)* cualquiera.
anyway, *see* **anyhow.**
anywhere, adv. en todas partes.
apart, adv. aparte; solo; *~ from* aparte de.
apartment, s. habitación f.
ape, s. mono m.
apologize, v. n. pedir perdon, disculparse.
apology, s. perdón m., disculpa f.
apparent, adj. aparente; manifiesto.
appeal, s. apelación f.; llamamiento m.; fuerza (f.) atractiva; — v. n. apelar; atraer.
appear, v. n. aparecer, presentarse.
appearance, s. aparición f., *(look)* aspecto m.
appendix, s. apéndice m.
appetite, s. apetito m.
applaud, v. n. aplaudir.
applause, s. aplauso m.
apple, s. manzana f.
applicant, s. solicitante m.
application, s. aplicación f.; solicitud f.
apply, v. a. aplicar, utilizar; v. n. cuadrar (con); *~ for* solicitar; *~ to* dirigirse a.
appoint, v. a. fijar; destinar; nombrar, designar.
appointment, s. destino m.; cita f.; nombramiento m.
appreciate, v. a. apreciar.
appreciation, s. estimación f., estima f.
apprentice, s. aprendiz m.
approach, s. aproximación f.; acceso m.; v. a. acercar, aproximar; v. n. acercarse, aproximarse.
appropriate, v. a. apropiarse; adj. apropiado.
approval, s. aprobación f.
approve, v. a. aprobar.
approximate, v. a. & n. aproximar(se); — adj. aproximativo.
apricot, s. albaricoque m., damasco m.
April, s. abril m.
apron, s. delantal m.
apt, adj. apto.
Arab, adj. & s. árabe (m).
arbitrary, adj. arbitrario.
arcade, s. arcada f.
arch, s. bóveda f. arco m.
architect, s. arquitecto m.
architecture, s. arquitectura f.
area, s. área f.
Argentine, adj. argentino.

argue, *v. a. & n.* discutir; argüir.
argument, *s.* argumento *m.*; discusión *f.*
arid, *adj.* árido.
arise, *v. n.* levantarse; *(come from)* resultar.
aristocratic, *adj.* aristocrático.
arm[1], *s.* brazo *m.*
arm[2], *s.* *(weapon)* arma *f.*
armament, *s.* armamento *m.*
armchair, *s.* sillón *m.*, butaca *f.*
army, *s.* ejército *m.*
around, *adv.* alrededor; *prep.* alrededor de.
arouse, *v. a.* despertar.
arrange, *v. a.* ordenar, arreglar; *v. n.* disponer.
arrangement, *s.* orden *f.*, arreglo *m.*; disposición *f.*
arrest, *v. a.* detener, arrestar; parar; — *s.* detención *f.*, arresto *m.*
arrival, *s.* llegada *f.*
arrive, *v. n.* llegar.
arrow, *s.* flecha *f.*
art, *s.* arte *m.*
artery, *s.* arteria *f.*
article, *s.* artículo *m.*
artificial, *adj.* artificial.
artillery, *s.* artillería *f.*
artist, *s.* artista *m. & f.*
artistic, *adj.* artístico.
as, *conj.* como, cuando; *pron.* tan; ~ *young* ~ tan joven como.
ascend, *v. n.* ascender.
ascent, *s.* ascensión *f.*
ascertain, *v. a.* averiguar; establecer.
ash(es), *s.* ceniza *f.*
ashamed, *adj.* avergonzado; *be* ~ *of* avergonzarse de.
ashore, *adv.* en la costa; *go* ~ desembarcar.
Asiatic, *adj.* asiático.
aside, *adv.* de lado; aparte.
ask, *v.a.* preguntar; pedir, rogar; ~ *about* informarse.
asleep, *adv.* durmiendo; *fall* ~ quedarse dormido, dormirse.
aspect, *s.* aspecto *m.*; punto de vista.
aspire, *v. n.* aspirar a.
ass, *s.* asno *m.*, burro *m.*
assail, *v. a.* atacar, asaltar.
assemble, *v. a.* reunir; *v. n.* reunirse.
assembly, *s.* reunión *f.*, asamblea *f.*
assign, *v. a.* asignar.
assist, *v. a.* ayudar.
assistance, *s.* asistencia *f.*
assistant, *s.* asistente *m.*
associate, *v. a.* asociar; *v. n.* asociarse.
association, *s.* asociación *f*
assume, *v. a.* asumir.
assumption, *s.* suposición *f.*; asunción *f.*
assure, *v. a.* asegurar.
astonish, *v. a.* sorprender.
astonishing, *adj.* sorprendente.
astonishment, *s.* sorpresa *f.*
at, *prep.* en; ~ *the station* en la estación; ~ *six o'clock* a las seis.
athlete, *s.* atleta *m. & f.*
athletic, *adj.* atlético.
athletics, *s. pl.* atletismo *m.*
atmosphere, *s.* atmósfera *f.*
atom, *s.* átomo *m.*
atomic, *adj.* atómico; ~ *bomb* bomba *(f.)* atómica; ~ *energy* energía *(f.)* atómica.
atrocity, *s.* atrocidad *f.*
attach, *v. a.* atar.
attaché, *s.* agregado *m.*; ~ *case* maletín *m.*
attack, *v. a.* atacar, asal-

tar; — *s.* ataque *m.*, asalto *m.*
attain, *v. a.* alcanzar, lograr.
attempt, *v. a.* intentar; — *s.* intento *m.*
attend, *v. a.* atender a; ~ *school* ir a la escuela.
attendance, *s.* asistencia *f.*
attention, *s.* atención *f.*; *pay* ~ prestar atención.
attentive, *adj.* atento.
attic, *s.* buhardilla *f.*
attitude, *s.* postura *f.*; conducta *f.*
attorney, *s.* abogado *m.*
attract, *v. a.* atraer.
attribute, *v. a.* atribuir; — *s.* atributo *m.*
auction, *s.* subasta *f.*
audience, *s.* audiencia *f.*; auditorio *m.*
auditorium, *s.* auditorio *m.*; aula *f.*
August, *s.* agosto *m.*
aunt, *s.* tía *f.*
Australian, *adj.* & *s.* australiano *(m.)*.
Austrian, *adj.* & *s.* austriaco *(m.)*.
authentic, *adj.* auténtico
author, *s.* autor *m.*
authority, *s.* autoridad *f.*; autorización *f.*
authorize, *v. a.* autorizar.
automatic, *adj.* automático.
automation, *s.* automatizacion *f.*
autumn, *s.* otoño *m.*
avail, *s. be of no* ~ no servir para nada; ser inútil.
available, *adj.* disponible; (estar) en venta.
avalanche, *s.* avalancha *f.*
avenge, *v. a.* vengar.
avenue, *s.* avenida *f.*
average, *s.* término *(m.)* medio; *on the* ~ por término medio; — *adj.* medio.
aversion, *s.* aversión *f.*
avoid, *v. a.* evitar.
await, *v. a.* esperar, aguardar.
awake, *v. a.* despertar; *v. n.* despertar(se); — *adj.* despierto.
aware, *adj.* consciente (de); *become* ~ hacerse cargo (de).
away, *adv.* ausente; *go* ~ irse, marcharse.
awful, *adj.* horrible.
awhile, *adv.* un rato.
awkward, *adj.* torpe; penoso.
axe, *s.* hacha *f.*
axis, *s.* eje *m.*
axle, *s.* eje *m.*
azure, *adj.* & *s.* azul *(m.)*.

B

baby, *s.* nene *m.*; bebé *m.*
baby-sitter, *s.* aya *f.*, niñera *f.* por horas.
bachelor, *s.* soltero *m.*; *(arts)* bachiller *m.*
back, *s.* espalda *f.*; *(football)* defensa *m.*; — *adj.* trasero; — *adv.* (hacia) atrás; *come* ~ volver, regresar; *some years* ~ hace unos años; — *v. n. (car)* dar marcha atrás; *(bet)* apostar (por).
background, *s.* fondo *m.*; segundo plano *m.*
backward, *adv.* (hacia) atrás; — *adj.* atrasado.
bacon, *s.* tocino *m.*
bad, *adj.* malo; *that's too* ~ ! ¡qué lástima!; ~ *luck* mala suerte *f.*
badly, *adv.* mal.
bag, *s.* saco *m.*; bolsa *f.*
baggage, *s.* bagaje *m.*; equipaje *m.*
bake, *v. a.* & *n.* cocer;

asar.
baker, *s.* panadero *m.*
bakery, *s.* panadería *f.*
balance, *s.* balanza *f.*; equilibrio *m.*; – *v. a.* sopesar; equilibrar.
balcony, *s.* balcón *m.*
bald, *adj.* calvo.
bale, *s.* bala *f.*; fardo *m.*
ball, *s.* pelota *f.*; bola *f.*; globo *m.*; *(dance)* baile *m.*
ballet, *s.* bailete *m.*; ballet *m.*
balloon, *s.* balón *m.*
ball(-point) pen, *s.* bolígrafo *m.*
Baltic, *adj.* báltico.
banana, *s.* plátano *m.*; banana *f.*
band, *s.* lazo *m.*; cinta *f.*; banda *f.*; – *v. a.* ~ *together* unirse.
bandage, *s.* venda *f.*; vendaje *m.*; – *v. a.* vendar.
bandit, *s.* bandido *m.*
bank[1], *s.* *(river)* orilla *f.*
bank[2], *s.* banca *f.*; banco *m.*
banknote, *s.* billete *m.* (de banco).
bankruptcy, *s.* bancarrota *f.*; quiebra *f.*
banner, *s.* bandera *f.*
banquet, *s.* banquete *m.*
baptism, *s.* bautismo *m.*
baptize, *v. a.* bautizar.
bar, *s.* *(iron)* barra *f.*; tribunal *m.*; *(place for drink)* bar *m.*; – *v. a.* barrear.
barber, *s.* barbero *m.*; peluquero *m.*
bare, *adj.* desnudo; – *v. a.* desnudar.
barefoot, *adv.* descalzo.
bargain, *s.* negocio *m.*; *into the* ~ por añadidura; compra *(f.)* de lance; – *v. n.* regatear.
barge, *s.* barcaza *f.*
bark, *s.* ladrido *m.*; –*v. n.* ladrar.
barley, *s.* cebada *f.*
barman, *s.* barman *m.*
barn, *s.* granero *m.*
barometer, *s.* barómetro *m.*
baron, *s.* barón *m.*
baroness, *s.* baronesa *f.*
barrack(s), *s.* *(pl.)* cuartel *m.*
barrel, *s.* barril *m.*; *(of gun)* cañón *m.*
barren, *adj.* árido, estéril.
barrier, *s.* barrera *f.*; obstáculo *m.*
barrister, *s.* abogado *m.*
base, *s.* base *f.*; – *v. a.* basar.
basement, *s.* fundamento *m.*; sótano *m.*
basic, *adj.* básico, fundamental.
basin, *s.* palangana *f.*; jofaina *f.*; cuenca *f.*
basis, *s.* base *f.*
basket, *s.* cesta *f.*; canasta *f.*, cesto *m.*
basket-ball, baloncesto *m.*
bass, *s.* bajo *m.*
bath, *s.* baño *m.*; *take a* ~ tomar un baño.
bathe, *v. a.* bañar; – *v. n.* bañarse.
bather, *s.* bañista *m.*, *f.*
bathing-costume, *s.* traje *(m.)* de baño.
bathroom, *s.* cuarto *(m.)* de baño.
battery, *s.* batería *f.*
battle, *s.* batalla *f.*
bay, *s.* golfo *m.*; bahía *f.*
be, *v. n.* ser, estar; *how are you?* ¿cómo está usted?; *I am twenty* tengo veinte años.
beach, *s.* playa *f.*
bead, *s.* perla *f.*; cuenta *f.*
beam, *s.* *(timber)* viga *f.*; *(light)* rayo *m.*; – *v. n.* (ir)radiar.

bean, *s.* judía *f.*; *French ~s* judías *(f. pl.)* verdes.
bear,[1] *s.* oso *m.*
bear[2], *v. a. (carry)* llevar; *(suffer)* sufrir, soportar; *(child)* dar a luz; *when were you born?* ¿cuándo nació usted?
beard, *s.* barba *f.*
bearing, *s.* conducta *f.*; relación *f.*; *beyond all ~* insoportable.
beast, *s.* bestia *f.*
beat, *v. a.* batir, golpear; vencer.
beautiful, *adj.* hermoso, guapo.
beauty, *s.* hermosura *f.*; belleza *f.*; *~ parlour* salón *(m.)* de belleza.
because, *conj.* porque.
beckon, *v. n.* hacer señas, llamar con señas.
become, *v. n.* hacerse, llegar a ser; convenir.
bed, *s.* cama *f.*; *go to ~* ir a la cama, acostarse.
bedclothes, *s. pl.* ropa *(f.)* de cama.
bedroom, *s.* dormitorio *m.*; alcoba *f.*
bee, *s.* abeja *f.*
beef, *s.* carne *(f.)* de vaca.
beef-steak, *s.* bistec *m.*
beer, *s.* cerveza *f.*
beetle, *s.* escarabajo *m.*
beetroot, *s.* remolacha *f.*
before, *adv.* antes; — *prep.* ante, delante de; — *conj.* antes de (que).
beg, *v. a.* rogar, pedir; *I ~ your pardon?* ¡Perdone! ¿Qué dijo usted?
beggar, *s.* mendigo *m.*
begin, *v. a. & n.* empezar, comenzar.
beginner, *s.* principiante *m.,f.*
beginning, *s.* comienzo *m.*; principio *m.*
behalf, *prep. on ~ of* en interés de; en nombre de.
behave, *v. n.* portarse, conducirse.
behaviour, *s.* conducta *f.*
behind, *adv.* detrás; atrás; — *prep.* detrás de, tras.
being, *s.* existencia *f.*; ser *m.*, criatura *f.*
Belgian, *adj & s.* belga.
belief, *s.* creencia *f.*
believe, *v. a.* creer; pensar.
bell, *s.* timbre *m.*; campanilla *f.*; *ring the ~* tocar el timbre.
belly, *s.* vientre *m.*
belong, *v. n.* pertenecer.
belongings, *s. pl.* efectos *m. pl.*; trastos *m. pl.*
beloved, *adj.* querido, amado.
below, *adv.* abajo, hacia abajo.
belt, *s.* cinturón *m.*
bench, *s.* banco *m.*
bend, *v. a.* curvar; — *v. n.* curvarse; — *s. (road)* curva *f.*
beneath, *adv.* abajo; — *prep.* debajo de.
benefit, *s.* beneficio *m.*; — *v. a. & n.* beneficiar.
bent, *s.* inclinación *f.*; — *adj. ~ on* empeñado en.
berry, *s.* baya *f.*
berth, *s.* litera *f.*; cama *f.*; camarote *m.*
beside, *prep.* al lado de.
besides, *adv.* además; — *prep.* además de.
best, *adj.* el (la) mejor; — *adv.* lo mejor
best-seller, *s.* libro *(m.)* de gran éxito.
bet, *v. a.* apostar; — *s.* apuesta *f.*
better, *adj.* mejor; *all the*

~ tanto mejor; — *v. a.* mejorar.
between, *prep.* entre, por entre.
beware, *v. n.* cuidarse de; — *int.* ~! ¡cuidado!
beyond, *prep.* más allá de; ~ *doubt* sin duda.
Bible, *s.* Biblia *f.*
bicycle, *s.* bicicleta *f.*
bid, *v. a.* mandar; ofrecer; — *s.* oferta *f.*
big, *adj.* grande; vasto.
bill, *s.* cuenta *f.*; ~ *of fare* lista *(f.)* de platos, menú *m.*; *(poster)* cartel *m.*
bin, *s.* recipiente *m.* dust ~ basurero *m.*
bind, *v. a.* atar; *fig.* obligar.
biography, *s.* biografía *f.*
biological, *adj.* biológico.
biology, *s.* biología *f.*
bird, *s.* pájaro *m.*, pajarillo *m.*
birth, *s.* nacimiento *m.*; parto *m.*
birthday, *s.* cumpleaños *m.*
birth-place, *s.* lugar *(m.)* de nacimiento.
biscuit, *s.* bizcocho *m.*; galleta *f.*
bishop, *s.* *(church)* obispo *m.*; *(chess)* alfil *m.*
bit, *s.* pedazo *m.*; pedacito *m.*
bite, *v. a.* morder; — *s.* mordedura *f.*; bocado *m.*
bitter, *adj.* amargo.
bitterness, *s.* amargura *f.*
black, *adj.* negro; ~ *coffee* café *m.*; — *v. a.* ennegrecer; ~ *shoes* limpiar los zapatos.
blackberry, *s.* zarzamora *f.*
blackbird, *s.* mirlo *m.*
blackboard, *s.* pizarra *f.*; encerado *m.*
blackmail, *s.* chantaje *m.*; — *v. a.* hacer chantaje, chantajear.
blacksmith, *s.* herrero *m.*
bladder, *s.* vejiga *f.*
blade, *s.* *(grass)* brizna *f.*; *(knife)* hoja *f.*; *razor* ~ hoja de afeitar.
blame, *v. a.* echar la culpa a, culpar; —*s*, culpa *f.*; reproche *m.*
blank, *s.* formulario *m.*
blanket, *s.* manta *f.*
bleed, *v. n.* sangrar; — *v. a.* desangrar.
blend, *v. a.* mezclar; — *v. n.* mezclarse; — *s.* mezcla *f.*
bless, *v. a.* bendecir; ~ *me!* ¡cielos!
blind, *adj.* ciego· ~ *alley* callejón *(m.)* sin salida.
block, *s.* *(buildings)* manzana *f.*; cuadra *f.*; bloque *m.*; *(traffic)* obstáculo *m.*; *v. a.* bloquear, obstruir.
blood, *s.* sangre *f.*
bloody, *adj.* sangriento.
bloom, *s.* floración *f.*; *fig.* prosperidad *f.*; — *v. n.* florecer; *fig.* prosperar.
blossom, *s.* flor *f.*; capullo *m.*; — *v. n.* estar en flor.
blot, *s.* mancha *f.*; — *v. a.* manchar.
blouse, *s.* blusa *f.*
blow[1], *v. n.* soplar; ~ *up* volar, hacer estallar.
blow[2], *s.* golpe *m.*
blue, *adj.* *azul.*
blunder, *s.* equivocación *f.* — *v. n.* cometer una equivocación, equivocarse.
blunt, *adj.* romo, obtuso.
board, *s.* tabla *f.*; plancha

f.; (meals) alimento *m.*, comida *f.*; *(council)* concejo *m.*, comisión *f.*; — v. *a.* alimentar; ~ *the ship* embarcar; — *v. n.* comer.
boarder, *s.* huésped *m.*
boarding-house, *s.* casa *(f.)* de huéspedes, pensión *f.*
boarding-school, *s.* internado *m.*
boast, *v. n.* jactarse; — *s.* jactancia *f.*
boat, *s.* barca *f.*; buque *m.*, barco *m.*
boat-train, *s.* tren *(m.)* de enlace con el buque.
bodily, *adj.* corporal.
body, *s.* cuerpo *m.*
boil[1], *v. a.* & *n.* hervir, cocer.
boil[2], *s.* furúnculo *m.*
boiler, *s.* caldera *f.*; termosifón *m.*
bold, *adj.* atrevido.
bolt, *s.* cerrojo *m.*; — *v. a.* echar el cerrojo; *v. n.* lanzarse.
bomb, *s.* bomba *f.*; — *v. a.* bombardear.
bond, *s.* lazo *m.*; obligación *f.*; contrato *m.*
bone, *s.* hueso *m.*
bonnet, *s.* gorra *f.*; cubierta *(f.)* del motor.
book, *s.* libro *m.*; — *v. a.* reservar, prenotar; *(ticket)* sacar, comprar.
bookcase, *s.* armario *(m.)* para libros, librería *f.*
booking-office, *s.* taquilla *f.*
book-keeper, *s.* contable *m.*; tenedor *(m.)* de libros.
book-keeping, *s.* contabilidad *f.*
book-maker, *s.* corredor *(m.)* de apuestas.
bookseller, *s.* librero *m.*
bookshelf, *s.* librería *f.*, estante *(m.)* para libros.
bookshop, librería *f.*
boot, *s.* bota *f.*
booth, *s.* barraca *f.*
booty, *s.* botín *m.*
border, *s.* frontera *f.*, borde *m.*; — *v. a.* orlar,
boring, *adj.* aburrido.
born, *pp.* nacido; *be* ~ nacer.
borrow, *v. a.* pedir prestado.
bosom, *s.* seno *m.*; pecho *m.*
boss, *s.* jefe *m.*, patrón *m.*
botanical, *adj.* botánico.
botany, *s.* botánica *f.*
both, *s.* ambos *m.*, ambas *f.*; los dos; — *conj.* ~ . . . *and* tanto . . . como.
bottle, *s.* botella *f.*; — *v. a.* embotellar.
bottom, *s.* fondo *m.*
bough, *s.* rama *f.*; ramo *m.*
boundary, *s.* límite *m.*
bouquet, *s.* ramillete *(m.)* de flores.
bow,[1] *s.* arco *m.*; *(knot)* nudo *m.*
bow[2], *v. n.* inclinarse; hacer una reverencia; — *s.* reverencia *f.*; *(ship)* proa *f.*
bowels, *s. pl.* intestinos *m. pl.*
bowl, *s.* tazón *m.*
box, *s.* caja *f.*, cajón *m.*; *(theatre)* palco *m.*
box-office, *s.* taquilla *f.*
boy, *s.* niño *m.*, muchacho *m.*; ~ *scout* explorador *m.*
bra, *s.* sostén *m.*
bracelet, *s.* pulsera *f.*; brazalete *m.*

brain, *s.* seso *m.; cerebro m.*
brainy, listo, cuerdo.
brake, *s.* freno *m.; — v. a.* frenar.
branch, *s.* rama *f.;* ramo *m.;* sucursal *f.; — v. n.* ramificarse, bifurcarse.
brand, *s.* marca *f.;* género *m.; — v. a.* marcar con hierro.
brave, *adj.* valiente; *v. n.* afrontar.
brawl, *s.* alboroto *m.*, pelea *f.; v. n.* alborotar, pelear.
bread, *s.* pan *m.; ~ and butter* pan con mantequilla.
breadth, *s.* anchura *f.*
break, *v. a.* romper; — *v. n.* romperse.
break-down, *s.* depresión *(f.)* nerviosa; *(car)* avería *f.*
breakfast, *s.* desayuno *m.; have ~* desayunar(se).
breast, *s.* pecho *m.;* seno *m.;* mama *f.*
breath, *s.* respiración *f.;* aliento *m.;* soplo *m.*
breathe, *v. a. & n.* respirar.
breed, *v. a.* criar; — *v. n.* reproducirse.
breeze, *s.* brisa *f.*
bribe, *s.* soborno *m.; — v. a.* sobornar.
brick, *s.* ladrillo *m.*
bricklayer, *s.* albañil *m.*
bride, *s.* novia *f.*; recién casada *f.*
bridegroom, novio *m.;* recién casado *m.*
bridge, *s.* puente *m.*
brief, *adj.* breve, sucinto.
briefcase, *s.* cartera *f.*
briefly, *adv.* brevemente.
bright, *adj.* brillante; claro; listo.
brighten, *v. a.* pulir; *v. n.* despejarse; iluminarse.
brightness, *s.* brillo *m.;* serenidad *f.*
brilliant, *adj.* brillante; — *s.* brillante *m.*
bring, *v. a.* traer; *~ up* educar.
brisk, *adj.* ágil, vivo.
British, *adj.* británico.
broad, *adj.* ancho.
broadcast, *v. a.* transmitir, radiar; *s.* emisión *f.*, transmisión *f.*
broadcasting, *s.* emisión *f.*
broken, *pp.* roto, quebrado.
bronze, *s.* bronce *m.*
brooch, *s.* broche *m.*
brook, *s.* arroyo *m.*
broom, *s.* escoba *f.*
brother, *s.* hermano *m.*
brother-in-law, *s.* cuñado *m*
brown, *adj.* pardo, moreno.
bruise, *s.* contusión *f.; — v. a.* contusionar.
brush, cepillo *m.; — v. a.* cepillar.
brute, *s.* bruto *m.*, bestia *f.*
bucket, *s.* cubo *m.*, balde *m.*
bud, *s.* capullo *m.*, brote *m.; — v. n.* brotar.
budget, *s.* presupuesto *m.; — v. a.* asignar.
buffet, *s.* buffet *m.*, aparador *m.;* ambigú *m.*
bug, *s.* chinche *f.*
build, *v. a.* construir, edificar; — *s.* figura *f.*
builder, *s.* arquitecto *m.*
building, *s.* edificio *m.*
built-in, *adj. ~ wardrobe* armario *(m.)* empotrado.
bulb, *s.* tubérculo *m.;* bombilla *f.*
bull, *s.* toro *m.*

bullet, *s.* bala *f.*
bulletin, *s.* boletín *m.*
bun, *s.* bollo *m.;* panecillo *m.*
bunch, *s.* ~ *of flowers* ramillete *(m.)* de flores; ~ *of keys* manojo *(m.)* de llaves.
bundle, *s.* lío *m.;* manojo *m.;* — *v. a.* atar.
buoy, boya *f.*
burden, *s.* carga *f.;* peso *m.;* — *v. a.* cargar.
burglar, *s.* ladrón *m.*
burial, *s.* entierro *m.;* funeral *m.*
burn, *v. a.* & *n.* quemar; — *s.* quemadura *f.*
burst, *v. a.* & *n.* reventar, estallar; — *s.* estallido *m.*
bury, *v. a.* enterrar, sepultar.
bus, *s.* autobús *m.*
bush, *s.* arbusto *m.*, maleza *f.*
business, *s.* ocupación *f.*, oficio *m.;* asunto *m.;* negocio *m.*
businessman, *s.* hombre *(m.)* de negocios.
bus-stop, parada *(f.)* del autobús.
bust, *s.* busto *m.*
busy, *adj.* diligente; ocupado.
but, *conj.* pero; *next door* ~ *one* de aquí la segunda puerta.
butcher, *s.* carnicero *m.*
butter, *s.* mantequilla *f.*
butterfly, *s.* mariposa *f.*
button, *s.* botón *m.;* — *v. a.* abotonar, abrochar.
buy, *v. a.* comprar.
buyer, *s.* comprador *m.*
by, *prep.* cerca de; por; según; ~ *car* en coche; ~ *heart* de memoria; ~ *chance* casualmente; —*adv.* cerca; ~ *the way* a propósito; *close* ~ muy cerca.

C

cab, *s.* coche *(m.)* de punto; taxi *m.*
cabbage, *s.* col *f.*
cabin, *s.* cabaña *f.;* camarote *m.*; barraca *f.*
cabinet, *s.* armario *m.;* gabinete *m.*, caja *f.;* consejo *(m.)* de ministros.
cabinet-maker, *s.* ebanista *m.*
cable, *s.* cable *m.;* cablegrama *m.;* — *v. a.* mandar un cable, cablegrafiar.
café, *s.* café *m.*
cage, *s.* jaula *f.;* — *v. a.* enjaular.
cake, *s.* bizcocho *m.*, pastel *m.*
calculate, *v. a.* calcular.
calendar, *s.* calendario *m*
calf, *s.* ternero *m.;* becerro. *m.;* *(anatomy)* pantorrilla *f.*
call, *v. a.* llamar; ~ *on* visitar, ir a ver; ~ *up* llamar por teléfono; *to be* ~*ed for* en lista de correos; — *s.* llamada *f.;* visita *f.*
call-box, *s.* cabina *(f.)* telefónica.
calm, *adj.* calmoso, tranquilo; — *s.* calma *f.;* — *v. a.* calmar, tranquilizar.
camel, *s.* camello *m.*
camera, *s.* aparato *(m.)* fotográfico, cámara *(f.)* fotográfica.
camp, *s.* campo *m.*, campamento *m.*, colonia *f.;* — *v. n.* campar.
campaign, *s.* campaña *f.*
camping, *s.* camping *m.*

can¹, *I ~ do it* puedo hacerlo; *you ~ go* puede irse.
can², *s.* jarro *m.; (car)* bidón *m.*
canal, *s.* canal *m.*
canary, *s.* canario *m.*
cancel, *v. a.* cancelar, anular.
cancer, *s.* cancro *m.*
candle, *s.* vela *f.;* bugía *f.*
cane, *s.* cana *f.;* bastón *m.*
cannon, *s.* cañón *m.*
canoe, *s.* canoa *f.*
can-opener, *s.* abrelatas *m.*
canteen, *s.* cantina *f.;* ambigú *m.; (bottle)* cantimplora *f.*
canvas, *s.* lona *f.; (picture)* lienzo *m.*
cap, *s.* gorro *m.;* gorra *f.;* tapa *f.*
capable, *adj.* capaz (de).
capacity, *s.* capacidad *f.*
cape¹, *s.* capa *f.*
cape², *s.* cabo *m.*, promontorio *m.*
capital, *s. (money)* capital *m.; (town)* capital *f.; — adj.* capital.
captain, *s.* capitán *m.*
caption, *s.* leyenda *f.*
capture, *s.* captura *f.; — v. a.* capturar.
car, *s.* coche *m.,* automóvil *m.*, auto *m.*
caravan, *s.* caravana *f.;* coche *(m.)* vivienda.
carbon-paper, *s.* papel *(m.)* carbón.
card, *s.* naipe *m.*, carta *f.;* tarjeta *(f.)* de visita.
cardboard, *s.* cartón *m.*
cardigan, *s.* chaqueta *(f.)* de lana.
cardinal, *s.* cardenal *m.; — adj.* cardinal; *~ number* número *(m.)* cardinal; *the ~ points* los puntos cardinales.
care, *s.* preocupación *f.;* cuidado *m.; take ~!* ¡cuidado!; *c/o* al cuidado de; *— v. n.* preocuparse de; *I don't ~!* ¡qué me importa! *~ for* interesarse por.
career, *s.* carrera *f.*
careful, *adj.* cuidadoso; prudente, cauteloso.
careless, *adj.* descuidado, desatento.
caress, *s.* caricia *f.; — v. a.* acariciar.
cargo, *s.* cargamento *m.*
carnation, *s.* clavel *m.*
carpenter, *s.* carpintero *m.*
carpet, *s.* alfombra *f.*
carriage, *s.* vehículo *m.*, coche *m.*
carriage-way, *s.* autopista *f.; dual ~* carretera *(f.)* con dos pistas.
carrot, *s.* zanahoria *f.*
carry, *v. a.* llevar.
cart, *s.* carretón *m.;* carretilla *f.; — v. a.* transportar.
cartoon, *s.* caricatura *f.;* película *(f.)* de dibujos animados.
cartridge, *s.* cartucho *m.;* rollo *(m.)* de película.
carve, *v. a.* cortar; tallar.
case¹, *s.* caso *m.;* asunto *m.; in ~* caso que; *in any ~* de todos modos.
case², *s.* estuche *m.*, caja *f.*
cash, *s.* caja *f.;* metálico *m.;* moneda *(f.)* contante ; *pay ~* pagar al contado: *~ on delivery* por reembolso; *— v. a.* cobrar.
cash-book, *s.* libro *(m.)* de caja.
cashier, *s.* cajero *m.*
cask, *s.* barril *m.*

cast, *v. a.* echar; ~ *a vote* votar; *s.* tiro *m.*, lance *m.* *(theatre)* reparto *m.*; *(mould)* fundición *f.*

castle, *s.* castillo *m.*; ~*s in Spain* castillos en el aire; — *v. a.* enrocar (chess).
casual, *adj.* casual.
cat, *s.* gato *m.*
catalog(ue), *s.* catalogo *m.*
cataract, *s.* catarata *f.*
catastrophe, *s.* catástrofe *f.*
catch, *v. a.* coger, atrapar; *(arrest)* capturar; ~ *the train* alcanzar el tren; ~ *cold* coger un catarro.
category, *s.* categoría *f.*
cater, *v. a.* abastecer; cuidar de.
caterpillar, *s.* oruga *f.*
cathedral, *s.* catedral *f.*
catholic, *adj.* & *s.* católico *(m.)*; liberal.
cattle, *s.* ganado *m.*
cauliflower, *s.* coliflor *f.*
cause, *s.* causa *f.*; asunto *m.*; — *v. a.* causar.
caution, *s.* prudencia *f.*, precaución *f.*; ~ *money* caución *f.*; *(warning)* advertencia *f.*; — *v. a.* advertir.
cautious, *adj.* cauto, prudente.
cave, *s.* cueva *f.*
cavern, *s.* caverna *f.*
cavity, *s.* cavidad *f.*
cease, *v. a.* &. *n.* cesar.
ceaseless, *adj.* incesante.
cedar, *s.* cedro *m.*
ceiling, *s.* techo *m.*, cielo raso *m.*
celebrate, *v. a.* celebrar.
celebration, s. celebración *f.*
celery, *s.* apio *m.*
cell, *s.* celda *f.*; *(biology)* célula *f.*
cellar, *s.* sótano *m.*
cello, *s.* violoncelo *m.*
cement, *s.* cemento *m.*
cemetery, *s.* cementerio *m.*
centenary, *s.* centenario *m.*
central, *adj.* central; ~ *heating* calefacción *(f.)* central; — *adj.* céntrico.
centre, *s.* centro *m.*; — *v. a.* centralizar, concentrar.
century, *s.* siglo *m.*
cereal, *s.* cereales *m. pl.*
ceremony, *s.* ceremonia *f.*
certain, *adj.* seguro, cierto; *for* ~ sin falta; *make* ~ *of sg* cerciorarse de.
certainly, *adv.* ciertamente.
certificate, *s.* certificado *m.*; ~ *of birth* acta *(f.)* de nacimiento.
certify, *v. a.* certificar.
chain, *s.* cadena *f.*; — *v. a.* encadenar.
chair, *s.* silla *f.*; presidencia *f.* — *v. n.* presidir.
chairman, *s.* presidente *m.*
chalk, *s.* tiza *f.*
challenge, *s.* desafío *m.*; — *v. a.* desafiar.
chamber, *s.* cámara *f.*
champagne, *s.* champaña *m.*
champion, *s.* campeón *m.*
championship, *s.* campeonato *m.*
chance, *s.* oportunidad *f.*; posibilidad *f.*
chancellor, *s.* canciller *m.*
change, *s.* cambio *m.*; *for a* ~ para variar; — *v. a.* cambiar; *(clothes)* mudarse; ~ *train* cambiar de tren.
channel, *s.* canal *m.*; *the English* ~ La Mancha.

chap, *s.* mozo *m.*
chapel, *s.* capilla *f.*
chapter, *s.* capítulo *m.*
character, *s.* carácter *m.*; *(novel)* personaje *m.*
characteristic, *s.* característica *f.*; *adj.* característico.
charge, *s.* *(weapon, electricity)* carga *f.*; *(office)* posición *f.*; cargo *m.*; *(law)* acusación *f.*; ~ *account* cuenta *(f.)* de crédito; *take* ~ *of* hacerse cargo de; — *v. a.* cargar; *(entrust)* encargar; *(expenses)* cobrar; *(law)* acusar.
charity, *s.* caridad *f.*; beneficencia *f.*; limosna *f.*
charm, *s.* encanto *m.*; — *v. a.* encantar.
charming, *adj.* encantador.
chase, *v. a.* cazar; — *s.* caza *f.*, persecución *f.*
chassis, *s.* chasis *m.*
chat, *s.* charla *f.*; plática.
chatter, *v. n.* charlar; castañetear; — *s.* charla *f.*
cheap, *adj.* barato.
cheat, *v. a.* engañar; — *s.* engaño *m.*
check, *s.* cheque *m.*; *(bill)* cuenta *f.*; *(ticket)* marca *f.*; — *v. a.* *(control)* examinar; marcar; *(hinder)* trabar; ~ *up* control; ~ *out* marcharse.
checkmate, *s.* jaque *(m.)* mate; — *v. a.* dar jaque mate.
cheek, *s.* mejilla *f.*
cheeky, *adj.* insolente.
cheer, *s.* alegría *f.*; *give a* ~ dar vivas; — *v. a.* aplaudir.
cheerful, *adj.* alegre, animado.
cheerio, *int.* ¡hasta pronto! *(drinking)* ¡a su salud!
cheese, *s.* queso *m.*
chemical, *adj.* químico.
chemist, *s.* boticario *m.*, químico; ~*'s shop* farmacia *f.*
chemistry, *s.* química *f.*
cheque-book, *s.* talonario *(m.)* de cheques.
cherry, *s.* cereza *f.*; *(tree)* cerezo *m.*
chess, *s.* ajedrez *m.*
chest, *s.* cajón *m.*, armario *m.*; ~ *of drawers* cómoda *f.*; *(anatomy)* pecho *m.*
chestnut, *s.* castaña *f.*; — *adj.* marrón.
chew, *v. a.* mascar, masticar.
chicken, *s.* pollo *m.*, gallina *f.*
chief, *adj.* principal; — *s.* jefe *m.*
chiefly, *adv.* principalmente, sobre todo.
child, *s.* niño *m.*, niña *f.*
childhood, *s.* infancia *f.*
childish, *adj.* pueril.
childless, *adj.* sin hijos.
chill, *s.* frío *m.*; — *v. a.* helar; *fig.* enfriar.
chilly, *adj.* frío.
chimney, *s.* chimenea *f.*
chin, *s.* barba *f.*, barbilla *f.*
china, *s.* porcelana *f.*
Chinese, *adj.* chino.
chip, *s.* astilla *f.*; — *s. pl.* patatas *(f.)* fritas.
chocolate, *s.* chocolate *m.*
choice, *s.* elección *f.*; — *adj.* excelente.
choir, *s.* coro *m.*
choke, *v. a.* ahogar; *v. n.* atragantarse.
choose, *v. a.* elegir, escoger.
chop, *v. a.* cortar; — *s.* chuleta *f.*
Christian, *adj.* & *s.* cris-

tiano *(m.)*.
Christianity, *s.* cristianismo *m.*
Christmas, *s.* Pascua *f.*, Navidad *f.*; *Merry* ~! ¡Felices Pascuas! ~ *eve* Nochebuena *f.*
church, *s.* iglesia *f.*
cider, *s.* sidra *f.*
cigar, *s.* cigarro *m.*, puro *m.*, habano *m.*
cigarette, *s.* cigarrillo *m.*, pitillo *m.*
cigarette-case, *s.* pitillera *f.*
cigarette-holder, *s.* boquilla *f.*
cinder, *s.* ceniza *f.*
cine-camera, *s.* tomavistas *m.*
cinema, *s.* cine *m.*; cinematografía *f.*
circle, *s.* círculo *m.*; — *v. n.* dar vueltas.
circuit, *s.* circuito *m.*; *short* ~ corto circuito.
circular, *adj.* redondo; — *s.* circular *f.*
circulate, *v. a.* & *n.* circular.
circumstance, *s.* circunstancia *f.*; *under no* ~*s* en ningún caso.
circus, *s.* circo *m.*; plaza *(f.)* rotunda.
cite, *v. a.* citar.
citizen, *s.* ciudadano *m.*, ciudadana *f.*
citizenship, *s.* ciudadanía *f.*
city, *s.* ciudad *f.*
civil, *adj.* civil; ~ *service* servicio *(m.)* público; *(polite)* cortés.
civilian, ciudadano *m.*
civilize, *v. a.* civilizar.
claim, *s.* demanda *f.*, pretensión *f.*; — *v. a.* reclamar.
clap, *v. n.* aplaudir; — *s.* aplauso *m.*; palmada *f.*
class, *s.* clase *f.*; — *v. a.* clasificar.
classic, *adj.* & *s.* clásico *(m.)*
classify, *v. a.* clasificar.
class-room, *s.* sala *(f.)* de clase, aula *f.*
clause, *s.* cláusula *f.*
claw, *s.* garra *f.*; — *v. a.* agarrar.
clay, *s.* greda *f.*, arcilla *f*
clean, *adj.* limpio; — *v. a.* limpiar; ~ *out* vaciar; ~ *up* arreglar(se).
cleaning, *s.* limpieza *f.*
clear, *adj.* claro, limpio; — *adv.* por completo, del todo; — *v. a.* limpiar, aclarar.
clergy, *s.* clero *m.*
clergyman, *s.* clérigo *m.*
clerk, *s.* empleado *m.*, dependiente *m.*; secretario *m.*
clever, *s.* listo, inteligente.
client, *s.* cliente *m.*
climate, *s.* clima *m.*
climb, *v. a.* subir; — *s.* subida *f.*
cling, *v. n.* agarrarse de.
clinic, *s.* clínica *f.*
cloak, *s.* abrigo *m.*, capote *m.*, capa *f.*; — *v. a.* cubrir.
cloak-room, *s.* guardarropa *m.*; *(station)* consigna *f.*, depósito *(m.)* de equipajes.
clock, *s.* reloj *m.*
close, *adj.* cercano; *(shut)* cerrado *adv.* ~ *at hand* muy cerca; — *s.* final *m.*; — *v. a.* cerrar, terminar.
closet, *s.* gabinete *m.*; ropero *m.*, armario *m.*; (WC) retrete *m.*
cloth, *s.* tela *f.*; *lay the* ~ poner la mesa.
clothe, *v. a.* vestir.

clothes, *s. pl.* ropa *f.*
clothing, *s.* ropa *f.*
cloud, *s.* nube *f.*; — *v. a.* nublarse.
cloudy, *adj.* nublado.
club, *s.* club *m.*; maza *(f.)* de golf; *(cards)* trébol *m.*; — *v. a.* golpear.
clue, *s.* indicio *m.*, pista *f.*
clutch, *v. a.* agarrar; — *s.* embrague *m.*
coach, *s.* coche *m.*, vagón *m.*; *(person)* entrenador *m.*; — *v. a.* entrenar.
coal, *s.* carbón *m.*
coal-mine, *s.* hullera *f.*, mina *(f.)* de carbón.
coast, *s.* costa *f.*; — *v. n.* costear.
coat, *s.* abrigo *m.*, sobretodo *m.*; *(jacket)* chaqueta *f.*, americana *f.*; — *(paint)* mano *f.*; ~ *of arms* blasón *m.*, escudo *m.*; ~ *v. a.* cubrir.
cock, *s.* gallo *m.*; *(tap)* grifo *m.*; *(hammer)* gatillo *m.*; — *v. a.* amartillar.
cockpit, *s.* cabina *(f.)* del piloto.
cocktail, *s.* coctel *m.*
cocoa, *s.* cacao *m.*
coconut (coco), *s.* coco *m.*
cod, *s.* bacalao *m.*
code, *s.* cifras *f. pl.*; *(law)* código *m.*
coffee, *s.* café *m.*
coffee-mill, *s.* molinillo *(m.)* de café.
coffee-pot, *s.* cafetera *f.*
coffin, *s.* ataúd *m.*
coin, *s.* moneda *f.*
coincidence, *s.* coincidencia *f.*
coke, *s.* coque *m.*
cold, *adj.* frío; *I am* ~ tengo frío; — *s.* frío *m.*; catarro *m.*; ~ *in the head* constipado *m.*, resfrío *m.*
collaborate, *v. n.* cooperar.
collapse, *s.* colapso *m.*; — *v. n.* hundirse.
collar, *s.* cuello *m.*; — *v. a.* agarrar.
colleague, *s.* colega *m.*, compañero *m.*
collect, *v. a.* recoger; coleccionar; *(gather)* reunir(se).
collection, *s.* colección *f.*
college, *s.* colegiò *m.*; universidad *f.*
collide, *v. n.* chocar.
collision, *s.* colisión *f.*
colon,[1] *s.* dos puntos.
colon,[2] *(anatomy)* colón *m.*
colonel, *s.* coronel *m.*
colonial, *adj.* colonial.
colony, *s.* colonia *f.*
colour, *s.* color *m.*; ~*s* bandera *(f.)* nacional; — *v. a.* colorar.
colourless, *adj.* incoloro.
column, *s.* columna *f.*
comb, *s.* peine *m.*; — *v. a.* peinar.
combine, *v. a.* combinar; *v. n.* unirse; — *s.* segadora-trilladora *f.*; cartel *m.*
come, *v. n.* venir; *(arrive)* llegar; ~ *and see me* venga usted a verme; ~ *to know* llegar a saber; ~ *back* volver, regresar; ~ *in* entrar; ~ *up* subir.
comedy, *s.* comedia *f.*
comfort, *s.* comodidad *f.*; — *v. a.* consolar.
comfortable, *adj.* cómodo.
comic, *adj.* & *s.* cómico *(m.)*; — *s.* historietas *(f. pl.)* cómicas.
comma, *s.* coma *f.*
command, *v. a.* & *n.* comandar, ordenar; — *s.*

orden *f.*, mando *m.*
commander, *s.* comandante *m.*
commemorate, *v. a.* conmemorar.
commence, *v. a.* & *n.* empezar, comenzar, principiar.
comment, *s.* comentario *m.*; – *v. n.* hacer comentarios.
commentary, *s.* comentario *m.*
commerce, *s.* comercio *m.*
commercial, *adj.* comercial, mercantil.
commission, *s.* comisión *f.*; – *v. a.* encargar; nombrar, designar.
commissioner, *s.* comisionado *m.*, comisario *m.*
commit, *v. a.* cometer, perpetrar; *(to prison)* encerrar, meter; ~ *oneself* comprometerse.
committee, *s.* comisión *f.*, comité *m.*
common, *adj.* común.
commonwealth, *s.* unión *(f.)* de Estados.
communicate, *v. n.* comunicar.
communication, *s.* comunicación *f.*
communication-cord, *s.* freno *(m.)* de alarma.
community, *s.* comunidad *f.*
compact, *s.* contrato *m.*; *m.*; *(powder)* polvera *f.*; – *adj.* compacto; *fig.* conciso, breve.
companion, *s.* compañero *m.*
company, *s.* compañía *f.*
comparatively, *adv.* relativamente.
compare, *v. a.* comparar.
comparison, *s.* comparación *f.*
compartment, *s.* compartimiento *m.*
compass, *s.* brújula *f.*
compasses, *s. pl.* compás *m.*
compel, *v. a.* obligar.
competence, *s.* competencia *f.*
competition, *s.* competición *f.*
competitor, *s.* competidor *m.*
complain, *v. n.* quejarse.
complaint, *s.* queja *f.*; reclamación *f.*
complete, *adj.* completo; – *v. a.* completar, terminar.
complication, *s.* complicación *f.*
compliment, *s.* piropo *m.*, galantería *f.*; – *v. a.* felicitar.
comply, *v. a.* cumplir; ~ *with* conformarse a.
component, *s.* componente *m.*
compose, *v. a.* componer, formar; ~ *oneself* serenarse.
composer, *s.* compositor *m.*
composition, *s.* composición *f.*
compound, *adj.* & *pp.* compuesto; – *s.* composición *f.*, compuesto *m.*; – *v. a.* componer, mezclar.
comprehend, *v. a.* comprender.
comprehension, *s.* comprensión *f.*
compress, *v. a.* comprimir; – *s.* compresa *f.*
compromise, *s.* compromiso *m.*; – *v. n.* acordarse; comprometer.
compulsory, *adj.* obligatorio, de rigor.
comrade, *s.* camarada *m.*, compañero *m.*

conceal, *v. a.* ocultar, esconder.
conceited, *adj.* presumido
concentrate, *v. a.* concentrar.
concept, *s.* concepto *m.*
conception, *s.* concepción *f.*; opinión *f.*
concern, *v. a.* referirse a, interesar; *be ~ed for* inquietarse por; – *s.* casa *(f.)* comercial, empresa *f.*, *(anxiety)* angustia.
concert, *s.* concierto *m.*; – *v. n.* concertarse.
concession, *s.* concesión *f.*
concise, *adj.* conciso, breve.
conclude, *v. a.* concluir, terminar; *v. n.* llegar a la conclusión.
conclusion, *s.* conclusión *f.*; final *m.*, fin *m.*, cabo *m.*
concrete, *adj.* concreto; – *s.* cemento *m.*; hormigón *m.*
condemn, *v. a.* condenar.
condense, *v. a.* condensar.
condition, *s.* condición *f.*; estado *m.*
conduct, *s.* conducta *f.*, – *v. a.* cònducir, dirigir.
conductor, *s.* cobrador *m.*, revisor *m.*; *(orchestra)* director *m.*
cone, *s.* cono *m.*
confectioner, *s.* confitero *m.*, pastelero *m.*
confectionery, *s.* confitería *f.*, pastelería *f.*
confer, *v. a.* & *n.* conferir.
conference, *s.* conferencia *f.*, reunión *f.*
confess, *v. a.* confesar.
confidence, *s.* confianza *f.*
confident, *adj.* seguro; – *s.* confidente *m.*
confidential, *adj.* confidencial.
confine, *v. a.* limitar; *be ~ed to bed* tener que guardar cama.
confirm, *v. a.* confirmar.
conflict, *s.* conflicto *m.*; – *v. n.* luchar, chocar.
confront, *v. a.* confrontar.
confuse, *v. a.* confundir, desorientar.
confusion, *s.* confusión *f.*
congratulate, *v. a.* felicitar.
congratulation, *s.* felicitación *f.*, enhorabuena *f.*
congress, *s.* congreso *m.*
conjecture, *s.* conjetura *f.*; – *v. a.* conjeturar.
connect, *v. a.* conectar, relacionar: *~ with* enlazar con.
connection, *s.* conexión *f.*
conquer, *v. a.* conquistar, vencer.
conqueror, *s.* conquistador *m.*
conquest, *s.* conquista *f.*
conscience, *s.* conciencia *f.*
conscious, *adj.* consciente; *be ~ of* darse cuenta de.
consent, *s.* permiso *m.*; – *v. n.* consentir.
consequence, *s.* consecuencia *f.*
consequent, *adj.* consecuente, consiguiente.
consequently, *adv.* por lo tanto, por eso.
conservation, *s.* conservación *f.*
conservative, *adj.* conservador.
consider, *v. a.* considerar, estudiar, tomar en cuenta.
considerable, *adj.* considerable, bastante.
considerate, *adj.* atento, delicado.
consideration, *s.* consideración *f.*; *(payment)* retribución *f.*; *take into*

~ tener en cuenta.
consign, *v. a.* consignar; mandar.
consignment, *s.* consignación *f.*, envío *m.*
consist, *v. n.* consistir.
consistent, *adj.* lógico, razonable.
consolation, *s.* consuelo *m.*
consonant, *adj.* & *s.* consonante *(f.)*
conspicuous, *adj.* conspicuo.
constable, *s.* agente *(m.)* de policía, guardia *m.*
constant, *adj.* constante.
constitute, *v. a.* constituir.
constitution, *s.* constitución *f.*
construct, *v. a.* construir.
construction, *s.* construcción *f.*
consul, *s.* cónsul *m.*
consulate, *s.* consulado *m.*
consult, *v. a.* consultar; *v. n.* deliberar.
consultation, *s.* consulta *f.*, deliberación *f.*
consume, *v. a.* consumir.
consumer, *s.* consumidor *m.*
consumption, *s.* consumo *m.*; *(illness)* tisis *f.*, tuberculosis *f.*
contact, *s.* relación *f.*, contacto *m.*
contain, *v. a.* contener; ~ *oneself* contenerse.
container, *s.* recipiente *m.*
contemplate, *v. a.* contemplar; *(project)* proyectar.
contemporary, *adj.* & *s.* contemporáneo *(m.)*.
contempt, *s.* desprecio *m.*, menosprecio *m.*
content, *adj.* contento, satisfecho; — *s.* contento *m.*, satisfacción *f.*
contents, *s. pl.* contenido *m.*
continent, *s.* continente *m.*
continental, *adj.* continental.
continuation, *s.* continuación *f.*
continue, *v. a.* continuar; ~ *reading* seguir leyendo; *to be* ~*d* continuará.
continuous, *adj.* continuo.
contract, *s.* contrato *m.*; — *v. a.* contratarse; *(debt, illness)* contraer.
contradiction, *s.* contradicción *f.*
contrary, *adj.* & *s.* contrario *(m.)*; ~ *to* contrario a; *on the* ~ al contrario.
contrast, *s.* contraste *m.*, diferencia *f.*; — *v. n.* contrastar, hacer contraste; *(compare)* comparar.
contribute, *v. a.* contribuir; *v. n.* colaborar.
contribution, *s.* contribución *f.*; colaboración *f.*
control, *s.* control *m.*; dirección *f.*; ~*s* mando *m.*; — *v. a.* controlar; dirigir.
convenience, *s.* comodidad *f.*
convenient, *adj.* conveniente, cómodo, oportuno.
conversation, *s.* conversación *f.*
converse, *v. n.* conversar.
convert, *v. a.* convertir, transformar.
convey, *v. a.* transmitir, llevar.
conveyance, *s.* transporte *m.*; *(vehicle)* vehículo *m.*
conveyer, *s.* cinta *(f.)* transportadora.
convince, *v. a.* convencer.
cook, *v. a.* cocinar, gui-

sar; — *s.* cocinero *m.*, cocinera *f.*
cool, *adj.* fresco; — *v. a.* enfriar; *v. n.* enfriarse.
co-operative, *s.* cooperativa *f.*
copper, *s.* cobre *m.*
copy, *s.* copia *f.*; número *m.*; — *v. a.* copiar.
coral, *s.* coral *m.*
cord, *s.* cuerda *f.*
cordial, *adj.* & *s.* cordial *(m.)*.
cork, *s.* corcho *m.*; — *v. a.* tapar con corcho.
cork-screw, *s.* sacacorchos *m.*
corn, *s.* grano *m.*; trigo *m.*; *(on the foot)* callo *m.*
corned-beef, *s.* adobado *(m.)* de carne de vaca.
corner, *s.* *(street)* esquina *f.*; *(room)* rincón *m.*
corporal, *s.* cabo *m.*; — *adj.* corporal.
corporation, *s.* corporación *f.*
corps, *s.* cuerpo *m.*; *army* ~ cuerpo *(m.)* de ejército.
corpse, *s.* cadáver *m.*
correct, *adj.* correcto, exacto; — *v. a.* corregir.
correction, *s.* corrección *f.*
correspond, *v. n.* estar de acuerdo; ~ *with* escribir a.
correspondence, *s.* correspondencia *f.*
correspondent, *s.* corresponsal *m.*
corridor, *s.* corredor *m.*, pasillo *m.*
corrupt, *adj.* corrupto; — *v. a.* corromper; — *v. n.* corromperse.
corruption, *s.* corrupción *f.*
cosmetics, *s. pl.* cosmético *m.*
cost, *s.* precio *m.*; — *v. a.* costar.
costly, *adj.* costoso, caro.
costume, *s.* traje *m.*; *(fancy dress)* disfraz *m.*
cottage, *s.* casita *f.*, chalet *m.*
cotton, *s.* algodón *m.*
couch, *s.* diván *m.*
cough, *s.* tos *f.*; — *v. n.* toser.
council, *s.* concejo *m.*, junta *f.*
councillor, *s.* consejero *m.*, concejal *m.*
counsel, *s.* consejo *m.*; *(lawyer)* abogado *m.*; — *v. a.* aconsejar.
count [1], *v. a.* contar; — *s.* recuento *m.*
count [2], *s.* conde *m.*
countenance, *s.* cara f., aspecto *m.*; *(aid)* apoyo *m.*; — *v. a.* apoyar.
counter, *s.* mostrador *m.*; — *adj.* contrario.
countess, *s.* condesa *f.*
country, *s.* país *m.*; región *f.*; *in the* ~ en el campo, en provincias.
countryman, *s.* aldeano *m.*, campesino *m.*
countryside, *s.* paisaje *m.*
county, *s.* condado *m.*, distrito *m.*
couple, *s.* par *m.*; pareja *f.*; — *v. a.* acoplar.
courage, *s.* valor *m.*
courageous, *adj.* valiente, valeroso, bravo.
course, *s.* curso *m.*; *(way)* ruta *f.*, dirección *f.*; *(dish)* plato *m.*; *of* ~ claro, por supuesto.
court, *s.* patio *m.*; *(law)* juzgado *m.*; tribunal *m.*; *(royal)* Corte *f.*; —*v. a.* hacer la corte a.
courteous, *adj.* cortés.

courtesy, *s.* cortesía *f.*
courtyard, *s.* patio *m.*
cousin, *s.* primo *m.*, prima *f.*
cover, *v. a.* cubrir, tapar; *(embrace)* abarcar; *(distance)* recorrer; *(with a weapon)* apuntar; — *s.* tapa *f.*, tapadera *f.*; *(rug)* manta *f.*; *(furniture)* funda *f.*
cow, *s.* vaca *f.*
coward, *adj.* & *s.* cobarde *(m., f.)*.
crab, *s.* cangrejo *m.*
crack *s.* *(sound)* detonación *f.*; *(gap)* raja *f.*, grieta *f.*; — *v. a.* & *n.* rajar; forzar, cascar; ~ *jokes* decir chistes; — *adj.* grande; — *int.* ¡crac!
cracker, *s.* galleta *f.*
cradle, *s.* cuna *f.*; — *v. a.* mecer.
craft, *s.* habilidad *f*, astucia *f.*; *(profession)* profesión *f.*, oficio *m.* *(conveyance)* embarcación *f.*
craftsman, *s.* artesano *m.*
crane, *s.* grua *f.*; *(bird)* grulla *f.*
crash, *s.* choque *m.*; *(sound)* estrépito *m.*; — *v. n.* chocar.
crash-helmet, *s.* casco *(m.)* protector.
crave, *v. a.* anhelar, codiciar.
crawl, *v. n.* marchar lentamente; *(on all fours)* gatear; — *s.* *(swim)* crawl *m.*
crayon, *s.* lápiz *(m.)* de color.
crazy, *adj.* loco, extravagante.
cream, *s.* crema *f.*; *fig.* crema y nata *f.*
create, *v. a.* crear.
creation, *s.* creación *f.*
creator, *s.* creador *m.*
creature *s.* criatura *f.*; *(beast)* animal *m.*, bicho *m.*; *fig.* tipo *m.*
credentials, *s. pl.* credenciales *f. pl.*
credit, *s.* saldo *(m.)* a favor, crédito *m.*
creditor, *s.* acreedor *m.*
crew, *s.* tripulación *f.*; *(group)* cuadrilla *f.*
cricket, *s.* grillo *m.*; *(sport)* cricket *m.*
crime, *s.* delito *m.*, crimen *m.*
criminal, *adj.* & *s.* criminal *(m.)*.
crimson, *adj.* & *s.* carmesí *(m.)*.
cripple, *s.* cojo *(m.)*, estropeado *(m.)*; — *v. a.* estropear.
crisis, *s.* crisis *f.*
critic, *s.* crítico *m.*
critical, *adj.* crítico.
criticism, *s.* crítica *f.*
criticize, *v. a.* criticar.
crooked, *adj.* torcido; *fig.* deshonesto.
crop, *s.* cosecha *f.*; — *v. a.* cosechar; *(hair)* cortar; ~ *up* surgir.
cross, *s.* cruz *f.*; *(crossing)* cruce *m.*; — *v. a.* cruzar; atravesar.
crossing, *s.* cruce *m.*
crossroad, *s.* cruce *(m.)* de caminos.
cross-word (puzzle), *s.* crucigrama *m.*
crow, *s.* cuervo *m.*; *(cock's)* canto *m.*; — *v. n.* cantar.
crowd, *s.* multitud *f.*, muchedumbre *f.*; — *v. a.* abarrotar; — *v. n.* apiñarse.
crowded, *adj.* abarrotado, completamente lleno, de bote en bote.

crown, *s.* corona *f.; fig.* cumbre *f.;* — *v. a.* coronar.
crude, *adj.* bruto; *(rude)* tosco.
cruel, *adj.* cruel.
cruelty, *s.* crueldad *f.*
cruet, *s.* alcuza *f.*, vinagreras *f. pl.*
cruise, *s.* viaje *(m.)* marítimo; — *v. n.* rondar.
crumb, *s.* miga *f.*
crusade, *s.* cruzada *f.*
crush, *v. a.* aplastar; — *v. n.* aplastarse.
crust, *s.* corteza *f.*
cry, *v. n.* gritar; *(weep)* llorar; — *s.* grito *m.*, llanto *m.*
crystal, *s.* cristal *m.*
cub, *s.* cría *f.*, cachorro *m.*
cube, *s.* cubo *m.; (ice-)* cubito *m.; (of sugar)* terrón *m.*
cuckoo, *s.* cuclillo *m.*
cucumber, *s.* pepino *m.*
cue [1], *(theatre)* entrada *f.*
cue [2], *(billiards)* taco *m.*
cuff, *s.* puño *m.; (slap)* bofetada *f.;* — *v. a.* dar una bofetada a.
cultivate, *v. a.* cultivar.
cultural, *adj.* cultural.
culture, *s.* cultura *f.*
cup, *s.* taza *f.;* copa *f.*
cupboard, *s.* aparador *m.;* alacena *f.*, armario *m.*
cure, *v. a.* curar; — *v. n.* curarse; — *s.* cura *f.*
curiosity, *s.* curiosidad *f.;* rareza *f.*
curious, *adj.* curioso; *(odd)* raro.
curl, *s.* rizo *m.;* — *v. a.* rizar.
curly, *adj.* rizado.
currant, *s.* grosella *f.*
currency, *s.* dinero *m.; foreign* ~ divisa *f.*, moneda *(f.)* extranjera.
current, *s.* corriente *f.;* — *adj.* corriente, común; ~ *account* cuenta *(f.)* corriente.
curse, *s.* maldición *f.;* — *v. a.* maldecir.
curtain, *s.* cortina *f.; (theatre)* telón *m.*
curve, *s.* curva *f.;* — *v. a.* curvar; *v. n.* hacer una curva.
cushion, *s.* almohada *f.*, cojín *m.*
custard, *s.* natillas *f. pl.*
custom, *s.* costumbre *f.;* ~*s* impuestos *m. pl.;* aduana *f.*
customary, *adj.* usual, acostumbrado.
customer, *s.* cliente *m.*, parroquiano *m.*
customhouse, *s.* aduana *f.*
cut, *v. a.* cortar; *(hay)* segar; *off* cortar; ~ *out* recortar; ~ *up* dividir, cortar — *s.* cortadura *f.; (of dress)* corte *m.;* parte *f.;* rebaja *f.;* — *adj. (glass)* tallado.
cutlery, *s.* cuchillos *m. pl.*, cubiertos *m. pl.*
cutter, *s.* cortador *m.; (ship)* cuter *m.*
cycle, *s.* ciclo *m.;* bicicleta *f.;* — *v. n.* ir en bicicleta.
cylinder, *s.* cilindro *m.*

D

dad, daddy, *s.* papá *m.*
daily, *adj.* diario; — *adv.* diariamente; — *s.* diario *m.*, periódico *m.*
dainty, *adj.* delicado, fino.
dairy, *s.* lechería *f.*
daisy, *s.* margarita *f.*
dam, *s.* dique *m.*
damage, *s.* daños *m. pl.;* — *v. a.* estropear, ave-

riar.
damages, *s. pl.* indemnización *f.*
dame, *s.* dama *f.*
damn, *v. a.* condenar; — *int.* ¡caray! ~ *it!* ¡Caramba!
dance, *v. n.* bailar; — *s.* baile *m.*
dancer, *s.* bailarín *m.*, bailarina *f.*
Dane, *s.* dinamarqués *m.*, danés *m.*
danger, *s.* peligro *m.*
dangerous, *adj.* peligroso.
Danish, *adj.* danés.
dare, *v. n.* atreverse.
dark, *adj.* oscuro; — *s.* oscuridad *f.*
darkness, *s.* oscuridad *f.*
darling, *adj.* & *s.* querido *(m.)*, alma *f.*
darn, *v. a.* zurzir; — *s.* zurcido *m.*
dash, *v. a.* echar, tirar; — *v. n.* salir corriendo; ~ *it!* ¡demonio!
dash-board, *s.* salpicadero *m.*; cuadro *(m.)* de instrumentos, panel *m.*
data, *s. pl.* datos *m. pl.*
date [1], *(fruit)* dátil *m.*
date [2], *s.* fecha *f.*
daughter, *s.* hija *f.*
daughter-in-law, *s.* nuera *f.*
dawn, *s.* amanecer *m.*, madrugada *f.*; — *v. n.* amanecer.
day, *s.* día *m.*; ~ *by* ~ cada día; *some* ~ un día; *by* ~ de día; *the other* ~ hace poco; *a* ~ *off* día libre.
day-nursery, *s.* guardería *(f.)* infantil.
day-ticket, *s.* billete *(m.)* válido un día.
daytime, *adv.* de día.
deacon, *s.* diácono *m.*
dead, *adj.* & *s.* muerto *(m.)*.
deadly, *adj.* mortal.
deaf, *adj.* sordo.
deal, *v. a. (cards)* repartir, dar; ~ *in* traficar en; ~ *with* tratar *de*; — *s. (business)* negocio *m.*; *square* ~ buen trato *(m.)*; *a great* ~ *of* mucho, gran cantidad de.
dealer, *s.* comerciante *m.*, vendedor *m.*
dealing, *s.* distribución *f.*
dean, *s.* decano *m.*; *(church)* deán *m.*
dear, *adj.* querido; *oh* ~! ¡Dios mío!; *Dear Sir* Muy Señor Mío.
death, *s.* muerte *f.*
debt, *s.* deuda *f.*
debtor, *s.* deudor *m.*
decease, *s.* muerte *f.*; — *v. n.* morir, fallecer.
deceit, *s.* engaño *m.*, trampa *f.*
deceive, *v. a.* engañar.
December, *s.* diciembre *m.*
decent, *adj.* decente.
deception, *s.* decepción *f.*
decide, *v. a.* decidir.
decidedly, *adv.* decididamente.
decision, *s.* decisión *f.*, resolución *f.*
decisive, *adj.* decisivo.
deck, *s.* cubierta *f.*
deck-chair, *s.* silla *(f.)* de tijera.
declare, *v. a.* declarar; *v. n.* declararse.
decline, *v. a.* rehusar; — *v. n.* decaer; — *s.* declinación *f.*
decorate, *v. a.* decorar.
decoration, *s.* decoración *f.*; *(distinction)* condecoración *f.*
decrease, *v. a.* & *n.* disminuir; — *s.* disminución *f.*

decree, *s.* decreto *m.;* — *v. a.* decretar.
dedicate, *v. a.* dedicar.
deed, *s.* acción *f.*, obra *f.; (contract)* contrato *m.*
deep, *adj.* hondo, profundo.
deer, *s.* venado *m.*
defeat, *v. a.* vencer; — *s.* derrota *f.*
defect, *s.* defecto *m.*
defence, *s.* defensa *f.*
defend, *v. a.* defender.
defender, *s.* defensor *m.*
deficient, *adj.* deficiente.
defile, *v. n.* desfilar; — *s.* desfile *m.*
define, *v. a.* definir.
definite, *adj.* definitivo.
definition, *s.* definición *f.*
defy, *v. a.* desafiar.
degree, *s.* grado *m.; by ~s* gradualmente; *(title)* título *m.*
delay, *v. a.* demorar; — *s.* demora *f.*
delegate, *s.* delegado *m.;* — *v. a.* delegar.
delegation, *s.* delegación *f.*
deliberate, *adj.* deliberado; — *v. a.* deliberar.
delicate, *adj.* delicado; — *(wine)* exquisito; *(vase)* frágil
delicious, *adj.* delicioso.
delight, *s.* deleite *m.;* — *v.a.* deleitar, encantar.
delightful, *adj.* delicioso; encantador.
deliver, *v. a.* entregar, repartir; *(speech)* dar, pronunciar.
delivery, *s.* entrega *f.*
delusion, *s.* decepción *f.*
demand, *s.* demanda *f.;* petición *f.;* — *v. a.* exigir; insistir.
democracy, *s.* democracia *f.*
democrat, *s.* demócrata *m., f.*
democratic, *adj.* democrático.
demolish, *v. a.* demoler, derrumbar.
demonstration, *s.* demostración *f.;* manifestación *f.*
den, *s.* caverna *f.*
denial, *s.* denegación *f.*
denomination, *s.* denominación *f.;* valor *(m.)* nominal.
denounce, *v. a.* denunciar.
dense, *adj.* denso, espeso.
dental, *adj.* dental.
dentist, *s.* dentista *m.*
denture, *s.* dentadura *f.*
deny, *v. a.* negar.
deodorant, *adj.* desodorante.
depart, *v. n.* irse, partir.
department, *s.* departamento *m.;* ministerio *m.*
departure, *s.* partida *f.*, salida *f.*
depend, *v. n.* depender; *it ~s* depende; *~ on* confiar en.
dependent, *adj. & s.* dependiente *(m.).*
deplore, *v. a.* deplorar.
depose, *v. a.* deponer.
deposit, *s.* depósito *m.;* — *v. a.* depositar.
depot, *s.* depósito *m.*, almacén *m.*
depress, *v. a.* deprimir.
depression, *s.* depresión *f.*
deprive, *v. a.* privar.
depth, *s.* profundidad *f.*
deputy, *s.* diputado *m.; (substitute)* sustituto, vice-.
derive, *v. a.* derivar; — *v. n.* derivarse.
descend, *v. n.* descender, bajar.
descendant, *s.* descen-

diente *m.*
descent, *s.* descenso *m.; (birth)* descendencia *f.*
describe, *v. a.* describir.
description, *s.* descripción *f.*
desert[1], *s.* desierto *m.*
desert[2], *v. n.* desertar.
deserve, *v. a.* merecer.
design, *v. a.* diseñar, proyectar; — *s.* proyecto *m.*
desire, *s.* deseo *m.*; — *v. a.* desear.
desk, *s.* escritorio *m.*; *(office* despacho *m.*
desolate, *adj.* desolado, despoblado.
despair, *v. n.* desesperar; — *s.* desesperación *f.*
despatch, *see* **dispatch.**
desperate, *adj.* desesperado.
despise, *v. a.* despreciar.
despite, *prep.* a pesar de.
dessert, *s.* postre *m.*
dessert-spoon, *s.* cucharilla *f.*
destination, *s.* destinación *f.*
destine, *v. a.* destinar.
destiny, *s.* destino *m.*
destroy, *v. a.* destruir.
destruction, *s.* destrucción *f.*
detach, *v. a.* separar; destacar.
detachment, *s.* separación *f.*; destacamento *m.*
detail, *s.* detalle *m.*; — *v. a.* detallar.
detain, *v. a.* detener.
detective, *s.* detective *m.*
detergent, *s.* detergente *m.*
deteriorate, *v. a.* deteriorar; — *v. n.* deteriorarse.
determine, *v. a.* determinar; decidir.
detonation, *s.* detonación *f.*
develop, *v. a.* desarrollar; *(film)* revelar.
development, *s.* desarrollo *m.*; *(event)* cambio *m.*, acontecimiento *m.*
device, *s. (trick)* recurso *m.*, ardid *m.*; *(mechanism)* dispositivo m., aparato *m.*
devil, *s.* diablo *m.*, demonio *m.*
devoted, *adj.* fiel, aficionado.
devotion, *s.* devoción *f.*
devour, *v. a.* devorar.
dew, *s.* rocío *m.*
diabetes, *s.* diabetes *f.*
diadem, *s.* diadema *f.*
diagnosis, *s.* diagnosis *f.*
diagram, *s.* diagrama *m.*
dial *s.* cuadrante *m.*, esfera *f.*; disco *m.* — *v. a.* marcar.
dialect, *s.* dialecto *m.*
dialogue, *s.* diálogo *m.*
diameter, *s.* diámetro *m.*
diamond, *s.* diamante *m.*; — *adj.* de diamantes.
diaper, *s.* pañal *m.*
diarrhoea, *s.* diarrea *f.*
diary, *s.* diario *m.*
dictate, *v. a.* dictar.
dictation, *s.* dictado *m.*
dictionary, *s.* diccionario *m.*
die[1], *s.* dado *m.*
die[2], *v. n.* morir; *(motor)* pararse.
diet, *s.* dieta *f.*; — *v. n.* estar a dieta.
differ, *v. n.* diferir.
difference, *s.* diferencia *f.*; *it makes no* ~ no importa
different, *adj.* diferente, distinto.
difficult, *adj.* difícil.
difficulty, *s.* dificultad

f.
diffuse, *v. a.* difundir; — *adj.* difuso.
dig, *v. a.* excavar, sacar.
digest, *v. a.* digerir; — *s.* resumen *m.*, reseña *f.*
digestion, *s.* digestión *f.*
dignity, *s.* dignidad *f.*
diligence, *s.* diligencia *f.*
diligent, *adj.* diligente, aplicado.
dimension, *s.* dimensión *f.*
diminish, *v. a.* disminuir.
dine, *v. a.* comer, cenar.
dining-car, *s.* coche comedor *m.*
dining-room, *s.* comedor *m.*
dinner, *s.* cena *f.*, comida *f.*, *have* ~ cenar, comer.
dinner-jacket, *s.* smoking *m.*
diphtheria, *s.* difteria *f.*, difteritis *f.*
diploma, *s.* diploma *m.*
diplomacy, *s.* diplomacia *f.*
diplomatic, *adj.* diplomático.
direct, *v. a.* dirigir; — *adj.* directo; *fig.* recto.
direction, *s.* dirección *f.*, rumbo *m.*; *(command)* instrucción *f.*
directly *adv.* directamente
director, *s.* director *m.*
directory, *s.* libro *(m.)* de señas; guía *f.*
dirt, *s.* suciedad *f.*, basura *f.*
dirty, *adj.* sucio; — *v. a.* manchar.
disadvantage, *s.* desventaja *f.*
disagree, *v. n.* disentir; oponerse.
disagreeable, *adj.* desagradable.
disappear, *v. n.* desaparecer.
disappoint, *v. a.* desengañar.
disappointment, *s.* desengaño *m.*
disapprove, *v. a.* desaprobar.
disarm, *v. a.* desarmar.
disaster, *s.* desastre *m.*
disc, *s.* disco *m.*
discern, *v. a.* discernir.
discharge, *v. a.* descargar; *(duties)* desempeñar, cumplir; *(from the hospital)* dar de alta; — *s.* descarga *f.*; *(shot)* disparo *m.*
discipline, *s.* disciplina *f.*; — *v. a.* disciplinar.
discourage, *v. a.* desanimar.
discourse, *s.* discurso *m.*; — *v. a.* tratar de.
discover, *v. a.* descubrir.
discovery, *s.* descubrimiento *m.*
discreet, *adj.* discreto.
discretion, *s.* discreción *f.*, prudencia *f.*
discuss, *v. a.* discutir.
discussion, *s.* discusión *f.*
disease, *s.* enfermedad *f.*
disembark, *v. a.* & *n.* desembarcar.
disgrace, *s.* deshonra *f.*
disgraceful, *adj.* deshonroso, vergonzoso.
disguise, *s.* disfraz *m.*; — *v. a.* disfrazar.
disgust, *s.* disgusto *m.*; — *v. a.* disgustar; *I'm* ~*ed* me repugna, me disgusta.
disgusting, *adj.* repugnante.
dish, *s.* plato *m.*; — *v. a.* ~ *up* servir.
dishonest, *adj.* deshonesto.
dishonour, *s.* deshonor

m.; — *v. a.* deshonrar.
dish-water, *s.* lavadura *f.*, lavazas *f. pl.*
disinfect, *v. a.* desinfectar.
disk, *see* **disc.**
dislike, *v. a.* no querer; *I* ~ *it* no me gusta; — *s.* antipatía *f.*
dismiss, *v. a.* despedir.
disobedient, *adj.* desobediente.
disobey, *v. n.* desobedecer.
disorder, *s.* desorden *m.*
dispatch, *v. a.* despachar, enviar; — *s.* despacho *m.*
dispensary, *s.* farmacia *f.*; dispensario *m.*
dispense, *v. a.* dispensar; ~ *with* pasar sin.
disperse, *v. a.* dispersar; — *v. n.* dispersarse.
displease, *v. n.* desagradar.
disposal, *s.* disposición *f.*; *for* ~ por vender.
dispose, *v. a.* disponer.
disposition, *s.* disposición *f.*; *(mind)* genio *m.*
dispute, *v. n.* disputar, discutir; — *s.* disputa *f.*, discusión *f.*
disqualify, *v. a.* descalificar.
dissolve, *v. a.* disolver; — *v. n.* disolverse, desaparecer.
distance, *s.* distancia *f.*
distant, *adj.* dis'ante, lejano.
distinct, *adj.* claro, preciso, diferente, distinto.
distinguish, *v. a.* distinguir; ~ *oneself* distinguirse.
distort, *v.a.* torcer.
distract, *v.a.* distraer.
distress, *s.* angustia *f.*; *(danger)* peligro *m.*, apuro *m.*; — *v. a.* angustiar.
distribute, *v. a.* distribuir.
distribution, *s.* distribución *f*; *(mail)* reparto *m.*
district, *s.* distrito *m.*
disturb, *v. a.* molestar, perturbar.
dive, *v. n.* zambullirse; — *s.* zambullida *f.*; *(plane)* picada *f.*
diver, *s.* buzo *m.*
divide, *v. a.* dividir.
dividend, *s.* dividendo *m.*
divine, *adj.* divino; — *v. a.* adivinar.
diving, *s.* salto *(m.)* de palanca.
diving-board, *s.* trampolín *m.*, palanca *f.*
division, *s.* división *f.*
divorce, *s.* divorcio *m.*; — *v. n.* divorciarse.
dizzy, *adj.* mareado; *(speed)* vertiginoso.
do, *v. a.* hacer; *what can I* ~ *for you?* ¿en qué puedo servirle? ; *that will* ~ está bien, basta; *that won't* ~ no conviene; ~ *one's best* hacer todo lo posible; *nothing* ~*ing!* ¡qué se le va a hacer!; *I am done* estoy muerto de cansancio; *how* ~ *you* ~*?* !buenos días! (¡buenas noches!); ¡hola!; *he is* ~*ing well* está bien; le va bien; *I don't know* no sé; *so* ~ *I* yo también; *you like coffee, don't you?* le gusta el café, ¿verdad?; ~ *again* repetir.
dock, *s.* muelle *m.*; — *v. n.* atracar.

dockyard, *s.* astilleros *m. pl.*
doctor, *s.* médico *m.*, doctor *m.*; — *v. a.* curar, tratar.
document, *s.* documento *m.*
documentary, ~ *film* película *(f.)* documental.
dog, *s.* perro *m.*
doll, *s.* muñeca *f.*
dollar, s. dólar *m.*
dome, *s.* cúpula *f.*
domestic, *adj.* *(person)* casero; *(animal)* doméstico; – *s.* doméstica *f.*, criada *f.*
dominate, *v. n.* dominar.
dominion, *s.* dominio *m.*
donkey, *s.* burro *m.*, asno *m.*
door, *s.* puerta *f*; *next* ~ al lado; *out of* ~*s* al aire libre; fuera.
dormitory, *s.* dormitorio *m.*
dose, *s.* dosis *f.*
dot, *s.* punto *m.*
double, *adj.* doble; ~ *bed* cama *(f.)* de matrimonio; ~ *bedroom* habitación *(f.)* con dos camas; — *v. a.* duplicar, doblar.
doubt, *s.* duda *f.*; *no* ~ sin duda; — *v. n.* dudar.
doubtful, *adj.* dudoso.
doubtless, *adv.* sin duda, indudablemente.
dough, *s.* masa *f.*
dove, *s.* paloma *f.*
down, *adv.* abajo; *go* ~ bajar; ~ *in the country* en el campo; — *prep.* ~ *the river* río abajo.
downstairs, *adv.* (escaleras) abajo.
downward(s), *adv.* hacia abajo.
dozen, *s.* docena *f.*
draft, *s.* *(plan)* plano *m.*; *(air)* corriente *(f.)* de aire; *(chimney)* tiro *m.*; *(bank)* giro *m.*; — *v. a.* *(plan)* trazar; *(recruit)* reclutar.
drain, *v. a.* desecar; *fig.* agotar; — *s.* desagüe *m.*
drama, *s.* drama *m.*
dramatic, *adj.* dramático.
draper, *s.* pañero *m.*
drapery, *s.* paños *m. pl.*; *(ornament)* colgaduras *f pl.*
draught, *s.* tiro *m.*; tracción *f.*; *(drink)* trago *m.*; *(air)* corriente *(f.)* de aire; *(sketch)* esbozo *m.*; *(ship)* calado *m.*
draw, *v. a.* *(fetch)* sacar; *(at school; sketch)* dibujar; ~ *to an end* llegar a su fin; ~ *back* retirar(se); ~ *near* acercarse; ~ *out* sonsacar; ~ *up* *(sketch)* redactar; — *s.* *(lottery)* sorteo *m.*; *(game)* empate *m.*
drawer, s. gaveta *f.*; *chest of* ~*s* cajón *m.*; *(person)* dibujante *m.*; *s. pl.* calzoncillos *m. pl.*
drawing-pin, *s.* chinche *f.*
drawing-room, *s.* sala *f.*, salón *m.*
drawn, *adj.* empatado.
dread, *v. n.* temer, tener miedo; — *s.* miedo *m.*, terror *m.*
dreadful, *adj.* espantoso.
dream, *s.* sueño *m.*; — *v. n.* soñar.
dress, *s.* traje *m.*, vestido *m.*; — *v. a.* vestir; *(decorate)* arreglar; *(hair)* peinar; *(wound)* hacer la cura a.
dresser, *s.* aparador *m.*
dressing-gown, *s.* bata *f.*

dressmaker, *s.* modista *f.*
dress-suit *s.* frac *m.*
drift, *s.* corriente *f.*; propensión *f.*; — *v. a.* arrastrar; *v. n.* dejarse arrastrar; amontonarse.
drill, *s.* taladro *m.*; *(exercise)* entrenamiento *m.*; — *v. a.* perforar; entrenar, hacer ejercicios.
drink, *v. a.* beber; ~ *to sy's health* brindar por; — *s.* bebida *f.*; trago *m.*
drip, *v. n* gotear.
drive, *v. a.* *(car)* conducir; *(nail)* clavar; ~ *at* proponerse; ~ *away* echar; — *s.* *(road)* carretera *f.*; *(by car)* paseo *(m.)* en coche *(golf)* golpe *m.*; *(campaign)* campaña *f.*
driver, *s.* chófer *m.*, motorista *m.*
driving license, *s.* permiso *(m.)* de conductor.
drop, *s.* gota *f.*; — *v. a.* dejar caer; *v. n.* caerse, bajar; ~ *in* pasar por; venir (a ver).
drown, *v. n.* ahogarse.
drug, *s.* droga *f.*, medicina *f.*; narcótico *m.*; — *v. a.* narcotizar.
druggist, *s.* boticario *m.*
drunk, *adv.* borracho; *get* ~ emborracharse.
dry, *adj.* seco; ~ *land* tierra *(f.)* firme; *fig.* aburrido; — *v. a.* secar; ~ *up* secarse.
dry-clean, *v. a.* limpiar en seco.
dub, *v. a.* apodar; *(film)* sincronizar.
duchess, *s.* duquesa *f.*
duck, *s.* pato *m.*; — *v. n.* bajar, agachar; — *v. a.* zambullir.
due, *adj.* *the train is* ~ *at noon* el tren debe llegar al mediodía; *in* ~ *time* a su tiempo; — *s.* cuota *f.*; impuesto *m.*
duel, *s.* duelo *m.*
duke, *s.* duque *m.*
dull, *adj.* *(knife)* romo; *(sad)* triste; *(pain)* sordo; *(boring)* soso, aburrido; *(stupid)* torpe.
duly, *adv.* debidamente.
dumb, *adj.* mudo; *strike* ~ dejar atónito.
dummy, *s.* maniquí *m.*, *(cards)* muerto *m.*; *(theatre)* comparsa *f.*; *(imitation)* imitación *f.*; *(baby)* chupete *m.*
duplicate, *s.* copia *f.*
durable, *adj.* durable, duradero.
during, *prep.* durante.
dusk, *s.* crepúsculo *m.*, oscurecer *m.*
dusky, *adj.* oscuro, sombrío.
dust, *s.* polvo *m.*; *bite the* ~ morder el polvo; — *v. a.* quitar el polvo de.
dustbin, *s.* lata *(f.)* para la basura; cubo *m.*
dustman, *s.* basurero *m.*
dusty, *adj.* polvoriento.
Dutch, *adj.* holandés.
Dutchman, *s.* holandés *m.*
duty, *s.* deber *m.*; *on* ~ de guardia, de servicio; *off* ~ libre de servicio; *(taxes)* impuesto *m.*
duty-free, *adj.* libre de derechos.
dwarf, *s.* enano *m.*
dwell, *v. n.* vivir, habitar; ~ *on* insistir en.
dwelling, *s.* vivienda *f.*

casa *f.*
dwelling-house, *s.* casa *(f.)* de vivienda.
dye, *v. a.* teñir; — *s.* tinte *m.*

E

each, *pron.* cada; ~ *other* el uno al otro.
ear, *s.* oído *m.; I'am all ~s* soy todo oídos; *anat.* oreja *f.*
earl, *s.* conde *m.*
early, *adj.* pronto, rápido; ~ *life* juventud *f.*; ~ *riser* madrugador *m.*; — *adv.* temprano.
earn, *v. a.* ganar.
earnest, *adj.* serio; — *s. in* ~ en serio.
earth, *s.* mundo *m.*, tierra *f.*; — *v. a.* dar tierra.
earthquake, *s.* terremoto *m.*
ease, *s.* naturalidad *f.*; *live a life of* ~ llevar una vida desahogada; *be at* ~ estar tranquilo; *with* ~ con soltura; — *v. a.* aliviar.
east, *s.* este *m.*, *the Near East* el Oriente Cercano; *the Far East* el Extremo Oriente.
Easter, *s.* Pascua *(f.)* de Resurrección; Pascua Florida.
eastern, *adj.* del este, oriental.
easy, *adj.* fácil; *feel easier* sentirse mejor; — *adv. take it* ~! ¡tómelo con calma!
easy-chair, *s.* sillón *m.*, butaca *f.*
eat, *v. a.* comer; *I want something to* ~ quiero algo para comer.
ebb, *s.* reflujo *m.*; — *v. n.* disminuir, bajar.
echo, *s.* eco *m*; — *v. a. & n.* resonar; repetir.
economic(al), *adj.* económico.
economics, *s pl.* economía *(f.)* política.
economy, *s.* economía *f.*
edge, *s. (razor)* filo *m.*; *(book)* borde *m.*
edition, *s.* edición *f.*
editor, *s.* redactor *m.*
editorial, *adj. & s.* editorial *(m.)*, artículo *(m.)* de fondo.
educate, *v. a.* educar.
education, *s.* educación *f.*
effect, *s.* efecto *m.*, resultado *m.*; *in* ~ en realidad; *go into* ~ entrar en vigor; — *v. a.* efectuar, realizar.
effective, *adj.* de buen efecto; *become* ~ entrar en vigor.
effort, *s.* esfuerzo *m.*; intento *m.*
egg, *s.* huevo *m.*; *boiled* ~ huevo pasado por agua.
egg-cup, *s.* huevera *f.*
Egyptian, *adj. & s.* egipcio *(m.)*.
eight, *adj. & s.* ocho,
eighteen, *adj. & s.* diez y ocho, dieciocho.
eighth, *adj.* octavo.
eighty, *adj. & s.* ochenta.
either, *adj. & pron.* cualquiera de los dos; *on* ~ *side* a ambos lados; ~.. *or* o...o.
elastic, *adj. & s.* elástico *(m.)*; goma *f.*
elbow, *s.* codo *m.*
elder, *adj.* mayor.
elderly, *adj.* de cierta edad.
elect, *v. a.* elegir; — *adj.* electo.
election, *s.* elección *f.*

electric(al), *adj*. eléctrico.
electricity, *s*. electricidad *f*.
electron, *s*. electrón *m*.
electronic, *adj*. electrónico.
elegance, *s*. elegancia *f*.
elegant, *adj*. elegante.
element, *s*. elemento *m*.
elementary, *adj*. elemental
elephant, *s*. elefante *m*.
eleven, *adj*. & *s*. once.
eleventh, *adj*. undécimo.
else, *conj*. o; *or* ~ o si no; – *pron*. & *adj*. más; *everyone* ~ todos los demás; *nothing* ~ nada más.
elsewhere, *adv*. en otra parte.
embankment, *s*. *(river)* dique *m*.; *(railway)* calzada *f*.; *(port)* muelle *m*.
embark, *v*. *a*. embarcar.
embassy, *s*. embajada *f*.
embrace, *v*. *a*. abrazar; *(contain)* abarcar.
embroider, *v*. *a*. bordar.
emerge, *v*. *n*. emerger.
emergency, *s*. emergencia *f*.
emigrant, *s*. emigrante *m*., *f*.
emigrate, *v*. *n*. emigrar.
emigration, *s*. emigración *f*.
emit, *v*. *a*. emitir.
emotion, *s*. emoción *f*.
emperor, *s*. emperador *m*.
empire, *s*. imperio *m*.
employ, *v*. *a*. emplear; – *s*. empleo *m*.
employee, *s*. empleado *m*.
employer, *s*. patrón *m*.
employment, *s*. empleo *m*.
empty, *adj*. vacío; *I feel* ~ tengo hambre; – *v*. *a*. vaciar; *v*. *n*. vaciarse.
enable, *v*. *a*. permitir.
enclose, *v*. *a*. cercar; *(annex)* adjuntar; ~*d* adjunto.
encounter, *s*. encuentro *m*.; – *v*. *a*. encontrar, dar con.
encourage, *v*. *a*. estimular, animar, *fig*. fomentar.
encyclopaedia, *s*. enciclopedia *f*.
end, *s*. final *m*.; *(aim)* fin *m*.; *loose* ~*s* cabos *m*. *pl*.; – *v*. *n*. terminar.
endeavour, *v*. *n*. esforzarse; – *s*. esfuerzo *m*.
ending, *s*. fin *m*.; *(of a word)* desinencia *f*.
endless, *adj*. sin fin, infinito.
endorse, *v*. *a*. endosar.
endorsement, *s*. endoso *m*.
endow, *v*. *a*. dotar.
enemy, *s*. enemigo *m*.
energetic, *adj*. enérgico.
energy, *s*. energía *f*.
engage, *v*. *a*. *(room)* reservar; *(maid)* tomar.
engagement, *s*. compromiso *m*., cita *f*.; esponsales *m*. *pl*.
engine, *s*. motor *m*.; *(train)* locomotora *f*.
engineer, *s*. ingeniero *m*.; *(driver)* maquinista *m*.
English, *adj*. inglés; *the* ~ los ingleses.
Englishman, *s*. inglés *m*.
Englishwoman, *s*. inglesa *f*.
engrave, *v*. *a*. grabar.
enjoy, *v*. *a*. gozar de; ~ *oneself* divertirse.
enjoyment, *s*. goce *m*.; placer *m*.
enlarge, *v*. *a*. ampliar, agrandar.
enormous, *adj*. enorme.
enough, *adj*. suficiente;

adv. bastante; *that's* ~! ¡basta!
enquire, *see* **inquire.**
enrich, *v. a.* enriquecer.
ensign, *s.* bandera *f.*, enseña *f.*; *(person)* alférez *m.*
enter, *v. a.* entrar en; ~ *the army* ingresar en el ejército; *(name)* registrar, anotar.
enterprise, *s.* empresa *f.*
entertain, *v. a.* divertir, entretener.
entertainment, *s.* divertimiento *m.*; *(show)* espectáculo *m.*
enthusiasm, *s.* entusiasmo *m.*
enthusiastic, *adj.* entusiástico.
entire, *adj.* entero, todo.
entirely, *adv.* totalmente, completamente.
entitle, *v. a.* titular, denominar; *(authorize)* autorizar.
entrails, *s. pl.* vísceras *f. pl.*, entrañas *f. pl.*
entrance, *s.* entrada *f.*; ~ *examination* examen *(m.)* de ingreso.
entry, *s.* entrada *f.*; *(account)* partida *f.*; *(sports)* competidor *m.*
enumerate, *v. a.* enumerar.
envelop, *v. a.* envolver, cubrir.
envelope, *s.* sobre *m.*
envious, *adj.* envidioso.
environment, *s.* ambiente *m.*
envy, *s.* envidia *f.*; – *v. a.* envidiar.
epidemic, *s.* epidemia *f.*; – *adj.* epidémico.
equal, *adj.* & *s.* igual *(m., f.)*; – *v. n.* equivaler; – *v. n.* igualar.
equality, *s.* igualdad *f.*
equator, *s.* ecuador *m.*
equip, *v. a.* equipar.
equipment, *s.* equipo *m.*
err, *v. n.* errar, equivocarse.
errand, *s.* recado *m.*, mandado *m.*
error, *s.* error *m.*; *be in* ~ equivocarse.
escalator, *s.* escalera *(f.)* móvil, escalera rodante.
escape, *v. n.* fugarse, escaparse; *v. a.* evitar, escapar a; *it* ~*s me* no me viene a la memoria; – *s.* fuga *f.*
escort, *s.* escolta *f.*; – *v. a.* escoltar.
especial, *adj.* especial.
especially, *adv.* especialmente.
essay, *s.* ensayo *m.*; – *v. a.* ensayar, intentar.
essence, *s.* esencia *f.*
essential, *adj.* esencial.
establish, *v. a.* establecer.
establishment, *s.* establecimiento *m.*
estate, *s.* estado *m.*; *(property)* propiedad *f.*, finca *f.*; *real* ~ inmueble *m.*
esteem, *v. a.* estimar; – *s.* estima *f.*
eternal, *adj.* eterno.
eucharist, *s.* eucaristía *f.*
European, *adj.* & *s.* europeo.
evacuate, *v. a.* evacuar.
even, *adj.* *(surface)* liso; *(speed)* uniforme; *(number)* par; *(exact)* exacto; – *v. a.* igualar; – *adv.* hasta, aún; *not* ~ ni siquiera; ~ *if* aun cuando.
evening, *s.* tarde *f.* *(before sunset)*; noche *f.* *(after sunset)*; ~ *dress* vestido *(m.)* de noche, traje *(m.)* de etiqueta.

event, *s.* acontecimiento *m.*, suceso *m.*; *(sports)* competición *f.*
eventually, *adv.* eventualmente, finalmente.
ever, *adv.* alguna vez; *(always)* siempre; ~ *since* desde que; *for* ~ por siempre; *Yours* ~ suyo afectísimo; ~ *so much* muchísimo.
every, *adj.* & *pron.* cada, todos *m.pl.*; ~ *day* cada día, todos los días; ~ *other day* un día sí y otro no.
everybody, *pron.* todo el mundo.
everyday, *adj.* diario, cotidiano.
everyone, *pron.* todo el mundo.
everything, *pron.* todo.
everywhere, *adv.* en todas partes.
evidence, *s.* evidencia *f.*
evident, *adj.* evidente.
evil, *adj.* malo; — *s.* mal *m.*
exact, *adj.* exacto; — *v. a.* exigir.
exactly, *adv.* exactamente.
exaggerate, *v. a.* exagerar.
examination, *s.* examen *m.*; *medical* ~ reconocimiento *(m.)* médico.
examine, *v. a.* examinar; *(doctor)* reconocer; *(judge)* interrogar.
example, *s.* ejemplo *m.*; *for* ~ por ejemplo.
excavation, *s.* excavación *f.*
exceed, *v. a.* exceder.
exceedingly, *adv.* sumamente.
excel, *v. n.* sobresalir.
excellent, *adj.* excelente.
except, *v. a.* exceptuar; — *conj.* excepto.
exception, *s.* excepción *f.*
exceptional, *adj.* excepcional.
excess, *s.* exceso *m.*, sobrante *m.*; — *adj.* ~ *luggage* exceso de equipaje.
excessive, *adj.* excesivo.
exchange, *s.* cambio *m.*; *in* ~ *for* a cambio de; *(building)* bolsa *(f.)* de cambio; *foreign* ~ divisa *f.*; *rate of* ~ curso *m.*, cambio *m.*; *bill of* ~ giro *m.*; *telephone* ~ central *(f.)* telefónica; — *v. a.* cambiar.
excitement, *s.* excitación *f.*; agitación *f.*
exclaim, *v. n.* exclamar.
exclude, *v. a.* excluir.
excursion, *s.* excursión *f.*
excuse, *s.* razón *f.*; — *v. a.* perdonar, dispensar, disculpar; ~ *me* perdóneme.
execute, *v. a.* *(order)* cumplir; *(music)* ejecutar; *(criminal)* ejecutar.
execution, *s.* cumplimiento *m.*; ejecución *f.*
executive, *adj.* ejecutivo, directivo; ~ *board* consejo *(m.)* de administración; — *s.* ejecutor *m.*, director *m.*
exercise, *s.* ejercicio *m.*; — *v. a.* & *n.* hacer ejercicio, entrenar.
exhaust, *v. a.* agotar; *be* ~*ed* estar exhausto.
exhibit, *v. a.* exhibir; — *s.* exhibición *f.*, exposición *f.*; *(jury)* cuerpo *(m.)* de delito.
exile, *s.* destierro *m.*, exilio *m.*; — *v. a.* desterrar, exilar.
exist, *v. n.* existir.
existence, *s.* existencia *f.*

exit, *s.* salida *f.*
expect, *v. a.* esperar, contar con; *I ~ so* lo supongo.
expectation, *s.* expectación *f.*, expectativa *f.*
expedition, *s.* expedición *f.*
expense, *s.* gasto *m.*
expensive, *adj.* caro.
experience, *s.* experiencia *f.*; — *v. a.* pasar por, sufrir.
experiment, *s.* experimento *m.*; — *v. n.* experimentar.
experimental, *adj.* experimental.
expert, *adj. & s.* experto *(m.)*.
expire, *v. n.* expirar.
explain, *v. a.* explicar; justificar.
explanation, *s.* explicación *f.*
exploit, *s.* hazaña *f.*; — *v. a.* explotar.
exploration, *s.* exploración *f.*
explore, *v. a.* explorar.
explosion, *s.* explosión *f.*
export, *s.* exportación *f.*; — *v. a.* exportar.
exporter, *s.* exportador *m.*
expose, *v a.* exponer; revelar.
exposure, *s.* exposición *f.*; fotografía *f.*
express, *adj.* expreso; — *s. (train)* expreso *m.*; — *v. a.* exprimir; *~ oneself* expresarse.
expression, *s.* expresión *f.*
exquisite, *adj.* exquisito.
extend, *v. a.* extender; *(visa)* prorrogar; *(lenghten)* prolongar; *(congratulations)* expresar; — *v. n.* extenderse.
extension, *s.* extensión *f.*; prolongación *f.*
external, *adj.* externo.
extinguish, *v. a.* extinguir, apagar.
extra, *adj.* adicional, de más; — *s. (news-paper)* extra *m.*; *(theatre)* comparsa *f.*
extract, *s.* extracto *m.*; — *v. a.* extraer.
extraordinary, *adj.* extraordinario.
extremely, *adv.* sumamente.
extremity, *s.* extremidad *f.*
eye, *s.* ojo *m.*; *keep an ~ on* vigilar.
eyebrow, *s.* ceja *f.*
eyeglasses, *s. pl.* gafas *f. pl.*; lentes *m. pl.*
eyelid, *s.* párpado *m.*
eyepiece, *s.* ocular *m.*
eyeshade, *s.* guardavista *m.*; visera *f.*
eyesight, *s.* vis

F

fable, *s.* fábula *f.*
face, *s.* cara *f.*; *~ down* boca abajo; *~ to ~* cara a cara; *make ~s* hacer muecas; — *v. a.* hacer frente a; *the room ~s the street* el cuarto da a la calle.
facility, *s.* facilidad *f.*
fact, *s.* hecho *(m.)* verídico; *as a matter of ~* en realidad.
factory, *s.* fábrica *f.*
faculty, *s.* facultad *f.*
fade, *v. n.* desteñirse; *(flowers)* marchitarse.
fail, *v. n.* faltar; *~ to*

find no poder encontrar; — *s. without* ~ sin falta.
failure, *s.* fracaso *m.; heart* ~ ataque *(m.)* al corazón.
faint, *adj.* desfallecido; *(colour)* pálido; *(idea)* vago; — *v. n.* desmayarse.
fair,[1] *s.* feria *f.*
fair,[2] *adj. (hair)* rubio; *(nice)* bueno, bello; *(passable)* ni bien ni mal; ~ *price* precio *(m.)* razonable; — *adv.* honestamente, limpiamente.
fairly, *adv.* bastante.
faith, *s.* confianza *f.; in good* ~ de buena fe.
faithful, *adj.* fiel, leal.
faithfully, *adv.* fielmente, lealmente; *yours* ~ s. s. s. (su seguro servidor).
falcon, *s.* halcón *m.*
fall, *v. n.* caer, caerse; *(curtain)* bajar; ~ *ill* caer enfermo; ~ *back* retroceder; ~ *for* prenderse de; ~ *in love* enamorarse de; ~ *off* disminuir; ~ *through* fracasar; — *s.* caída *f.; (slope)* declive; *(water)* catarata *f.*
false, *adj.* falso; fingido; ~ *teeth* dentadura *(f.)* postiza.
fame, *s.* fama *f.*
familiar, *adj.* conocido, familiar; *be* ~ *with* estar familiarizado con.
family, *s.* familia *f.;* — *adj.* de familia.
famine, *s.* hambre *f.*
famous, *adj.* famoso.
fan[1], *s.* abanico *m.;* ventilador *m.;* — *v. a.* abanicar.
fan[2], *(sports)* aficionado *m.;* hincha *m.*
fancy, *s.* fantasía *f.;* imaginación *f.;* — *v. n.* imaginarse.
fantastic, *adj.* fantástico.
far, *adv,* lejos; *so* ~ hasta ahora; *how* ~ *is it?* ¿a qué distancia está? ~ *from it* muy al contrario; *by* ~ con mucho; *as* ~ *I know* que yo sepa; *as* ~ *as the town* hasta la ciudad; — *adj.* lejano; *on the* ~ *side of* al otro lado de.
fare, *s.* precio *(m.)* del billete; *(person)* viajero *m.; (food)* comida *f.;* — *v. n.* vivir; salir; *(eat)* comer.
farewell, *s.* despedida *f.; take one's* ~ *of sy* despedirse de.
farm, *s.* finca *f.;* granja *f.;* hacienda *f.;* — *v. a.* cultivar, labrar.
farmer, *s.* labrador *m.,* agricultor *m.,* granjero *m.*
farther, *adv.* más; más lejos.
fashion, *s.* moda *f.*
fashionable, *adj.* de moda, elegante.
fast[1], *s.* ayuno *m.;* — *v. n.* ayunar.
fast[2], *adj. (train)* rápido; *(watch)* estar adelantado; — *adv.* de prisa.
fasten, *v. a.* fijar; *(boat)* amarrar.
fat, *s.* gordo *m.;* — *adj.* grasiento, grueso, gordo.
fate, *s.* fortuna *f.,* suerte *f.*
father, *s.* padre *m.*
father-in-law, *s.* suegro *m.*
fault, *s.* culpa *f.;* defecto *m.;* falta *f.*

faultless, *adj.* sin defectos, impecable.
faulty, *adj.* defectuoso.
favour, *s.* favor *m.; ask a ~ of sy* pedir un favor a; — *v. a.* preferir.
favourable, *adj.* favorable.
favourite, *adj.* preferido, favorito.
fear, *s.* temor *m.*, miedo *m.;* — *v. a.* temer.
fearful, *adj. (shy)* tímido, miedoso; *(terrible)* terrible, espantoso.
fearless, *adj.* valiente, intrépido.
feast, *s.* fiesta *f.;* banquete *m.;* — *v. a.* celebrar; convidar; *v. n.* deleitarse.
feat, *s.* hecho *m.*, hazaña *f.*
feather, *s.* pluma *f.*
feature, *s.* facción *f.;* — *v. a.* exhibir.
February, *s.* febrero *m.*
federation, *s.* (con)federación *f.*
fee, *s.* honorario *m.;* cuota *f.*
feeble, *adj.* débil.
feed, *v. a.* dar de comer; *~ up* engordar; *I'm fed up* estoy harto de; — *s.* pienso *m.*
feel, *v. a.* sentir, palpar, tocar; *v. n.* sentirse; *do you ~ hungry?* ¿tiene usted hambre? *I ~ like a Coca-Cola* me apetece una Coca-Cola.
fellow, *s.* hombre *m.;* tipo *m.*
fellowship, *s.* amistad *f.*
felt, *s.* fieltro *m.*
female, *s.* hembra *f.;* — *adj.* femenino; *~ child* niña *f.;* chica *f.*
femimine, *adj.* femenino.
fencing, *s.* esgrima *f.*
ferry, *s.* ferry *m.*, transbordo *m.;* — *v. n.* transbordar.
ferry-boat, *s.* transbordador *m.*
fertile, *adj.* fértil.
fertilize, *v. a.* fertilizar.
fertilizer, *s.* fertilizante *m.*
festival, *s.* fiesta *f.*, festival *m.*
fetch, *v. a.* traer.
fever, *s.* fiebre *f.*
few, *adj. & pron.* pocos, unos cuantos; *quite a ~* bastante; *~er* menos.
fiancé, *s.* novio *m.*
fiancée, *s.* novia *f.*
fibre, *s.* fibra *f.*
fiction, *s.* ficción *f.*, fantasía *f.; (literature)* novela *f.*
field, *s.* campo *m.; (war)* campaña *f.*
fiery, *adj.* ardiente, fogoso.
fifteen, *adj. & s.* quince.
fifth, *adj.* quinto.
fifty, *adj. & s.* cincuenta.
fig, *s.* higo *m.; I don't care a ~ for it* ¡no me importa un comino!
fight, *v. n.* pelear; *fig.* luchar; — *s.* pelea *f.*, lucha *f.*
fighter, *s.* luchador *m.; (plane)* avión *(m.)* de caza, caza *m.*
figure, *s.* figura *f.*, tipo *m.;* línea *f.; (number)* cifra *f.;* número *m.; (drawing)* dibujo *m.;* — *v. a.* figurar.
file¹, *s.* lima *f.*, — *v. a.* limar.
file², *s.* archivo *m.;* fila *f.*
fill, *v. a.* llenar; *v. n.* llenarse.
film, *s.* película *f.;* — *v. a. & n.* filmar.
fin(s), *s.* aleta *f.*
final, *adj.* final, último; — *~s (sports)* final *f.;* examen *(m.)* final.

finally, *adv.* finalmente, por último, en fin.
finance, *s.* finanzas *f. pl.;* — *v. a.* financiar.
financial, *adj.* financiero.
find, *v. a.* hallar, encontrar; ~ *out* averiguar; — *s.* hallazgo *m.*
fine¹, *s.* multa *f.;* — *v. a.* multar.
fine², *adj.* fino; *that's* ~! ¡qué bueno!
finger, *s.* dedo *m.; first* ~ índice *m.*
finger-nail, *s.* uña *f.*
finish, *v. a.* terminar, acabar; — *s.* final *m.*, fin *m.*
fir, *s.* abeto *m.*
fire, *s.* fuego *m.*; incendio *m.; be on* ~ arder; *set on* ~ prender fuego a; — *v. a.* disparar.
fire-alarm, *s.* alarma *(m.)* de incendios.
fire-arm, *s.* arma *(f.)* de fuego.
fire-brigade, *s.* cuerpo *(m.)* de bomberos.
fire-engine, *s.* bomba *(f.)* de incendios.
fire-escape, *s.* escalera *(f.)* de salvamento.
fireplace, *s.* chimenea *f.*, hogar *m.*
fire-station, *s.* cuartel *(m.)* de bomberos.
firework(s), *s. (pl.)* fuegos *(m. pl.)* artificiales.
firm¹, *s.* casa *f.*
firm², *adj.* firme.
firmament, *s.* firmamento *m.*
firmness, *s.* firmeza *f.*
first, *adj.* primero; ~ *aid* primeros auxilios *m. pl.;* — *adv.* primero; por primera vez.
firstly, *adv.* primeramente.
first-rate, *adj.* de primer orden, de primera categoría.
fish, *s.* pez *m. (alive);* pescado *m. (dish);* — *v. n.* pescar.
fisherman, *s.* pescador *m.*
fish-hook, *s.* anzuelo *m.*
fishing-rod, *s.* caña *(f.)* de pescar.
fist, *s.* puño *m.*
fit¹, *s.* ataque *m.*
fit¹, *adj.* apto; — *v. n.* sentar, encajar; *this key doesn't* ~ esta llave no sirve; *the coat* ~*s me* el abrigo me sienta bien.
five, *adj.* &. *s.* cinco.
fix, *v. a.* fijar; — *s.* lío *m.*
flag, *s.* bandera *f.;* — *v. a.* embanderar.
flame, *s.* llama *f.* luz *f.;* — *v. n.* llamear.
flank, *s.* costado *m.*, flanco *m.* — *v. a.* flanquear.
flannel, *s.* franela *f.*
flash, *v. n.* destellar, brillar; — *v. a.* proyectar; — *s.* instante *m.;* ~ *of light* destello *m.*
flashlight, *s.* linterna *(f.)* eléctrica.
flat¹, *s.* piso *m.*, apartamiento *m.*
flat², *adj.* plano, llano, liso.
flatter, *v. a.* adular.
flattery, *s.* adulación *f.*
flavour, *s.* sabor *m.;* — *v. a.* sazonar.
flax, *s.* lino *m.*
flea, *s.* pulga *f.*
flee, *v. n.* huir.
fleet, *s.* flota *f.*
flesh, *s.* carne *f.*
flight¹, *s.* vuelo *m.;* ~ *of stairs* escalera *f.*
flight², *s. (escape)* huida *f.*, fuga *f.; put to* ~ poner en fuga.

flirt, *s.* coqueta *f.*; — *v. n.* flirtear.
float, *v. n.* flotar ; — *v. n.* poner a flote; *(loan)* emitir; — *s.* balsa *f.*
flood, *s.* inundación *f.*; — *v. a.* inundar.
floor, *s.* piso *m.*, suelo *m.*; *ground* ~ planta *(f.)* baja, piso bajo.
flour, *s.* harina *f.*
flourish, *v. n.* prosperar.
flow, *v. n.* fluir; — *s.* corriente *f.*, flujo *m.*
flower, *s.* flor *f.*; — *v. n.* florecer.
flower-bed, *s.* macizo *m.*
flu, *s.* gripe *f.*
fluent, *adj.* fluente, fluido.
fluid, *s.* & *adj.* fluido *(m.)*, líquido *(m.)*
flute, *s.* flauta *f.*
fly[1], *s.* mosca *f.*
fly[2], *v. n.* volar; ir en avión.
foam(-)rubber, *s.* espuma *(f.)* de goma.
focus, *s.* foco *m.*, centro *m.*; — *v. a.* enfocar.
fog, *s.* neblina *f.*, niebla *f.*; — *v. a.* ofuscar.
fog-horn, *s.* sirena *(f.)* de niebla.
fold, *s.* arruga *f.*, redil *m.*; *(pleat)* pliegue *m.*; — *v. a.* doblar; *(arms)* cruzar.
foliage, *s.* follaje *m.*
folk, *s.* gente *f.*; familia *f.*
follow, *v. a.* seguir; *do you* ~ *me?* ¿me entiende usted?; *as* ~*s* como sigue.
follower, *s.* partidario *m.*
following, *adj.* siguiente.
folly, *s.* tontería *f.*
fond, *adj.* aficionado, cariñoso, tierno; *I'm very* ~ *of flowers* me gustan muchísimo las flores.
food, *s.* comida *f.*
fool, *s.* tonto, necio; — *v. a.* engañar.
foolish, *adj.* tonto; ~ *thing* tontería *f.*
foot, *s.* pie *m.*; *on* ~ a pie, de pie.
football, *s.* fútbol *m.*
footlight(s), *s.* *(pl.)* candilejas *f. pl.*
footstep, *s.* huella *f.*, pisada *f.*, paso *m.*
for[1], *prep.* para; por; *leave* ~ *London* salir para Londres; ~ *a year* por un año.
for[2], *conj.* porque, como.
forbidden, *adj.* & *pp.* *it is* ~ está prohibido.
force, *s.* violencia *f.*; *by* ~ a la fuerza; armed ~*s* fuerzas *(f. pl.)* armadas; *police* ~ policía *f.*; *legal* ~ vigencia *f.*; *come into* ~ entrar en vigor; — *v. a.* forzar, obligar.
forearm, *s.* antebrazo *m.*
forecast, *s.* pronóstico *m.*; — *v. a.* & *n.* pronosticar.
forefinger, *s.* (dedo) índice *m.*
foreground, *s.* primer plano *m.*
forehead, *s.* frente *f.*
foreign, *adj.* extranjero; ~ *affairs* asuntos *(m. pl.)* exteriores; *Foreign Office* Ministerio de Asuntos Exteriores; ~ *trade* comercio *(m.)* exterior.
foreigner, *s.* extranjero *m.*, forastero *m.*
forenoon, *s.* mañana *f.*
foresee, *v. a.* prever.
forest, *s.* bosque *m.*

foretell, *v. a.* predecir, pronosticar.
foreword, *s.* prefacio *m.*
forge, *s.* fragua *f.*; — *v. a.* forjar; *(falsify)* falsificar.
forgery, *s.* falsificación *f.*
forget, *v. a.* olvidar(se); *I* ~ no recuerdo.
forgive, *v. a.* perdonar.
fork, *s.* tenedor *m.*; *(road)* empalme *m.*, bifurcación *f.*; — *v. n.* bifurcarse.
form, *s.* forma *f.*; *(school)* año *m.*, grado *m.*; — *v. a.* formar; ~ *a line* hacer cola.
formal, *adj.* formal; ceremonioso.
formality, *s.* formalidad *f.*
formation, *s.* formación *f.*
former, *adj.* primero, antiguo, ex-.
formerly, *adv.* anteriormente.
formula, *s.* fórmula *f.*
fortify, *v. a.* fortificar.
fortnight, *s.* quince días.
fortunate, *adj.* afortunado.
fortunately, *adj.* afortunadamente, por suerte.
fortune, *s.* fortuna *f.*, dicha *f.*; *(riches)* bienes *m. pl.*
forty, *adj.* & *s.* cuarenta.
forward, *adj.* delantero; — *adv.* adelante; *look* ~ *to* esperar con ilusión; — *s.* *(football)* delantero *m.*; — *v. a.* reexpedir.
foul, *adj.* *(play)* sucio; *(air)* viciado; *(weather)* malo; — *s.* irregularidad *f.*
found, *v. a.* fundar.
foundation, *s.* fundación *f.*; *(base)* cimientos *m. pl.*
founder, *s.* fundador *m.*
fountain, *s.* fuente *f.*
fountain-pen, *s.* pluma *(f.)* fuente, pluma estilográfica.
four, *adj.* & *s.* cuatro.
fourteen, *adj.* & *s.* catorce.
fourth, *adj.* & *s.* cuarto.
fowl, *s.* aves *f. pl.*, pollo *m.*
fox, *s.* zorro *m.*
fraction, *s.* fracción *f.*, trozo *m.*
fracture, *s.* fractura *f.*; — *v. a.* fracturar.
fragile, *adj.* frágil.
fragrant, *adj.* fragante.
frail, *adj.* frágil.
frame, *(picture)* marco *m.*; *(house)* armadura *f.*; *(constitution)* constitución *f.*; complexión *f.*; — *v. a.* *(picture)* poner marco *a*; *(construct)* construir.
framework, *s.* armazón *m.*; armadura *f.*
frank, *adj.* franco.
frankness, *s.* franqueza *f*, sinceridad *f.*
fraternal, *adj.* fraternal.
fraud, *s.* fraude *m.*
free, *adj.* libre; ~ *of charge* gratis; ~ *of duty* libre de derechos aduaneros; — *v. a.* libertar, poner en libertad.
freedom, *s.* libertad *f.*
freely, *adv.* libremente, con toda libertad.
freeze, *v. n.* helar; — *v. a.* congelar.
freight, *s.* carga *f.*; *(charges)* flete *m.*; — *v. a.* cargar; fletar.
French, *adj.* francés.
French-bean, *s.* judías *(f. pl.)* verdes.
Frenchman, *s.* francés *m.*
Frenchwoman, *s.* francesa

f.
frequent, *adj.* frecuente — *v. a.* frecuentar.
frequently, *adv.* frecuentemente.
fresh, *adj.* fresco; *(air)* puro, *(water)* dulce; *(new)* nuevo; — *adv.* recién.
friction, *s.* fricción *f.*
Friday, *s.* viernes *m.*
fridge, *s.* frigorífico *m.*; nevera *f.*
friend, *s.* amigo *m.*; *make ~s with* hacerse amigo.
friendly, *adj.* amistoso.
friendship, *s.* amistad *f.*
fright, *s.* susto *m.*, miedo *m.*
frighten, *v. a.* asustar.
frivolous, *adj.* frívolo.
frock, *s.* falda *f.*; hábito *(m.)* de fraile.
frog, *s.* rana *f.*
from, *prep.* de; *where do you come ~?* ¿de dónde es usted?; *~ beginning to end* desde el principio al fin; *~ day to day* de día en día.
front, *s.* fachada *f.*; *(war)* frente *m.*; *in ~* delante; *in ~ of* delante de; frente a; — *adj.* *~ row* primera fila *f.*; — *v. n.* enfrentarse.
front-door, *s.* puerta *(f.)* principal.
frontier, *s.* frontera *f.*
frost, *s.* helada *f.*; frío *m.*; — *v. a.* congelar.
frosty, *adj.* helado, frío.
frozen, *adj.* helado, congelado.
fruit, *s.* fruta *f.*, fruto *m.*
fruitful, *adj.* fecundo, fértil.
fruit-tree, *s.* árbol *(m.)* frutal.
frustrate, *v. a.* frustrar.
fry, *v. a.* freir; *fried eggs* huevos *(m.)* al plato.
frying-pan, *s.* sartén *f.*
fuel, *s.* combustible *m.*
fulfil, *v. a.* cumplir.
full, *adj.* lleno; *of ~ age* mayor de edad.
fully, *adv.* enteramente, completamente.
fun, *s.* diversión *f.*, gracia *f.*
function, *s.* función *f.*; — *v. n.* funcionar.
fund, *s.* fondo *m.*
funeral, *s.* entierro *m.*
funnel, *s.* embudo *m.*; *(of a ship)* chimenea *f.*
funny, *adj.* gracioso; *(strange)* extraño, raro.
fur, *s.* piel *f.*
fur-coat, *s.* abrigo *(m.)* de piel.
furious, *adj.* furioso.
furnace, *s.* caldera *f.*
furnish, *v. a.* amueblar; *(provide)* proporcionar.
furnished, *adj.* amueblado.
furniture, *s.* muebles *m. pl.*
furrier, *s.* peletero *m.*
further, *adv.* más; *~ on* más lejos.
furthermore, *adv.* además.
fury, *s.* furia *f.*
fuse, *v. a.* fundir; — *v. n.* fundirse; — *s.* fusible *m.*, plomo *m.*
fuss, *s.* alboroto *m.*; — *v. n.* alborotar.
future, *s.* futuro *m.* porvenir *m.*; — *adj.* futuro, venidero.

G

gain, *v. a.* ganar, conquistar; *(reach)* alcanzar; *v. n.* *(watch)* adelantarse; — *s.* ganancia *f.*

gait, *s.* manera *(f.)* de andar.
gall, *s.* bilis *f.*
gallery, *s.* galería *f.; picture* ~ galería de pinturas.
gallon, *s.* galón *m.*
gallop, *s.* galope *m.*; – *v. n.* galopar.
gambling, *s.* juego *(m.)* de azar.
game, *s.* juego *m.; play a* ~ jugar una partida; *(hunting)* caza *f.*
gamekeeper, *s.* guardabosque *m.*
gang, *s.* pandilla *f.*, cuadrilla *f.*
gangway, *s.* pasillo *m.;* escalerilla *(f.)* de embarco.
gaol, *see* **jail.**
garage, *s.* garaje *m.*, cochera *f.*
garden, *s.* jardín *m.*, huerta *f.*
gardener, *s.* jardinero *m.*
garlic, *s.* ajo *m.*
garment, *s.* prenda *(f.)* de vestir.
garter, *s.* liga *f.*
gas, *s.* gas *m.;* ~ *stove* cocina *(f.)* de gas; – *v. a.* gasear.
gasometer, *s.* gasómetro *m.*
gas-pipe, *s.* tubo *(m.)* de gas.
gas-range, *s.* cocina *(f.)* de gas.
gas-works, *s.* fábrica *(f.) or* compañía *(f.)* de gas.
gate, *s.* puerta *f.*, entrada *f.*
gateway, *s.* puerta *(f.)* cochera.
gather, *v. a.* recoger; *(from words)* deducir; *v. n.* reunirse.
gay, *adj.* alegre.
gaze, *v. a.* mirar con fijeza; – *s.* mirada *(f.)* fija.
gazetteer, enciclopedia *f.;* diccionario *(m.)* geográfico.
gear, *s.* equipo *m.; engranaje m.; (car)* cambio *(m.)* de velocidades; – *v. n.* embragar.
general, *s.* & *adj.* general *(m.); in* ~ en general
generally, *adv.* general. mente.
generation, *s.* generación *f.*
generator, *s.* generador *m.*
generosity, *s.* generosidad *f.*
generous, *adj.* generoso.
genial, *adj.* cordial, afable.
genius, *s.* genio *m.*
gentle, *adj. (hand)* cuidadoso; *(knock)* leve; *(person)* apacible, bondadoso.
gentleman, *s.* caballero *m.*
gently, *adv.* delicadamente.
genuine, *adj.* genuino.
geographical, *adj.* geográfico.
geography, *s.* geografía *f.*
geology, *s.* geología *f.*
geometric, *adj.* geométrico.
geometry, *s.* geometría *f.*
germ, *s.* germen *m.*
German, *adj.* & *s.* alemán.
gesticulate, *v. n.* gesticular.
gesture, *s.* gesto *m.*
get, *v. a.* recibir, conseguir; *(have)* tener; ~ *me?* ¿me entiende usted?; ~ *one's hair cut* cortarse el pelo; ~ *home* llegar a casa; ~ *better* mejorar; ~ *dress-*

ed vestirse; ~ *ill* caer enfermo; *it is ~ting late* ya es tarde; ~ *married* casarse; ~ *old* envejecer; ~ *tired* cansarse; ~ *along* marcharse; *fig.* llevarse bien; ~ *at* llegar hasta, alcanzar; ~ *away* alejarse; ~ *down* bajar; ~ *in* meter, entrar; *(arrive)* llegar; ~ *off* apearse; bajarse: ~ *on* subir, proseguir, continuar; ~ *out* salir, bajarse; ~ ~ *up* levantarse.

geyser, *s.* calentador *(m.)* de agua.

ghost, *s.* fantasma *m.*

giant, *s.* gigante *m.*; — *adv.* gigantesco.

gift, *s.* regalo *m.*, obsequio *m.*; *(talent)* talento *m.*

gifted, *adj.* talentoso.

gild, *v. a.* dorar.

gin, *s.* ginebra *f.*

ginger, *s.* jengibre *m.*

gingerbread, *s.* pan *(m.)* de especies; alajú *m.*

gipsy, *s.* gitano *m.*

giraffe, *s.* jirafa *f.*

girdle, *s.* cinturón *m.*; faja *f.*; — *v. a.* ceñir, cercar.

girl, *s.* niña *f.*; *(older)* muchacha *f.*, chica *f*; ~ *friend* amiga *f.*

give, *v. a.* dar; *(gift)* regalar; ~ *a toast* brindar por; ~ *a hand* ayudar; ~ *birth* dar a luz; ~ *away* regalar; *(secret)* divulgar; ~ *back* dvolver; ~ *up* dejar, aebandonar.

glacier, *s.* glaciar *m.*

glad, *adj.* contento, alegre; *be* ~ estar contento, alegrarse.

gladness, *s.* gozo *m.*, alegría *f.*

glance, *v. n.* echar una mirada; ~ *through (a book)* hojear; *(gleam)* brillar, relucir; — *s.* mirada *f.*, ojeada *f.*

glass, *s.* vidrio *m.*; *a ~ of wine* un vaso *or* una copa de vino: *~es* gafas *f. pl.*, anteojos *m. pl.* — *v. a.* vidriar.

glazier, *s.* vidriero *m.*

gleam, *s.* destello *m.*; — *v. n.* destellar.

glide, *v. n.* resbalar, deslizarse; *(aviation)* planear.

glider, *s.* planeador *m.*

glimpse, *s.* ojeada *f.*, vistazo *m.*; *catch a ~ of* avistar; — *v. a.* dar un vistazo *a.*

glitter, *v. n.* brillar; — *s.* resplandor *m.*

globe, *s.* esfera *f.*, globo *m.*

gloom, *s.* oscuridad *f.*; *fig.* tristeza *f.*

gloomy, *adj.* sombrío; *fig.* triste, melancólico.

glorious, *adj.* glorioso.

glory, *s.* gloria *f.*; — *v. n.* gloriarse.

glove, *s.* guante *m.*

glow-worm, *s.* luciérnaga *f.*

glue, *s.* cola *f.*

gnat, *s.* mosquito *m.*

gnaw, *v. a. & n.* roer.

go, *v. n.* ir, andar, marchar; *let's ~!* ¡vámonos!; ~ *shopping* ir de compras; ~ *bad* echarse a perder; ~ *mad* volverse loco; *I'm going to ask you a favour* le pediré a usted un favor; ~ *abroad* ir al extranjero; ~ *across* cruzar; ~ *away* irse, marcharse; ~ *back* volver, regresar; ~ *down* bajar; *(sun)* ponerse; ~ *on* conti-

nuar; ~*out* salir; *(light)* apagarse; ~ *to pieces* romperse en mil pedazos; ~*under* hundirse; ~ *up* subir; ~ *with* acompañar; *fig.* ir con.
goal, *s.* meta *f.; (sports)* gol *m.*, tanto *m.*
goal-keeper, *s.* portero *m.*
goat, *s.* cabra *f.*
God, *s.* Dios; ~ *bless you!* ¡Dios le bendiga!; *(sneezing)* ¡Salud!
goddess, *s.* diosa *f.*
godfather, *s.* padrino *m.*
godmother, *s.* madrina *f.*
goggles, *s. pl.* anteojos *(m. pl.)* de automovilista.
gold, *s.* oro *m.*
golden, *adj.* dorado.
golf, *s.* golf *m.*
golf-club, *s.* palo *(m.)* de golf.
goloshes, *s. pl.* chanclos *m. pl.*
good, *adj* bueno; *(ticket)* válido; *it is no* ~ no sirve para nada; *she has* ~ *looks* es muy guapa; *very* ~*!* ¡muy bien!; ~ *heavens!* ¡cielos!; *a* ~ *many* mucho; — *s.* bueno *m.*; bien *m.*; ~*s* bienes *m. pl.*; ~*s train* tren *(m.)* de carga.
good-bye, *int.* ¡adiós!
good-looking, *adj.* guapo, bien parecido.
goodness, *s.* bondad *f.*
good-tempered, *adj.* cordial, afable.
goodwill, *s.* buena voluntad *f.*
goose, *s.* ganso *m.*
gooseberry, *s.* uva *(f.)* espina.
gospel, *s.* evangelio *m.*
gossip, *s.* chisme *m.*; *(person)* chismoso; — *v. n.* chismear.
Gothic, *adj.* gótico.
gout, *s.* gota *f.*
govern, *v. a.* & *n.* gobernar.
governess, *s.* institutriz *f.*
government, *s.* gobierno *m.*
governor, *s.* gobernador *m.*
gown, *s.* bata *f.*; vestido *m.*
grace, *s.* gracia *f.*; *with a good* ~ de buena gana; *with a bad* ~ de mala gana; *say* ~ rezar el benedícite.
graceful, *adj.* garboso.
gracious, *adj.* afable.
grade, *s.* grado *m.*; — *v. a.* clasificar.
gradual, *adj.* gradual.
graduate, *v. n.* graduarse; — *s.* graduado *m.*
grain, *s.* grano *m.*
grammar, *s.* gramática *f.*
grammar-school, *s.* instituto *m.*
grammatical, *adj.* gramatical, gramático.
gramme, *s.* gramo *m.*
gramophone, *s.* gramófono *m.*
grand, *adj.* magnífico.
grandchild, *s.* nieto *m.* nieta *f.*
granddaughter, *s.* nieta *f.*
grandfather, *s.* abuelo *m.*
grandma, *s.* abuelita *f.*
grandmother, *s.* abuela *f.*
grandpa, *s.* abuelito *m.*
grandson, *s.* nieto *m.*
grape, *s.* uva *f.*
grape-fruit, *s.* toronja *f.*
grant, *v. a.* conceder; *take for* ~*ed* tomar por cierto: — *s.* concesión *f.*;

subvención *f.*
graph, *s.* gráfica *f.*
graphic, *adj.* gráfico.
grasp, *v. a.* agarrar; *(meaning)* comprender; — *s.* conocimiento *m.*
grass, *s.* hierba *f.*, césped *m.*
grate, *s.* parrilla *f.*; *(on the window)* reja *f.*; — *v. a.* raspar, rayar.
grateful, *adj.* agradecido.
gratitude, *s.* gratitud *f.*
grave,[1] *s.* sepulcro *m.*, tumba *f.*
grave,[2] *adj.* grave.
gravity, *s.* gravedad *f.*
gravy, *s.* salsa *f.*
gray, *adj.* gris.
grease, *s.* grasa *f.*; — *v. a.* engrasar.
great, *adj.* gran, grande; *a ~ deal* mucho.
greatly, *adv.* muy; mucho.
greatness, *s.* grandeza *f.*
greed, *s.* codicia *f.*
greedy, *adj.* codicioso.
Greek, *adj.* & *s.* griego.
green, *adj.* verde.
greengrocer, *s.* verdulero *m.*
greenhouse, *s.* invernadero *m.*, invernáculo *m.*
greet, *v. a.* saludar.
greeting(s), *s. (pl.)* saludo(s) *m. (pl.)*.
grey, *adj.* gris.
grief, *s.* dolor *m.*
grieve, *v. a.* afligir, lastimar; *v. n.* afligirse.
grill *s.* parrilla *f.*; *v.a.* asar a la parrilla.
grim, *adj.* torvo; horrendo.
grin, *s.* mueca *f.*; — *v. n.* hacer muecas.
grind, *v. a.* moler; *(teeth)* rechinar.
grinder, *s.* molinillo *m.*; *(tooth)* muela *f.*
grip, *v. a.* agarrarse a; — *s.* empuñadura *f.*
grocer, *s.* especiero *m.*
grocery, *s.* tienda *(f.)* de comestibles, *or* ultramarinos.
groom, *s.* mozo *(m.)* de cuadra; *(bride-)* novio *m.*; — *v. a.* cuidar de.
gross, *s.* grueso *m.*; *(12 dozens)* gruesa *f.*; — *adj.* grosero; *(error)* craso; — *~ weight* peso *(m.)* bruto.
ground, *s.* tierra *f.*, terreno *m.*; *~ floor* planta *(f.)* baja.
group, *s.* grupo *m.*; — *v. a.* agrupar.
grow, *v. n.* crecer; *~ up* desarrollarse.
growl, *s.* gruñido *m.*; — *v. n.* gruñir, refunfuñar.
grown-up, *adj.* & *s.* adulto *m.*
growth, *s.* desarrollo *m.*, crecimiento *m.*
grudge, *v. a.* envidiar; — *s.* rencor *m.*; *bear a ~ against sy* guardar rencor a.
gruff, *adj.* ceñudo, áspero.
grunt, *s.* gruñido *m.*; — *v. n.* gruñir.
guarantee, *s.* garantía *f.*; — *v. a.* garantizar.
guard, *s.* guardia *m.*; *(railway)* revisor *m.*; guardatrén *m.* — *v. a.* vigilar.
guardian, *s.* guardián *m.*
guess, *v. a.* acertar, adivinar; *(think)* suponer; — *s.* conjetura *f.*, suposición *f.*
guest, *s.* huésped *m.*, convidado *m.*
guide, *v. a.* guiar; — *s.* guía *m.*, *f.*
guide-book, *s.* guía *f.*

guilt, *s.* delito *m.*, culpa *f.*
guilty, *adj.* culpable; *plead* ~ reconocerse culpable.
guinea, *s.* guinea *f.*
guitar, *s.* guitarra *f.*
gulf, *s.* golfo *m.*
gull, *s.* gaviota *f.*
gullet, *s.* esófago *m.*
gum,[1] *s.* goma *f.*
gum,[2] *(anatomy)* encía *f.*
gun, *s.* fusil *m.*, cañón *m.*
gunpowder, *s.* pólvora *f.*
gust, *s.* ráfaga *f.*
gutter, *s.* canalón *m.*
gymnasium, *s.* gimnasio *m.*
gymnastics, *s. pl.* gimnasia *f.*
gym-shoes, *s. pl.* calzado *(m.)* de gimnasia.

H

haberdashery, *s.* pañería *f.*, mercería *f.*
habit, *s.* costumbre *f.*
hail,[1] *s.* granizo *m.*; — *v. n.* granizar.
hail,[2] *v. a.* aclamar; *(taxi)* llamar; ~ *from* venir de.
hair, *s.* pelo *m.*, cabello *m.*
hairdresser, *s.* peluquero *m.*
hairy, *adj.* velludo, peludo; *(not shaved)* barbudo.
half, *s.* mitad *f.*; ~ *an hour* media hora *f.*; *an hour and a* ~ una hora y media; — *adj.* medio; — *adv.* medio, a medias.
half-way, *adv.* a medio camino.
hall, *s.* vestíbulo *m.*; salón *m.*; *city* ~ ayuntamiento *m.*
halt, *s.* alto *m.*; *come to a* ~ pararse, interrumpirse; — *v. n.* hacer alto.
ham, *s.* jamón *m.*
hammer, *s.* martillo *m.*; — *v. a.* martillar.
hand, *s.* mano *f.*; *at* ~ a mano; *on* ~ a mano, disponible; *give a* ~ ayudar; *have a* ~ *in* tomar parte en; ~*s off!* ¡quita!; ~*s up!* ¡arriba las manos!; *(on a watch)* manecilla *f.*; *(worker)* obrero *m.*; *(play)* mano *f.*; — *v. a.* entregar, dar; ~ *in* presentar; ~ *on* transmitir, pasar; ~ *out* distribuir.
handbag, *s.* bolso *m.*, cartera *(f.)* de señora.
handbook, *s.* manual *m.*
handful, *s.* puñado *m.*
handicap, *s.* impedimento *m.*, obstáculo *m.*; handicap *m.*; — *v. a.* perjudicar, estorbar.
handkerchief, *s.* pañuelo *m.*
handle, *s.* mango *m.*, palo *m.*; — *v. a.* manejar; tocar, manosear; *(trade)* tener.
hand-made, *adj.* hecho a mano.
handsome, *adj.* guapo; *(generous)* generoso.
handwriting, *s.* letra *f.*, escritura *f.*
handy, *adj.* hábil; *(useful)* útil, a la mano.
hang, *v. a.* colgar; *(head)* bajar, inclinar; ~ *it!* ¡que el diablo se lo lleve!; ~ *sy* ahorcar; *v. n.* estar colgado; ~ *about* gandulear, vagar; ~ *back* quedar atrás; *fig.* vacilar; ~ *up* colgar.
hanger, *s.* colgador *m.*,

gancho *m.*
happen, *v. n.* pasar, ocurrir, suceder.
happiness, *s.* felicidad *f.*
happy, *adj.* feliz; contento, alegre.
harbour, *s.* puerto *m.*; – *v. a.* abrigar.
hard, *adj.* duro; *(time)* difícil; *(work)* fuerte; *(worker)* asiduo; *(man)* severo; *(word)* injurioso; *get* ~ endurecerse; ~ *cash* dinero *(m.)* contante; – *adv.* duramente.
hardly, *adv.* apenas; ~ *ever* casi nunca.
hardware, *s.* ferretería *f.*
hare, *s.* liebre *f.*
harm, *s.* daño *m.*; – *v. a.* dañar.
harmful, *adj.* dañoso, nocivo.
harmless, *adj.* innocuo, inofensivo.
harmony, *s.* armonía *f.*
harp, *s.* arpa *f.*
harsh, *adj.* áspero.
hart, *s.* ciervo *m*.
harvest, *s.* cosecha *f.*; – *v. a.* & *n.* cosechar.
harvester, *s.* segadora *f*
haste, *s.* prisa *f.*; *make* ~ apresurarse, darse prisa.
hasty, *adj.* rápido, precipitado; *(decision)* ligero, irreflexivo.
hat, *s.* sombrero *m.*
hatchet, *s.* hacha *f.*
hate, *v. a.* odiar, aborrecer; – *s.* odio *m.*
hateful, *adj.* odioso.
hatred, *s.* odio *m.*
have, *v. a.* tener; ~ *a try* intentar; *let me* ~ *your key* déme usted su llave; ~ *tea* tomar un té; ~ *dinner* comer; ~ *lunch* almorzar; *what will you* ~? ¿que desea usted?; ~ *a drink* tomar un trago; ~ *a game* jugar un partido; *I* ~ *to leave early* tengo que salir temprano; *I* ~ *nothing to do with it* no tengo nada que ver con ello; *I'd better leave* será mejor que me vaya; *I* ~ *a new suit made* me hago hacer un nuevo traje.
haversack, *s.* mochila *f.*
hawk, *s.* halcón *m.*
hay, *s.* heno *m.*; *make* ~ hacer heno.
hazard, *s.* azar *m.*
H-bomb, *s.* bomba *(f.)* de hidrógeno.
he, *pron.* él; (animal) macho *m.*
head, *s.* cabeza *f.*; *(of the family)* cabeza *m.*; *(chief)* director *m.*; *(of a page)* principio *m.*; *(of cattle)* res *f.*; ~ *first* de cabeza; *keep one's* ~ mantener la calma; *lose one's* ~ perder los estribos; – *v. a.* estar a la cabeza de.
headache, *s.* dolor *(m.)* de cabeza.
heading, *s.* encabezamiento *m.*, título *m.*; – *(sports)* cabezada *f.*
headlight, *s.* faro *m.*, linterna *(f.)* delantera.
headline, *s.* titular *m.*
headmaster, *s.* director *(m.)* de escuela.
headquarters, *s. pl.* jefatura *f.*, cuartel *(m.)* general.
heal, *v. a.* sanar; *v. n.* curarse, cicatrizarse.
health, *s.* salud *f.*; *to your* ~! ¡a su salud!
healthy, *adj.* sano, bien de salud.
heap, *s.* montón *m.*; – *v.*

a. amontonar.
hear, *v. a.* oir; ~ *of* enterarse de; ~ *say* oir decir.
heart, *s.* corazón *m.; take sg to* ~ tomar algo a pecho; *by* ~ de memoria; *in the* ~ *of the town* en el centro de la ciudad; *(cards)* copas *f. pl.*
hearth, *s.* hogar *m.*
hearty, *adj.* cordial; ~ *eater* comilón *m.*
heat, *s.* calor *m.; fig.* acaloramiento *m.;* — *v. a.* calentar; *v. n.* calentarse.
heating, *s.* calefacción *f.*
heaven, *s.* cielo *m.; Heaven forbid!* ¡no quiera Dios!, ¡Dios me libre!; *Good Heaven!* ¡Dios mío!; *for Heaven's sake!* ¡por amor de Dios!
heavy, *adj.* pesado; *(rain)* fuerte; *(work)* duro; ~ *drinker* muy bebedor.
Hebrew, *adj. & s.* hebreo.
hedge, *s.* seto *m.;* — *v. a.* cercar con un seto.
heed, *s.* cuidado *m.*, atención *f.*; *take* ~ *of sg* tener cuidado de; — *v. n.* atender.
heedless, *adj.* desatento.
heel, *s.* talón *m.*
height, *s.* altura *f.; fig.* colmo *m.*, crisis *f.*
heir, *s.* heredero *m.*
heiress, *s.* heredera *f.*
helicopter, *s.* helicóptero *m.*
hell, *s.* infierno *m.; go to* ~*!* ¡vete al infierno!
hello, *int.* ¡hola!
helm, *s.* timón *m.*
helmet, *s.* casco *m.*
help, *v. a.* ayudar; ~ *yourself* sírvase usted; *it can't be* ~*ed!* ¡qué se le va a hacer! ¡no hay remedio!; *I can't* ~ *laughing* no puedo menos de reírme; — *s.* ayuda *f.;* ~*!* ¡socorro!
helpful, *adj.* útil.
helpless, *adj.* inútil.
hen, *s.* gallina *f.*
hence, *adv.* de aquí; *a week* ~ de hoy en ocho días; — *conj.* por lo tanto, en consecuencia.
her, *pron.* la; I *see* ~ la veo; *give* ~ *it* désela; *to* ~ a ella, le.
herb, *s.* hierba *f.;* planta *(f.)* medicinal.
here, *adv.* aquí.
heritage, *s.* herencia *f.*
hero, *s.* héroe *m.*
heroic, *adj.* heroico.
heroine, *s.* heroína *f.*
herring, *s.* arenque *m.*
hers, *pron.* suyo, de ella.
herself, *pron.* ella misma.
hesitate, *v. n.* vacilar.
hiccough, hiccup, *s.* hipo *m.;* — *v. n.* hipar, tener hipo.
hide, *v. a.* esconder, ocultar; *v. n.* esconderse, ocultarse.
hiding-place, *s.* escondrijo *m.*, escondite *m.*
high, *adj.* alto; *(opinion, temperature)* elevado; *(note)* agudo; ~ *and low* todo el mundo; por todas partes; *High Street* calle principal; *adv.* en alto; *play* ~ jugar fuerte *or* grueso.
highland, *s.* tierras *(f. pl.)* altas.
highness, *s.* altitud *f.; fig.* majestad *f.*, sublimidad *f.*
highway, *s.* carretera *f.*
hike, *v. n.* caminar; — *s.* caminata *f.*
hiker, *s.* excursionista *m.*,

caminante *m.*, *f.*
hiking, *s.* excursionismo *m.*
hill, *s.* colina *f.*
him, *pron.* le.
himself, *pron.* él mismo.
hinder, *v. a.* impedir.
hindrance, *s.* impedimento *m.*, estorbo *m.*
hint, *s.* indicio *m.*, indirecta *f.*; – *v. n.* insinuar.
hip, *s.* cadera *f.*
hire, *s. have for* ~ alquilar; – *v. a.* alquilar; *(person)* emplear.
his, *pron.* su, suyo, de él.
hiss, *s.* siseo *m.*; – *v. n.* sisear.
historic, *adj.* histórico.
history, *s.* historia *f.*
hit, *v. a.* pegar, dar en; ~ *a blow* golpear; ~ *it* dar en el blanco; – *s.* golpe *m.*; blanco *m.*; *it's a* ~ es sensacional.
hitch-hiking, *s.* autostop *m.*
hoarse, *adj.* ronco.
hobby, *s.* afición *f.*, pasatiempo *m.*
hockey, *s.* hockey *m.*
hoist, *v. a.* alzar, elevar; *(flag)* izar.
hold, *v. a.* tener; ~ *sy* sostener; *(meeting)* celebrar; *(office)* ocupar; *(opinion)* sostener; ~ ~ *guilty* juzgar culpable; ~ *back* retener; detenerse; *(himself)* refrenarse; ~ *off* mantener(se) alejado; ~ *on* aguantar; *(wait)* detenerse; ~ *out* resistir; ~ ~ *up* parar, detener; – *s. get* ~ *of* obtener; *take* ~ *of* agarrar.
holder, *s.* mango *m.*; *(person)* propietario *m.*
hole, *s.* agujero *m.*, hoyo *m.*
holiday, *s.* día *(m.)* festivo, día de fiesta; vacaciones *f. pl.*; *go on* ~ tomarse unas vacaciones.
holiday-maker, *s.* veraneante *m.*, *f.*
hollow, *adj.* & *s.* hueco *(m.)*, vacío *(m.)*; – *v. a.* excavar.
holly, *s.* acebo *m.*
holy, *adj.* sagrado, santo.
home, *s.* casa *f.*; hogar *m.*; asilo *m.*; *at* ~ en casa; *make yourself at* ~ esta usted en su casa; – *adj.* casero, doméstico; ~ *affairs* asuntos *(m. pl.)* internos; *Home Office* Ministerio de la Gobernación; ~ *trade* comercio *(m.)* interior; – *adv.* a casa; *go* ~ volver *or* regresar a casa.
homeless, *adj.* sin domicilio; sin patria.
homely, *adj.* simple, sencillo.
home-made, *adj.* hecho en casa, casero.
homesick, *adj.* nostálgico.
homeward, *adv.* hacia casa.
honest, *adj.* honrado, honesto.
honesty, *s.* honradez *f.*
honey, *s.* miel *f.*
honeymoon, *s.* luna *(f.)* de miel, viaje *(m.)* de novios.
honour, *s.* honor *m.*; *in* ~ *of* en honor de; – *v. a.* honrar.
hood, *s.* capota *f.*
hoof, *s.* casco *m.*
hook, *s.* gancho *m.*; *(fishing)* anzuelo *m.*; *(blow)* crochet *m.*; – *v. a.* enganchar.

hooligan, *s.* gamberro *m.*
hope, *s.* esperanza *f.;* — *v. a. & n.* esperar.
hopeful, *adj.* esperanzado, lleno de esperanza.
hopeless, *adj.* desesperanzado, desesperado.
horizon, *s.* horizonte *m.*
horizontal, *adj.* horizontal.
horn, *s.* asta *f.*, cuerno *m.;* bocina *f.*
horrible, *adj.* horrible.
horror, *s.* horror *m.*
horse, *s.* caballo *m.*
horseback, *s. on* ~ a caballo.
horseman, *s.* jinete *m.*
hose, *s.* calcetines *m. pl.; (water-)* manguera *f.*
hospitable, *adj.* hospitalario.
hospital, *s.* hospital *m.*
hospitality, *s.* hospitalidad *f.*
host, *s.* dueño *(m.)* de la casa, anfitrión *m.*, patrón *m.*
hostel, *s.* refugio *m.*; *youth* ~ albergue *(m.)* juvenil.
hostess, *s.* dueña *(f.)* de la casa.
hot, *adj.* caliente; *I'm* ~ tengo calor.
hotel, *s.* hotel *m.*
hot-water-bottle, *s.* bolsa *(f.)* de agua caliente.
hound, *s.* sabueso *m.;* — *v. a.* perseguir.
hour, *s.* hora *f.;* ~ *by* ~ de hora en hora; *office* ~*s* horas de servicio.
house, *s.* casa *f.; keep* ~ mantener casa; *(theatre)* teatro *m.*, público *m.;* — *v. a.* alojar.
household, *s.* familia *f.*, casa *f.*
housekeeper, *s.* ama *(f.)* de llaves.
housewife, *s.* ama *(f.)* de casa.
housework, *s.* quehaceres *(m. pl.)* domésticos.
housing, *s.* vivienda *f.;* ~ *conditions* condiciones *(f. pl.)* de viviendas; ~ *estate* colonia *f.*
hovercraft, barca *(f.)* de almohada neumática.
how, *adv.* cómo; ~ *are you?* ¿cómo está usted?; ~ *is it?* ¿por qué?; ~ *much?* cuánto (pago)?
however, *conj.* no obstante; — *adv.* por muy, por mucho.
huge, *adj.* enorme.
hullo, *int.* ¡eh!; *(phone)* ¡oiga! ¡diga! ¡dígame!
human, *adj.* humano.
humanity, *s.* humanidad *f.*
humble, *adj.* humilde.
humorous, *adj.* divertido.
humour, *s.* humor *m.; be in a good* ~ estar de buen humor; *sense of* ~ sentido *(m.)* de humor.
hundred, *adj. & s.* ciento.
hundredth, *adj.* centésimo.
Hungarian, *adj. & s.* húngaro *(m.).*
hunger, hambre *f.;* — *v. n.* sentir hambre de.
hungry, *adj.* hambriento; *I'm* ~ tengo hambre.
hunt, *v. a. & s.* cazar, buscar; — *s.* caza *f.*, cacería *f.*
hunter, *s.* cazador *m.*
hurricane, *s.* huracán *m.*
hurry, *s.* prisa *f.; I'm in a* ~ tengo prisa; — *v. n.* apresurarse; ~ *up!* ¡dése prisa!
hurt, *v. a.* herir; *fig.* ofender; *get* ~ estar resentido; — *s.* herida *f.;* ofendida *f.*
husband, *s.* marido *m.*, esposo *m.*

hut, *s.* choza *f.*
hydrant, *s.* boca *(f.)* de riego.
hydrogen, *s.* hidrógeno *m.*
hygiene, *s.* higiene *f.*
hymn, *s.* himno *m.*
hyphen, *s.* guión *m.*

I

I, *pron.* yo.
ice, *s.* hielo *m.*; *(~ cream)* helado *m.*, granizado *m.*
icy, *adj.* helado.
idea, *s.* idea *f.*; *(purpose)* intención *f.*
ideal, *adj.* ideal; magnífico; — *s.* modelo *m.*, ideal *m.*
identical, *adj.* idéntico.
identity, *s.* identidad *f.*; *~ card* documento *(m.)* de identidad.
idle, *adj.* perezoso, holgazán, desocupado; — *v. n.* holgazanear.
idleness, *s.* pereza *f.*
if, *conj.* si; *as ~* como si; *even ~* aunque; *~ I were you* en su lugar.
ignition, *s.* ignición *f.*, encendido *m.*
ignorant, *adj.* ignorante; *be ~ of* ignorar.
ignore, *v. a.* no hacer caso.
ill, *adj.* enfermo; — *s.* mal *m.*; — *adv. be ~ at ease* no estar a gusto.
illegal, *adj.* ilegal.
illiterate, *adj.* iletrado; — *s.* analfabeto *m.*
illness, *s.* enfermedad *f.*
illusion, *s.* ilusión *f.*
illustrate, *v. a.* ilustrar.
illustration, *s.* ilustración *f.*
image, *s.* imagen *f.*; vivo retrato *m.*
imagine, *v. a.* imaginar.
imitate, *v. a.* imitar.
immediate, *adj.* inmediato; urgente.
immense, *adj.* inmenso, enorme.
immigrant, *adj.* & *s.* inmigrante *(m., f.)*.
immigration, *s.* inmigración *f.*
impact, *s.* impacto *m.*, choque *m.*
impatience, *s.* impaciencia *f.*
impatient, *adj.* impaciente.
impel, *v. a.* empujar.
imperial, *adj.* imperial.
impertinent, *adj.* impertinente.
implement, *s.* herramienta *f.*
implore, *v. a.* & *n.* implorar.
import, *v. a.* importar; — *s.* importación *f.*
importance, *s.* importancia *f.*
important, *adj.* importante.
importer, *s.* importador *m.*
impose, *v. a.* imponer; *~ on* engañar.
impossible, *adj.* imposible.
impregnate, *v. a.* impregnar.
impression, *s.* impresión *f.*
imprison, *v. a.* encarcelar.
improve, *v. a.* mejorar, perfeccionar: *v. n.* mejorarse.
improvement, *s.* mejoría *f.*, mejora *f.*
impulse, *s.* impulso *m.*
in, *prep.* en; *a foot ~ length* un pie de largo, *~ all* en todo; *~ a week* en una semana; *~ the morning* por la maña-

na; — *adv.* dentro; *come* ~! ¡adelante!
incapable, *adj.* incapaz.
inch, *s.* pulgada *f.*; ~ *by* ~ poco a poco, palmo a palmo.
incident, *s.* incidente *m.*
incidentally, *adv.* incidentalmente.
incline, *v. a.* inducir; *be* ~*d* inclinarse; — *s.* pendiente *m.*, cuesta *f.*
include, *v. a.* incluir, comprender.
inclusive, *adj.* inclusivo.
income, *s.* ingresos *m. pl.*; renta *f.*
income-tax, *s.* impuesto *(m.)* sobre la renta.
incompetent, *adj.* incompetente.
inconvenient, *adj.* inconveniente.
increase, *v. a.* & *n.* aumentar; — *s.* aumento *m.*
incredible, *adj.* increíble.
indeed, *adv.* verdaderamente, claro.
independence, *s.* independencia *f.*
independent, *adj.* independiente.
index, *s.* índice *m.*; ~ *finger* dedo *(m.)* índice.
Indian, *adj.* & *s.* indio *(m.)*; ~ *corn* maíz *m.*
india-rubber, *s.* goma *(f.)* de borrar.
indicate, *v. a.* indicar.
indicator, *s.* indicador *m.*
indifferent, *adj.* indiferente.
indigestion, *s.* indigestión *f.*
indirect, *adj.* indirecto.
indispensable, *adj.* indispensable.
individual, *adj.* individual; orginal; — *s.* individuo *m.*, individual *m.*
indoors, *adv.* en casa.
induce, *v. a.* inducir.
indulge, *v. a.* mimar, ~ *in* permitirse.
indulgence, *s.* indulgencia *f.*
industrial, *adj.* industrial.
industrious, *adj.* industrioso, aplicado, trabajador.
industry industria *f.*
inevitable, *adj.* inevitable.
inexpensive, *adj.* barato.
inexperienced, *adj.* inexperto.
infamous, *adj.* infame.
infant, *s.* criatura *f.*, niño *m.*
infantry, *s.* infantería *f.*
infant-school, *s.* escuela *(f.)* de párvulos.
infection, *s.* infección *f.*
infinitive, *s.* infinitivo *m.*
infirmary, *s.* enfermería *f.*
inflame, *v. a.* inflamar.
inflammable, *adj.* inflamable.
inflict, *v. a.* infligir.
influenza, *s.* influenza *f.*, gripe *f.*
inform, *v. a.* informar, avisar.
informal, *adj.* familiar, de confianza.
information, *s.* información *f.*
ingenious, *adj.* ingenioso.
ingenuity, *s.* ingeniosidad *f.*, inventiva *f.*
ingratitude, *s.* ingratitud *f.*
inhabit, *v. a.* & *n.* habitar.
inhabitant, *s.* habitante *m.*
inherit, *v. a.* heredar.
inheritance, *s.* herencia *f.*
initiative, *s.* iniciativa *f.*
injection, *s.* inyección *f.*
injury, *s.* herida *f.*; *fig.* injuria *f.*
injustice, *s.* injusticia *f.*

ink, *s.* tinta *f.*; — *v. a.* entintar, echar tinta a.
inland, *s.* tierra *(f.)* adentro; ~ *trade* comercio *(m.)* interior.
inn, *s.* posada *f.*, parador *m.*
inner, *adj.* interior.
innocent, *adj.* inocente.
innumerable, *adj.* innumerable, innúmero, sin número *(m)*.
inoculate, *v. a.* inocular, vacunar.
in-patient, *s.* hospitalizado *m.*
inquire, *v. a.* & *n.* preguntar, indagar, averiguar.
inquiry, *s.* indagación *f.*, averiguación *f.*; ~ *office* oficina *(f.)* de informaciones.
inscription, *s.* inscripción *f.*
insect, *s.* insecto *m.*
insensible, *adj.* insensible.
inseparable, *adj.* inseparable.
insert, *v. a.* insertar, añadir.
inside, *adj.* & *s.* interior *(m.)*; *(sports) left, right* ~ interior *(m.)* izquierda, derecha; — *adv.* por dentro; *let's go* ~ entremos.
insist, *v. n.* insistir.
inspect, *v. a.* inspeccionar.
inspection, *s.* inspección *f.*
inspector, *s.* inspector *m.*
inspire, *v. a.* inspirar.
instalment, *s.* plazo *m.*; parte *f.*
instance, *s.* ejemplo *m.*; ocasión *f.*; *for* ~ por ejemplo.
instant, *adj.* inmediato; — *s.* instante *m*; momento *m.*; *this* ~ ahora mismo.
instead, *adv.* en lugar de esto; *prep.* ~ *of* en vez de.
instinct, *s.* instinto *m.*
institute, *s.* instituto *m.*; — *v. a.* instituir.
institution, *s.* institución *f.*
instruct, *v. a.* & *n.* enseñar; *(command)* dar órdenes.
instruction, *s.* instrucción *f.*; enseñanza *f.*
instructive, *adj.* instructivo.
instrument, *s.* instrumento *m.*; *fig.* medio *m.*
insufficient *adj.* insuficiente.
insult, *s.* insulto *m.*; — *v. a.* insultar, ofender.
insurance, *s.* seguro *m.*
intact, *adj.* intacto.
integral, *adj.* integral.
integrity, *s.* integridad *f.*
intelligence, *s* inteligencia *f.*; ~ *service* Inteligencia *f.*
intelligent, *adj.* inteligente.
intend, *v. a.* intentar, querer, pensar.
intense, *adj.* intenso.
intensity, *s.* intensidad *f.*
intent, *s.* intento *m.*; — *adj.* resuelto, decidido.
intention, *s.* intención *f.*
intercontinental, *adj.* intercontinental.
interest, *s.* interés *m.*; *be of* ~ tener importancia; *rate of* ~ tipo *(m.)* de interés; — *v. a.* interesar.
interesting, *adj.* interesante.
interfere, *v. n.* meterse, intervenir.
interior, *adj.* & *s.* interior *(m.)*.

intermission, *s.* intermedio *m.*, descanso *m.*
internal, *adj.* interno; ~ *combustion engine* motor *(m.)* de combustión interna.
international, *adj.* & *s.* internacional *(m.)*.
interpret, *v. a.* interpretar.
interpretation, *s.* interpretación *f.*
interpreter, *s.* intérprete *m.*, *f.*
interrupt, *v. a.* interrumpir.
interval, *s.* intervalo *m.*
interview, *s.* entrevista *f.*; — *v. a.* entrevistar.
intimate, *adj.* íntimo; — *v. a.* sugerir; comunicar.
into, *prep.* en; *translate* ~ *English* traducir al inglés.
introduce, *v. a.* presentar.
introduction, *s.* prefacio *m.*, introducción *f.*; *letter of* ~ carta *(f.)* de presentación.
invalid[1], *adj.* indispuesto, enfermizo.
invalid[2], *adj.* no válido.
invasion, *s.* invasión *f.*
invent, *v. a.* inventar.
invention, *s.* invento *m.*
inventor, *s.* inventor *m.*
invest, *v. a.* investir; *(money)* invertir.
investigate, *v. a.* investigar.
investigation, *s.* investigación *f.*
investment, *s.* inversión *f.*
invitation, *s.* invitación *f.*
invite, *v. a.* convidar, invitar; provocar.
involuntary, *adj.* involuntario.
inward(s), *adv.* hacia adentro.
iris, *s.* iris *m.*; *(flower)* lirio *m.*
Irish, *adj.* irlandés.
Irishman, *s.* irlandés *m.*
Irishwoman, *s.* irlandesa *f.*
iron, *s.* hierro *m.*; plancha *f.*; — *v. a.* planchar.
ironical, *adj.* irónico.
ironware, *s.* ferretería *f.*
ironworks, *s.* fundición *(f.)* de hierro *(m.)*
irony, *s.* ironía *f.*
irregular, *adj.* irregular.
irrelevant, *adj.* insignificante, fútil.
irresolute, *adj.* irresoluto.
irrigation, *s.* irrigación *f.*, riego *m.*
irritate, *v. a.* irritar, molestar.
island, *s.* isla *f.*
isle, *s.* isla *f.*
isolate, *v. a.* aislar.
isolation, *s.* aislamiento *m.*
issue, *s.* edición *f.*; emisión *f.*; tema *m.*; — *v. a.* publicar.
it, lo; *I don't see it* no lo veo; *it's I* soy yo; *that's it* eso es; *it is cold* hace frío.
Italian, *adj* & *s.* italiano.
item, *s.* entrada *f.*, item *m.*, artículo *m.*
its, *pron.* su.
itself, *pron.* sí mismo.
ivory, *s.* marfil *m.*
ivy, *s.* hiedra *f.*

J

jack, *s.* gato *m.*; ~ *of hearts* sota *(f.)* de corazones; — *v. a.* ~ *up* alzar con gato.
jacket, *s.* chaqueta *f.*, americana *f.*

jail, *s.* cárcel *f.*
jam [1], *v. a.* atestar; *~med with people* atestado de gente; *~ on the brakes* frenar bruscamente; — *s.* atropello *m.; be in a ~* estar apurado.
jam [2], *s.* mermelada *f.*
January, *s.* enero *m.*
Japanese, *adj.* & *s.* japonés *(m.).*
jar, *s.* tarro *m.*
jaw, *s.* quijada *f.*, mandíbula *f.*
jazz, *s.* jazz *m.*
jealous, *adj.* celoso.
jealousy, *s.* celos *m. pl*
jelly, *s.* jalea *f.*
jersey, *s.* jersey *m.*
jet, *s.* chorro *m.; ~ plane* avión *(m.)* a reacción; *~ propulsion* propulsión *(f.)* a reacción.
Jew, *s.* judío *m.*
jewel, *s.* joya *f.*, alhaja *f.*, piedra *(f.)* preciosa
jeweller, *s.* joyero *m.*
jewellery *s.* joyería *f.*
job, *s.* empleo *m.*, trabajo *m.* deber *m.*; *~ work* destajo *m.*; — *v. n.* destajar.
jockey, *s.* jockey *m.*, jinete *m.*
join, *v. a.* juntar, acoplar; *v. n.* juntarse; ingresar; ir con, unirse.
joiner, *s.* carpintero *m.*
joint, *s.* empalme *m.*, juntura *f.*; — *adj.* mancomunado.
joint-stock company, *s.* sociedad *(f.)* anónima.
joke, *s.* chiste *m.*, broma *f.*; — *v. n.* bromear.
jolly, *adj.* alegre, jovial.
journal, *s.* revista *f.*, periódico *m.*
journalist, *s.* periodista *m.*, *f.*
journey, *s.* viaje *m.*, —*v. n.* viajar.
joy, *s.* alegría *f.*, gozo *m.*
joyful, *adj.* alegre.
judge, *s.* juez *m.*; — *v. a.* & *n.* juzgar.
jug, *s.* jarro *m.*
Jugoslav, *adj.* & *s.* yugoslavo *(m.).*
juice, *s.* zumo *m.*, jugo *m.*
July, *s.* julio *m.*
jump, *v. n.* saltar; — *s.* salto *m.*; *long ~* salto de longitud; *high ~* salto de altura.
jumper, *s.* blusa *(f.)* de punto, pulóver *m.*
junction, *s.* unión *f.*; *(of roads)* cruce *m.*
June, *s.* junio *m.*
junior, adj. menor; *I am three years his ~* soy tres años menor que él; *John Smith, Jr.* John Smith, hijo; — *adj.* juvenil.
jury, *s.* jurado *m.*
juryman, *s.* jurado *m.*
just [1], *adj.* justo, exacto.
just [2], *adv.* justamente, precisamente; *~ the same* da lo mismo; *~ now* ahora mismo; *~ in time* en buen momento; *~ a minute* sólo un minuto; un momento.
justice, *s.* justicia *f.*
justify, *v. a.* justificar.
juvenile, *adj.* juvenil.

K

keel, *s.* quilla *f.*
keen, adj. afilado, aguzado; *~ appetite* muy buen apetito; *be ~ on* tener entusiasmo por.

keep, *v. a.* guardar, conservar; *(family)* mantener; *(boarders)* tener; ~ *accounts* llevar los libros; ~ *one's word* cumplir su palabra; *v. n.* quedarse; *(milk, butter)* conservarse; ~ *working* trabajar sin cesar; ~ *waiting* hacer esperar; ~ *away* mantener *or* quedar alejado; ~ *back* retener; ~ *on* continuar, seguir.
keeper, *s.* guardián *m.*
kennel, *s.* perrera *f.*
kerb, *s.* borde *(m.)* de la acera.
kernel, *s.* semilla *f.*, pepita *f.*; *fig.* médula *f.*
kettle, *s.* caldera *f.*, tetera *f.*, hervidor *m.*
key, *s.* llave *f.*; *fig.* clave *f.*; *(of typewriter)* tecla *f.*
kid, *s.* cabrito *m.*; *(child)* pequeño *m.*, niño *m.*; — *v. n.* bromear.
kidnap, *v. a.* secuestrar.
kidney, *s.* riñón *m.*
kill, *v. a.* matar; *be* ~*ed* perder la vida.
kilogram(me), *s.* kilogramo *m.*, kilo *m*
kilometre, *s.* kilómetro *m.*
kind, *s.* clase *f.*; raza *f.*, especie *f.*; *all* ~*s of* toda clase de; — *adj.* amable; *be so* ~ *as to* tenga la bondad de.
kindle, *v. a.* encender.
kindly, *adj.* bondadoso; — *adv.* amablemente.
kindness, *s.* bondad *f.*, amabilidad *f.*
king, *s.* rey *m.*
kingdom, *s.* reino *m.*
kipper, *s.* arenque *(m.)* ahumado.
kiss, *s.* beso *m* ; — *v. a.* besar.
kit, *s.* equipo *m.*; herramientas *f. pl.*, caja *(f.)* de herramientas.
kitchen, *s.* cocina *f.*; ~ *garden* huerta *f.*
kitchenette, *s.* nicho *(m.)* para cocinar.
kite, *s.* cometa *(f.)* de papel.
knapsack, *s.* mochila *f.*
knee, *s.* rodilla *f.*
kneel, *v. n.* arrodillarse.
knife, *s.* cuchillo *m.*; — *v. a.* apuñalar, dar una cuchillada a.
knight, *s.* caballero *m.*
knit, *v. a.* & *n.* tejer, hacer puntò.
knob, *s.* tirador *m.*
knock, *s.* golpe *m.*, ruido *m.*; — *v. n.* llamar a la puerta; *v. a.* pegar, golpear; ~ *against* tropezar con; ~ *down* desarmar; *(price)* rebajar; ~ *out* poner fuera de combate.
knocker, *s.* aldaba *f.*
knot, *s.* nudo *m.*; *v. a.* anudar.
know, *v. a.* conocer; ~ *by sight* conocer de vista; saber; *he* ~*s French* sabe francés; *let* ~ informar.
knowledge, *s.* conocimiento *m.*; *to my* ~ según tengo entendido.
known, *adj.* conocido; *make* ~ publicar, comunicar.
knuckle, *s.* juntura *(f.)* de los dedos, nudillo *m.*

L

L, *s.* libra *f.*
label, *s.* rótulo *m.*, etiqueta *f.*; — *v. a.* rotular.

laboratory, *s.* laboratorio *m.*
labour, *s.* trabajo *m.*; — *v. n.* trabajar; esforzarse.
labourer, *s.* jornalero *m.*, peón *m.*
lace, *s.* encaje *m.*; cordón *m.*; — *v. a.* enlazar.
lack, *s.* falta *f.*; *for* ~ *of* a falta de; — *v. n.* faltar; no tener.
lad, *s.* mozo *m.*, muchacho *m.*
ladder, *s.* escalera *f.*; *(on stocking)* carrera *f.*
ladle, *s.* cucharón *m.*
lady, *s.* señora *f.*, dama *f.*
lake, *s.* lago *m.*
lamb, *s.* cordero *m.*
lame, *adj.* cojo.
lamp, *s.* lámpara *f.*
lamp-shade, *s.* pantalla *f.*
land, *s.* tierra *f.*; campo *m.*; *by* ~ por tierra; *native* ~ patria *f.*; — *v. n. (ship)* atracar; *(plane)* aterrizar.
landing, *s.* desembarco *m.*; aterrizaje *m.*
landing-strip, *s.* pista *(f.)* de aterrizaje.
landlady, *s.* propietaria *f.*, casera *f.*
landlord, *s.* propietario *m.*, casero *m.*
landscape, *s.* paisaje *m.*
language, *s.* idioma *m.*, lengua *f.*
lantern, *s.* linterna *f.*, farol *m.*
lard, *s.* manteca *(f.)* *or* grasa *(f.)* de cerdo; — *v. a.* mechar.
larder, *s.* despensa *f.*
large, *adj.* grande.
last, *adj.* último; ~ *but one* penúltimo; *at* ~ por fin, al fin; ~ *week* la semana pasada; ~ *night* anoche; — *v. n.* durar.
lasting, *adj.* duradero.
latch-key, *s.* llave *(f.)* de la casa.
late, *adj.* tardío; *(dead)* difunto; *(news)* reciente; — *adv.* tarde *be* ~ llegar tarde.
lately, *adv.* recientemente.
later (on), *adv.* más tarde.
latest, *adj.* último; *the* ~ *news* últimas noticias *f. pl.* — *adv.* por último.
Latin, *adj.* latino; — *s. (language)* latín *m.*
latter, *adj.* último.
laugh, *s.* risa *f.*; — *v. n.* reir(se); ~ *at* reirse de.
laughter, *s.* risa *f.*
launch, *v. a.* lanzar; *(ship)* botar, echar al agua; — *s.* lancha *f.*
laundry, *s.* lavandería *f.*; ropa *(f.)* limpia, ropa sucia.
lavatory, *s.* retrete *m.*, water *m.*
lavish, *adj.* pródigo; — *v. a.* prodigar.
law, *s.* ley *f.*; derecho *m.*
law-court, *s.* juzgado *m.*, tribunal *m.*
lawful, *adj.* legal, lícito.
lawn, *s.* césped *m.*
lawn-tennis, *s.* tenis *m.*
lawyer, *s.* abogado *m.*
lay, *v. a.* poner, colocar, situar; ~ *the cloth* poner la mesa; ~ *off* despedir; dejar, cesar; ~ *up* acumular.
layer, *s.* capa *f.*
lazy, *adj.* perezoso, holgazán.
lead[1], *s.* plomo *m.*; *(pencil)* mina *f.*
lead[2], *v. a.* conducir; *(life)* llevar; *(orchestra)*

dirigir; — *v. n. (street)* llevar; *(cause)* dar lugar *a; (cards)* ser mano; — *s.* delantera *f.*, ventaja *f.*, *(theatre)* papel *(m.)* principal.
leader, *s.* líder *m.; director m.;* jefe *m.*, caudillo *m.*
leadership, *s.* direccion *f.*
leaf, *s.* hoja *f.; (of book)* página *f.*
lean [1], *v. n.* inclinarse; *(prop)* apoyarse; *v. a.* apoyar; ~ *back* reclinarse; ~ *on* depender de; ~ *out* asomarse.
lean [2], *adj.* magro, flaco.
leap, *v. n.* saltar; — *s.* salto *m.*
learn, *v. a.* aprender.
learned, *adj.* culto, erudito.
learning, *s.* estudio *m.*, saber *m.*
least, *adj.* menor; at ~ por lo menos.
leather, *s.* cuero *m.*
leave [1], *v. a.* dejar; ~ *it to me* déjelo de mi cuenta; *v. n.* salir; ~ *behind* dejar atrás; ~ *for* salir para; ~ *out* omitir.
leave, [2] *s.* licencia *f.;* permiso *m.; take ~ of* despedirse de; *go on ~* ir de vacaciones.
lecture, *s.* conferencia *f.;* — *v. n.* hablar.
lecturer, *s.* conferenciante *m ;* docente *m.*
left, *adj.* izquierdo; — *s.* izquierda *f.; to the ~* a la izquierda.
left-luggage office, *s.* depósito *(m.)* de equipajes.
leg, pierna *f.; (of animal, of chair)* pata *f.*
legal, *adj.* legal.
legend, *s.* leyenda *f.*
legitimate, *adj.* legítimo.
leisure, *s.* horas *(f. pl.)* libres; *be at ~* estar desocupado.
lemon, *s.* limón *m.*
lemonade, *s.* limonada *f.*
lend, *v. a.* prestar; *~ an ear* escuchar; *~ a hand* ayudar.
length, *s.* largo *m.*, longitud *f.*
lengthen, *v. a.* alargar; *v. n.* alargarse.
lens, *s.* lente *f.*
less, *adj. & adv.* menos.
lesser, *adj.* menor.
lesson, *s.* lección *f.;* clase *f.*
lest, *conj.* a fin de que no.
let, *v. a.* dejar; *~ go* soltar; *let's o* vamos; *have you rooms to let?* ¿tiene usted habitaciones para alquilar?; *~ alone* dejar en paz; *~ down* bajar; *fig.* fallar; *~ off* dejar ir; *(weapon)* descargar; *~ out* alquilar; — *s.* alquiler *m.*
letter, *s.* carta *f.; (type)* letra *f.; ~ of credit* carta de crédito.
letter-box, *s.* buzón *m.*
lettuce, *s.* lechuga *f.*
level, *s.* nivel *m.;* — *adj.* llano; *~ crossing* paso *(m.)* a nivel; — *v. a.* igualar.
lever, *s.* palanca *f.*
lexicon, *s.* diccionario *m.*
liability, *s.* obligación *f.*
liar, *adj. & s.* mentiroso.
liberal, *adj.* liberal; generoso.
liberty, *s.* libertad *f.*
librarian, *s.* bibliotecario *m.*

library, *s.* biblioteca *f.; lending* ~ biblioteca circulante.
licence, license, *s.* licencia *f.; driving* ~ carnet *(m.)* de conductor.
lick, *v. a.* lamer.
lid, *s.* tapa *f.*, tapadera *f.*
lie,[1] *s.* mentira *f.;* – *v. n.* mentir.
lie,[2] *v. n.* estar acostado *or* echado; *here* ~*s* aquí yace; *(be situated)* estar situado, quedar; ~ *down* acostarse, echarse; – *s.* situación *f.*, posición *f.*
lieutenant, *s.* teniente *m.*
life, *s.* vida *f.;* biografía *f.*
life-belt, *s.* salvavidas *m.*
lifeless, *adj.* inanimado, sin vida.
lift, *v. a.* levantar; *v. n. (fog)* disiparse; – *s.* levantamiento *m.; give sy a* ~ ayudar a; llevar en su coche.
light,[1] *s.* luz *f.;* lumbre *f.*, fuego *m.; give a* ~ dar lumbre; *turn on the* ~ encender la luz; *bring to* ~ sacar a la luz; – *v. a.* encender; ~ *up* iluminar.
light[2] *adj.* ligero; ~ *blue* azul claro.
lighten, *v. a.* aliviar; – *v. n.* aliviarse.
lighter, *s.* encendedor *m.*, mechero *m.*
lighthouse, *s.* faro *m.*
lighting, *s.* alumbrado *m.*
lightness, *s.* ligereza *f.*
lightning, *s.* relámpago *m.*
like,[1] *adj.* igual, parecido; *what is he* ~*?* ¿qué aspecto tiene? — *s.* igual *m.*
like[2], *v.a.* querer; *I'd* ~ *to* quisiera.
likely, *adj.* verosímil; – *adv.* probablemente.
likeness, *s.* semejanza *f.*, parecido *m.*
likewise, *adv.* asimismo.
lily, *s.* lirio *m.*
limb, *s.* miembro *m.; (of the tree)* rama *f.*
limit, *s.* límite *m.;* – *v. a.* limitar.
imited, *pp.* limitado; ~ *company* compañía *(f.)* de responsabilidad limitada, sociedad *(f.)* anónima.
line, *s.* línea *f.; drop a* ~ mandar unas líneas; — *v. a. (paper)* rayar; *(coat)* forrar; ~ *up* alinearse.
linen, *s.* ropa *(f.)* blanca.
lining, *s.* forro *m.*
links, *s. pl.* campo *(m.)* de golf.
lion, *s.* león *m.*
lip, *s.* labio *m.; (of a pitcher)* pico *m.*
lipstick, barra *(f.) or* lápiz *(m.)* de labios.
liquid, *adj.* & *s.* líquido.
liquor, *s.* bebida *(f.)* alcohólica.
list, *s.* lista *f.;* – *v. a.* hacer una lista.
listen, *v. n.* oir; escuchar
listener, *s.* oyente *m., f.*
literal, *adj.* literal.
literary, *adj.* literario.
literature, *s.* literatura *f.*
litter, *s.* basura *f.; (stretcher)* camilla *f.; (animals)* camada *f.*
little, *adj.* pequeño; ~ *money* poco dinero.
live, *v. n.* vivir; *long* ~*!* ¡viva!; – *adj.* vivo.
lively, *adj.* vivo, animado.
liver, *s.* hígado *m.*
living-room, *s.* sala *(f.)* de estar.
load, *s.* carga *f.;* — *v. a.* cargar.
loaf, *s.* pan *m.*

loan, *s.* préstamo *m.; —* *v. a.* prestar.
lobby, *s.* vestíbulo *m.*
lobster, *s.* langosta *f.*
local, *adj.* local.
locate, *v. a.* situar; hallar.
location, *s.* situación *f.*, ubicación *f.*
lock,[1] *s.* mechón *m.*
lock,[2] *s.* cerradura *f.*, candado *m.; (on river)* esclusa *f.; — v. a.* cerrar (con llave).
locksmith, *s.* cerrajero *m.*
lock-up, *s.* calabozo *m.*
lodge, *s.* casucha *f.*, portería *f.; — v. a.* alojar; *v. n.* alojarse.
lodger, *s.* inquilino *m.*, huésped *m., f.*
lodging(s), *s. (pl.)* alojamiento *m.*, vivienda *f.*
logical, *adj.* lógico.
loin, *s.* lomo *m.*
lonely, *adj.* solitario, solo.
long,[1] *adj.* largo; *a ~ time ago* hace mucho; *— s. before ~* en poco tiempo; *— adv. all day ~* todo el día; *how ~?* ¿cuánto tiempo? *so ~!* ¡hasta pronto!; *any ~er* más tiempo.
long,[2] *v. n. ~ for* anhelar, codiciar.
long-play(ing), *adj.* (record) disco *(m.)* de larga duración.
look, *v. n.* mirar; *~ here!* ¡escúcheme!; *~ like* parecerse; *~ after* cuidar; *~ at* mirar; *~ for* buscar; *~ forward to* aguardar con impaciencia; *~ up* buscar; *~ out!* ¡cuidado!; — *s.* mirada *f.*
looking-glass, *s.* espejo *m.*
loose, *adj.* flojo, suelto; *(life)* licencioso.
loosen, *v. a.* soltar.
lord, *s.* señor *m.; House of Lords* Cámara *(f.)* de los Lores.
lordship, *s.* autoridades *f. pl.; his ~* su excelencia.
lorry, *s.* camión *m.*, furgón *m.*
lose, *v. a.* perder; *~ heart* desanimarse; *~ the train* perder el tren.
loss, *s.* pérdida *f.; be at a ~* no saber qué hacer.
lost, *adj. & pp.* perdido; *~ property office* sección *(f.)* de objetos perdidos.
lot, *s.* suerte *f.; (ground)* lote *m.; a ~ of* mucho.
loud, *adj.* fuerte; *(colour)* chillón.
loud-speaker, *s.* altoparlante *m.*, altavoz *m.*
lounge, *v. n.* holgazanear; — *s.* salón *m.*, vestíbulo *m.*
lounge-suit, *s.* traje *(m.)* para la tarde.
love, *s.* amor *m.; be in ~* estar enamorado; *fall in ~ with sy* enamorarse de; *— v. a.* querer.
lovely, *adj.* bello, hermoso, guapo.
lover, *s.* amante *m.*
low, *adj.* bajo; *~ gear* primera velocidad *(f.) ~ opinion* mala opinión.
lower, *adj.* más bajo; — *v. a.* bajar; *(flag)* arriar.
lowland, *s.* llanura *f.*, país *(m.)* bajo.
loyal, *adj.* leal, fiel.
loyalty, *s.* lealtad *f.*
lubricate, *v. a.* lubricar.
luck, *s.* suerte *f.; bad ~* mala suerte.
lucky, *adj.* afortunado.
luggage, *s.* equipaje *m.*
luggage-rack, *s.* portaequipajes *m.*

luggage-van, *s.* furgón *(m.)* de equipajes.
luminous, *adj.* luminoso.
lump, *s.* bola *f.*, grumo *m.*, *(of sugar)* terrón *m.*
lunch, *s.* almuerzo *m.*; – *v. n.* almorzar.
luncheon, *s.* almuerzo *m.*
lung, *s.* pulmón *m.*
lustre, *s.* lustre *m.*; *(lamp)* lustro *m.*
lute, *s.* lira *f.*
luxurious, *adj.* lujoso.
luxury, *s.* lujo *m.*
lyric, *adj.* lírico.

M

macaroni, *s.* macarrones *m. pl.*
machine, *s.* máquina *f.*
machinery, *s.* maquinaria *f.*
mackintosh, *s.* impermeable *m.*
mad, *adj.* loco; *(dog)* rabioso; *be ~ after sg* anhelar.
madam, *s.* señora *f.*
madness, *s.* locura *f.*
magazine, *s.* revista *f.*
magistrate, *s.* magistrado *m.*
magnet, *s.* imán *m.*
magnetic, *adj.* magnético.
magneto, *s.* magneto *m.*
magnificent, *adj.* magnífico.
magnify, *v. a.* ampliar; *~ing glass* lente *(f.)* de aumento, lupa *f.*
maid, *s.* criada *f.*, sirvienta; *old ~* solterona *f.*
maiden, soltera *f.*; *~ name* nombre *(m.)* de soltera.
mail, *s.* correo *m.*; Correos *m.*; – *v. a.* echar al correo.
mail-boat, *s.* buque *(m.)* correo.
main, *adj.* principal; *in the ~* en general.
maintain, *v. a.* mantener; sostener.
majestic, *adj.* majestuoso.
majesty, *s.* majestad *f.*
major, *adj.* mayor; principal; – *s.* comandante *m.*, mayor *m.*; *~ general* general *(m.)* de brigada.
majority, *s.* mayoría *f.*
make, *v. a.* hacer; *(mistake)* cometer; *(money)* ganar; *(peace)* firmar; *(war)* hacer; *~ fun of* burlarse de; *~ a fool of sy* poner en ridículo; *~ known* hacer saber; *~ ready* preparar; *~ sense* tener sentido; *~ sure* cerciorarse; *~ the acquaintance of* conocer a; *~ use of* servirse de; *~ up (face)* pintarse; *(invent)* inventar; – *s.* fabricación *f.*, producto *m.*
maker, *s.* fabricante *m.*
male, *adj.* & *s.* macho *(m.)*.
mammal, *s.* mamífero *m.*
man, *s.* hombre *m.*; – *v. a.* tripular.
manage, *v. a.* manejar; *~ to do sg* lograr hacer.
management, *s.* administración *f.*, dirección *f.*
manager, *s.* gerente *m.*, director *m.*, administrador *m.*
manhood, *s.* virilidad *f.*
manicure, *s.* manicura *f.* – *v. a.* hacer la manicura.
manifest, *adj.* manifiesto; – *v. a.* manifestar.
manipulate, *v. a.* manipular.
mankind, *s.* humanidad *f.*
manly, *adj.* varonil.
manner, *s.* manera *f.*;

~s costumbres *f. pl.*
manoeuvre, *s.* maniobra *f.*; .– *v. n.* maniobrar.
manpower, *s.* mano *(f.)* de obra.
manual, *adj.* & *s.* manual *(m.)*.
manufacture, *s.* fabricación *f.*; – *v. a.* fabricar.
manufacturer, *s.* fabricante *m.*
manuscript, *adj.* & *s.* manuscrito *(m.)*.
many, *adj.* mucho(s); *a good* ~ mucho; *how* ~? ¿cuántos?; ~ *a time* a menudo.
map, *s.* mapa *m.*
marble, *s.* mármol *m.*
march, *v. n.* marchar; – *s.* marcha *f.*
March, *s.* marzo *m.*
mare, *s.* yegua *f.*
margin, *s.* margen *m.*
marine, *adj.* marino; – *s.* marina *f.*
mariner, *s.* marinero *m.*, marino *m.*
mark, *s.* marca *f.*, seña *f.*, señal *f.*; *hit the* ~ dar en el blanco; *(school)* punto *m.*, nota *f.* *price* ~ etiqueta *f.*; – *v. a.* marcar, señalar.
market, *s.* mercado *m.*
market-price, *s.* precio *(m.)* de mercado.
marmalade, *s.* mermelada *f.*
marriage, *s.* matrimonio *m.*
married, *adj.* casado, casada.
marry, *v. a.* casar; – *v. n.* casarse.
marshal, *s.* mariscal *m.*; – *v. a.* ordenar, guiar.
marvel, *s.* maravilla *f.*; – *v. n.* maravillarse.
marvellous, *adj.* maravilloso.
masculine, *adj.* masculino.
mask, *s.* máscara *f.*, careta *f.*
mass,[1] *s.* misa *f.*
mass,[2] *s.* masa *f.*, montón *m.*; ~ *meeting* mítin *(m.)* popular; ~ *production* producción *(f.)* en serie.
mast, *s.* mástil *m.*
master, *s.* *(school)* maestro *m.*; *(owner)* amo *m.*, dueño *m.*; – *v. a.* dominar.
masterpiece, *s.* obra *(f.)* maestra.
match,[1] *s.* fósforo *m.*, cerilla *f.*
match,[2] *s.* encuentro *m.*, competición *f.*; *(marriage)* partido *m.*; *(equal)* igual *m.*; *they're a good* ~ hacen una buena pareja; *I'm no* ~ *for him* no puedo competir con él; – *v. a.* igualar.
match-box, *s.* caja *(f.)* de fósforos, *or* cerillas.
mate,[1] *s.* *(chess)* mate *m.*
mate,[2] *s.* compañero *m.*; *(marine)* primer oficial *m.*; *(wife)* consorte *f.*, mujer *f.*; – *v. a.* aparear.
material, *s.* materia *f.*; *raw* ~ materia prima; *writing* ~s efectos *(m. pl.)* de escritorio; – *adj.* material.
mathematical, *adj.* matemático.
mathematics, *s.* matemáticas *f. pl.*
matrimony, *s.* matrimonio *m.*
matter, *s.* materia *f.*; *(theme)* tema *m.*; *(business)* asunto *m.*, causa

f.; what's the ~? ¿qué pasa?; — *v n.* importar.
mattress, *s.* colchón *m.*
mature, *adj.* maduro; — *v. a. & n.* madurar.
maturity, *s.* madurez *f.*
maximum, *adj. & s.* máximo *(m.).*
may, *v. n.* poder; ~ *I come in?* ¿puedo entrar?; ~ *I have this dance?* ¿quiere usted concederme este baile?
May, *s.* mayo *m.*
maybe, *adv.* tal vez, quizás.
mayor, *s.* alcalde *m.*
me, *pron.* me; *give* ~ *some of that* déme usted un poco de aquello; *it's* ~ soy yo; *is this for* ~? es esto para mí?
meadow, *s.* pradera *f.*
meal, *s.* comida *f.*
mean[1], *s.* término *(m.)* medio; *in the* ~ *time* entretanto.
mean,[2] *v. a. & n.* proponerse, intentar.
mean,[3] *adj.* malo.
meaning, *s.* sentido *m.;* significado *m.; what's the* ~ *of this?* ¿qué significa esto?
means, *s.pl.* medios *m. pl.;* *(money)* dinero *m.; by all* ~ a todo trance, sin falta.
meantime, *adv.* mientras tanto, entretanto.
meanwhile, *see* **meantime.**
measure, *s.* medida *f.; in some* ~ hasta cierto punto; — *v. a.* medir.
measurement, *s.* medida *f.; take sy's* ~*s* tomar las medidas de.
meat, *s.* carne *f.;* ~ *pie* empanada *f.*
mechanic, *s.* mecánico *m.*
mechanical, *adj.* mecánico.
mechanics, *s. pl.* mecánica *f.*
mechanism, *s.* mecanismo *m.*
mechanize, *v. a.* mecanizar.
medal, *s.* medalla *f.*
medical, *adj.* médico.
medicine, *s.* medicina *f.;* ~ *chest* botiquín *m.*
mediocre, *adj.* mediocre.
meditate, *v. n.* meditar.
medium, *s.* medio *m.; through the* ~ *of* por medio de; — *adj.* medio; ~*-sized* de tamaño mediano.
meet, *v. a.* encontrar; *pleased to* ~ *you* tengo mucho gusto en conocerle; *will the bus* ~ *the train?* ¿empalmará el ómnibus con el tren?; *(demands)* satisfacer; — *v. n.* ~ *with an accident* tener un accidente; *(assemble)* reunirse.
Mexican, *adj. & s.* mejicano *(m.).*
microbe, *s.* microbio *m.*
microfilm, *s.* microfilm *m.;* — *v.n.* microfilmar.
microphone, *s.* micrófono *m.*
microscope, *s.* microscopio *m.*
middle, *adj.* medio; *Middle Ages s.* edad *(f.)* media; — *s.* centro *m.,* medio *m.*
middle-aged, *adj.* de edad madura.
midnight, *s.* media noche *f.*
might, *s.* poder *m.,* fuerza *f.*
mighty, *adj.* poderoso.
migrate, *v. n.* vagar.

mild, *adj.* *(weather)* templado; *(cheese)* blando, fresco; *(disposition)* suave.
mile, *s.* milla *f.*
mileage, *s.* kilometraje *m.*
military, *adj.* militar.
milk, *s.* leche *f.*; — *v. a.* & *n.* ordeñar.
milkman, *s.* lechero *m.*
mill, *s.* molino *m.*, molinillo *m.*; *(factory)* fábrica *f.*; — *v. a.* moler.
miller, *s.* molinero *m.*
milliner, *s.* modista *f.*, sombrérera *f.*
million, *s.* millón *m*
mince, *v. a.* despedazar: — *s.* carne *(f.)* picada.
mind, *s.* mente *f.*; *call to* ~ recordar; *change one's* ~ cambiar de opinión; *have a* ~ tener
meeting, *s.* sesión *f.*, junta *f.*, mítin *m.*
melody, *s.* melodía *f.*
melon, *s.* melón *m.*
melt, *v. a.* derretir; *v. n.* derretirse, disolverse.
member, *s.* socio *m.*, miembro *m.*
memorial, *s.* monumento *(m.)* conmemorativo; memorial *m.*
memory, *s.* memoria *f.*; *in* ~ *of sy* en recuerdo de.
mend, *v. a.* remendar; *v. n.* restablecerse.
mention, *v. a.* mencionar; *don't* ~ *it!* no hay de que; — *s.* mención *f.*
menu, *s.* menú *m.*, lista *(f.)* de platos.
merchandise, *s.* mercancía *f.*, mercadería *f.*
merchant, *s.* comerciante *m.*
mere, *adj.* mere, puro.
meridian, *s.* meridiano *m.*
merit, *s.* mérito *m.*; — *v. a.* merecer.
merry, *adj.* alegre; *a* ~ *Christmas!* ¡Felices Pascuas!; *make* ~ estar alegre.
mess, *s.* lío *m.*; *in a* ~ desarreglado, revuelto; — *v. a.* enredar; ensuciar.
message, *s.* recado *m.*, mensaje *m.*
messenger, *s.* mensajero *m.*
metal, *s.* metal *m.*
meteorology, *s.* meterología *f.*
method, *s.* método *m.*
metre, *s.* metro *m.*
metropolis, *s.* metrópoli *f.*
ganas de; *have in* ~ pensar en; *keep in* ~ tener presente; *make up one's* ~ decidir, resolver; — *v. a.* cuidar, tener cuidado a; *I don't* ~ me da lo mismo; *never* ~ no se moleste.
mine,[1] *pron.* mío; *a friend of* ~ uno de mis amigos.
mine,[2] *s.* mina *f.*; — *v. a.* extraer, explotar.
miner, *s.* minero *m.*
mineral, *adj.* & *s.* mineral *(m.)*; ~ *water* agua *(f.)* mineral.
miniature, *s.* miniatura *f.*
minimum, *adj* & *s.* mínimo *(m.)*
minister, *s.* ministro *m.*; — *v. n.* atender.
ministry, *s.* ministerio *m.*
minor, *adj.* menor; — *s.* menor *(m. f.)* de edad.
minority, *s.* minoridad *f.*
minus, *adj.* menos, sin.
minute[1], *s.* minuto *m.*
minute[2], *adj.* menudo.
miracle, *s.* milagro *m.*
mirror, *s.* espejo *m.*
miscarry, *v. n.* fracasar.
miscellaneous, *adj.* mis-

celáneo.
mischief, *s.* travesura *f.*, maldad *f.*
miserable, *adj.* miserable.
misery, *s.* miseria *f.*
misfortune, *s.* mala suerte *f.*, desgracia *f.*
miss, *v. a.* *(train)* perder; *(sy)* no encontrar; *be ~ing* faltar; — *s.* falta *f.*
Miss, *s.* señorita *f.*
missile, *s.* cohete *m.*
mission, *s.* misión *f.*
mist, *s.* niebla *f.*, neblina *f.*
mistake, *s.* error *m.*, culpa *f.*, falta *f.*, equivocación *f.*; *sorry, my ~* lo siento, ha sido culpa mía; *make a ~* equivocarse, cometer un error; *by ~* sin querer; — *v. a.* confundir.
Mister, *s.* señor *m.*
mistress, *s.* señora *f.*, *(of the house)* dueña *f.*; *(lover)* amante *f.*
mistrust, *s.* desconfianza *f.*; — *v. n.* desconfiar.
misty, *adj.* nebuloso, brumoso.
misunderstand, *v. a.* entender mal.
misunderstanding, *s.* equivocación *f.*
mix, *v. a.* mezclar; *(drinks)* preparar; *v. n.* relacionarse, mezclarse.
mixture, *s.* mezcla *f.*, mixtura *f.*
mob, *s.* muchedumbre *f.*, gentío *m.*
mobility, *s.* movilidad *f.*
mock, *v. a.* burlar; — *s.* burla *f.*
mockery, *s.* burla *f.*, mofa *f.*
model, *s.* modelo *m.*; — *v. a.* modelar, planear.
moderate, *adj.* moderado; *v. a.* moderar.
moderation, *s.* moderación *f.*
modern, *adj.* moderno.
modest, *adj.* modesto.
modesty, *s.* modestia *f.*
modify, *v. a.* modificar.
moist, *adj.* húmedo.
moisten, *v. a.* humedecer; mojar; *v. n.* mojarse.
moisture, *s.* humedad *f.*
molar, *s.* muela *f.*, molar *m.*
moment, *s.* momento *m.*; *in a ~* en seguida; *at the ~* por ahora.
momentary, *adj.* momentáneo.
monarch, *s.* monarca *m.*
monarchy, *s.* monarquía *f.*
Monday, *s.* lunes *m.*
money, *s.* dinero *m.*; *make ~* ganar dinero.
money-order, *s.* giro *(m.)* postal.
monkey, *s.* mono *m.*
monograph, *s.* monografía *f.*
monopolize, *v. a.* monopolizar.
monopoly, *s.* monopolio *m.*
monstrous, *adj.* monstruoso.
month, *s.* mes *m.*
monthly, *adj.* mensual; — *adv.* mensualmente; — *s.* periódico *(m.)* mensual.
monument, *s.* monumento *m.*
monumental, *adj.* monumental.
mood, *s.* humor *m.*, genio *m.*
moon, *s.* luna *f.*; *full ~* luna llena; — *v. a. ~ about* vagar.

moonlight, *s.* claro *(m.)* de luna.
moor, *s.* pantano *m.*, ciénaga *f.*; — *v. a.* amarrar.
moral, *adj.* moral, ético; — *s.* moraleja *f.*
more, *adj.* más; *have some* ~ sírvase usted.
moreover, *adv.* además (de eso).
morning, *s.* mañana *f.*; *in the* ~ por la mañana; *good* ~ buenos días; ~ *paper* diario *(m.)* de la mañana.
mortal, *adj.* mortal.
mortality, *s.* mortalidad *f.*
mosquito, *s.* mosquito *m.*
moss, *s.* musgo *m.*
most, *adj.* & *s.* lo máximo, lo más; ~ *people* la mayoría de la gente; ~ *of them* la mayor parte de ellos; ~ *interesting* interesantísimo; ~ *likely* muy probable.
mostly, *adv.* en su mayor parte, por lo común.
motel, *s.* parador *m.*
moth, *s.* polilla *f.*
mother, *s.* madre *f.*
mother-in-law, *s.* suegra *f.*
mother-tongue, *s.* lengua *(f.)* madre.
motion, *s.* movimiento *m.*, *(proposal)* moción *f.*, proposición *f.*; — *v. n.* hacer señas; indicar.
motionless, *adj.* inmóvil.
motive, *s.* motivo *m.*
motor, *s.* motor *m.*; — *v. n.* ir en automóvil.
motor-bike, *s.* motocicleta *f.*, moto *f.*
motor-boat, *s.* lancha *(f.)* motora.
motor-car, *s.* automóvil *m.*
motor-coach, *s.* autocar *m.*
motor-cycle, *s.* motocicleta *f.*, moto *f.*
motorway, *s.* autopista *f.*
mount, *s.* monte *m.*; — *v. a.* subir; ~ *a horse* montar a caballo; *v. n.* subir, aumentar.
mountain, *s.* montaña *f.*
mountainous, *adj.* montañoso.
mountain-range, *s.* sierra *f.*, cordillera *f.*
mourn, *v. a.* deplorar la muerte de, llevar de luto.
mouse, s. ratón *m.*
moustache, *s.* bigote *m.*
mouth, *s.* boca *f.*; *fig.* entrada *f.*
move, *v. a.* mover; *(propose)* proponer; *v. n.* moverse; *keep moving* circular; ~ *off* alejarse; — *s.* movimiento *m.*, paso *m.*; *(chess)* jugada *f.*; *get a* ~ *on* apresurarse.
movement, *s.* movimiento *m.*
movie, *s.* película *f.*; cine *m.*
mow, *v. a.* segar.
mower, *s.* segador *m.*; *(machine)* segadora *f.*
much, *adj.* mucho; *how* ~? ¿cuánto cuesta?; *thank you very* ~ muchas gracias; *too* ~ demasiado; *so* ~ tanto.
mud, *s.* fango *m.*, cieno *m.*, barro *m.*
muddy, *adj.* fangoso.
mug, *s.* tazón *m.*
mule, *s.* mula *f.*
multiple, *adj.* múltiple.
multiplication, *s.* multiplicación *f.*

multiply, *v. a.* multiplicar.
multitude, *s.* multitud *f.*
municipal, *adj.* municipal.
murder, *s.* asesinato *m.*; *v. a.* asesinar.
murderer, *s.* asesino *m.*
muscle, *s.* músculo *m.*
museum, *s.* museo *m.*
mushroom, *s.* seta *f.*; hongo *m.*
music, *s.* música *f.*
musical, *adj.* musical.
music-hall, *s.* teatro *(m.)* de variedades.
musician, *s.* músico *m.*
must[1], *v. n.* deber, tener que; *I* ~ *go* tengo que irme; *you* ~ *not go* no debe ir.
must[2], *s.* moho *m.*; *(of grape)* mosto *m.*
mustard, *s.* mostaza *f.*
muster, *s.* inspección *f.*, revista *f.*; — *v. a.* pasar revista.
mute, *adj.* mudo; — *v. a.* hacer callar, silenciar.
mutton, *s.* carnero *m.*
mutual, *adj.* mutuo.
muzzle, *s.* hocico *m.*; *(of dog)* bozal *m.*; *(of arms)* cañón *m.*, boca *f.*; — *v. a.* silenciar.
my, *pron.* mi, mío; ~ *gloves* mis guantes.
myself, *pron.* yo mismo.
mysterious, *adj.* misterioso.
mystery, *s.* misterio *m.*
myth, *s.* mito *m.*

N

nail, clavo *m.*; *(finger-)* uña *f.*; — *v. a.* & *n.* clavar.
nail-brush, *s.* cepill(it)o *(m.)* de uñas.
naked, *adj.* desnudo.
name, *s.* nombre *m.*; *(of a book)* título *m.*; *(fame)* fama *f.*; *by* ~ de nombre; *what's your* ~? ¿cómo se llama usted?; — *v. a.* nombrar.
namely, *adv.* a saber.
nap, *s.* sueñecillo *m.*
napkin, *s.* servilleta *f.*
narrow, *adj.* estrecho; — *v. a.* reducir; *v. n.* reducirse, estrecharse.
nation, *s.* nación *f.*, país *m.*
national, *adj.* nacional.
nationalization, *s.* nacionalización *f.*
nationality, *s.* nacionalidad *f.*
native, *adj.* nativo; ~ *land* patria *f.*; ~ *language* lengua *(f.)* maternal; — *s.* indígena *m.*, *f.*
natural, *adj.* natural.
nature, *s.* naturaleza *f.*; *by* ~ por naturaleza.
naughty, *adj.* travieso, díscolo, desobediente.
naval, *adj.* naval.
navigable, *adj.* navegable.
navy, *s.* marina *(f.)* de guerra, armada *f.*
near, *adv.* cerca; ~ *at hand* próximo; ~ *by* cerca de aquí; *draw* ~ acercarse; — *prep.* cerca de; ~ *the station* cerca de la estación; — *adv.* cercano; — *v. n.* acercarse.
nearly, *adv.* aproximadamente, casi.
neat, *adj.* aseado, limpio.
necessary, *adj.* necesario.
necessity, *s.* necesidad *f.*
neck, *s.* nuca *f.*; *(of a bottle)* cuello *m.*
necklace, *s.* cadena *f.*, collar *m.*
necktie, *s.* corbata *f.*

need, *s.* necesidad *f.*; – *v. a.* necesitar; *v. n.* hacer falta.
needle, *s.* aguja *f.*
needless, *adj.* inútil, innecesario.
negative, *adj.* & *s.* negativo (*m.*), – *v. a.* negar, refutar.
neglect, *v. a.* descuidar; – *s.* abandono *m.*, descuido *m.*
negligence, *s.* negligencia, *f.*, descuido *m.*
negotiation, *s.* negociación *f.*
Negro, *s.* negro *m.*
neighbour, *s.* vecino *m.*
neighbourhood, *s.* vecindad *f.*
neither, *conj.* ~ ... *nor* ni ... ni; – *pron.* ninguno de los dos.
nephew, *s.* sobrino *m.*
nerve, *s.* nervio *m.*
nervous, *adj.* nervioso; ~ *breakdown* agotamiento *(m.)* nervioso.
nest, *s.* nido *m.*
net[1], *s.* red *f.*; – *v. a.* enredar.
net[2], *adj.* neto.
neutral, *adj.* neutral.
never, *adv.* nunca, jamás; ~ *again* nunca más.
nevertheless, *conj.* no obstante, sin embargo.
new, *adj.* nuevo; *New Year's Eve* Noche *(f.)* de Año Nuevo.
news, *s.* noticias *f. pl.*; *what's the* ~? ¿qué hay de nuevo?
newspaper, *s.* periódico *m.*
next, *adj.* siguiente, próximo; ~ *day* el día siguiente; ~ *year* el año que viene; ~ *time* la próxima vez; – *adv.* después; *who comes* ~? ¿quién sigue?; *what* ~? ¿y ahora qué?; *prep.* ~ *to* al lado de.
nice, *adj.* agradable; bonito; ~ *and warm* un calor agradable.
nickname, *s.* apodo *m.*, – *v. a.* apodar.
niece, *s.* sobrina *f.*
night, *s.* noche *f.*; *last* ~ anoche; *good* ~! ¡buenas noches!; *at* ~ de noche; ~ *and day* día y noche.
night-porter, *s.* portero *(m.)* de noche.
nightingale, *s.* ruiseñor *m.*
nightmare, *s.* pesadilla *f.*
nine, *adv.* & *s.* nueve.
nineteen, *adv.* & *s.* diecinueve.
ninety, *adj.* & *s.* noventa *(m.)*.
ninth, *adj.* noveno.
nitrogen, *s.* nitrógeno *m.*
no, no; *whether or* ~ sí o no; *adj.* ningún; ~ *smoking* prohibido fumar.
nobility, *s* . nobleza *f.*
noble, *adj.* & *s.* noble *(m.)*.
nobody, *pron.* & *s.* nadie.
nod, *v. a.* afirmar con la cabeza, inclinar la cabeza, cabecear.
noise, *s.* ruido *m.*
noiseless, *adj.* silencioso.
noisy, *adj.* ruidoso.
nomination *s.* nombramiento *m.*
none, *pron.* & *s.* ningún, ninguno; ~ *but* únicamente; ~ *too* no demasiado; ~ *too soon* a buena hora; ~ *the less* no obstante, sin embargo.
nonsense, *s.* tontería *f.*
non-smoker, *s.* no-fumador *m.*
non-stop, *adj.* continuo, interrumpido.

noon, *s.* mediodía *m.*
nor, ni; *neither you ~ I* ni usted ni yo.
normal, *adj.* normal.
north, *s.* norte *m.*
northern, *adj.* del norte.
northwest, *s.* noroeste *m.*
nose, *s.* nariz f.; *fig.* olfato *m.*
not, no; *~ at all* de ninguna manera; *~ a ...* ninguno.
notable, *adj.* notable.
note, *s.* nota *f.*, anotación *f.*; *take ~s* tomar notas; *(music)* nota *(f.)* de música; — *v. a.* anotar; darse cuenta de.
note-book, *s.* cuaderno *m.*, libreta *f.*
noted, *adj.* célebre, famoso.
nothing, nada; *I have ~ to do* no tengo nada que hacer; *good for ~* tunante *m.*; *~ else* nada más; *~ less than* nada menos que.
notice, *s.* aviso *m.*; *until further ~* hasta nueva orden; *give ~ to sy* despedir; *at short ~* a corto plazo; — *v. a.* darse cuenta de.
notify, *v. a.* notificar.
notion, *s.* noción *f.*
nought, nada, cero.
noun, *s.* substantivo *m.*, nombre *m.*
nourish, *v. a.* alimentar, nutrir.
novel, *s.* novela *f.*; — *adj.* reciente, moderno.
novelist, *s.* novelista *m.*, *f.*
novelty, novedad *s. f.*
November, *s.* noviembre *m.*
now, ahora; *by ~* ya; *from ~ on* de ahora en adelante; *just ~* ahora mismo; *~ and then* de vez en cuando; *~ that* ahora que; — *int. ~ then!* ¡ahora bien!
nowadays, *adv.* hoy día.
nowhere, *adv.* por ninguna parte.
nuclear, *adj.* nuclear; *~ bomb* bomba *(f.)* nuclear; *~ fission* fisión *(f.)* nuclear; *~ power station* central *(f.)* de energía atómica.
number, *s.* número *m.*; — *v. a.* numerar.
number-plate, *s.* placa *(f.)* de matrícula, *or* matrícula *f.*
numerous, *adj.* numeroso.
nun, *s.* monja *f.*
nurse, *s.* niñera *f.*; *(sick)* enfermera *f.*; — *v. a.* cuidar.
nursery, *s.* cuarto *(m.)* de los niños; *~ school* jardín *(f.)* de la infancia; *(of trees)* plantel *m.*
nut, *s.* nuez *f.*; *(screw)* tuerca; *~s* loco, chiflado.
nutrition, *s.* nutrición *f.*
nylon, *s.* nailón *m.* nilón *m.*

O

oak, *s.* roble *m.*
oar, *s.* remo *m.*
oath, juramento *m.*
obedient, *adj.* obediente.
obey, *v. n.* obedecer.
object, *s.* objeto *m.*; *(intention)* propósito *m.*; — *v. n.* oponerse a.
objection, *s.* objeción *f.*
obligation, *s.* obligación *f.*
oblige, *v. a.* obligar; *be ~d to* tener que; *I am much ~d* estoy muy agradecido.
obscure, *adj.* obscuro; — *v. a.* obscurecer.

observation, *s.* observación *f.*
observe, *v. a.* observar, advertir, darse cuenta de; *(rules)* cumplir, obedecer.
observer, *s.* observador *m.*
obstacle, *s.* obstáculo *m.*
obstinate, *adj.* terco, obstinado.
obtain, *v.* a. obtener, adquirir.
occasion, *s.* ocasión *f.*
occasional, *adj.* ocasional.
occupation, *s.* ocupación *f.*; trabajo *m.*, oficio *m.*
occupy, *v. a.* ocupar; tomar; apoderarse de; *be occupied in* estar ocupado con.
occur, *v. n.* ocurrir; *it ~s to me* se me ocurre.
ocean, *s.* océano *m.*
o'clock, *adv. at seven ~* a las siete.
October, *s.* octubre *m.*
odd, *adj.* *(number)* impar; *three shillings ~* tres chelines y pico; *(person)* raro.
of, *prep.* de; *the book ~ the student* el libro del estudiante; *it is very kind ~ you* es usted muy amable; *two ~ them* dos de ellos; *most ~ all* lo más; *a friend ~ mine* un amigo mío.
off, *adv. & prep. he is ~ to London* salió para Londres; *a mile ~* a una milla de distancia; *day ~* día *(m.)* libre; *~ duty* no estar de servicio.
offence, *s.* ofensa *f.*; *(fault)* culpa *f.*, delito *m.*
offend, *v. a.* ofender; pecar, cometer una falta.
offensive, *adj.* ofensivo; — *s.* ofensiva *f.*
offer, *v. a.* ofrecer; — *s.* oferta *f.*
office, *s.* oficina *f.*; *(charge)* cargo *m.*; despacho *m.*
officer, *s.* oficial *m.*
official, *adj.* oficial; — *s.* oficial *m.*
often, *adv.* a menudo, con frecuencia.
oil, *s.* aceite *m.*; — *v. a.* engrasar.
ointment, *s.* unguento *m.*, crema *f.*
old, *adj.* viejo; *fig.* antiguo; *grow ~* envejecer; *how ~ are you?* ¿qué edad tiene usted? *I'm thirty years ~* tengo treinta años.
old-fashioned, *adj.* fuera de moda.
omlet(te) *s.* tortilla *f.*
omit, *v. a.* omitir.
on, *prep. & adv.* a; *~ the left* a la izquierda; *~ Sunday* el domingo; *~ April 3rd* el tres de abril; *~ sale* de venta; *~ the contrary* al contrario; *~ credit* al fiado; *~ foot* a pie; *~ duty* de servicio; *~ purpose* de propósito, a sabiendas.
once, *adv.* una vez; *at ~* en seguida, inmediatamente; *~ more* otra vez.
one, *adj. & s.* uno; *~ of us* uno de nosotros; *~ has to be careful* hay que tener cuidado; *I prefer this ~* prefiero esto.
onion, *s.* cebolla *f.*
onlooker, *s.* espectador *m.*
only, *adj.* único; — *adv.* unicamente, solamente.

open, *adj.* abierto; *in the ~ air* al aire libre; *be ~ with* ser franco con; — *v. a.* abrir; *v. n.* abrirse.
opening, *s.* abertura *f.*; *(beginning)* apertura *f.*; inauguración *f.*
opera, *s.* ópera *f*
operate, *v. a.* hacer funcionar; *v. n. ~ on* operar, hacer una operación.
operating-theatre, *s.* sala *(f.)* de operaciones.
operation, *s.* funcionamento *m.*; *(military, medical)* operación *f.*
operative, *adj.* operativo, operatorio; — *s.* operario *m.*
opinion, *s.* opinión *f.*
opponent, *s.* oponente *m.*
opportunity, *s.* oportunidad *f.*
oppose, *v. a.* & *n.* oponer.
opposite, *adj.* contrario, opuesto.
opposition, *s.* oposición *f.*
oppress, *v. a.* oprimir.
oppression, *s.* opresión *f.*
optic, *adj.* óptico.
optimism, *s.* optimismo *m.*
option, *s.* opción *f.*
optional, *adj.* facultativo.
or, *conj.* o; *either . . . ~* o. . .o.
oral, *adj.* oral.
orange, *s.* naranja *f.*
orator, *s.* orador *m.*
orbit, *s.* órbita *f.*
orchard, *s.* huerto *m.*
orchestra, *s.* orquesta *f.*
order, *s.* orden *m.*; *(command)* orden *f.*; *fill an ~* enviar el pedido; — *v. a.* ordenar, mandar.
ordinary, *adj.* ordinario, corriente.
organ, *s.* órgano *m.*
organic, *adj.* orgánico.
organism, *s.* organismo *m.*
organization, *s.* organización *f.*
organize, *v. a.* organizar.
Orient, *adj.* oriente; — *s.* oriente *m.*; — *v. a.* orientar; *v. n.* orientarse.
Oriental, *adj.* oriental.
origin, *s.* origen *m.*
original, *adj.* original; primero, primitivo; — *s.* original *m.*
ornament, *s.* ornamento *m.*; — *v. a.* ornar, decorar.
ornamental, *adj.* ornamental.
orphan, *adj.* & *s.* huérfano *(m.)*, huérfana *(f.)*.
other, *adj.* otro; *the ~ day* el otro día; *on the ~ hand* por otra parte; *every ~ day* un día sí otro no.
otherwise, *adv.* de otro modo; si no.
ought, *v. n.* deber, tener que.
ounce, *s.* onza *f.*
our, *adj.* &. *pron.* nuestro.
ours, *pron.* nuestro.
ourself, -ves, *pron.* nosotros mismos.
oust, *v. a.* desalojar, expulsar.
out, *adv.* fuera; *be ~* estar fuera.
outboard-motor, *s.* motor *(m.)* fuera de bordo, fuerabordo *m.*
outdoor(s), *adv.* al aire libre, fuera.
outer, *adj.* exterior, más lejano.
outfit, *s.* equipo *m.*; ajuar *m.*

outline, *s.* silueta *f.*, contorno *m.*; *(summing up)* resumen *m.*; – *v. a.* hacer un resumen de.
outlook, *s.* vista *f.*, perspectiva *f.*; modo *(m.)* de ver.
output, *s.* producción *f.*
outrage, *s.* atrocidad *f.*; – *v. a.* ultrajar.
outrageous, *adj.* ultrajoso, infame.
outside, *adj.* exterior, de fuera; – *adv.* fuera; – *s.* exterior *m.*
outsider, *adj.* & *s.* forastero, extraño.
outskirts, *s. pl.* afueras *f. pl.*, arrabal *m.*
outward, *adj.* externo, exterior.
outwards, *adv.* al exterior.
oven, *s.* horno *m.*
over, *prep.* & *adv.* sobre; *all* ~ por todo; ~ *there* allí; *it is* ~ ha terminado.
overalls, *s.* mono *(m.)* de mecánico.
overcoat, *s.* abrigo *m.*, gabán *m.*
overcome, *v. a.* vencer.
overcrowded, *adj.* hacinado, atestado.
overdo, *v. a.& n.* exagerar; *(meat) it is overdone* está muy hecho.
overexpose, *v. a.* sobre(e)xponer.
overflow, *v. a.* inundar; *v. n.* desbordar; – *s.* inundación *f.*
overhear, *v. a.* oir por casualidad.
overlook, *v. a.* mirar, dar a; *(miss)* olvidar, pasar por alto; *(forgive)* tolerar.
overseas, *adv.* en ultramar; – *adj.* ultramarino.
overtake, *v. a.* alcanzar, pasar; *fig.* sorprender.
overtime, *s.* horas *(f. pl.)* extra; – *v. n.* trabajar horas extraordinarias.
overturn, *v. a.* derribar, trastornar; – *v. n.* derrumbarse, volcarse.
owe, *v. a.* deber; *how much do I* ~ *you?* cuánto le debo?
owing to, *prep.* debido a.
own, *adj.* propio; *my* ~ mío; – *v. a.* tener; ser de alguien.
owner, *s.* propietario *m.*
ox, *s.* buey *m.*
oxygen, *s.* oxígeno *m.*

P

pace, *s.* paso *m.*; *(speed)* velocidad *f.*
pacific, *adj.* pacífico; *The Pacific* el Océano Pacífico.
pack, *s.* carga *f.*; ~ *of cards* baraja *f.*; – *v. a.* empaquetar.
package, *s.* paquete *m.*
pact, *s.* pacto *m.*
pad, *s.* cojín *m.*; *(writing-)* bloc *(m.)* de papel; – *v. a.* rellenar.
paddle, *s.* canalete *m.*; – *v. n.* impeler con canalete.
page, *s.* página *f.*
pail, *s.* cubo *m.*
pain, *s.* dolor *m.*
painful, *adj.* doloroso, penoso.
paint, *s.* pintura *f.*; – *v. a.* pintar.
painter, *s.* pintor *m.*;

(house-) pintor de brocha gorda.
painting, *s.* pintura *f.*, cuadro *m.*
pair, *s.* par *m.*
palace, *s.* palacio *m.*
palate, *s.* paladar *m.*; *fig.* gusto *m.*
pale, *adj.* pálido.
palm[1], *s.* palma *f.*
palm[2], *s.* *(tree)* palmera *f.*
pan, *s.* cacerola *f.*, olla *f.*
pane, *s.* cristal *m.*, vidrio *m.*
panel, *s.* panel *m.*, tablero *m.*
panic, *s.* pánico *m.*, terror *m.*
panorama, *s.* panorama *m.*
pansy, *s.* pensamiento *m.*
pant, *v. n.* jadear.
pantry, *s.* despensa *f.*
pants, *s. pl.* calzoncillos *m. pl.*
paper, *s.* papel *m.*; documento *m.*
parade, *s.* parada *f.*, desfile *m.*; — *v. n.* desfilar.
paradise, *s.* paraíso *m.*
paragraph, *s.* párrafo *m.*
parallel, *adj.* & *s.* paralelo *m.*; *draw a* ~ establecer un paralelo.
paralize, *v. a.* paralizar.
parcel, *s.* paquete *m.*, bulto *m.*
parchment, *s.* pergamino *m.*
pardon, *s.* indulto *m.*, perdón *m.*; *I beg your* ~ perdone usted, dispense usted; *I beg your* ~? no le he entendido; ¿quiere hacer el favor de repetirlo?; — *v. a.* perdonar.
parent, *s.* progenitor *m.*; *the* ~*s* los padres.
parish, *s.* parroquia *f.*
Parisian, *adj.* & *s.* parisiense *(m.)*.
park, *s.* parque *m.*; — *v. a.* estacionar, dejar, aparcar.
parking, *s.* estacionamiento *m.*; *no* ~ prohibido el estacionamiento.
parliament, *s.* parlamento *m.*
parlour, *s.* salón *m.*, sala *f.*
parrot, *s.* loro *m.*
parsley, *s.* perejil *m.*
parson, *s.* párroco *m.*, cura *m.*
part, *s.* parte *f.*; *(of actor)* papel *m.*; *(for a car)* repuesto *m.*, pieza *f.*; *take* ~ *in* tomar parte en; — *v. a.* partir; *v. n.* romperse; separarse.
partake, *v. n.* tener parte de, beneficiar de.
partial, *adj.* parcial.
participant, *s.* participante *m.*, *f.*
participation, *s.* participación *f.*
particular, *adj.* particular; — *s.* detalle *m.*
partly, *adv.* en parte, en cierto modo.
partner, *s.* compañero *m.*, socio *m.*; *(dancing)* pareja *f.*
partridge, *s.* perdiz *f.*
party, *s.* partido *m.*; *(feast)* fiesta *f.*
pass, *v. a.* pasar; *(bill, examination)* aprobar; *(sentence)* pronunciar; *v. n.* pasar; *let* ~ pasar por alto; ~ *away* fallecer; ~ *for* tener *or* considerar por; ~ *on* pasar, transmitir; ~ *out* desmayarse; ~ *through* pasar por.
passage, *s.* pasaje *m.*; *(cor-*

ridor) pasillo *m.*
passenger, *s.* pasajero *m.*
passer-by, *s.* transeúnte *m.*
passion, *s.* pasión *f.; be in* ~ estar en cólera.
passive, *adj.* pasivo.
passport, *s.* pasaporte *m.*
past, *adj.* & *s.* pasado *(m.).; in the* ~ antes; ~ *danger* fuera del peligro; *it's half* ~ *four* son las cuatro y media.
paste, *s.* pasta *f.*
pastime, *s.* pasatiempo *m.*
pastry, *s.* pastel *m.*, pastelito *m.*
pat, *v. a.* acariciar.
patch, *s.* remiendo *m.*; parche *m.*; — *v. a.* remendar.
patent, *adj.* patente; patentado; — *s.* patente *f.*; — *v. a.* sacar la patente de.
path, *s.* sendero *m.*
patience, *s.* paciencia *f.*
patient, *adj.* paciente; — *s.* enfermo *m.*, paciente *m.*
patriot, *s.* patriota *m.*
patriotic, *adj.* patriótico.
patron, *s.* parroquiano *m.*, cliente *m.*
pattern, *s.* patrón *m.*, molde *m.*, dibujo *m.*
pause, *s.* descanso *m.*, parada *f.*; — *v. n.* hacer una pausa.
pave, *v. a.* & *n.* pavimentar.
pavement, *s.* pavimento *m.*, empedrado *m.*
pavilion, *s.* pabellón *m.*
paw, *s.* pata *f.*
pay, *v. a.* pagar; *order to* ~ orden *(f.)* de pago; ~ *a visit* hacer una visita; — *s.* paga *f.*, sueldo *m.*
payable, *adj.* pagable.
pay-day, *s.* día *(m.)* de pago.
payment, *s.* pago *m.*, pagamiento *m.*
pea, *s.* guisante *m.*
peace, *s.* paz *f.*
peaceful, *adj.* pacífico, tranquilo.
peach, *s.* melocotón *m.*
peak, *s.* cima *f.*, cúspide *f.*
pear, *s.* pera *f.*
pearl, *s.* perla *f.*
peasant, *s.* campesino *m.*, labriego *m.*
peculiar, *adj.* peculiar, raro.
peel, *s.* cáscara *f.*, pellejo *m.* ; — *v. a.* pelar.
peer,[1] *s.* noble *m.*
peer,[2] *v. n.* escudriñar.
peg, *s.* clavija *f.*; — *v. a.* fijar.
pen, *s.* pluma *f.*
penalty, *s.* castigo *m.*; multa *f.*; ~ *area* área *(f.)* de castigo.
pencil, *s.* lápiz *m.*
penetrate, *v. a.* penetrar.
penicillin, *s.* penicilina *f.*
peninsula, *s.* península *f.*
penknife, *s.* cortaplumas *m.*, navaja *f.*
penny, *s.* penique *m.*
pension, *s.* pensión *f.*; *(boarding-house)* casa *(f.)* de huéspedes; — *v. a.* pensionar.
people, *s.* gente *f.*, país *m.*; *many* ~ mucha gente; — *v. a.* poblar.
pepper, *s.* pimienta *f.*; *red* ~ pimienta roja.
per, *prep.* por; ~ *annum* anualmente; ~ *cer* porciento *m.*; ~ *d* al día; ~ *person* persona.
perceive, *v. a.* p
perch,[1] *s.* perc
perch,[2] *s.* *(fish)*

perfect, *adj.* perfecto; — *v. a.* perfeccionar.
perfectly, *adv.* perfectamente.
perforate, *v. a.* perforar.
perform, *v. a.* hacer, ejecutar.
performance, *s.* función *f.*, representación *f.*; *(of a job)* desempeño *m.*; *(of a machine)* rendimiento *m.*
perfume, *s.* perfume *m.*; — *v. a.* perfum(e)ar.
perhaps, *adv.* quizás.
peril, *s.* peligro *m.*
period, *s.* período *m.*; tiempo *m.*; *(full stop)* punto *m.*
periodical, *adj.* & *s.* periódico *(m.).*
perish, *v. n.* perecer.
perishable, *adj.* perecedero.
permanent, *adj.* permanente; ~ *wave* permanente *f.*
permission, *s.* permiso *m.*
permit, *v. a.* permitir; — *s.* permiso *m.*
Persian, *adj.* & *s.* persa.
person, *s.* persona *f.*; *in* ~ personalmente.
personal, *adj.* personal
personality, *s.* personalidad *f.*
perspiration, *s.* transpiración *f.*, sudor *m.*
persuade, *v. a.* persuadir.
pessimist, *s.* pesimista *m.*, *f.*
pet, *adj.* preferido; — *v. a.* mimar.
petition, *s.* petición *f.*; — *v. a.* suplicar.
petrol, *s.* gasolina *f.*, nafta *f.*; ~ *station* surtidor *m.*
petroleum, *s.* petróleo *m.*
petticoat, *s.* enaguas *f. pl.*
etty, *adj.* mezquino.
phase, *s.* fase *f.*
pheasant, *s.* faisán *m.*
phial, *s.* redoma *f.*
philosopher, *s.* filósofo *m.*
philosophical, *adj.* filosófico.
philosophy, *s.* filosofía *f.*
phone, *s.* teléfono *m.*; — *v. n.* telefonear.
phosphorus, *s.* fósforo *m.*
photograph, *s.* fotografía *f.*, foto *f.*, retrato *m.*; — *v. a.* fotografiar, retratar.
phrase, *s.* frase *f.*
physical, *adj.* físico.
physician, *s.* médico *m.*
physicist, *s.* físico *m.*
physics, *s. pl.* física *f.*
pianist, *s.* pianista *m.*, *f.*
piano, *s.* piano *m.*
pick, *v. a.* coger; *(lock)* abrir con ganzúa; ~ *out* escoger; ~ *up* recoger; ~ *up speed* ganar velocidad; — *s.* pico *m.*
pickle, *s.* encurtido *m.*, pepinillo *m.*
picnic, *s.* merienda *f.*, jira *(f.)* campestre; — *v. n.* ir de campo.
picture, *s.* cuadro *m.*, fotografía *f.*, retrato *m.*; *(cinema)* película *f.*; — *v. a.* figurar; imaginarse.
picturesque, *adj.* pintoresco.
pie (meat), *s.* pastel *m.*, tarta *f.*
piece, *s.* pieza *f.*; *(of paper)* pedazo *m.*, trozo *m.*
pier, *s.* muelle *m.*
pierce, *v. a.* perforar.
piety, *s.* piedad *f.*
pig, *s.* cerdo *m.*, puerco *m.*; *fig.* cochino *m.*
pigeon, *s.* paloma *f.*

pigeon-hole, *s.* palomar *m; (office)* casilla *f.;* — *v. a.* clasificar.
pile, *s.* pila *f.*, montón *m.;* — *v. a.* ~ *up* apilar.
pilgrim, *s.* peregrino *m.*, romero *m.*
pill, *s.* píldora *f.*
pillar, *s.* pilar *m.*, columna *f.*
pillar-box, *s.* buzón *m.*
pillow, *s.* almohada *f.*
pilot, *s.* piloto *m.;* — *v. a.* pilotear.
pin, *s.* alfiler *m.;* broche *m.;* — *v. a.* fijar; adornarse con.
pinch, *v. a.* pellizcar; — *s.* pellizco *m.; a* ~ *of salt* un pizco de sal.
pine, *s.* pino *m.*
pineapple, *s.* piña *f.*
pink, *adj.* rosado; — *s.* color *(m.)* de rosa; *(flower)* lave *m.*
pint, *s.* pinta *f.*
pioneer, *s.* pionero *m.*, iniciador *m.;* — *v. a.* abrir(se) paso.
pious, *adj.* piadoso.
pipe, *s.* tubo *m.*, cañeria *f.; smoke a* ~ fumar en pipa.
pipe-line, *s.* cañería *f.*, tubería *f.*
pit, *s.* hoyo *m.*
pitcher, *s.* jarro *m.*
pitiful, *adj.* lastimoso.
pitiless, *adj.* despiadado.
pity, *s.* lástima *f.*, compasión *f.;* — *v. a.* compadecer.
place, *s.* sitio *m.*, lugar *m.; take* ~ *(seat)* tomar asiento; *fig.* tener lugar, ocurrir; *(post)* puesto *m.;* — *v. a.* colocar, poner.
plague, *s.* plaga *f.*
plain, *adj.* sencillo, corriente; *in* ~ *English* claramente, en buen romance; *in* ~ *clothes* en traje de paisano; — *s.* llanura *f.*, planicie *f.*
plan, *s.* plan *m.;* — *v. a.* planear, proyectar.
plane[1], *s.* aeroplano *m.*, avión *m.; (level)* nivel *m.;* — *adj.* plano.
plane,[2] *s. (tree)* plátano *m.*
planet, *s.* planeta *f.*
plank, *s.* tablón *m.*
plant, *s.* planta *f.;* fábrica *f.;* — *v. a.* plantar, sembrar.
plantation, *s.* plantación *f.*
plaster, *s.* estuco *m.*, repello *m.; (on wound)* parche *m.*
plastic, *adj.* plástico, sintético.
plastics, *s. pl.* materiales *(m. pl.)* plásticos.
plate, *s.* plancha *f.*, lámina *f.; (dish)* plato *m.;* — *v. a.* enchapar.
platform, *s.* plataforma *f.; (on a station)* andén *m.*
platinum, *s.* platino *m.*
platter, *s.* fuente *f.*
play, *s.* juego *m.; (theatre)* representación *f.;* obra *(f.)* teatral; *fair* ~ juego limpio; *foul* ~ vileza *f.;* — *v. a. & n.* jugar; ~ *a part* hacer un papel de; ~ *a joke* gastar una broma; ~ *the piano* tocar el piano.
player, *s.* jugador *m.*
playground, *s.* patio *(m.)* de recreo.
playmate, *s.* compañero *(m.)* de juego.
plaything, *s.* juguete *m.*

plead, *v. a.* *(beg)* suplicar, pedir; *(a lawsuit)* defender; *~ guilty (not guilty)* declararse culpable (inocente).
pleasant, *adj.* agradable.
please, *v. a. & n.* agradar, gustar; *be ~d with* estar contento con; *shut the door ~* cierre la puerta, por favor.
pleasure, *s.* placer *m.*; *take ~ in* complacerse en; *with ~* con mucho gusto; *at ~* a gusto.
plentiful, *adj.* copioso, abundante.
plenty, *adj. & s.* mucho, abundante; *~ of books* bastantes libros; *~ more* mucho más.
plot, *s.* conspiración *f.*, complot *m.*; *(of a play)* trama *f.*; *~ of land* solar *m.*, lote *m.*; — *v. a.* conspirar.
plough, *s.* arado *m.*; — *v. a.* arar.
pluck, *v. a.* desplumar; — *s.* valor *m.*, ánimo *m.*
plug, *s.* tapón *m.*, enchufe *m.*; — *v. a.* enchufar.
plum, *s.* ciruela .
plume, *s.* pluma *f.*
plunge, *v. a.* zambullir; *v. n.* zambullirse; — *s.* zambullida *f.*
plural, *adj. & s.* plural *(m.)*.
plus, más.
pocket, *s.* bolsillo *m.*; *~ dictionary* diccionario *(m.)* de bolsillo.
pocket-book, *s.* agenda *f.*, cartera *f.*
pocket-money, *s.* dinero *(m.)* de bolsillo.
poem, *s.* verso *m.*, poema *m.*
poet, *s.* poeta *m.*
poetic(al), *adj.* poético.
poetry, *s.* poesía *f.*
point, *s.* punto *m.*; *(of a pencil)* punta *f.*; *(sports)* tanto *m.*, punto *m.*; *decimal ~* coma; *three ~ six* tres coma seis; — *v. a.* señalar; *(weapon)* apuntar; *~ out* indicar, mostrar.
poison, *s.* veneno *m.*; — *v. a.* envenenar.
poisonous, *adj.* venenoso.
polar, *adj.* polar.
pole,[1] *s.* poste *m.*, palo *m.*
pole,[2] *s.* polo; *The North Pole* el Polo Norte.
Pole, *adj. & s.* polaco.
police, *s.* policía *f.*
policeman, *s.* agente *(m.)* de policía.
police-station, *s.* comisaría *f.*
policy, *s.* política *f.*; *insurance ~* póliza *(f.)* de seguro.
polite, *adj.* cortés.
political, *adj.* político.
politician, *s.* político *m.*
politics, *s.* política *f.*
pond, *s.* estanque *m.*
pony, *s.* jaca *f.*, caballito *m.*
pool,[1] *s.* charco *m.*; *swimming ~* piscina *f.*
pool,[2] *s.* puesta *f.*; — *v. a. & n.* reunir.
poor, adj. pobre.
pope, *s.* papa *m.*
poplar, *s.* álamo *m.*
poppy, *s.* amapola *f.*
popular, *adj* popular.
popularity, *s.* popularidad *f.*
population *s.* población *f.*
pore, *s.* poro *m.*
pork, *s.* puerco *m.*

port, [1] *s.* puerto *m.*; *reach* ~ llegar a puerto.
port, [2] *s.* babor *m.*
port, [3] *s* *(wine)* vino de oporto *m.*
portable, *adj.* portátil.
porter, *s.* portero *m.*; *(railway)* mozo *(m.)* de estación; *(beer)* cerveza *(f.)* de malta.
portfolio, *s.* cartera *f.*
portion, *s.* porción *f.*, parte *f.*
portrait, *s.* retrato *m.*
Portuguese, *adj.* & *s.* portugués *(m.)*.
position, *s.* posición *f.*; *(place)* sitio *m.*; *(employment)* puesto *m.*, empleo *m.*
positive, *adj.* positivo.
possess, *v. a.* poseer.
possession, *s.* posesión *f.*; *take* ~ *of* apoderarse de.
possibility, *s.* posibilidad *f.*
possible, *adj.* posible; *as early as* ~ lo antes posible.
post, [1] *s.* poste *m.*, pilar *m.*; *(employment)* puesto *m.*, cargo *m.*; *(military)* puesto *(m.)* de guardia; — *v. a.* fijar, colocar.
post, [2] *s.* Correos *m. pl.*; *send by* ~ enviar por correo; — *v. a.* llevar al correo.
postage, *s.* franqueo *m.*
poster, *s.* cartel *m.*
posterity, *s.* posteridad *f.*
postman, *s.* cartero *m.*
post-office, *s.* oficina *(f.)* de Correos, estafeta *f.*
postpone, *v. a.* aplazar.
postscript, *s.* posdata *f.*
pot, *s.* olla *f.*
potato, *s.* patata *f.*
pottery, *s.* cerámica *f.*
poultry, *s.* aves *(f. pl.)* de corral.
pound, *s.* libra *f.*; *(money)* libra esterlina.
pour, *v. a.* echar; ~ *out* vaciar.
poverty, *s.* pobreza *f.*
powder, *s.* polvos *m. pl.*; *(gun-)* pólvora *f.*; — *v. a.* pulverizar; ~*ed milk* leche *(f.)* en polvo; *v. n.* empolvarse.
power, *s.* potencia *f.*, poder *m.*; *the Great Powers* las grandes potencias.
powerful, *adj.* poderoso.
power-station, *s.* central *(f.)* de energía eléctrica.
practical, *adj.* práctico.
practice, *s.* práctica *f.*; *(of a doctor)* clientela *f.*
practise, *v. a.* hacer ejercicios, practicar.
praise, *v. a.* alabar, elogiar; — *s.* alabanza *f.*, elogio *m.*
pray, *v. n.* rezar, orar.
preach, *v. a.* & *n.* predicar.
preacher, *s.* predicador *m.*
precede, *v. n.* preceder.
precious, *adj.* valioso, precioso.
precise, *adj.* preciso.
precisely, *adj.* precisamente.
precision, *s.* precisión *f.*
predict, *v. a.* predecir, pronosticar.
prefabricated, *adj.* prefabricado.
preface, *s.* prefacio *m.*
prefer, *v. a.* preferir a.
preferable, *adj.* preferible.
preference, *s.* preferencia *f.*
pregnant, *adj.* preñada,

encinta, embarazada.
prejudice, *s.* *(bias)* prejuicio *m.*; *(harm)* perjuicio *m.*; — *v. a.* prejuzgar.
preliminary, *adj.* & *s.* preliminar *(m.)*.
premier, *adj.* primero; — *s.* primer ministro *m.*
premises, *s. pl.* casa *(f.)* y anejos.
premium, *s.* prima *f.*
preparation, *s.* preparativo *m.*; *(product)* producto *m.*, preparación *f.*
prepare, *v. a.* preparar; *v. n.* prepararse.
preposition, *s.* preposición *f.*
presbyterian, *adj.* & *s.* presbiteriano *(m.)*.
prescribe, *v. a.* prescribir; *(doctor)* recetar.
prescription, *s.* receta *f.*
presence, *s.* presencia *f.*
present, [1] *adj.* presente; *at the ~ time* hoy día; — *s.* presente *m.*; *at ~* ahora; *for the ~* por ahora.
present, [2] *v. a.* presentar; — *s.* regalo *m.*
preserve, *v. a.* preservar; — *s.* compota *f.*; mermelada *f.*; *(hunting)* coto *m.*, vedado *m.*
president, *s.* presidente *m.*
press, *v. a.* *(button)* apretar, tocar; *(suit)* planchar; *time ~es* el tiempo apremia; — *s.* prensa *f.*
pressure, *s.* presión *f.*; urgencia *f.*
prestige, s. prestigio *m.*
pretend, *v. a.* aparentar, simular.
pretension, *s.* pretensión *f.*
pretext, *s.* pretexto *m.*
pretty, *adv.* bonito; — *adv. ~ well* bastante bien.
prevail, *v. n.* prevalecer, predominar.
prevent, *v. a.* impedir, evitar.
previous, *adj.* previo.
pre-war, *adj.* de anteguerra, de preguerra.
prey, *s.* botín *m.*, presa *f.*
price, *s.* precio *m.*; premio *m.*
price-list, *s.* lista *(f.)* de precios.
pride, *s.* orgullo *m.*; — *take ~ in sg* enorgullecerse de.
priest, *s.* sacerdote *m.*, cura *m.*
primary, *adj.* primario, primero.
prime, *adj.* primero; — *s. in the ~ of life* en la flor de la vida.
Prime Minister, *s.* primer ministro *m.*
primitive, *adj.* primitivo.
prince, *s.* príncipe *m.*
princess, *s.* princesa *f.*
principal, *adj.* & *s.* principal *(m.)*.
principle, *s.* principio *m.*, teoría *f.*; *in ~* en principio.
print, *s.* tipo *m.*, letra *f.*; *(from negative)* copia *f.*; — *v. a.* imprimir, tirar; copiar; escribir en letras de imprenta.
printed matter, *s.* impreso *m.*
printing office, *s.* imprenta *f.*
priority, *s.* prioridad *f.*
prison, *s.* cárcel *f.*, prisión *f.*
prisoner, *s.* preso *m.*; *~ of war* prisionero

m.; take ~ capturar.
private, *adj.* particular; *keep sg* ~ tener en secreto; — *s.* soledad *f.; in* ~ en privado; *(soldier)* soldado *(m.)* raso.
privilege, *s.* privilegio *m.*; — *v. a.* privilegiar.
prize, *s.* premio *m.*; ~ *scholarship* beca *f.*; — *v. a.* apreciar.
probability, *s.* probabilidad *f.*
probable, *adj.* probable.
problem, *s.* problema *m.*
process, *s.* proceso *m.*; — *v. a.* elaborar, transformar; *v. n.* desfilar.
procession, *s.* procesión *f.*
proclaim, *v. a.* proclamar.
proclamation, *s.* proclamación *f.*
procure, *v. a.* lograr, conseguir.
produce,[1] *v. a.* producir; *(play)* montar; presentar.
produce,[2] *s.* producto *m.*
producer, *s.* producente *m.*, productor *m.*; *(of a play)* director *(m.)* de producción.
product, *s.* producto *m.*
production, *s.* producción *f.*; ~ *line* cadena *f.*
productive, *adj.* productivo.
profession, *s.* profesión *f.*
professional, *adj.* & *s.* profesional *(m.)*.
professor, *s.* profesor *m.*
profile, *s.* perfil *m.*
profit, *s.* beneficio *m.*, ganancia *f.*; — *v. n.* aprovechar, sacar provecho.
profitable, *adj.* provechoso.
programme, *s.* programa *m.*
progress, *s.* progreso *m.*; *be in* ~ estar en curso, estar en marcha; — *v. n.* progresar, marchar, andar.
progressive, *adj.* progresivo.
prohibit, *v. a.* prohibir.
project, *v. a.* proyectar; *v. n.* *(protrude)* sobresalir, resaltar; — *s.* proyecto *m.*
projectile, *s.* proyectil *m.*
projector, *s.* proyector *m.*
prolong, *v. a.* prolongar.
promise, *s.* promesa *f.*; *break one's* ~ faltar a su promesa; — *v. a.* prometer.
promising, adj. muy prometedor.
promote, *v. a.* promover, fomentar.
promotion, *s.* ascenso *m.*, promoción *f.*
prompt, *adj.* pronto; — *v. a.* impulsar; *(at school)* soplar; *(at theatre)* apuntar.
pronoun, *s.* pronombre *m.*
pronounce, *v. a.* pronunciar.
pronunciation, *s.* pronunciación *f.*
proof, *s.* prueba *f.*
propagate, *v. a.* propagar; *v. n.* propagarse.
propeller, *s.* hélice *f.*
proper, *adj.* propio, correcto.
property, *s.* propiedad, *f.*
prophecy, *s.* profecía *f.*
prophet, *s.* profeta *m.*
proportion, *s.* proporción *f.*; *out of* ~ desproporcionado.
propose, *v. a.* proponer; ~ *sy's health* brindar a la salud de;

v. n. proponerse, tener intención de.
proposition, *s.* proposición *f.*, propuesta *f.*; *(affair)* negocio *m.*
prose, *s.* prosa *f.*
prospect, *s.* perspectiva *f.* — *v. n.* hacer sondeos.
prospectus, *s.* prospecto *m.*
prosper, *v. n.* prosperar.
prosperity, *s.* prosperidad *f.*
prosperous, *adj.* próspero.
protect, *v. a.* proteger.
protection, *s.* protección *f.*
protest, *v. n.* protestar, quejarse; — *s.* protesta *f.*
Protestant, *adj.* & *s.* protestante *(m.)*.
proud, *adj.* orgulloso.
prove, *v. a.* probar, demostrar; ~ *to be bad* resultar malo.
proverb, *s.* refrán *m.*
provide, *v. a.* proporcionar, proveer; *be ~d for* estar asegurado; *v. n.* ~ *for sy* cuidarse de.
province, *s.* provincia *f.*; competencia *f.*, incumbencia *f.*
provincial, *adj.* provincial.
provision, *s.* provisión *f.*; preparativos *m. pl.*
provoke, *v. a.* provocar; irritar.
prudent, *adj.* prudente.
psalm, *s.* salmo *m.*
psychological, *adj.* psicológico.
psychology, *s.* psicología *f.*
public, *adj.* & *s.* público.
publication, *s.* publicación *f.*
publicity, *s.* publicidad *f.*
publish, *v. a.* publicar.
publisher, *s.* editor *m.*
pudding, *s.* postre *m.*
pull, *v. a.* tirar de; *(tooth)* sacar, extraer; ~ *at* tirar de; ~ *down* bajar; *(building)* derribar, tumbar; ~ *off* sacar, quitar; ~ *up (car)* parar; — *s.* tirón *m.*; *(holder)* mango *m.*
pulse, *s.* pulso *m.*
pump, *s.* bomba *f.*; — *v. n.* bombear; ~ *up* inflar.
pumpkin, *s.* calabaza *f.*
punch, *v. a.* picar, marcar; *(beat)* dar un puñetazo; — *s.* puñetazo *m.*; *(ticket-)* perforador *m.*
punctual, *adj* puntual.
puncture, *s.* pinchazo *m.*, punzada *f.*; — *v. a.* pinchar.
punish, *v. a.* castigar.
punishment, *s.* castigo *m.*, pena *f.*
pupil, *s.* alumno *m.*, discípulo *m.*
puppy, *s.* cachorro *m.*, perrito *m.*
purchase, *s.* compra *f.*; *make ~s* hacer compras; — *v. a.* comprar.
pure, *adj.* puro.
purge, *v. a.* purgar; — *s.* purga *f.*
purify, *v. a.* purificar.
purity, *s.* puridad *f.*
Purple, *adj.* morado; — *s.* púrpura *f.*
Purpose, *s.* objeto *m.*, propósito *m.*; *on ~* a propósito; *to no ~* en vano; — *v. a.* proponerse, intentar.
Purse, *s.* bolso *m.*, portamonedas *m.*
Pursue, *v. a.* perseguir; ~ *a profession* ejercer una

profesión.
pursuit, *s.* persecución *f.;* ocupación *f.*
push, *v. a.* empujar: *(button)* apretar, tocar; – *s.* empujón *m.*
puss(y), *s.* gatito *m.*, minino *m.*
put, *v. a.* poner; *(facts)* exponer; *~ sg right* arreglar, reparar; *~ a question* hacer una pregunta; *~ an end to sg* poner fin a; *~ aside* ahorrar; *~ away* poner de lado; *~ back* poner a su lugar; *~ in order* poner en orden; *~ off* dejar; *~ on* ponerse; *~ on speed* aumentar la velocidad; *~ on the light* encender la luz; *~ out (light)* apagar; *through* ejecutar; *(on the phone)* poner con; *~ to bed* acostar; *~ up at a hotel* alojar (se).
puzzle, *s.* enigma *m.;* rompecabezas *m.;* – *v. a.* dejar perplejo.
pyjamas, *s pl.* pijama *m*
pyramid, *s.* pirámide *f.*

Q

qualification, *s.* calificación *f.;* requisito *m.*
qualify, *v. a.* calificar.
quality, *s.* calidad *f.*
quantity, *s.* cantidad *f.*
quarrel, *s.* riña *f.*, disputa *f.*, disgusto *m.;* – *v. n.* reñir, disputar.
quart, *s.* litro *m.*
quarter, *s.* cuarto *m.*, cuarta parte *f.; at a ~ to three* a las tres menos cuarto; *it's a ~ past six* son las seis y cuarto; – *v. a. (divide)* cuartear; *(put up)* alojar.
quarterly, *adj.* trimestral; – *s.* revista *(f.)* trimestral.
quarters, *s. pl.* vivienda *f.*, morada *f.*
quartz, *s.* cuarzo *m.*
quay, *s.* muelle *m.*, (des)-embarcadero *m.*
queen, *s.* reina *f.*
queer, *adj.* extraño, raro
quench, *v. a.* apagar.
query, *s.* pregunta *f.;* – *v. a.* interrogar; poner en duda.
quest, *s.* busca *f.*, búsqueda *f.; in ~ of* en busca de.
question, *s.* pregunta *f.;* – *v. a.* interrogar; dudar.
questionnaire, *s.* cuestionario *m.*
queue, *s.* fila *f.*, cola *f.; stand in ~* hacer cola.
quick, *adj.* rápido; – *adv.* pronto.
quiet, *adj.* quieto, tranquilo; *be ~* callarse, no hacer ruido; – *s.* tranquilidad *f.;* – *v. a.* aquietar, calmar.
quilt, *s.* acolchado *m.;* – *v. a.* colchar.
quit, *v. a.* dejar; renunciar a; – *adj. we are ~s* quedamos iguales.
quite, *adv.* completamente; *~ well* bastante bien; *~ right!* ¡justo! ¡exacto!
quiz, *v. a.* interrogar; – *s.* quiz *m.*
quotation, *s.* citación *f;* *(market)* curso *m.*, cotización *f.*

quote, *v. a.* citar; *(prices)* cotizar.

R

rabbit, *s.* conejo *m.*
race,[1] *s.* carrera *f.; the ~s* carreras *(f. pl.)* de caballos; *(boot-)* regata *f.;* — *v. n.* ir a la carrera.
race,[2] *s.* raza *f.*
rack, *s. (luggage-)* red *f.*
racket,[1] *s. (tennis)* raqueta *f.*
racket,[2] *s. (noise)* bulla *f.,* estruendo *m.*
radar, *s.* radar *m.*
radiate, *v. a. & n.* radiar.
radiator, *s.* radiador *m.*
radio, *s.* radio *f.; ~ set* aparato *(m.)* de radio; — *v. a.* radiar.
radioactive, *adj.* radioactivo.
radish, *s.* rábano *m.*
radius, *s.* radio *m.*
rag, *s.* trapo *m.*
rage, *s.* rabia *f.,* ira *f* · — *v. n.* rabiar.
ragged, *adj.* andrajoso.
raid, *s.* correría *f.; (police-)* batida *f.,* redada *f.;* — *v. a.* atracar.
rail, *s. (railway)* riel *m.; by ~* por ferrocarril; *(banister)* baranda *f.*
railway, *s.* ferrocarril *m.; ~ station* estación *(f.)* de ferrocarril.
rain, *s.* lluvia *f.;* — *v. n.* llover.
rainbow, *s.* arco *(m.)* iris.
rainfall, *s.* lluvias *f. pl.*
rainy, *adj.* lluvioso.
raise, *v. a. (prices)* aumentar; *(hat)* quitarse; *(glass)* brindar por; *(army)* reclutar; (family) criar; *(hand)* levantar; *(money)* recoger; — *s. (of salary)* aumento *m*; *(hill)* colina *f.*
raisin, *s.* pasa *f.*
rally, *v. a.* reunir; — *s.* reunión *f.,* mítin *m.*
rampart, *s.* bastión *m.;* dique *m.*
ranch, *s.* hacienda *f.*
range, *s. (of prices)* escala *f.; ~ of mountains* cordillera *f.,* cadena *(f.)* de montañas; *be within ~* estar a tiro; — *v. a.* alinear.
rank, *s.* grado *m.*
ransom, *s.* rescate *m.;* — *v. a.* rescatar.
rapid, *adj* rápido.
rare, *adj.* raro.
rash, *adj.* imprudente.
raspberry, *s.* frambuesa *f.*
rat, *s.* rata *f.*
rate, *s.* at the *~ of six per cent* a razón de seis por ciento; *at any ~* en todo caso; *at this ~* a este paso; *first-~* de primera; *(speed)* velocidad *f.; postage ~* tarifa *(f.)* postal.
rather, *adv. it is ~ cold* hace un poco de frío; *I'd ~ have ice cream* preferiría tomar helado.
ration, *s.* porción *f.,* ración *f.;* — *v. a.* racionar.
raven, *s.* cuervo *m.*
raw, *adj* crudo; *~ material* materia prima.
ray, *s.* rayo *m.*
razor, *s.* navaja *(f.)* de afeitar.
razor-blade, *s.* hoja *(f.)* de afeitar.
reach, *v. a.* alcanzar; *~ the city* llegar a la ciudad; — *s.* alcance *m.*
react, *v. n.* reaccionar.

reaction, *s.* reacción *f.*
reactor, *s.* reactor *m.*
read, *v. a.* leer.
reader, *s. (person)* lector *m.; (book)* libro *(m.)* de lectura.
readiness, *s.* prontitud *f.*, diligencia *f.*
ready, *adj.* preparado, listo.
real, *adj.* verdadero.
reality, *s.* realidad *f.*
realize, *v.a.* realizar; *(profit)* ganar; obtener; *(know)* comprender, darse cuenta de.
really, *adv.* verdaderamente, en realidad, de verdad.
realm, *s.* reino *m.*
reappear, *v. n.* reaparecer.
rear,[1] *v. a.* criar; *(horse)* encabritarse.
rear,[2] *s.* parte *(f.)* posterior; — *adj.* de atrás.
reason, *s.* razón *f.; listen to* ~ ser razonable; *(motive)* motivo *m.;* — *v. a. & n.* discutir, razonar.
reasonable, *adj.* razonable, justo.
recall, *v. a.* recordar; *(ambassador)* retirar.
receipt, *s.* recibo *m.;* — *v. a.* poner el recibí.
receive, *v. a.* recibir.
receiver, *s.* receptor *m.*
recent, *adj.* reciente.
recently, *adv.* recientemente.
reception, *s. (greeting)* recibimiento *m.; (party)* recepción *f.*
receptionist, *s.* recepcionista *m.*
recipe, *s.* receta *f.*
recital, *s.* recitación *f.*
recite, *v. a.* recitar.
reckless, *adj.* imprudente, temerario.
reckon, *v. a.* calcular, contar; *(think)* creer; ~ *on* contar con.
recognize, *v. a.* reconocer.
recollect, *v. a.* recordar.
recommend, *v. a.* recomendar.
recommendation, *s.* recomendación *f.*
reconstruction, *s.* reconstrucción *f.*
record, *s.* registro *m.; (sports)* record *m.; (disk)* disco *m.; be on* ~ estar registrado; — *v. a.* registrar; *(song)* grabar.
recorder, *s.* registrador *m.*
recover, *v. a.* recobrar; ~ *oneself* recobrar la serenidad; *v. n.* restablecerse.
rector, *s.* rector *m.*
recur, *v. n.* recurrir.
red, *adj.* rojo, colorado.
red-tape, *s.* balduque *m,* burocratismo *m.*
reduce, *v. a.* reducir.
reduction, *s.* reducción *f.*
reed, *s.* juncal *m.*, caña *f.*
reel, *s.* carrete *m.*, bobina *f.;* — *v. a.* devanar.
re-elect, *v. a.* reelegir.
refer, *v. n.* referirse; ~ *to* hablar de.
referee, *s.* árbitro *m.;* — *v. a.* dirigir.
reference, *s.* referencia *f.; (information)* información *f.;* ~ *book* manual *m.*
refine, *v. a.* refinar.
reflect, *v. a.* reflejar.
reflection, *s.* reflexión *f.*
reform, *v. a.* corregir, reformar; — *s.* re-

forma *f.*
reformation, *s.* reformación *f.*
refrain, *s.* estribillo *m.;* — *v. n.* evitar, reprimir.
refresh, *v. a.* refrescar.
refreshment, *s.* refresco *m.; ~ room* buffet *m.*, ambigú *m.*
refrigerator, *s.* frigorífico *m.*, nevera *f.*
refuge, *s* refugio *m.*
refugee, *s.* refugiado *m.*
refusal, *s.* rechazo *m.*
refuse, *v. a.* rechazar, no querer aceptar; decir que no, negarse; — *s.* basura *f.*
refute, *v. a.* refutar.
regard, *v. a.* considerar; — *s.* consideración *f.*, respeto *m.; in this ~* a este respecto.
regent, *s.* regente *m.*
regime, *s.* régimen *m.*
regiment, *s.* regimiento *m.*
region, *s.* región *f.*, comarca *f.*
regret, *v. a. & n.* sentir; — *s.* pena *f.*
regular, *adj.* regular, corriente, normal.
regulate, *v. a.* regular.
regulation, *s.* regla *f.*, reglamento *m.*
reign, *s.* reinado *m.;* — *v. n.* reinar.
rein, *s.* rienda *f.*
relate, *v. a.* relatar, contar; *be ~d to* estar emparentado con.
relation, *s.* relación *f.*; *(person)* pariente *m.*
relative, *adj.* relativo; *be ~ to* depender de; — *s.* pariente *m.*, *f.*
relax, *v. a. & n.* relajar; descansar.
release, *v. a.* soltar, relevar; — *s.* liberación *f.*
reliable, *adj.* seguro, digno de confianza.
relic, *s.* reliquia *f.*
relief, *s.* alivio *m.;* descanso *m.*
religion, *s.* religión *f.*
religious, *adj.* religioso.
relish, *s.* sabor *m.;* gusto *m.; with ~* con gusto; — *v. a.* tomar gusto en *or* a.
reluctant, *adj* mal dispuesto, renitente.
rely, *v. n. ~ on* depender de, contar con.
remain, *v. n.* quedar.
remainder, *s.* resto *m.*
remark, *v. a.* observar, hacer comentarios; — *s.* observación *f.*
remarkable, *adj.* notable.
remedy, *s.* remedio *m.;* — *v. a.* remediar.
remember, *v. a.* recordar, acordarse de.
remembrance, *s.* recuerdo *m.*
remind, *v. a.* recordar.
remit, *v. a.* remitir.
remittance, *s.* remisión *f.*, giro *m.*
remorse, *s.* remordimiento *m.*
remote, *adj.* remoto; *~ control* telemando *m.*, mando *m.* remoto.
removal, *s.* alejamiento *m.*
remove, *v. a.* quitar.
remuneration, *s.* remuneración *f.;* premio *m.*
render, *v. a. (service)* prestar; *~ an account* dar cuenta de.
renew, *v. a.* renovar.
renounce, *v. a.* renunciar a.
rent, *s.* alquiler *m.;* — *v. a.* alquilar.
reorganization, *s.* reor-

ganización *f.*
reorganize, *v. a.* reorganizar.
repair, *v. a.* reparar, remediar, componer, remendar; — *s.* reparación *f.*
repay, *v. a.* reembolsar.
repeat, *v. a.* repetir.
repent, *v. a.* arrepentirse de.
repetition, *s.* repetición *f.*
replace, *v. a.* reemplazar.
reply, *v. a.* contestar, responder; — *s.* respuesta *f.*
report, *v. a.* informar, hacer un informe, dar cuenta de; *(to the police)* denunciar; — *s.* informe *m.*; *weather* ~ boletín *(m.)* meteorológico; *(school)* libreta *(f.)* de calificaciones; certificado *m.*; *(noise)* estampido *m.*
reporter, *s.* periodista *m.*, reportero *m.*
represent, *v. a.* representar.
representation, *s.* representación *f.*
representative, *adj.* representativo; típico; — *s.* diputado *m.*
reproach, *v. a.* reprochar; — *s.* reproche *m.*
reproduce, *v. a.* reproducir.
reproduction, *s.* reproducción *f.*
reptile, *s.* reptil *m.*
republic, *s.* república *f.*
republican, *adj.* & *s.* republicano *(m.)*.
reputation, *s.* reputación *f.*, fama *f.*
request, *s.* petición *f.*; ~ *stop* parada *(f.)* discrecional.
require, *v. a.* requerir, necesitar.
requirement, *s.* requisito *m.*, condición *f.*; *(claim)* exigencia *f.*
research, *s.* investigación *f.*
resemble, *v. a.* parecerse.
resent, *v. a.* resentirse por.
reserve, *v. a.* reservar; — *s.* reserva *f.*
reside, *v. n.* residir.
residence, *s.* residencia *f.*, domicilio *m.*
resident, *s.* residente *m.*
resist, *v. n.* resistir.
resistance, *s.* resistencia *f.*
resolute, *adj.* resuelto.
resolution, *s.* resolución *f.*
resolve, *v. a.* resolver.
resort, *v. n.* ~ *to* recurrir *a*; — *s.* recurso *m.*; *summer* ~ lugar *(m.)* de veraneo.
respect, *s.* respeto *m.*; *(standpoint)* respecto *m.*; *in every* ~ en todos respectos; *in many* ~*s* en muchos puntos; *with* ~ *to* con respecto a; — *v. a.* respetar.
espectable, *adj.* respetable.
respectful, *adj.* respetuoso.
respective, *adj.* respectivo.
respiration, *s.* respiración *f.*
responsibility, *s.* responsabilidad *f.*
responsible, *adj.* responsable; *be* ~ *for* ser causa de.
rest, *s.* descanso *m.*; *at* ~ parado; *set at* ~ tranquilizar; — *v. n.* des-

resume, *v. a.* recomenzar, reanudar.
retain, *v. a.* retener.
retire, *v. n.* retirarse.
retreat, *v. n.* retirarse; – *s.* retiro *m.*
return, *v. a.* devolver; *v.* cansar.
restaurant, *s.* restaurante *m.*, restorán *m.*
restless, *adj.* inquieto.
restoration, *s.* restauración *f.*
restore, *v. a.* restaurar; *be ~d to health* ser restablecido; *~to life* salvar la vida a.
result, *s.* resultado *m.*; – *v. n.* *~ in* terminar en; *~ from sg* resultar.
n. regresar, volver; *~ thanks for sg* dar las gracias por; – *s.* vuelta *f.*, regreso *m.*; *by ~ of post* a vuelta de correo; *many happy ~s* feliz cumpleaños; *~s* rédito *m.*; provecho *m.*
reveal, *v. a.* revelar.
revenge, *s.* venganza *f.*; – *v. a.* vengar.
revenue, *s.* renta *s.*
reverend, *adj.* reverendo.
reverse, *adj.* contrario; *~ gear* marcha *(f.)* atrás; – *v. a.* dar vuelta a; *(decision)* revocar; – *s.* revés *m.*; *~s* contratiempos *m. pl.*
review, *s.* revista *f.*; – *v. a.* repasar; hacer la crítica de.
revolution, *s.* revolución *f.*
reward, *s.* recompensa *f.*, gratificación *f.*; – *v. a.* recompensar, premiar.
rheumatism, *s.* reumatismo *m.*
rhyme, *s.* rima *f.*; – *v. n.* rimar.
rhythm, *s.* ritmo *m.*
rib, *s.* costilla *f.*
ribbon, *s.* cinta *f.*
rice, *s.* arroz *m.*
rich, *adj.* rico; *(land)* fértil.
rid, *v. a.* librar; *get ~ of* librarse de, quitarse.
riddle, *s.* acertijo *m.*
ride, *v. a.* montar, andar; *~ a bicycle* montar en bicicleta; *v. n.* ir, pasear; – *s.* paseo *m.*, viaje *m.*; *give sy a ~* llevar en su coche.
ridiculous, *adj.* ridículo.
right, *adj.* derecho; *on the ~ side* a la derecha; *be ~* tener razón; *that's ~* eso es; *all ~!* bien; – *s.* derecho *m.*; *by ~* legítimamente; con razón; *by ~ of* a causa de; *keep to the ~!* llevar la derecha; – *adv.* bien; *~ now* en este momento; *~ away* ahora mismo; – *v. a.* enderezar; restaurar, reparar.
rim, *s.* borde *m.*; *(hat)* ala *f.*
ring,[1] *s.* anillo *m.*; *(sports)* ring *m.*, ruedo *m.*, pista *f.*
ring,[2] *v. a.* *~ the bell* tocar el timbre; *v. n.* *the bell ~s* suena el timbre; *~ out* sonar; *~ up* llamar por teléfono, – *s.* timbre *m.*
riot, *s.* tumulto *m.*, motín *m.*
rip, *v. a.* rasgar.
ripe, *adj.* maduro; *grow ~* madurar.
ripen, *v. a. & n.* madurar.
rise, *v. n.* levantarse, ponerse en pie; *(prices)* subir; *(river)* crecer; *(to a post)* ascen-

der; *(sun)* salir; — *s.* subida *f.*
risk, *s.* riesgo *m.;* — *v. n.* arriesgarse.
risky, *adj.* arriesgado.
rival, *adj.* & *s.* rival *(m.);* — *v. a.* competir.
river, *s.* río *m.*
road, *s.* carretera *f.*, camino *m.;* ~ *map* mapa *(m.);* itinerario.
roast, *v. a.* asar; — *adj.* & *s.* asado *(m.);* ~ *beef* rosbif *m.*, carne *(f.)* de vaca asada; ~ *meat* asado *m.*
rob, *v. a.* robar.
robber, *s.* ladrón *m.*
robbery, *s.* robo *m.*
robe, *s.* hábito *(m.)* talar, toga *f.; (dressing gown)* bata *f.*
rock,[1] *s.* roca *f.*, escollo *m.*
rock,[2] *v. a.* mecer; *v. n.* balancearse.
rocket, *s.* cohete *m.;* ~ *plane* avión *(m.)* cohete.
rocket-range, *s.* rampa *(f.)* de lanzamiento de cohetes.
rocky, *adj.* rocoso.
rod, *s.* varilla *f.*, barra *f.; (fishing)* caña *(f.)* de pescar.
roll, *s. (coil)* rollo *m.; (list)* lista *f.;* ~ *of bills* fajo *(m.)* de billetes; *(bread)* panecillo *m.;* — *v. n. (ball)* rodar; *(ship)* balancearse; ~ *up* enrollar; *(sleeves)* remangarse.
Roman, *adj.* & *s.* romano *(m.);* ~ *Catholic* católico romano; ~ *type* letra *(f.)* romana.
romantic, *adj.* romántico.
romanticism, *s.* romanticismo *m.*
roof, *s.* tejado *m.;* ~ *of the mouth* paladar *m.*
room, *s.* cuarto *m.*, habitación *f.; (place)* sitio *m.;* ~ *and board* pensión *(f.)* completa.
root, *s.* raíz *f.; fig.* origen *m.; take* ~ arraigar; — *v. a.* ~ *out* desarraigar.
rope, *s.* cuerda *f.*, soga *f.*
rose, *s.* rosa *f.*
rotten, *adj.* podrido, malo.
rough, *adj. (sea)* tempestuoso, agitado; *(ground)* quebrado; *(to the touch)* áspero; ~ *draft* borrador *m.*
round, *adj.* redondo; ~ *cheeks* mejillas *(f. pl.)* llenas; ~ *trip ticket* billete *(m.)* de ida y vuelta; — *adv.* alrededor, en círculo; *all the year* ~ todo el año; *go* ~ dar la vuelta a; — *prep.* alrededor, a la vuelta de; — *s. (daily)* recorrido *m.; (of drinks)* ronda *f.; (sports)* asalto *m.;* — *v. a.* redondear; *v. n.* redondearse.
route, *s.* ruta *f.*, vía *f.*
routine, rutina *f.*, marcha *f.;* ~ *work* trabajo *(m.)* rutinario.
row,[1] *s.* fila *f.*
row,[2] *v. n.* remar; — *s.* remar m.
row,[3] *s. (quarrel)* pelea *f.*
royal, *adj.* real, regio.
rub, *v. a.* frotar; *(clothes)* restregar; *v. n.* ~ *against* rozar contra; ~ *in* machacar; ~ *out* borrar; — *s.* fricción *f.*
rubber, *s.* caucho *m.*, ~*s* chanclos *m. pl.*
rubbish, *s.* basura *f.*
ruby, *s.* rubí *m.*
rude, *adj.* rudo; *fig.* des-

cortés.
rug, *s.* alfombra *f.; (bed)* manta *f.*
rugged, *adj.* accidentado, aspero.
ruin, *s.* ruina *f.; — v. a.* arruinar, dañar.
rule, *s.* regla *f.; (domination)* dominio *m.;* mando *m.; as a ~* por regla general; *— v. a. & n.* regir, gobernar; *~ out* excluir.
ruler, *s.* regla *f.; (person)* gobernante *m.*
rumour, *s.* rumor *m.*
run, *v. n.* correr; *(road)* pasar; *(engine)* andar, marchar; *(law)* estar en vigor; *(horse)* correr; *(story)* decir; *(stocking)* hacerse carreras; *v. a. (machine)* manejar; *(rope)* pasar; *(shop)* conducir, dirigir; *~ dry* secarse; *~ away* huir, escaparse; *~ down* pararse; *(car)* atropellar; *~ for* presentarse; *~ off* fugarse; *~ out* acabarse; *~ over* derramarse; *— s.* carrera *f.;* viaje *m.; (on goods)* demanda *f.; in the long ~* a la larga, al fin y al cabo.
runner, *s.* corredor *m.; (of a sled)* patín *m.*
runway, *s.* pista *(f.)* de despegue, (*or*) aterrizaje.
rural, *adj.* rural.
rush, *v. n.* darse prisa; *~ through* hacer de prisa; *— s.* aglomeración *f.; the ~ hours* horas *(f. pl.)* de máxima circulación.
Russian, *adj. & s.* ruso.
rust, *s.* herrumbre *f.,* orín *m.; — v. n.* oxidarse.
rustic, *adj.* rústico.
rye, *s.* centeno *m.*

S

sack, *s.* saco *m.; give sy the ~* echar, despedir; *— v. a.* ensacar; *(plunder)* saquear.
sacred, *adj.* sagrado.
sacrifice, *s.* sacrificio *m.; — v. a.* sacrificar.
sad, *adj.* triste.
saddle, *s.* silla *(f.)* de montar; *— v. a.* ensillar.
sadness, *s.* tristeza *f.*
safe, *adj.* seguro; *(saved)* a salvo; *~ and sound* sano y salvo; *— s.* caja *(f.)* fuerte, caja de caudales.
safely, *adv.* sin peligro, a salvo.
safety, *s.* seguridad *f.; ~ pin* imperdible *m.*
sail, *s.* vela *f.; — v. n.* navegar; hacerse a la mar, zarpar; *~ for Spain* embarcarse para España; *v. a. ~ a boat* gobernar un barco.
sailor, *s.* marinero *m.*
saint, *adj. & s.* santo *(m.).*
sake, *s. for my ~* por mí.
salad, *s.* ensalada *f.*
salary, *s.* salario *m.,* sueldo *m.*
sale, *s.* venta *f.; for ~* en venta; *~s* liquidación *f.*
salesman, *s.* vendedor *m.*
salmon, *s.* salmón *m.*
saloon, *s.* salón *m.*
salt, *s.* sal *f.; — adj.* salado; *— v. a.* salar.
salt-cellar, *s.* salero *m.*
salvation, *s.* salvación *f.*
same, *adj.* mismo ; *at the ~ time* al mismo tiempo; *it is all the ~ to me* a mí me da lo mismo; *all the ~* no obstante, a pesar de todo; *the ~ to you* lo

mismo digo.
sample, *s.* muestra *f.*; — *v. a.* probar.
sanatorium, *s.* sanatorio *m.*
sand, *s.* arena *f.*; *~s* playa *f.*
sandal, *s.* sandalia *f*
sandwich, *s.* emparedado *m.*, bocadillo *m.*
sane, *adj.* cuerdo, sano.
sanitary, *adj.* higiénico.
sardine, *s.* sardina *f.*
satellite, *s.* satélite *m.*
satin, *s.* satén *m.*
satisfaction, *s.* satisfacción *f.*
satisfactory, *adj.* satisfactorio.
satisfy, *v. a.* satisfacer; *be satisfied* estar convencido.
Saturday, *s.* **sábado** *m.*
sauce, *s.* salsa *f.*
saucepan, *s.* sartén *f.*
saucer, *s.* platillo *m.*
sausage, *s.* salchicha *f.*
savage, *adj.* salvaje.
save, *v.a.* salvar; *(trouble)* ahorrar, evitar; *(keep)* guardar; *(stamps)* coleccionar; *(the goal)* parar; — *prep.* salvo.
savings, *s. pl.* ahorros *m. pl.*; *~ bank* caja *(f.)* de ahorros.
say, *v. a.* decir; *that is to ~* es decir; *what did you ~?* ¿cómo dijo usted?; *so to ~* para así decirlo; *let us ~* digamos; *he is said* dicen que él; — *s.* opinión *f.*
scale,[1] *s.* escala *f.*, graduacion *f.*; — *v. a.* escalar.
scale,[2] *s.* *(of fish)* escama *f.*; — *v. a.* escamar.
scales, *s.* balanza *f.*
scandal, *s.* escándalo *m.*
scar, *s.* cicatriz *f.*; — *v. n.* cicatrizarse.
scarce, *adj.* escaso, raro.
scarcely, *adv.* apenas.
scare, *v. a.* asustar; — *s.* susto *m.*
scarf, *s.* bufanda *f.*
scarlet, *adj.* escarlata; *~ fever* escarlatina *f.*
scatter, *v. a.* esparcir, dispersar.
scene, *s.* escena *f.*; *behind the ~s* entre bastidores; *make a ~* hacer escenas; *a beautiful ~* una hermosa vista.
scenery, *s.* decoración *f.*
scent, *s.* olor *m.*; *(of dog)* olfato *m.*; — *v. a.* husmear, rastrear.
schedule, *s.* programa *m.*; plan *m.*; *(train)* horario *m.*; *according to ~* puntualmente.
scheme, *s.* proyecto *m.*, esquema *m.*; — *v. a.* proyectar, idear.
scholar, *s.* escolar *m.*, estudiante *m.*; — *(scientist)* sabio *m.*, erudito *m.*; *(holder of scholarship)* becario *m.*
school, *s.* escuela *f.*; *primary ~* escuela primaria; *public ~* escuela secundaria; *trade ~* escuela profesional.
schoolmaster, *s.* profesor *m.*; maestro *m.*, director *(m.)* de escuela.
schoolroom, *s.* sala *(f.)* de clase, aula *f.*, auditorio m.
science, *s.* ciencia *f.*
scientific, *adj.* científico.
scientist, *s.* hombre *(m.)* de ciencia.
scissors, *s. pl.* tijeras *f. pl.*
scooter, *s.* patinete *m.*
scope, *s.* alcance *m.*; *be within the ~ of* estar al alcance de.

scorch, *v. a.* chamuscar.
score, *s. (cut)* entalladura *f.*; *(debt)* deuda *f.*: *(sports)* tanto *m.*; *(musical)* partitura *f.* *(twenty)* veintena *f.*; — *v. a.* entallar; *(game)* ganar puntos, marcar; ~ *a goal* marcar un gol; *(music)* instrumentar.
scorn, *s.* desprecio *m.*; — *v. a.* despreciar.
Scotch, *adj.* & *s.* escocés *(m.)*; *the* ~ los escoceses; *(drink)* whisky *m.*
scout, *s.* explorador *m.*; — *v. a.* explorar.
scramble, *v. n.* trepar; *~d eggs* huevos *(m. pl.)* revueltos.
scrape, *v. a.* raspar; *s.* lío *m.* enredo *m.*; *get into ~s* meterse en un lío.
scratch, *v. a.* arañar, rasguñar; — *s.* rasguño *m.*, raspadura *f.*
scream, *v. n.* gritar; — *s.* grito *m.*
screen, *s.* pantalla *f.*; *(fender)* biombo *m.*
screw, *s.* tornillo *m.*; — *v. a.* atornillar; ~ *on* enroscar.
screw-driver, *s.* destornillador *m.*
sculptor, *s.* escultor *m.*
sculpture, *s.* escultura *f.*
sea, *s.* mar *m.*; *be at* ~ navegar; *fig.* estar confuso; *go to* ~ zarpar, hacerse a la mar.
seal,[1] *s.* foca *f.*
seal,[2] *s.* sello *m.*; — *v. a.* ~ *up* cerrar con lacre.
seam, *s.* costura *f.*
seaman, *s.* marinero *m.*
seaport, *s.* puerto *(m.)* marítimo, **(or)** de mar.
search, *v. a.* buscar; *(a person)* registrar; — *s.* registro *m.*; *in ~ of* en busca de.
search-light, *s.* proyector *m.*
season, *s.* estación *f.*; temporada *f.*; — *v. a.* *(food)* sazonar, condimentar.
seat, *s.* asiento *m.*; *(theatre)* localidad *f.*; *(residence)* residencia *f.*; — *v. n.* sentarse, tomar asiento; *be ~ed* tome usted asiento.
second, *adj.* &*s.* segundo *(m)*; — *v. a.* apoyar, secundar.
secondary, *adj.* secundario; ~ *school* instituto *(m.)* secundario.
second-hand, *adj.* de segunda mano, de ocasión.
secret, *adj.* & *s.* secreto *(m.)*.
secretary, *s.* secretario *m.*; *Secretary of State* ministro *(m.)* de Estado.
section, *s.* sección *f.*, parte *f.*; *(of town)* barrio *m.*
secure, *adj.* seguro; — *v. a.* asegurar, garantizar; *(get)* obtener, conseguir.
security, *s.* seguridad *f.*, garantía *f.*; ***securities s. pl.*** títulos *m.*, valores *m.*, bonos *m.*
sedative, *adj.* & *s.* sedante *(m.)*, sedativo *(m.)*.
seduce, *v. a.* seducir.
see, *v. a.* ver; *let me ~!* ¡a ver!; *~ you again* hasta la vista; *~ you on Tuesday* hasta martes; *I ~!* ya lo veo, comprendo; *come to ~ me* venga a verme; *~ sy home*

acompañar a casa; ~ *off* despedir; ~ *to* encargarse de, cuidar de.
seed, *s.* semilla *f.*; — *v. n.* sembrar,
seek, *v. a.* buscar.
seem, *v. n.* parecer.
seize, *v. a.* agarrar; *(take away)* confiscar; *(opportunity)* aprovechar; *(arrest)* detener; *(understand)* comprender.
seldom, *adv.* raramente, rara vez.
select, *v. a.* elegir; — *adj.* selecto.
selection, *s.* selección *f.*
self, *pron & s.* mismo.
selfish, *adj.* egoista.
selfishness, *s.* egoísmo *m.*
self-service, *adj. & s.* autoservicio *(m.)*.
sell, *v. a.* vender; ~ *off* liquidar.
seller, *s.* vendedor *m.*
send, *v. a.* enviar, mandar; *(telegram)* mandar, poner; ~ *for* llamar.
sender, *s.* remitente *m., f.*; expedidor *m.*
senior, *adj.* mayor; — *s.* decano *m.*
sense, *s.* sentido *m.*
senseless, *adj.* insensible; insensato, sin sentido.
sensible, *adj.* sensato, cuerdo.
sensitive, *adj.* sensible.
sensual, *adj.* sensual.
sentence, *s.* sentencia *f.*; frase *f.*; — *v. a.* condenar, sentenciar.
sentry, *s.* centinela *m.*
separate, *adj.* separado; — *v. a.* separar; *v. n.* separarse.
separation, *s.* separación *f.*
September, *s.* septiembre *m.*
serenade, *s.* serenata *f.*
sergeant, *s.* sargento *m.*
serial, *adj.* periódico; ~ *number* número *(m.)* de orden.
series, *s.* serie *f.*
serious, *adj.* serio.
servant, *s.* criado *m.*; *public* ~ funcionario *m.*
serve, *v. a.* servir.
service, *s.* servicio *m.*; *civil* ~ administración *(f.)* pública, servicio *(m.)* público; *be of* ~ ser útil; *I'm at your* ~ estoy a sus órdenes.
session, *s.* sesión *f.*
set, *v. a.* poner, colocar; *(type)* componer; *(price)* fijar; ~ *an example* dar ejemplo; *v. n.* *(sun)* ponerse; ~ *off* salir; ~ *up* poner, establecer; — *s.* colección *f.*; *(radio)* aparato *m.*; — *adj.* terco, obstinado; ~ *price* precio *(m.)* fijo.
setting, *s.* disposición *f.*, arreglo *m.*; *(of types)* composición *f.*
settle, *v. a.* establecer; *(claim)* satisfacer; ~ *down* establecerse; ~ *up* arreglar.
settlement, *s.* acuerdo *m.*, arreglo *m.*; *(colony)* caserío *m.*
seven, *adj. & s.* siete.
seventeen, *adj. & s.* diecisiete.
seventh, *adj.* séptimo.
seventy, *adj. & s.* setenta.
several, *adj.* varios *pl.*
severe, *adj.* severo; *(winter)* duro.
sew, *v. a.* coser.
sewing-machine, *s.* máquina *(f.)* de coser.
sex, *s.* sexo *m.*
sexual, *adj.* sexual.
shabby, *adj.* raído, gas-

tado.
shade, *s.* sombra *f.*; — *v. a.* sombrear.
shadow, *s.* sombra *f.*
shady, *adj.* sombreado; sombrío.
shaft, *s.* mango *m.*; *(pit)* pozo *m.*
shake, *v. a.* sacudir; *(medicament)* agitar.
shall, *v. n. I ~ go* iré; *~ I wait?* ¿debo esperar?
shame, *s.* vergüenza *f.*; *v. a.* avergonzar.
shameful, *adj.* vergonzoso.
shameless, *adj.* descarado, desvergonzado.
shampoo, *s.* champú *m.*
shape, *s.* forma *f.*; estado *m.*; *I'm in bad ~* me siento mal; — *v. a.* modelar, dar forma.
share, *s.* parte *f.*; *(stock)* acción *f.*; — *v. a.* compartir, repartir.
shareholder, *s.* accionista *m.*, *f.*
sharp, *adj.* afilado; *(mind)* agudo; — *adv. at five o'clock ~* a las cinco en punto.
sharpen, *v. a.* afilar.
shave, *v. a.* afeitar; *v. n.* afeitarse; — *s.* afeite *m.*
shawl, *s.* chal *m.*; mantón *m.*
she, *pron.* ella; — *s.* hembra *f.*
shed,[1] *v. a.* verter, echar.
shed,[2] *s.* cobertizo *m.*
sheep, *s.* oveja *f.*
sheet, *s. (of paper)* pliego *m.*, hoja *f.*; *(of bed)* sábana *f.*
shelf, *s.* estante *m.*
shell, *s.* concha *f.*; cáscara *f.*; *(bullet)* proyectil *m.*; — *v. a. (peas)* desgranar; bombardear.
shelter, *s.* albergue *m.*, refugio *m.*; — *v. a.* albergar.
shepherd, *s.* pastor *m.*
shield, *s.* escudo *m.*; — *v. a.* proteger, amparar.
shift, *v. a. & n.* mudar, cambiar; — *s.* cambio *m.*; *(in work)* turno *m.*
shine, *v. n.* brillar; — *s.* brillo *m.*
ship, *s.* barco *m.*; — *v. a.* embarcar; *v. n.* embarcarse.
shipment, *s.* embarque *m.*, cargamento *m.*
shipwreck, *s.* naufragio *m.*
shipyard, *s.* astilleros *m. pl.*
shirt, *s.* camisa *f.*
shiver, *v. n.* tiritar; — *s.* tiritón *m.*
shock, *s.* choque *m.*; — *v. a.* chocar; *be ~ed at* escandalizarse de.
shocking, *adj.* espantoso chocante.
shoe, *s.* zapato *m.*; *(horse-)* herradura *f.*: — *v. a.* herrar.
shoe-cream, *s.* pomada *(f.)* para calzado.
shoe-lace, *s.* cordón *(m.)* de zapato.
shoemaker, *s.* zapatero *m.*
shoot, *v. n.* disparar; tirar; *(car)* salir disparado; *v. a. (photo)* tomar.
shooting, *s.* disparo *m.*; *(hunting)* caza *f.*; *(film)* rodaje *m.*
shop, *s.* tienda *f.*; — *v. a.* ir de compras.
shop assistant, *s.* dependiente *m.*, dependienta
shopkeeper, *s.* tendero *m.*
shore, *s.* orilla *f.*, costa *f.*, playa *f.*
short, *adj.* corto; *~ cut* atajo *m.*; *~ story* cuento *m.*; *in a ~ time* dentro de poco; — *adv. cut ~* interrumpir; *run*

~ *of sg* quedarse falto de; — *s.* ~*s* pantalones *(m. pl.)* cortos.
shorten, *v. a.* acortar, abreviar.
shorthand, *s.* taquigrafía *f.*
shortly, *adv.* en breve, dentro de poco.
shot, *s.* disparo *m.*, tiro *m.*; *(person)* tirador *m.*; *(photo)* instantánea *f.*; *(drink)* trago *m.*, sorbo *m.*; *(injection)* inyección *f.*
shoulder, *s.* hombro *m.*
shout, *s.* grito *m.*; — *v. n.* gritar.
show, *v. a.* enseñar, mostrar; indicar; *(prove)* probar, justificar; ~ *in* hacer entrar; ~ *off* presumir; ~ *up* presentarse, aparecer; — *s.* espectáculo *m.*, función *f.*
shower, *s.* chubasco *m.*, aguacero *m.*, lluvia *f.*; *(bath)* ducha *f.*
shrewd, *adj.* astuto.
shrill, *adj.* agudo, penetrante.
shrine, *s.* relicario *m.*
shrink, *v. n.* encogerse.
shrub, *s.* arbusto *m.*, mata *f.*
shrug, *v. n.* encogerse de hombros.
shudder, *s.* estremecimiento *m.*; — *v. n.* estremecerse.
shut, *v. a.* cerrar; ~ *in* encerrar; ~ *up* cerrar; *(be silent)* callarse.
shutter, *s.* persiana *f.*; *(photo)* obturador *m.*
shy, *adj.* tímido.
sick, *adj.* enfermo; *be* ~ sentirse mal, vomitar; *feel* ~ sentir náuseas; *fall* ~ caer enfermo; *be* ~ *of* estar harto de.
sicken, *v. n.* enfermar.
sickness, *s.* enfermedad *f.*
side, *s.* lado *m.*; *on all* ~*s* por todas partes; — *adj.* lateral.
sigh, *s.* suspiro *m.*; — *v. n.* suspirar.
sight, *s.* vista *f.*; *by* ~ de vista; *see the* ~*s* visitar los lugares interesantes; — *v. a.* notar, avistar.
sightseeing, *s.* el visitar los lugares interesantes.
sign, *s.* señal *f.*; *(signboard)* letrero *m.*; — *v. a.* firmar; ~ *on* contratar.
signal, *s.* señal *f.*; — *v. a.* hacer señales a.
signature, *s.* firma *f.*
significant, *adj.* significante, significativo.
signify, *v. a.* significar.
silence, *s.* silencio *m.*; — *v. a.* acallar.
silent, *adj.* silencioso; callado; *v. n. keep* ~ callarse.
silk, *s.* seda *f.*
silly, *adj.* tonto.
silver, *s.* plata *f.*; — *v. a.* azogar, platear.
silvery, *adj.* plateado.
similar, *adj.* semejante, similar.
simple, *adj.* sencillo; simple.
simplicity, *s.* sencillez *f.*
sin, *s.* pecado *m.*; — *v. n.* pecar.
since, *adv. & prep.* desde; *ever* ~ desde entonces; — *conj.* puesto que.
sincere, *adj.* sincero.
sinew, *s.* tendón *m.*
sinful, *adj.* pecaminoso.
sing, *v. a. & n.* cantar.
singer, *s.* cantante *m.*, *f.*
single, *adj.* solo; *(not married)* soltero.

singlet, *s.* camiseta *f.*
singular, *adj.* singular.
sinister, *adj.* siniestro.
sink, *v n.* hundirse; *v. a.* abrir, excavar; – *s.* fregadero *m.*, pila *f.*
sip, *v. a.* sorber, chupar; –*s.* sorbo *m.*, trago *m.*
sir, *s.* señor *m.*
sister, *s.* hermana *f.*
sister-in-law, *s.* cuñada *f.*
sit, *v. n.* sentarse; *be ~ting* estar sentado; *~ down* sentarse; *~ for* posar; *~ up* incorporarse; *(all night)* estarse levantado.
site, *s.* solar *m.*, sitio *m.*
sitting-room, *s.* cuarto *(m.)* de estar.
situation, *s.* situación *f.*
six, *adj.* & *s.* seis.
sixteen, *adj.* &. *s.* dieciséis.
sixth, *adj.* sexto.
sixty, *adj.* & *s.* sesenta.
size, *s.* tamaño *m.*, número *m.*
skate, *s.* patín *m.*; – *v. n.* patinar.
skeleton, *s.* esqueleto *m.*; *~ key* ganzua *f.*, llave *(f.)* maestra.
sketch, *s.* croquis *m,*; – *v. a.* dibujar.
ski, *s.* esquí *m.*; – *v. n.* esquiar.
skiff, *s.* bote *m.*, canoa *f*
skilful, *adj.* hábil, diestro.
skill, *s.* habilidad *f.*, destreza *f.*
skilled, *adj.* diestro, experto, especializado.
skin, *s.* piel *f.*; – *v. a.* desollar.
skip, *v. a.* & *n.* saltar.
skirt, *s.* falda *f.*; – *v. a.* orillar, orlar.
skull, *s.* cráneo *m.*
sky, *s.* cielo *m.*
slab, *s.* placa *f.*
slack, *adj.* flojo.
slacken, *v. a.* aminorar, disminuir.
slacks, *s. pl.* pantalones *m. pl.*
slander, *s.* calumnia *f.*; – *v. a.* calumniar.
slate, *s.* pizarra *f.*; – *v. a.* empizarrar.
slaughther, *s.* matanza *f.*; – *v. a.* matar.
slave, *s.* esclavo *m.*
slay, *v. a.* matar.
sledge, *s.* trineo *m.*; – *v. n.* ir en trineo.
sleep, *v. n.* dormir; – *s.* sueño *m.*
sleeping-car, *s.* coche-cama *m.*
sleepy, *adj.* soñóliento.
sleeve, *s.* manga *f.*
sleigh, *s.* trineo *m.*; – *v. n.* ir en trineo.
slender, *adj.* delgado.
slice, *s.* tajada *f.*, rebanada *f.*; – *v. a.* cortar en tajadas, rebanar.
slide, *v. n.* deslizarse, resbalar.
slight, *adj.* leve, ligero; – *v. a.* desairar; – *s.* desprecio *m.*, desaire *m.*
slim, *adj.* delgado.
sling, *s.* nudo *(m.)* corredizo; cabestrillo *m.*
slip, *s.* *(of paper)* trozo *m.*, tira *f.*; *(fault)* imprudencia *f.*, pata *f.*; *(combination)* combinación *f.*; *pillow ~* funda *f.*; *give the ~* dar esquinazo; – *v n.* resbalar; *(escape)* escapar; *it ~ped my memory* se me olvidó; *v. a.* echar; *~ away* escabullirse.
slipper, *s.* zapatilla *f.*, pantufla *f.*
slot, *s.* ranura *f.*
slow, *adj.* lento; *(child)*

retrasado; – *adv.* despacio; – *v. a.* retardar; *v. n.* atrasar.
slum, *s.* calle *(f.)* sucia; *~s* barrios *(m. pl.)* bajos, tugurios *m. pl.*
slumber, *v. n.* dormitar; – *s.* sueño *(m.)* ligero.
sly, *adj.* astuto, taimado.
small, *adj.* pequeño; *~ change* suelto *m.*; *~ talk* charla *f.*
smallpox, *s.* viruelas *f. pl.*
smart, *adj.* listo; elegante.
smell, *s.* olfato *m.*; olor *m.*; – *v. a.* oler.
smile, *s.* sonrisa *f.*; – *v. n.* sonreir.
smoke, *s.* humo *m.*; – *v. n.* fumar; *v. a.* ahumar.
smooth, *adj.* llano; *(sea)* tranquilo; *(wine)* suave; *(person)* lisonjero; – *v. a.* alisar; *(way)* allanar.
smuggle, *v. a.* pasar de contrabando; *v. n.* hacer contrabando.
snack, *s.* merienda *f.*
snail, *s.* caracol *m.*
snake, *s.* serpiente *f.*, culebra *f.*
snap, *s.* instantánea *f.*: – *v. a.* sacar una instantánea.
sneeze, *s.* estornudo *m.*; – *v. n.* estornudar.
snore, *v. n.* roncar; – *s.* ronquido *m.*
snow, *s.* nieve *f.*; – *v. n.* nevar.
snug, *adj.* cómodo, íntimo.
so, *adv.* así; *that's not ~!* ¡eso no es cierto!; *~ I see* ya lo veo; *and ~ on* etcétera; *~ much* tanto; *~ that* a fin de que; *~ long!* ¡hasta luego!
soak, *v. a.* empapar, remojar.
soap, *s.* jabón *m.*; – *v. a.* enjabonar.
sober, *adj.* sobrio; – *v. a.* desembriagar.
social, *adj.* social.
socialism, *s.* socialismo *m.*
socialist, *adj.* & *s.* socialista *(m., f.)*.
society, *s.* sociedad *f.*
sock, *s.* calcetín *m.*
socket, *s.* enchufe *m.*
soda, *s.* soda *f.*, agua *(f.)* de Seltz.
sofa, *s.* sofá *m.*, canapé *m.*
soft, *adj.* blando, suave; *~-boiled eggs* huevos *(m. pl.)* pasados por agua.
soil, *s.* tierra *f.*; – *v. a.* ensuciar.
soldier, *s.* soldado *m.*
sole, *s.* suela *f.*, *(fish)* lenguado *m.*; – *v. a.* poner suelas.
solemn, *adj.* solemne.
solicit, *v. a.* solicitar.
solicitor, *s.* abogado *m.*
solid, *adj.* & *s.* sólido *(m.)*
solidarity, *s.* solidaridad *f.*
solitude, *s.* soledad *f.*
soluble, *adj.* soluble.
solution, *s.* solución *f.*
solve, *v. a.* resolver, solucionar.
some, *adj.* algo, poco, algún; algunos, pocos; *to ~ extent* hasta cierto punto; *~ twenty boys* unos veinte muchachos.
somebody, *pron.* alguien.
someone, *pron.* alguien.
something, *pron.* algo.
sometime, *adv.* algún día.
sometimes, *adv.* a veces; algunas veces.
somewhat, *adv.* algo, un poco.
somewhere, *adv.* en al-

guna parte.
son, *s.* hijo *m.*
song, *s.* canción *f.*
son-in-law, *s.* yerno *m.*
soon, *adv.* pronto; *as ~ as* tan pronto como; *as ~ as possible* lo antes posible; *~er or later* tarde o temprano.
soprano, *s.* soprano *f.*
sore, *adj.* mal, lastimado; *I've a ~ throat* me duele la garganta; *get ~* ofenderse; — *s.* llaga *f.*
sorrow, *s.* aflicción *f.*; — *v. n.* afligirse.
sorry, *adj.* triste; *so ~!* ¡lo siento mucho!
sort, *s.* clase *f.*
soul, *s.* alma *f.*
sound,[1] *s.* sonido *m.*; — *v. n.* sonar.
sound[2], *adj.* sano, bueno.
soup, *s.* sopa *f.*
sour, *adj.* agrio, ácido.
source, *s.* fuente *f.*; *fig.* origen *m.*; motivo *m.*
south, *s.* sur *m.*; — *adj.* del sur; — *adv.* hacia el sur.
southern, *adj.* meridional, al sur, del sur.
sovereign, *adj.* & *s.* soberano *(m.)*.
sow[1], *s.* puerca *f.*, marrana *f.*
sow,[2] *v. a.* sembrar.
space, *s.* espacio *m.*; *~ vehicle* nave *(f.)* espacial; — *v. a.* espaciar, separar.
space-flight, *s.* vuelo *(m.)* orbital.
spaceman, *s.* astronauta *m.*, cosmonauta *m.*
space-ship, *s.* nave *(f.)* espacial.
space-suit, *s.* traje *(m.)* espacial.
spacious, *adj.* espacioso.
spade, *s.* pala *f.*, azada *f.*; *(card)* espada *f.*; — *v. n.* cavar con pala, remover la tierra.
Spaniard, *s.* español *m.*
Spanish, *adj.* español.
spanner, *s.* llave *(f.)* inglesa.
spare, *v. a.* ahorrar; sobrar; conceder; — *adj.* *~ parts* piezas *(f. pl.)* de repuesto; *~ time* momentos *(m. pl.)* libres.
spark, *s.* chispa *f.*; — *v. n.* chispear.
sparrow, *s.* gorrión *m.*
speak, *v. a.* & *n.* hablar.
speaker, *s.* orador *m.*, conferencista *m.*
spear, *s.* lanza *f.*
special, *adj.* especial; — *s.* edición *(f.)* extra.
specialist, *s.* especialista *m.*
specially, *adv.* especialmente.
species, *s.* especie *f.*
specific, *adj.* específico.
specify, *v. a.* especificar.
specimen, *s.* muestra *f.*, espécimen *m.*
speck, *s.* motita *f.*
spectacle, *s.* espectáculo *m.*
spectacles, *s.* gafas *f. pl.*, anteojos *m. pl.*
spectator, *s.* espectador *m.*
speech, *s.* discurso *m.*
speed, *s.* velocidad *f.*; prisa *f.*; — *v. n.* apresurarse; *~ up* acelerar.
speedway, *s.* autódromo *m.*; autopista *f.*
speedy, *adj.* rápido.
spell[1], *v. a.* deletrear; *how do you your ~ name?* ¿cómo se escribe su nombre?
spell[2], *s.* encanto *m.*
spelling, *s.* deletreo *m.*, ortografía *f.*

spend, *v. a.* gastar; *(night)* pasar.
sphere, *s.* esfera *f.*
spice, *s.* especia *f.*; – *v. a.* condimentar, sazonar.
spider, araña *f.*
spill, *v. a.* derramar.
spin, *v. a.* & *n.* hilar.
spinach, espinaca *f.*
spine, *s.* columna *(f.)* vertebral; espinazc *m.*
spinster, *s.* solterona *f.*
spiral, *adj.* & *s.* espiral *(f.)*.
spirit, *s.* espíritu *m.*; – *v. a.* entusiasmar; ~ ~ *away* hurtar.
spirits, *s. pl.* alcohol *m.*; *low* ~ mal humor *m.*; *in high* ~ de buen humor.
spiritual, *adj.* espiritual.
spit,[1] *v. a.* & *n.* escupir; – *s.* saliva *f.*
spit,[2] *s.* asador *m.* (a rotación).
splash, *v. a.* salpicar; – *s.* salpicadura *f.*
splendid, *adj.* espléndido.
splendour, *s.* esplendor *m.*
split, *v. a.* dividir, repartir; ~ *hairs* pararse en pelillos; *a* ~*ting headache* un tremendo dolor de cabeza; – *s.* grieta *f.*, hendedura *f.*
spoil, *v. a.* pillar; *fig.* echar a perder; *(child)* mimar; – *s.* botín *m.*
spokesman, *s.* portavoz *m.*
sponge, *s.* esponja *f.*
spontaneous, *adj.* espontáneo.
spoon, *s.* cuchara *f.*
spoonful, *s.* cucharada *f.*
sport, *s.* deporte *m.*; *he is a real* ~ es un buen muchacho.
spot, *s.* mancha *f.*; *(place)* lugar *m.*, punto *m.*; – *on the* ~ en el sitio; – *v. a.* manhcar; *(see)* reconocer, distinguir.
spotless, *adj.* inmaculado.
spray, *s.* rociada *f.*; – *v. a.* rociar.
spread, *v. a.* extender; *v. n.* extenderse; – *s.* propagación *f.*
spring,[1] *s.* primavera *f.*
spring,[2] *v. n.* saltar, dar un salto; lanzarse; ~ *back* rebotar; ~ *from* proceder; – *s.* origen *m.*; *(water-)* manantial *m.*; *(watch-)* resorte *m.*, muelle *m.*
sprinkle, *v. a.* rociar; *v. n.* *(rain)* lloviznar.
spur, *s.* espuela *f.*; *fig.* impulso *m.*; – *v. a.* estimular.
spy, *s.* espía *m.*; – *v. n.* espiar.
square, *s.* cuadrado *m.*; plaza *f.*; – *adj.* ~ *foot* pie *(m.)* cuadrado; *(honest)* honrado; *a* ~ *meal* una comida abundante; – *v. a.* arreglar, ajustar.
squeeze, *v. a.* *(lemon)* exprimir; *(hand)* apretar, estrujar.
squint, *v. n.* bizcar.
squire, *s.* terrateniente *m.*
squirrel, *s.* ardilla *f.*
stab, *v. a.* apuñalar; – *s.* punzada *f.*
stability, *s.* estabilidad *f.*
stable, *s.* caballeriza *f.*; establo *m.*
stack, *s.* pila *f.*, montón *m.*; *v. a.* apilar, amontonar.
stadium, *s.* estadio *m.*
staff, *s.* báculo *m.*; *(personnel)* personal *m.*
stag, *s.* ciervo *m.*
stage, *s.* escenario *m.*,

teatro *m.*; *(period)* período *m.*; — *v. a.* representar.
stagger, *v. n.* tambalearse.
stain, *v. a.* manchar; — *s.* mancha *f.*
stairs, *s. pl.* escalera *f.*
staircase, *s.* escalera *f.*, escalerón *m.*
stake, *s.* estaca *f.*, palo *m.*; *(game)* postura *f.*; — *v. a.* estacar; *fig.* arriesgar.
stale, *adj.* rancío, viejo.
stall, *s.* pesebre *m.*; *(market)* tenderete *m.*; puesto *m.*; *(seat)* butaca *f.*; — *v. n.* atascar; *v. a.* entretener.
stammer, *v. n.* tartamudear.
stamp, *s.* sello *m.*, estampilla *f.*; — *v. a.* poner sello, franquear; *(mark)* marcar, sellar; *(feet)* patalear; ~ *on* pisar.
stand, *v. n.* estar de pie; estar situado; *(remain)* quedarse; *v. a.* poner; *I can't* ~ *him* no puedo soportarle; ~ *aside* apartarse; ~ *for* estar partidario de; ~ *off* mantenerse a distancia; ~ *out* destacarse; resistir; ~ *up* levantarse; — *s.* tribuna *f.*, plataforma *f.*; *(market)* puesto *m.*
standard, *s.* bandera *f.*; ~ *of living* nivel *(m.)* de vida; norma *f.*; — *adj.* corriente; ~ *weight* peso *(m.)* legal.
standstill, *s.* parada *f.*, suspensión *f.*
star, *s.* estrella *f.*; — *v. n.* figurar como estrella.
start, *v. n.* partir, ponerse en camino; *v. a.* empezar; *(engine)* poner en marcha; *(frighten)* asustar; — *s.* principio *m.*; *(fright)* susto *m.*
strarve, *v. n.* morir de hambre; *v. a.* hacer morir de hambre.
state, *s.* estado *m.*, situación *f.*; *(country)* Estado *m.*; — *v. a.* declarar.
statement, *s.* declaración *f.*; ~ *of account* estado *(m.)* de cuentas.
statesman, *s.* estadista *m.*, político *m.*
station, *s.* estación *f.*; *police* ~ comisaría *f.*; — *v. a.* apostar; *fig.* destinar.
stationer, s. papelero *m.*
statistical, *adj.* estadístico.
statistics, *s. pl.* estadística *f.*
statute, *s.* estatuto *m.*
stay *v. n.* permanecer, quedarse; *(in a place)* alojarse, parar; — *s.* estancia *f.*, temporada *f.*
steady, *adj.* firme: constante; — *v. a.* sostener.
steak, *s.* solomillo *m.*, biftec *m.*
steal, *v. a.* robar, hurtar.
steam, *s.* vapor *m.*; — *v. n.* evaporarse; ~ *out* zarpar.
steam-engine, *s.* máquina *(f.)* de vapor.
steamer, *s.* vapor *m.*, barco *m.*
steel, s. acero *m.*; — *v. a.* fortalecer; *v. n.* fortalecerse.
steep, *adj.* escarpado, empinado; *(price)* exorbitante.

steeple, *s.* campanario *m.*, torre *f.*
steeple-chase, *s.* carrera (*f.*) de obstáculos.
steer, *v. a.* (*ship*) gobernar, dirigir; (*car*) conducir, manejar.
steering-gear, *s.* mando *m.*
steering-wheel, *s.* rueda (*f.*) del timón; volante *m.*
stem, *s.* tallo *m.*
step, *v. n.* poner el pie, pisar; ~ *this way!* ¡por aquí! ~ *aside* ponerse a un lado; ~ *in* entrar; ~ *off* bajarse, apearse; ~ *on* pisar; ~ *up* subir; – *s.* paso *m.*; ~ *by* ~ paso a paso; ~*s* escalones *m. pl.*
stepmother, *s.* madrastra *f.*
stereo, *adj.* estéreo-.
stereotype, *s.* estereotipia *f.*; – *adj.* estereotípico; – *v. a.* estereotipar.
sterility, *s.* esterilidad *f.*
stern,[1] *adj.* duro, severo.
stern,[2] *s.* popa *f.*
stew, *v. a.* estofar; – *s.* guisado *m.*
steward, *s.* administrador *m.*; (*on ship*) camarero *m.*
stewardess, *s.* camarera *f.*; (*on plane*) azafata *f.*
stick, *s.* palo *m.*, bastón *m.*; – *v. a.* pinchar, poner; (*glue*) pegar; (*pig*) matar; ~ *out* sobresalir; ~ *to* seguir en, no abandonar.
sticky, *adj.* pegajoso.
stiff, *adj.* tieso, duro; *a* ~ *neck* torticolis *m.*
still,[1] *adj.* quieto; *stand* ~ estarse quieto; – *s.* calma *f.*
still,[2] *adv.* todavía, aún.
stimulate, *v. a.* estimular.
sting, *v. a.* picar; – *s.* picadura *f.*
stink, *v. n.* heder, apestar; – *s.* hedor *m.*
stipulate, *v. a.* estipular.
stir, mover, menear; provocar, excitar; *v. n.* moverse; – *s.* conmoción *f.*
stock, *s.* surtido *m.*; (*share*) acción *f.*; (*cattle*) ganado *m.*; *take* ~ hacer inventario; – *v. a.* tener en existencia.
stock-exchange, *s.* Bolsa *f.*
stockholder, *s.* accionista *m.*, *f.*
stocking, *s.* media *f.*
stomach, *s.* estómago *m.*
stone, *s.* piedra *f.*; *precious* ~ piedra preciosa; – *v. a.* apedrear.
stony, *adj.* pedregoso.
stool, *s.* taburete *m.*
stoop, *v. n.* inclinarse, doblarse.
stop, *v. a.* parar; (*pay*) suspender; (*hinder*) impedir, detener; *v. n.* pararse; – *s.* parada *f.*
store, *s.* provisión *f.*; tienda *f.*; ~*s* almacén *m.* – *v. a.* acumular.
stork, *s.* cigüeña *f.*
storm, *s.* tormenta *f.*, tempestad *f.*; – *v. a.* asaltar.
stormy, *adj.* tempestuoso, borrascoso.
story,[1] *s.* cuento *m.*, historieta *f.*; relato *m.*, información *f.*; *short* ~ cuento *m.*, novela (*f.*) corta.
story,[2] *s.* piso *m.*
stout, *adj.* gordo, corpulento.
stove, *s.* estufa *f.*; hornilla *f.*; fogón *m.*

straight, *adj.* *(road)* recto; *(honest)* honrado.
straighten, *v. a.* poner en orden, arreglar.
strait, *adj.* & *s.* estrecho *(m.)*.
strand, *s.* playa *f.*; *(of pearls)* sarta *f.*; — *v. n.* encallar(se).
strange, *adj.* extraño, raro.
stranger, *s.* forastero *m.*, extranjero *m.*, desconocido *m.*
strap, correa *f.*; — *v. a.* amarrar, sujetar.
strategy, *s.* estrategia *f.*
straw, *s.* paja *f.*
strawberry, *s.* fresa *f.*
streak, *s.* raya *f.*, lista *f.*; — *v. a.* rayar.
stream, *s.* corriente *f.*, río *m.*, arroyo *m.*; — *v. n.* afluir; salir a torrentes.
street, *s.* calle *f.*
strength, *s.* fuerza *f.*
strenghten, *v. a.* reforzar; *v. n.* fortalecerse, cobrar fuerzas.
stress, *s.* énfasis *m.*; — *v. a.* recalcar, subrayar.
stretch, *v. a.* tender, extender; *(shoes)* ensanchar; — *s.* *(of road)* trecho *m.*
stretcher, *s.* camilla *f.*
strew, *v. a.* esparcir.
strict, *adj.* estricto.
strike, *v. a.* pegar, golpear; ~ *a match* encender un fósforo ;~ *a bargain* llegar a un acuerdo; ~ *work* estar en huelga; *v. n.* *(clock)* dar; — *s.* golpe *m.*; huelga *f.*
striking, *adj.* sorprendente.
string, *s.* cuerda *f.*, cordel *m.*; ~ *of pearls* collar *(m.)* de perlas; — *v. a.* tender.
strip, *v. a.* descortezar; *v. n.* desnudarse; — *s.* tira *f.*, franja *f.*
stripe, *s.* raya *f.*, lista *f.*; — *s.* galones *m. pl.*
stroke, *s.* golpe *m.*; *(swimming)* brazada *f.*; *(apoplexy)* ataque *m.*; ~ *of luck* suerte *f.*; — *v. a.* acariciar.
stroll, *s.* paseo *m.*; *go for a* ~ dar un paseo; — *v. n.* pasear.
strong, *adj.* fuerte, resistente; ~ *tea* té *(m.)* cargado.
structure, *s.* estructura *f.*
struggle, *v. n.* luchar; — *s.* lucha *f.*; ~ *for life* lucha por la vida.
student, *s.* estudiante *m.*
study, *s.* estudio *m.*; — *v. n.* & *s.* estudiar.
stupid, *adj.* tonto, estúpido.
stupidity *s.* tontería *f.*
sturdy, *adj.* fuerte, robusto.
style, manera *f.*, estilo *m.*, moda *f.*
subdue, *v. a.* dominar, sojuzgar.
subject, *adj.* ~ *to* sujeto a; — *s.* tema *m.*; *(person)* súbdito *m.*; — *v. a.* someter.
sublime, *adj.* sublime.
submarine, *adj.* & *s.* submarino *(m.)*.
submission, *s.* sumisión *f.*
submit, *v. a.* someter.
subordinate, *adj.* subordinado; — *v. a.* subordinar.
subscribe, *v. a.* suscribir; *v. n.* ~ *to* suscribirse, abonarse a.
subscriber, *s.* su(b)scriptor *m.*; abonado *m.*

subsidy, *s.* subsidio *m.*
subsist, *v. n.* subsistir.
substance, *s.* sustancia *f.*
substantial, *adj.* sustancial, sustancioso.
substitute, *s.* su(b)stituto *m.*; — *v. a.* su(b)stituir.
subtle, *adj.* sutil, ingenioso.
subtract, *v. a.* su(b)straer, restar.
suburb, *s.* suburbio *m.*
subway, *s.* paso *(m.)* subterráneo.; metro *m.*
succeed, *v. n.* suceder; *v. a.* lograr, tener éxito.
success, *s.* éxito *m.*
successful, *adj.* afortunado, próspero.
succession, *s.* sucesión *f.*
successive, *adj.* sucesivo.
successor, *s.* sucesor *m.*
such, *adj.* & *pron.* tal; así; ~ *as* tal como; ~ *is life!* ¡así es la vida!
suck, *v. a.* chupar.
sudden, *adj.* repentino, súbito; *all of a* ~ de repente.
suffer, *v. n.* sufrir.
sufficient, *adj.* suficiente.
suffocate, *v. a.* sofocar, asfixiar; *v. n.* sofocarse, asfixiarse.
sugar, *s.* azúcar *m.*; — *v. a.* azucarar.
suggest, *v. a.* sugerir, proponer; insinuar.
suggestion, *s.* sugestión *f.*, sugerencia *f.*
suicide, *s.* suicidio *m.*; *(person)* suicida *m.*, *f.*
suit, *s. (dress)* traje *m.*; *(lawyer's)* pleito *m.*; *(cards) follow* ~ jugar el mismo palo; — *v. n.* venir bien, convenir; *this hat* ~*s me* este sombrero me va bien.
suitable, *adj.* apropiado, adecuado.
suitcase, *s.* maleta *f.*
suitor, *s.* pretendiente *m.*; *(law)* demandante *m.*
sulphur, *s.* azufre *m.*
sum, *s.* suma *f.*; — *v. a.* sumar; ~ *up* resumir.
summary, *adj.* sumario; — *s.* resumen *m.*, compendio *m.*
summer, *s.* verano *m.*
summit, *s.* cima *f.*, cumbre *f.*
summon, *v. a.* citar.
sun, *s.* sol *m.*; — *v. n.* tomar el sol.
Sunday, *s.* domingo *m.*
sunny, *adj.* (a)soleado.
sunrise, *s.* amanecer *m.*, salida *(f.)* del sol.
sunset, *s.* crepúsculo *m.*, puesta *(f.)* del sol.
sunshine, *s.* luz *(f.)* del sol.
sunstroke, *s.* insolación *f.*
superb, *adj.* soberbio.
superfluous, *adj.* superfluo.
superintendent, *s.* superintendente *m.*
superior, *adj.* & *s.* superior *(m.)*.
superiority, superioridad *f.*
supermarket, *s.* supermercado *m.*
supersonic, *adj.* supersónico.
superstition, *s.* superstición *f.*
superstitious, *adj.* supersticioso.
supper, *s.* cena *f.*
supply, *v. a.* suplir; proporcionar; — *s.* provisión *f.*, abastecimiento *m.*; *(store)* surtido *m.*; ~ *and demand* oferta *(f.)* y demanda *(f.)*.

support, *v. a.* aguantar, resistir; *fig.* mantener, apoyar; — *s.* soporte *m.*; sostén *m.*; *fig.* mantenimiento *m.*, sustento *m.*
suppose, *v. a.* suponer.
suppress, *v. a.* suprimir.
suppression, *s.* supresión *f.*
supreme, *adj.* supremo.
sure, *adj.* seguro; *be* ~ estar seguro; *make* ~ asegurarse; — *adv.* claro, por supuesto, ciertamente.
surely, *adv.* ciertamente, sin duda.
surface, *s.* superficie *f.*
surgeon, *s.* cirujano *m.*
surpass, *v. a.* sobrepasar, superar.
surprise, *s.* sorpresa *f.*; — *v. a.* sorprender.
surprising, *adv.* sorprendente.
surrender, *v. n.* rendirse, capitular; — *s.* rendición *f.*, capitulación *f.*
surround, *v. a.* rodear.
surroundings, *s.* ambiente *m.*; alrededores *m. pl.*, cercanías *f. pl.*
survive, *v. a.* & *n.* sobrevivir.
survivor, *adj.* & *s.* sobreviviente *(m., f.)*.
suspect, *v. a.* sospechar; *adj.* sospechoso.
suspenders, *s.* liga *f.*; *(braces)* tirantes *m. pl.*
suspicion, *s.* sospecha *f.*
suspicious, *adj.* sospechoso; receloso.
swallow,[1] *v. a.* tragar.
swallow,[2] *s.* golondrina *f.*
swan, *s.* cisne *m.*
swarm, *s.* enjambre *m.*; — *v. n.* enjambrar.
swear, *v. n.* jurar; ~ *in* jurar, prestar juramento.
sweat, *s.* sudor *m.*; — *v. n.* sudar.
sweater, *s.* suéter *m.*, jersey *m.*
Swedish, *adj.* sueco.
sweep, *v. a.* barrar; ~ *aside* derribar; — *s.* barredura *f.*; extensión *f.*, dimensión *f.*
sweet, *adj.* dulce; — *s.* ~*s* dulces *m. pl.*; caramelos *m. pl.*
sweetheart, *s.* enamorado *m.*, enamorada *f.*, cariño *m.*, novia *f.*
sweetness, *s.* dulzor *m.*, suavidad *f.*
swell, *v. n.* aumentar, crecer; *v. a.* hinchar; — *adj.* estupendo; elegante.
swift, *adj.* rápido, veloz.
swim, *v. n.* nadar; — *s.* nadada *f.*; natación *f.*
swindler, *s.* embustero *m.*, estafador *m.*
swine, *s.* puerco *m.*, cerdo *m.*
swing, *v. a.* mecer, balancear; *v. n.* mecerse; — *s.* columpio *m.*
Swiss, *adj.* suizo.
switch, *s.* *(railway)* aguja *f.*; *(electric)* conmutador *m.*; *(stick)* varita *f.*, varilla *f.* — *v. a.* cambiar (de sitio); ~ *off* apagar (la luz); ~ *on* encender (la luz).
swollen, *adj.* hinchado.
syllable, *s.* sílaba *f.*
symbol, *s.* símbolo *m.*
symmetrical, *adj.* simétrico.
sympathy, *s.* simpatía *f.*
symphony, *s.* sinfonía *f.*
symptom, *s.* síntoma *m.*
synagogue, *s.* sinagoga *f.*
syndicate, *s.* sindicato *m.*
synthetic, *adj.* sintético.
syringe, *s.* jeringa *f.*

syrup, *s.* jarabe *m.*, almíbar *m.*
system, *s.* sistema *m.*, método *m.*
systematic(al), *adj.* sistematico, metódico.

T

table, *s.* mesa *f.*; ~ *of contents* sumario *m.*, índice *m.*
table-cloth, *s.* mantel *m.*
tablet, *s.* tableta *f.*, pastilla *f.*
tail, *s.* rabo *m.*, cola *f.*; *heads or* ~*s* cara o cruz; – *v. a.* seguir de cerca.
tailor, *s.* sastre *m.*; – *v. a.* cortar.
take, *v. a.* tomar, coger; *(to a place)* llevar; *(accept)* aceptar; *(advice)* seguir; *(last)* durar; *(pictures)* sacar, tomar; ~ *a bath* bañarse; ~ *advantage of* aprovechar; ~ *a seat, please* tome asiento, por favor; ~ *place* tener lugar; ~ *down* bajar, descolgar; ~ *off* *(hat)* quitarse; *(plane)* despegar; ~ *out* sacar; *(spot)* quitar.
tale, *s.* cuento *m.*
talent, *s.* talento *m.*, aptitud *f.*
talk, *s.* discurso *m.*; – *v. n.* hablar.
talkative, *adj.* locuaz.
tall, *adj.* alto.
tame, *adj.* domesticado; manso; — *v. a.* domesticar.
tank, *s.* tanque *m.* *(petrol)* depósito *m.*
tape, *s.* cinta *f.*
tape-recorder, *s.* magnetófono *m.*, grabador *(m.)* de sonido.
tapestry, *s.* tapiz *m.*
tariff, *s.* tarifa *f.*
task, *s.* tarea *f.*
taste, *s.* gusto *m.*; sabor *m.*; – *v. a.* probar; *v. n.* saber.
tasteless, *adj.* soso, insípido; *fig.* de mal gusto.
tavern, *s.* taberna *f.*, posada *f.*
tax, *s.* impuesto *m.*; – *v. a.* poner impuestos.
taxi, *s.* taxi *m.*
tea, *s.* té *m.*, merienda *f.*
teach, *v. a.* enseñar.
teacher, *s.* maestro *m.*, profesor *m.*
team, *s.* equipo *m.*
tea-pot, *s.* tetera *f.*
tear,[1] *s.* lágrima *f.*
tear,[2] *v. a.* romper, ~ *down* derribar; ~ *out* arrancar; – *s.* rasgadura *f.*, roto *m.*
tease, *v. a.* fastidiar, molestar.
teaspoon, *s.* cucharita *f.*
technical, *adj.* técnico.
technique, *s.* técnica *f.*
teenager, *s.* adolescente *m.*, *f.*
telecast, *s.* transmisión *(f.)* televisiva.
telecommunication, *s.* telecomunicación *f.*
telegram, *s.* telegrama *m.*
telegraph, *s.* telégrafo *m.*; – *v. n.* telegrafiar.
telephone, *s.* teléfono *m.*, – *v. n.* telefonear.
telephone-box, cabina *(f.)* telefónica.
telephone-exchange, *s.* central *(f.)* telefónica
telescope, *s.* telescopio *m.*
teleprinter, telex, *s.* teletipo *m.*, teleimpresor *m.*
television, *s.* televisión *f.*
television-set, *s.* televi-

sor *m.*
televise, *v. a.* transmitir por televisión, televisar.
tell, *v. a.* decir; *I was told* me han dicho; *(a story)* contar.
temper, *s.* humor *m.*
temperature, *s.* temperatura *f.*
tempest, *s.* tempestad *f.*
temporary, *adj.* provisorio.
tempt, *v. a.* tentar.
temptation, *s.* tentación *f.*
ten, *adj.* & *s.* diez *(m.).*
tenant, *s.* inquilino *m.*
tendency, *s.* tendencia *f.*
tender, *adj.* tierno; delicado.
tennis, *s.* tenis *m.*
tense, *adj.* tenso, nervioso; — *s.* tiempo *m.* *(verb).*
tension, *s.* tensión *f.*
tent, *s.* tienda (de campaña).
tenth, *adj.* décimo.
term, *s.* período *m.*, semestre *m.; (name)* nombre *m.; ~s* condiciones *f. pl.; come to ~s* llegar a un arreglo; *be on good ~s* estar en buenas relaciones.
terminate, *v. a.* & *n.* terminar.
terminus, *s.* estación *(f.)* terminal.
terrace, *s.* terraza *f.*
terrible, *adj.* terrible.
territory, *s.* territorio *m.*
test, *s.* examen *m.*, prueba *f.*; – *v. a.* examinar, analizar, probar.
testify, *v. a.* testificar, declarar.
testimony, *s.* testimonio *m.*
text, *s.* texto *m.*
text-book, *s.* libro *(m.)* de texto.
than, *conj.* que.
thank, *v. n.* dar las gracias; *~ you* gracias; – *s. ~s* gracias *f. pl.*
thankful, *adj.* agradecido.
that,[1] *adj.* & *pron.* ese, aquel; *~ is to say* es decir; *~'s all* eso es todo.
that,[2] *conj.* que.
thaw, *s.* deshielo *m.;* – *v. n.* deshelarse.
the, el, la; los, las.
theatre, *s.* teatro *m.*
their, *pron.* su, sus, de ellos *(m.),* de ellas *(f.).*
theirs, *pron.* de ellos *(m.),* de ellas *(f.).*
them, *pron.* ellos, les, los *(m.);* ellas, las *(f.).*
theme, *s.* tema *m.*
themselves, *pron.* se; ellos mismos *(m.);* ellas mismas *(f.).*
then, *adv.* entonces, luego, después.
thence, *adv.* de allí; por eso.
theology, *s.* teología *f.*
theory, *s.* teoría *f.*
there, *adv.* allí; *~ is, ~ are* hay.
thereby, *adv.* ahí, de este modo.
therefore, *conj.* por lo tanto, por eso.
thermometer, *s.* termómetro *m.*
thermo-nuclear, *adj.* termonuclear.
thermos, *s.* termos *m.*
these, *adj.* & *pron.* estos *(m.),* estas *(f.).*
they, *pron.* ellos *(m.),* ellas *(f.).*
thick, *adj.* grueso; *(soup)* espeso.
thief, *s.* ladrón *m.*

thigh, *s.* muslo *m.*
thimble, *s.* dedal *m.*
thin, *adj.* delgado, flaco; *(soup)* claro.
thing, *s.* cosa *f.*
think, *v. a.* & *n.* pensar, creer; *I* ~ *so* creo que sí; ~ *about* pensar en; ~ *out* inventar.
third, *adj.* tercero.
thirst, *s.* sed *f.*
thirsty, *adj. be* ~ tener sed.
thirteen, *adj.* & *s.* trece.
thirty, *adj.* & *s.* treinta.
this, *adj.* & *pron.* esto; éste; ésta; ~ *far* hasta aquí; ~ *much* tanto.
thorn, *s.* espina *f.*
thorough, *adj.* completo, cuidadoso.
thoroughfare, *s.* paso *m.*; *no* ~ prohibido el paso.
those, *adj.* & *pron.* esos, aquellos *(m.)*; esas, aquellas *(f.)*.
though, *conj.* aunque; *as* ~ como si.
thought, *s.* pensamiento *m.*; consideración *f.*
thoughtless, *adj.* imprudente, desatento.
thousand, *adj.* mil.
thrash, *v. a.* trillar.
thread, *a.* hilo *m.*; *(of screw)* rosca *f.*; *v. a.* enhebrar.
threat, *s.* amenaza *f.*
threaten, *v. a.* amenazar.
three, *adj.* & *s.* tre *(m.)*.
threshold, *s.* umbral *m.*
throat, *s.* garganta *f.*
throne, *s.* trono *m.*
throng, *s.* muchedumbre *f.*, — *v. n.* apiñarse.
through, *prep.* & *adv.* por; a través de; — *adj.* directo; ~ *train* tren *(m.)* directo.
throughout, *prep.* & *adv.* durante todo; ~ *the world* en el mundo entero.
throw, *s.* tiro *m.*, tirada *f.*; — *v. a.* tirar; ~ *away* tirar; ~ *up* renunciar.
thrust, *s.* empuje *m.*; — *v. a.* empujar.
thumb, *s.* pulgar *m.*
thunder, *s.* trueno *m.*; — *v. n.* tronar.
Thursday, *s.* jueves *m.*
thus, *adv.* así, de este modo.
ticket, *s.* billete *m.*
tide, *s.* marea *f.*; *high* ~ pleamar *f.*, marea alta; *low* ~ bajamar *f.*, marea baja.
tie, *s.* corbata *f.*; *(bond)* lazo *m.*; — *v. a.* atar, amarrar; ~ *(score)* empatar.
tiger, *s.* tigre *m.*
tight, *adj.* estrecho, apretado; *(drunk)* borracho.
till,[1] *prep.* hasta; — *conj.* hasta que.
till,[2] *v. a.* cultivar, labrar.
timber, *s.* tronco *m.*, madera *(f.)* de construcción.
time, *s.* tiempo *m.*; *what's the* ~? ¿qué hora es?; *(period)* época *f.*
timetable, *s.* guía *(f.)* de ferrocarriles; horario *m.*
timid, *adj.* tímido.
tin, *s.* lata *f.*, estaño *m.*, bote *m.*
tin-opener, *s.* abrelatas *m.*
tint, *s.* matiz *m.*, tono *m.*; — *v. a.* teñir.
tiny, *adj.* chiquito, menudo.
tip,[1] *s.* punta *f.*; extremo

m.; — *v. a.* ~ *up* volcar; *v n.* volcarse.

tip,[2] *s.* propina *f.*; — *v. a.* dar propina.

tire,[1] *v. a.* cansar; aburrir.

tire,[2] *s.* llanta *f.*, cubierta *f.*, neumático *m.*

tired, *adj.* cansado; *I'm* ~ estoy cansado.

tiresome, *adj.* pesado, aburrido.

tissue, *s.* tejido *m.*; gasa *f.*; *toilet* ~ papel *(m.)* higiénico.

title, *s.* título *m.*; — *v. a.* titular.

to, *prep.* a; *go* ~ *town* ir a la ciudad; *what do you say* ~ *this?* ¿qué dice de esto?; *I've come* ~ *see you* he venido para verle; *it's five minutes to six* son las seis menos cinco.

toast, *s.* *(bread)* tostada *f.*; *(drink)* brindis *m.*

tobacco, *s.* tabaco *m.*

tobacconist, *s.* tabaquero *m.*

today, *adv.* hoy.

toe, *s.* dedo *(m.)* del pie.

together, *adv.* juntos; *gather* ~ reunir(se).

toilet, *s.* tocado *m.*; *(table)* tocador *m*; *(W. C.)* excusado *m.*, retrete *m.*

tomato, *s.* tomate *m.*

tomb, *s.* tumba *f.*

tomorrow, *adv.* mañana *f.*; ~ *morning* mañana por la mañana.

ton, *s.* tonelada *f.*

tone, *s.* sonido *m.*, tono *m.*; — *v. a.* entonar.

tongs, *s. pl.* tenazas *f. pl.*

tongue, *s.* lengua *f.*

tonight, *adv.* esta noche.

tonnage, *s.* tonelaje *m.*

tonsil, *s.* amígdala *f.*

too, *adv.* demasiado; ~ *bad!* ¡qué lástima!; *(also)* también.

tool, *s.* herramienta *f.*; instrumento *m.*

tooth, *s.* diente *m.*; *(molar)* muela *f.*

toothache, *s.* dolor *(m.)* de muelas.

toothbrush, *s.* cepillo *(m.)* de dientes.

toothpaste, *s.* pasta *(f.)* dentífrica.

toothpick, *s.* mondadientes *m.*

top, *s.* cima *f.*, cumbre *f.*; *on* ~ *of* encima de; — *adj.* máximo; último; *at* ~ *speed* a la velocidad máxima; ~ *floor* último piso *m.*

torch, *s.* antorcha *f.*, lámpara *f.*, linterna *f.*

torment, *s.* tormento *m.*; — *v. a.* atormentar.

torrent, *s.* torrente *m.*

tortoise, *s.* tortuga *f.*

total, *adj.* & *s.* total *(m.)*; — *v. a.* sumar, hacer la suma.

touch, *s.* tacto *m.*; contacto *m.*; *a* ~ *of salt* una pizca de sal; — *v. a.* tocar; *fig.* afectar; *(affect)* conmover.

tough, *adj.* duro; ~ *luck* mala suerte *f.*

tour, *s.* jira *f.*; — *v. n.* viajar, hacer una jira.

tourism, *s.* turismo *m.*

tourist, *s.* turista *m.*, *f.*

tow, *s.* barcaza *f.*, remolque *m.*; — *v. a.* remolcar.

toward(s), *prep.* hacia.

towel. *s.* toalla *f.*

tower, *s.* torre *f.*

town. *s.* ciudad *f.*

town hall, *s.* municipalidad *f.*, ayuntamiento *m.*
toy, *s.* juguete *m.*
trace, *s.* huella *f.*, rastro *m.*; señal *f.*; – *v. a.* marcar, señalar.
track, *s.* pista *f.*
tractor, *s.* tractor *m.*
trade, *s.* comercio *m.*; oficio *m.*; – *v. a.* & *n.* comerciar.
trade-mark, *s.* marca *(f.)* de fábrica.
tradesman, *s.* comerciante *m.*, negociante *m.*
trade(s)-union, *s.* sindicato *m.*
tradition, *s.* tradición *f.*
traditional, *adj.* tradicional.
traffic, *s.* tráfico *m.*; ~ *lights* señales *f pl.*, luz *(f.)* de tráfico.
tragedy, *s.* tragedia *f.*
trail, *s.* sendero *m.*, huella *f.*
train, *s.* tren *m.*; *go by* ~ ir en tren; – *v. a.* enseñar, entrenar; *v. n.* entrenarse.
trainer, *s.* entrenador *m.*
tram, *s.* tranvía *m.*
transact, *v. a.* ~ *business* hacer un negocio.
transatlantic, *adj.* transatlántico.
transfer, *s.* traslado *m*, traspaso *m.*; ~ *ticket* billete *(m.)* de trasbordo; – *v. a.* trasladar, transferir.
transform, *v. a.* transformar.
transfusion, *s.*, transfusión *f.*
transistor, *adj.* & *s.* transistor *(m.)*.
transit, *s.* tránsito *m.*; ~ *visa* visado *(m.)* de tránsito.
translate, *v. a.* traducir.
translation, *s.* traducción *f.*, versión *f.*
translator, *s.* traductor *m.*
transmission, *s.* transmisión *f.*
transmit, *v. a.* transmitir.
transmitter, *s.* transmisor *m.*
transparent, *adj.* tra(n)sparente.
transport, *s.* transporte *m.*; —*v. a.* transportar.
travel, *s.* viaje *m.*; — *v. n.* viajar.
traveller, *s.* viajero *m.*
traverse, *s.* traversa *f.*; – *v. a.* atravesar, cruzar.
tray, *s.* bandeja *f.*
treacherous, *adj.* traicionero.
tread, *v. a.* & *n.* pisar.
treason, *s.* traición *f.*
treasure, *s.* tesoro *m.*
treasury, *s.* tesorería *f.*
treat, *s.* placer *m.*; *(of guests)* convidada *f.*; – *v. a.* tratar; *(guests)* convidar.
treaty, *s.* tratado *m.*, pacto *m.*
tree, *s.* árbol *m.*
tremendous, *adj.* tremendo, formidable.
trench, *s.* trinchera *f.*
trespass, *s.* traspaso *m.*; — *v. a.* traspasar; *no ~ing!* ¡prohibido el paso!
trial, *s.* prueba *f.*; *(law)* proceso *m.*, juicio *m.*; *(affliction)* mortificación *f.*
triangle, *s.* triángulo *m.*
tribe, *s.* tribu *f.*, raza *f.*
tribute, *s.* tributo *m.*
trick, *s.* maña *f.*; *(card)* baza *f*; – *v. a.* engañar.
trifle, *s.* bagatela *f.*;

— *v. n.* jugar con.
trim, *v. a.* igualar; *(hair)* cortar un poco.
trip, *s.* viaje *m.*; — *v. n.* brincar; *(stumble)* tropezar.
triple, *adj.* triple; — *v. a.* triplicar.
triumph, *s.* triunfo *m.*; — *v. n.* triunfar.
trivial, *adj.* trivial.
trolley, *s.* carreta *f.*; *tea* ~ carrito *(m.)* de servicio.
trolley-bus, *s.* trolebús *m.*
troop, *s.* tropa *f.*; —*v. n.* apiñarse.
trophy, *s.* trofeo *m.*
tropic(al), *adj.* tropical.
tropics, *s. pl.* trópicos *m. pl.*
trot, *s.* trote *m.*; — *v. n.* trotar.
trouble, *s.* apuro *m.*, dificultad *f.*; *get into* ~ meterse en un lío; *what's the* ~? ¿qué le pasa?; — *v. a.* molestar, incomodar.
troublesome, *adj.* molesto.
trousers, *s. pl.* pantalones *m. pl.*
trout, *s.* trucha *f.*
truck, *s.* carreta *f.*; vagón *(m.)* de mercancías; camión *m.*
true, *adj.* verdadero; leal; *(story)* verídico.
truly, *adv.* sinceramente, de verdad; *Yours very* ~ Suyo affmo. (afectísimo).
trumpet, *s.* trompeta *f.*
trunk, *s.* tronco *m.*; *(bag)* baúl *m.*
trunk-call, *s.* conferencia *(f.)* interurbana.
trust, *s.* confianza *f.*; *hold in* ~ guardar en depósito; *(company)* trust *m.*; — *v. a.* & *n.* tener confianza en; confiar; dar crédito.
trustee, *s.* síndico *m.*
truth, *s.* verdad *f.*
try, *s.* intento *m.*; — *v. a.* probar, tratar de; *(case)* juzgar; ~ *on* probarse; ~ *out* hacer una prueba.
tub, *s.* *(bathtub)* baño *m.*; *(washtub)* tina *f.*
tube, *s.* tubo *m.*
Tuesday, *s.* martes *m.*
tug-boat, *s.* remolcador *m.*
tuition, *s.* enseñanza *f.*, instrucción *f.*
tumble, *s.* tumbo *m.*, caída *f.*; — *v. n.* caer, derribar.
tumour, *s.* tumor *m.*
tune, *s.* melodía *f.*, tonada *f.*; *out of* ~ desafinado; — *v. a.* afinar; ~ *in* sintonizar.
tunnel, *s.* túnel *m.*
turbine, *s.* turbina *f.*
turbo-jet, ~ *engine* motor *(m.)* a turboreacción.
turbo-prop, *s.* avión *(m.)* a turbopropulsión, de turbohélices.
turf, *s.* césped *m.*; hipódromo *m.*
turkey, *s.* pavo *m.*
Turkish, *adj.* turco; ~ *towel* toalla *(f.)* de baño.
turn, *s.* vuelta *f.*; *(in line)* turno *m.*; *by* ~*s* por turno, alternativamente; — *v. a.* dar vuelta a; *(corner)* doblar; *(stomach)* revolver; *(ankle)* torcer; *v. n.* volverse; ~ *away* rechazar; ~ *in* entrar; ~ *into* cambiar por; ~ *off (gas,*

water) cerrar la llave de; *(light)* apagar; ~ *on* abrir; *(light)* encender; ~ *out* echar; ~ *to* recurrir a.
turning, *s.* bocacalle, *f.*; ángulo *m.*
turnip, *s.* nabo *m.*
tutor, *s.* instructor *m.*, preceptor *m.*; – *v. a.* instruir.
twelfth, *adj.* duodécimo.
twelve, *adj.* & *s.* doce.
twenty, *adj.* & *s.* veinte.
twice, *adv.* dos veces.
twig, *s.* ramita *f.*
twilight, *s.* crepúsculo *m.*
twin, *s.* gemelo *m.*, mellizo *m.*; ~ *beds* camas *(f. pl.)* gemelas.
twist *v. a.* torcer.
twitter, *s.* gorjeo *m.*; – *v. n.* gorjear.
two, *adj.* & *s.* dos *(m.)*.
two-seater, *adj.* de dos asientos.
type, *s.* tipo *m.*; clase *f.*, estilo *m.*; *(letter)* tipo *(m.)* de letra; – *v. a.* escribir a máquina.
type-script, *s.* escrito *(m.)* mecanografiado.
typewriter, *s.* máquina *(f.)* de escribir.
typist, *s.* mecanógrafo *m.*, mecanógrafa *f.*
tyre, *s.* llanta *f.*, cubierta *f.*, neumático *m.*
tyranny, *s.* tiranía *f.*

U

ugly, *adj.* feo.
ultraviolet, *adj.* ultravioleta.
umbrella, *s.* paraguas *m.*
unable, *adj.* incapaz.
unaccustomed, *adj.* desacostumbrado.
unanimous, *adj.* unánime.
unauthorized, *adj.* desautorizado, sin autorización.
unaware, *adj.* no enterado; *be* ~ *of* ignorar.
unbearable, *adj.* insoportable.
uncertain, *adj.* incierto, inseguro.
unchangeable, *adj.* inalterable, irrevocable.
uncle, *s.* tío *m.*
uncomfortable, *adj.* incómodo, molesto.
uncommon, *adj.* insólito, desacostumbrado.
unconscious, *adj.* inconsciente, sin conocimiento.
uncover, *v. a.* descubrir.
undamaged, *adj.* intacto, entero, sano y salvo.
undecided, *adj.* indeciso; pendiente.
undeniable, *adj.* innegable, indiscutible.
under, *prep.* bajo, debajo de.
underclothes, *s.* ropa *(f.)* interior.
underdeveloped, *adj.* subdesarrollado, atrasado.
underdone, *adj.* un poco crudo.
undergo, *v. a.* sufrir, padecer, experimentar.
undergraduate, *s.* estudiante *(m.)* universitario no licenciado.
underground, *adj.* subterráneo; – *s.* metro *m.*, metropolitano *m.*; *(illegality)* ilegalidad *f.*
underline, *v. a.* subrayar.
understand, *v. a.* comprender, entender; *make oneself understood* ha-

cerse entender.
undertake, *v. a.* emprender.
underwear, *s.* ropa *(f.)* interior.
undisturbed, *adj.* imperturbado.
undo, *v. a.* desatar, deshacer.
undress, *v. n.* desnudarse; *v. a.* desnudar.
uneasy, *adj.* inquieto, molesto.
uneducated, *adj.* ineducado.
unemployed, *adj.* desocupado, sin trabajo.
unemployment, *s.* falta *(f.)* de trabajo.
unequal, *adj.* desigual.
uneven, *adj.* impar; *(surface)* escabroso, accidentado.
unexpected, *adj.* inesperado.
unfair, *adj.* incorrecto.
unfavorable, *adj.* desfavorable.
unfinished, *adj.* inacabado, sin terminar.
unfortunate, *adj.* desafortunado, infeliz, desgraciado.
unhappy, *adj.* infeliz, desdichado.
unhealthy, *adj.* malsano, insalubre; *(look)* enfermizo.
uniform, *adj.* & *s.* uniforme *(m.)*.
union, *s.* unión *f.*; *(trade-)* sindicato *m.*
unique, *adj.* único *m.*
unit, *s.* unidad *f.*
unite, *v. a.* unir; *v. n.* unirse.
unity, *s.* unidad *f.*
universal, *adj.* universal.
universe, *s.* universo *m.*
unjust, *adj.* injusto.
unkind, *adj.* poco amable, duro.
unknown, *adj.* desconocido.
unless, *conj.* a menos que, a no ser que.
unlike, *adj.* diferente, distinto.
unload, *v. a.* descargar.
unlock, *v. a.* abrir, abrir con llave.
unmarried, *adj.* & *s.* soltero *(m.)*, soltera *(f.)*.
unnecessary, *adj.* innecesario.
unoccupied, *adj.* libre, desocupado.
unpack, *v. a.* & *n.* desempaquetar; deshacer las maletas.
unpaid, *adj.* impagado, no pagado.
unpleasant, *adj.* desagradable.
unpopular, *adj.* impopular.
unprecedented, *adj.* inaudito, sin precedente.
unprejudiced, *adj.* imparcial, sin prejuicios.
unprepared, *adj.* sin preparación, improvisado, improviso.
unqualified, *adj.* sin calificación; absoluto.
unreasonable, *adj.* irrazonable.
unselfish, *adj.* desinteresado.
unsettled, *adj.* indeciso, pendiente; ~ *account* cuenta *(f.)* sin saldar.
unsolved, *adj.* no resuelto.
unsteady, *adj.* inconstante.
unsuccessful, *adj.* vano, infructuoso, sin resultado.
untidy, *adj.* desordenado, mal cuidado.
until, *prep.* hasta; — *conj.* hasta que.
unusual, *adj.* raro, extra-

ordinario.
unwell, *adv.* no bien. mal; enfermo; *be ~* sentirse mal.
unwilling, *adj.* & *adv.* de mala gana, de mala voluntad.
unworthy, *adj.* indigno.
up, *adv.* arriba; *be ~* estar levantado.
uphill, *adv.* cuesta arriba.
upholsterer, *s.* tapicero *m.*
upon, *see* **on**; *~ my word!* ¡palabra!
upper, *adj.* superior, de arriba; *the Upper House* la Cámara Alta, el senado.
upright, *adj.* erecto, recto; *(honest)* honrado.
upset, *v. a.* *(person)* perturbar, contrariar, trastornar; *(thing)* volcar; desarreglar.
upside down, *adv.* patas arriba; revuelto, en desorden.
upstairs, *adv.* arriba.
up-to-date, *adj.* moderno, al día, de ultima moda.
urge, *v. a.* instar; — *s.* impulso *m.*, deseo *m.*
urgent, *adj.* urgente.
us, *pron.* nos; *of ~* de nosotros; *let ~ go!* ¡vámonos!
use, *s.* uso *m.*; *be of no ~* ser inútil, no servir para nada; *make ~ of* aprovechar; *what's the ~ of arguing?* ¿para qué sirve discutir?; — *v. a.* usar; *be ~d to* acostumbrar; *~ up* gastar.
useful, *adj.* útil.
useless, *adj.* inútil.
usher, *s.* acomodador *m.*; *(judiciary)* ujier *m.*; — *v. a.* introducir; anunciar.
usual *adj.* usual, acostumbrado.
usually, *adv.* usualmente, por lo común.
utensil, *s.* utensilio *m.*
utility, *s.* utilidad *f.*
utilize, *v. a.* utilizar.
utmost, *adj* sumo; *do one's ~* hacer lo más que pueda; *to the ~* a más no poder.
utter,[1] *adj.* completo.
utter,[2] *v. a.* proferir, declarar.
utterly, *adv.* completamente.

V

vacancy, *s.* vacante *f.*
vacant, *adj.* vacante, desocupado, vacío, libre.
vaccination, *s.* vacuna *f.*
vacuum-cleaner, *s.* aspirador *m.*
vain, *adj,* vano; *in ~* en vano, en balde.
valid, *adj.* válido, valedero.
validity, *s.* validez *f.*
valley, *s.* valle *m.*
valuable, *adj.* valioso; — *s.* *~s* objetos *(m.)* de valor.
value, *s.* valor *m.*; — *v. a.* valuar; *fig.* estimar, apreciar.
valve, *s.* válvula *f.*
van, *s.* vagón *(m.)* de mercancías; camion *m.*
vanity, *s.* vanidad *f.*
vapour, *s.* vapor *m.*
various, *adj.* varios *pl.*, diversos *pl.*
varnish, *s.* barniz *m.*; — *v. a.* barnizar.
vary, *v. a.* & *n.* variar, cambiar.
vase, *s.* florero *m.*
vast, *adj.* vasto.

vault, *s.* bóveda *f.*
veal, *s.* carne *(f.)* de ternera.
vegetable, *adv.* vegetal; — *s.* legumbre *f.*, verdura *f.*, hortaliza *f.*
vehicle, s. vehículo *m.*
veil, *s.* velo *m.*; — *v. a.* velar.
vein, *s.* vena *f.*
velvet, *s.* terciopelo *m.*
vengeance, *s.* venganza *f.*
venison, *s.* venado *m.*
ventilation, *s.* ventilación *f.*
ventilator, *s.* ventilador *m.*
verb, *s.* verbo *m.*
verdict, *s.* veredicto *m.*, fallo *m.*, sentencia *f.*; opinión *f.*
verge, *s.* borde *m.*
verify, *v. a.* verificar, comprobar.
vermicelli, *s.* tallarines *m. pl.*, fideos *m. pl.*
verse, *s.* verso *m.*
vertical, *adj.* vertical.
very, *adv.* muy; — *adv.* mismo; *the ~ day* el mismo día.
vessel, *s.* *(container)* vasija *f.*; *(ship)* barco *m.*
vest, *s.* camiseta *f.*
vestry, *s.* sacristía *f.*
veteran, veterano *m.*
vex, *v. a.* irritar, molestar.
via, *adv.* & *prep.* por, por la vía de.
vibrate, *v. a.* & *n.* vibrar.
vice, *s.* vicio *m.*
vice-president, *s.* vicepresidente *m.*
vicinity, *s.* vecindad *f.*
victim, *s.* víctima *f.*
victorious, *adj.* victorioso.
victory, *s.* victoria *f.*
victuals, *s. pl.* comestibles *m. pl.*, víveres *m. pl.*
view, *s.* vista; opinión *f.*
vigorous, *adj.* vigoroso.
vigour, *s.* vigor *m.*
vile, *adj.* bajo, vil.
village, *s.* aldea *f.*, pueblo *m.*
villain, *s.* malvado *m.*
vine, *s.* vid *f.*, parra *f.*
vinegar, *s.* vinagre *m.*
vineyard, *s.* viña *f.*, viñedo *m.*
vintage, *s.* vendimia *f.*
violate, *v. a.* violar.
violent, *adj.* violento.
violet, *s.* violeta *f.*
violin, *s.* violín *m.*
violinist, *s.* violinista *m.*, *f.*
violoncello, *s.* violoncelo *m.*
virgin, *adj.* & *s.* virgen *(f.)*
virtue, *s.* virtud *f.*
virtuous, *adj.* virtuoso.
visible, *adj.* visible.
visibility, *s.* visibilidad *f.*
vision, *s.* visión *f.*
visit, *s.* visita *f.*; — *v. a.* visitar.
visitor, *s.* visitante *m.*, *f.*
vitamin, *s.* vitamina *f.*
vivid, *adj.* vivo, brillante.
vocabulary, *s.* vocabulario *m.*
vocation, *s.* ocupación *f.*, profesión *f.*, oficio *m.*
voice, *s.* voz *f.*
void, *adj.* nulo, sin efecto; *be ~ of sg* faltar; — *s.* *(emptiness)* vacío *m.*; — *v. a.* anular.
volcano, *s.* volcán *m.*
volume, *s.* volumen *m.*
voluntary, *adj.* ;voluntario.
volunteer, *s.* voluntario *m.*; — *v. n.* ofrecerse a hacer algo.
vomit, *v. a.* & *n.* vomitar.
vote, *s.* voto *m.*; votación

f.; — *v. n.* votar.

voter, *s.* votante *m., f.,* votador *m.*

voucher, *s.* recibo *m.*

vow, *s.* voto *m.*, promesa *f.*; — *v. n.* hacer voto.

voyage, *s.* viaje *(m.)* por mar.

vulgar, *adj.* vulgar, ordinario, soez; *(joke)* verde.

W

wage, *s.* sueldo *m.*, salario *m.*; *daily* ~ jornal *m.*; *living* ~ mínimo *(m.)* vital.

wag(g)on, *s.* carro *(m.)* de cuatro ruedas; vagón *m.*

waist, *s.* cintura *f.*

waistcoat, *s.* chaleco *m.*

wait, *v. n.* esperar; ~ *on sy* atender a.

waiter, *s.* camarero *m.*, mozo *m.*

waiting-room, *s.* sala *(f.)* de espera.

wake,[1] *v. a.* despertar; *v. n.* despertarse.

wake,[2] *s.* estela *f.*

walk, *s* paseo *m.*; *take a* ~ dar un paseo; *(way)* camino *m.*; *(gait)* modo *(m.)* de andar; — *v. n.* caminar, andar, ir a pie.

walkie-talkie, *s.* radiorreceptor *(m.)* portátil.

walking-tour, *s.* excursión *(f.)* a pie; caminata *f.*

wall, *s.* pared *f.*; tapia *f.*; muralla *f.*

wallet, *s.* cartera *f.*

wall-paper, *s.* papel *(m.)* pintado.

wall-socket, *s.* enchufe *m.*

walnut, *s.* *(nut)* nuez *f.*; *(tree)* nogal *m.*

waltz, *s.* vals *m.*

wander, *v. n.* vagar, extraviarse.

want, *s.* necesidad *f.*; *for* ~ *of sg* a falta de; — *v. a.* querer.

war, *s.* guerra *f.*

ward, *s.* tutela *f.*; *(hospital)* sala *f.*; — *v. a.* defender, parar.

wardrobe, *s.* armario *m.*; *(clothes)* ropero *m.*, guardarropa *m.*

ware, *s.* mercancía *f.*

warehouse, *s.* almacén *m.*, depósito *m.*

warm, *adj.* caliente; cálido; *(greetings)* caluroso, afectuoso, cariñoso; *it's* ~ hace calor; *I'm* ~ tengo calor; *s.* calor *m.*; — *v. a.* ~ *up* calentar; *v. n.* calentarse.

warn, *v. a.* advertir, avisar.

warning, *s.* advertencia *f.*, aviso *m.*

warrant, *s.* autorización *f.*; — *a.* garantizar.

warrior, *s.* combatiente *m.*, soldado *m.*, guerrero *m.*

wash, *v. a.* lavar; *v. n.* lavarse; — *s.* lavado *m.*, lavadura *f.*; ropa *(f.)* lavada.

wash-basin, *s.* jofaina *f.*, palangana *f.*, lavamanos *m.*

washing-machine, *s.* lavaropas *m.*, máquina *(f.)* de lavar; lavadora *f.*

washing-up, *s.* fregado *m.*

wash-stand, *s.* lavabo *m.*

was , *s.* avispa *f.*

waste, *s.* desperdicio *m.*, desechos *m. pl.*; —*v. a.* perder.
watch, *v. a.* observar; ~ *your step!* ¡tenga cuidado!; *v. n.* tener cuidado, velar; — *s.* servicio *m.*, guardia *f.*; *(clock)* reloj *m.*; *my* ~ *is fast* tengo el reloj adelantado.
watch-maker, *s.* relojero *m.*
watchman, *s.* vigilante *m.*, sereno *m.*
water, *s.* agua *f.*; *by* ~ por barco; — *v. a.* *(flowers)* regar; *(horses)* dar de beber; *(wine)* aguar.
watercolour, *s.* acuarela *f.*
waterfall, *s.* ascada *f.*, catarata *f.*
watering-place, *s.* estación *(f.)* balnearia.
waterproof, *adj.* & *s.* impermeable *(m.)*.
wave, *s.* ola *f.*, onda *f.*; ~ *length* longitud *(f.)* de onda; — *v. a.* & *n.* ondear; *(hand)* agitar las manos, hacer señas.
wax, *s.* cera *f.*
way, *s.* camino *m.*; *fig.* modo *m.*, manera *f.*; *a long* ~ muy lejos; *by the* ~ a propósito.
we, *pron.* nosotros *m.*, nosotras *f.*
weak, *adj.* débil.
weaken, *v. a.* debilitar, extenuar; — *v. n.* debilitarse.
weakness, *s.* debilidad *f.*
wealth, *s.* riqueza *f.*
wealthy, *adj.* rico.
weapon, *s.* arma *f.*
wear, *s.* ropa *f.*, trajes *m. pl.*; — *v. a.* llevar, usar; *(last)* durar.
weather, *s.* tiempo *m.*
weather-forecast, *s.* pronóstico *(m.)* del tiempo.
weave, *v. a.* tejer.
weaver, *s.* tejedor *m.*
web, *s.* *(cloth)* tela *f.*; *(spider)* tela de araña.
wedding, *s.* matrimonio *m.*, boda *f.*
wedding-ring, *s.* anillo *(m.)* de boda.
Wednesday, *s.* miércoles *m.*
weed, *s.* maleza *f.*, mala hierba *f.*; — *v. a.* escardar, desherbar.
week, *s.* semana *f.*
week-day, *s.* día *(m.)* de semana, día laborable.
weekly, *adj.* semanal; — *s.* revista *(f.)* semanal.
weep, *v. n.* llorar.
weigh, *v. a.* & *n.* pesar; ~ *anchor* llevar anclas.
weight, *s.* peso *m.*; *fig.* importancia *f.*
welcome, *adj.* & *int.* ~*!* ¡bienvenido!
welfare, *s.* bienestar *m.*
well, *adv.* bien; *very* ~*!* ¡muy bien!
wellbeing, *s.* bienestar *m.*
wellbred, *adj.* bien educado.
well-informed, *adj.* bien informado.
well-to-do, *adj.* acomodado, adinerado.
west, *s.* oeste *m.*, poniente *m.*; — *adj.* occidental.
western, *adj.* occidental, oeste.
wet, *adj.* mojado; *(paint)* fresco; *get* ~ mojarse; *v. a.* mojar.
whale, *s.* ballena *f.*

wharf, *s.* muelle *m.*
what, *pron* qué; ~ *time is it?* ¿qué hora es?; ~*'s the news?* ¿qué hay de nuevo?; ~ *for?* ¿por qué?; — *int.* ~! ¡cómo!
whatever, *pron. do ~ you want* haga usted lo que quiera; *he has no money ~* no tiene ningún dinero.
wheat, *s.* trigo *m.*
wheel, *s.* rueda *f.*; — *v. a.* conducir, llevar.
when, *adv.* cuando; ~? ¿cuándo?
whence, *adv.* de donde; ~? ¿de dónde?
whenever, *conj.* siempre que.
where, *adv.* donde, por donde; ~? ¿dónde?
wherefore, *adv.* por esto; ~? ¿por qué?
wherein, *adv.* en que; ~? ¿en qué?
wherever, *adv.* dondequiera que.
whether, *conj.* si.
which, *pron.* que, el cual; ~? ¿cuál?; ~ *book?* ¿qué libro?; ~ *way?* ¿por dónde?
whichever, *pron.* cualquiera.
while, *conj.* mientras que; — *s.* rato *m.*
whirlwind, *s.* torbellino *m.*, remolino *m.*
whisper, *v. a.* cuchichear.
whistle, *s.* silbido *m.*; pito *m*; — *v. n.* silbar.
white, *adj.* blanco.
Whitsun, *s.* Pentecostés *m.*
who, *pron.* quien, que; ~? ¿quién?
whoever, *pron.* quienquiera.
whole, *adj.* todo, entero; ~ *lot* gran cantidad *f.*; — *s.* totalidad *f.*; *on the ~* en general.
wholesale, *adj.* & *adv.* al por mayor.
wholesome, *adj.* sano, saludable.
wholly, *adv.* enteramente.
whom, *pron.* a quien; ~? ¿a quién?
whose, *pron.* de quien, cuyo; ~? ¿de quién?
why, *adv.* & *conj.* ¿por qué?; — *int.* ~! ¡cómo!
wicked, *adj.* malo, malvado.
wide, *adj.* ancho.
widow, *s.* viuda *f.*
widower, *s.* viudo *m.*
wife, *s.* mujer *f.*, esposa *f.*, señora *f.*
wig, *s.* peluca *f.*
wild, *adj.* salvaje; *(flower)* silvestre; *fig.* bárbaro.
wilful, *adj.* premeditado.
will, *s.* voluntad *f.*; *(testament)* testamento *m.*; *at ~* a voluntad; — *v. n.* querer; *he ~ come today* vendrá hoy.
willing, *adj. be ~* estar dispuesto.
willingly, *adv.* con placer; voluntariamente.
willow, *s.* sauce *m.*
win, *v. a.* ganar; vencer.
wind,[1] viento *m.*
wind,[2] *v. n. (road)* torcer; ~ *oneself* enroscarse; *v. a. (watch)* dar cuerda a.
windmill, *s.* molino *(m.)* de viento.
window, *s.* ventana *f.*, ventanilla *f.*
windscreen, *s.* parabrisas

m.
windy, *adj.* ventoso.
wine, *s.* vino *m*
wing, *s.* ala *f.*; *(theatre)* bastidor *m.*; *(football)* exterior *m.*, ala *f.*; — *v. n.* volar.
wink, *v. n.* guiñar; — *s.* guiño *m.*
winner, *s.* vencedor *m.*, ganador *m.*
winter, *s.* invierno *m.*
wipe, *v. a.* *(dry)* secar; *(clean)* limpiar.
wire, *s.* alambre *m.*; hilo *m.*; *(telegram)* telegrama *m.*; — *v. n.* telegráfiar.
wireless, *s.* telégrafo *(m.)* sin hilos; radio *f.*
wisdom, *s.* sabiduría *f.*; *(judgment)* juicio *m.*
wise, *adj.* sensato, juicioso; listo, sabio, serio.
wish, *s.* deseo *m.*, voto *m.*; — *v. a.* gustar, desear.
wit, *s.* agudeza *f.*, ingenio *m.*
with, *prep.* con; ~ *you* contigo; ~ *me* conmigo; ~ *him* con él.
withdraw, *v. a.* retirar; *v. n.* retirarse.
within, *prep.* dentro de.
without, *prep.* sin; — *adv.* por fuera.
withstand, *v. n.* resistir, aguantar.
witness, *s.* testigo *m.*
witty, *adj.* ingenioso, agudo.
wolf, *s.* lobo *m.*
woman, *s.* mujer *f.*; ~ *doctor* doctora *f.*
wonder, *s.* maravilla *f.*, admiración *f.*; — *v. n.* preguntarse; *I ~!* no lo sé; estoy curioso de saberlo.
wonderful, *adj.* maravilloso, estupendo.
wood, *s.* madera *f.*; *(forest)* bosque *m.*; *(fire)* leña *f.*
wooden, *adj.* de madera.
wool, *s.* lana *f.*
woollen, *adj.* de lana.
word, *s.* palabra *f.*; *(news)* noticia *f.*
work, *s.* trabajo *m.*; *(composition)* obra *f.*; *set to ~* poner manos a la obra; *~s* fábrica *f.*, planta *(f.)* industrial; *public ~s* servicios *(m. pl.)* públicos; — *v. n.* trabajar; *~ out* preparar; resolver.
worker, *s.* trabajador *m.*, obrero *m.*
workshop, *s.* taller *m.*
world, *s.* mundo *m.*; *all the ~ over* en el mundo entero.
worldly, *adj.* terrestre.
world-politics, *s.* política *(f.)* mundial.
world-war, *s.* guerra *(f.)* mundial.
worm, *s.* gusano *m.*, lombriz *f.*
worn, *adj.* *(tired)* agotado; *(used)* usado.
worry, *s.* preocupación *f.* — *v. n.* preocuparse; *don't ~!* ¡descuide usted!; *v. n.* molestar.
worse, *adj.* peor; *get ~* empeorar.
worst, *adj.* & *adv.* peor; *at ~* a lo peor.
worth, *s.* valor *m.*, mérito *m.*; — *adj.* *what is it ~?* ¿cuánto vale?; *it is ~ while* vale la pena.
worthless, *adj.* sin valor.
worthy, *adj.* digno.
wound, *s.* herida *f.*; — *v. a.* herir.

wounded, *adj.* & *s.* herido.
woven, *adj.* tejido, textil.
wrap, *v. a.* envolver.
wrapper, *s.* envoltura *f.*, embalaje *m.*, faja *f.*
wrath, *s.* cólera *f.*, ira *f.*
wreath, *s.* *(funeral)* corona *f.*; *(decoration)* guirnalda *f.*
wreck, *s.* destrucción *f.*, ruina *f.*; restos *(m. pl.)* de un naufragio; — *v. a.* destrozar.
wrench, *s.* llave *(f.)* para tuercas.
wrestle, *v. n.* luchar.
wrestler, *s.* luchador *m.*
wretched, *adj.* miserable, desdichado.
wring, *v. a.* retorcer.
wrinkle, *s.* arruga *f.*; — *v. a.* arrugar.
wrist, *s.* muñeca *f.*
write, *v. a.* escribir.
writer, *s.* escritor *m.*
writing-desk, *s.* escritorio *m.*
written, *adj.* escrito.
wrong, *adj.* equivocado, incorrecto; *be* ~ no tener razón, estar equivoçado; — *adv.* mal; — *v. a.* ofender, agraviar.

X

Xmas, *s.* Navidad *f.*
X-ray, *s.* *(ray)* rayo *(m.)* X; *(picture)* radiografía *f.*; — *v. a.* radiografiar.

Y

yacht, *s.* yate *m.*
yard *s.* yarda *(court-)* patio *m.*
year, *s.* año *m.*
yearly, *adj.* anual; — *adv.* anualmente, cada año.
yeast, *s.* levadura *f.*
yell, *s.* grito *m.*, alarido *m.*; — *v. n.* gritar, dar alaridos.
yellow, *adj.* amarillo; ~ *fever* fiebre *(f.)* amarilla.
yes, sí.
yesterday, *adv.* ayer.
yet, *adv.* todavía, aún, sin embargo; *as* ~ hasta ahora, todavía; *not* ~ todavía no, aún no.
yield, *v. a.* producir; ~ *to sy* rendirse.
yolk, *s.* yema *f.*
you, *pron.* usted; ustedes *pl.*; *let me help* ~ permítame que le ayude; *I love* ~ yo te quiero.
young, *adj.* joven; ~ *girl* chica *f.*, muchacha *f.*; ~ *lady* señorita *f.*; — *s.* cachorros *m. pl.*, crías *f. pl.*
youngster, *s.* mozo *m.*, muchacho *m.*
your, *pron.* su, sus; tu, tus; vuestro, vuestros.
yours, *pron.* el suyo, el de usted; el tuyo; el vuestro; *a friend of* ~ uno de sus amigos.
yourself, usted mismo, tú mismo.
youth, *s.* juventud *f.*; *(person)* joven *m.*, muchacho *m.*

Z

zeal, *s.* celo *m.*

zealous, *adj.* celoso.
zero, *s.* cero *m.*
zigzag, *s.* zigzag *m.*; — *v. n.* zigzaguear.
zinc, *s.* zinc *m.*
zipper, *s.* cremallera *f.*
zone, *s.* zona *f.*, región *f.*
zoo, *s.* jardín *(m.)* zoológico, zoo *m.*
zoology, *s.* zoología *f.*

SPANISH-ENGLISH DICTIONARY

A

a, *prep.* at, on, to; by; *a la mesa* at table; *a las diez* at ten o'clock; *a caballo* on horseback; *a pie* on foot; *poco a poco* little by little; *voy a la ciudad* I go to town; *voy a verle* I'll go to see him.
abad, *s. m.* abbot,
abajo, *adv.* below, down, downstairs.
abandonado, *adj.* negligent, untidy.
abandonar, *v. a.* abandon, leave.
abandono, *s. m.* abandonment.
abanico, *s. m.* fan.
abedul, *s. m.* birch(-tree).
abeja, *s. f.* bee.
abertura, *s. f.* opening, aperture.
abeto, *s. m.* fir(-tree).
abierto, *adj.* open.
abogado, *s. m.* lawyer, solicitor.
abolición, *s. f.* abolition.
abolir, *v. a.* abolish.
abominable, *adj.* abominable.
abominar *de, v. n.* abhor.
abonado, *s. m.* subscriber.
abonar, *v. a.* pay, settle; improve; fertilize; *v. n.* *~se a* subscribe.
abono, *s. m.* subscription; fertilizer; *(theatre)* seasonticket.
abordar, *v. n.* go aboard; reach port.
aborrecer, *v. a.* abhor.
abotonar. *v. a.* button.
abrazar, *v. a.* embrace, hug.
abrazo, *s. m.* embrace, hug.
abrelatas, *s. m.* tin-opener
abreviar, *v. a.* abbreviate.
abrigar, *v. a.* warm; shelter, protect; *v. n.* *~se* dress warmly.
abrigo, *s. m.* overcoat; shelter.
abril, *s. m.* April.
abrir, *v. a.* open, unlock.
absolutamente, *adv.* absolutely.
absoluto, *adj.* absolute; *en ~* (not) at all.
absorbente, *adj.* absorbent.
absorber, *v. a.* absorb.
abstenerse, *v. n.* abstain.
abstinencia, *s. f.* abstinence.
abstinente, *adj.* abstinent, teetotal.
abstracto, *adj.* abstract.
absurdo, *adj.* absurd; — *s. m.* absurdity.
abuela, *s. f.* grandmother.
abuelo, *s. m.* grandfather.
abuelos, *pl. m.* grandparents.
abundancia, *s. f.* abundance.
abundante, *adj.* abundant.
aburrido, *adj.* boring, dull, bored.
aburrir, *v. a.* bore, tire; *v. n.* *~se* be bored.
abusar *de, v. n.* abuse.
abuso, *s. m.* abuse.
acá, *adv.* here, this way; *por ~* around here.
acabado, *adj.* finished; exhausted, worn out.
acabar, *v. a.* finish, end, terminate; put an end to; *~ con* exhaust; *~ de* have just (done sg); *acabo de llegar* I've just arrived; *~ por* end by; *v. n.* *~se* run out.
academia, *s. f.* academy.

acaecer, *v. n.* happen.
acalorar, *v. a.* warm (up); incite; *v. n.* *~se* become heated or excited.
acampar, *v. n.* camp, be encamped; *~se* pitch camp.
acariciar, *v. a.* caress, pet.
acaso, *s. m.* coincidence, chance; — *adv.* perhaps, maybe.
acatarrarse, *v. n.* catch cold.
acaudalado, *adj.* well-to-do, well-off.
acceder *a*, *v. n.* assent, agree; fulfil, comply.
accesorio, *adj.* & *s. m.* accessory.
accidentado, *adj.* uneven.
accidental, *adj.* accidental.
accidente, *s. m.* accident, mishap, chance.
acción, *s. f.* action; plot (of a drama); share.
accionamiento, *s. m.* drive, propulsion.
accionista, *s. m.* shareholder.
acedía, *s. f.* gastric acid.
aceitar, *v. a.* oil, grease.
aceite, *s. m.* oil; *~ de hígado de bacalao* cod-liver oil; *~ mineral* crude oil.
aceleración, *s. f.* acceleration.
acelerado, *adj.* accelerated.
acelerador, *s. m.* accelerator.
acelerar, *v. a.* accelerate.
acento, *s.m.* stress, accent, pronunciation.
acentuar, *v. a.* accent.
aceptación, *s. f.* acceptance.
aceptar, *v. a.* accept.
acera, *s. f.* pavement.
acerca de, *prep.* concerning.
acercar, *v. a.* bring near; *v. n.* *~se a* approach.
acero, *s. m.* steel.
acertado, *adj.* skilful, clever.
acertar, *v. a.* guess right; *~ con* locate, find; *~ en* hit the mark.
acertijo, *s. m.* riddle.
ácido, *adj.* sour; — *s. m.* sourness, acid.
aclamación, *s. f.* acclamation, cheers.
aclamar, *v. a.* acclaim, applaud.
aclarar, *v. a.* make clear, clarify; *v. n.* brighten, clear up.
aclimatar, *v. n.* acclimatize.
acoger, *v. a.* lodge, receive.
acogida, *s. f.* reception.
acometer, *v. a.* attack.
acometida, *s. f.* attack.
acomodado, *adj.* well-to-do.
acomodador, *s. m.* usher.
acomodar, *v. a.* put, place; *v. n.* *~se* adapt oneself, make oneself comfortable.
acompañamiento, *s. m.* accompaniment.
acompañar, *v. a.* accompany, see off.
acondicionar, *v. a.* form, shape; prepare, dress (dish).
aconsejar, *v. a.* advise; *v. n.* *~se de* consult sy.
acontecer, *v. n.* happen, occur.
acontecimiento, *s. m.* event, ocurrence.
acorazado, *s. m.* battleship.
acordar, *v. a.* agree to, on; *v. n.* *~se de* remember, recollect.
acostar, *v. a.* put to bed;

lay; *v. n.* ~*se* go to bed.
acostumbrar, *v. a.* accustom, be accustomed; *v. n.* ~*se* get accustomed, get used.
acre, *adj.* acrid, pungent.
acrecer, *v. a.* augment.
acreditado, *adj.* accredited; reliable; of good reputation; solvent.
acreditar, *v. a.* accredit.
acreedor, *s. m.* creditor.
acróbata, *s. m.* acrobat.
acta, *s. f.* protocol, record; *levantar* ~ protocol, record.
actitud, *s. f.* attitude.
activar, *v. a.* promote; set in motion.
actividad, *s. f.* activity.
activo, *adj.* active; – *s. m.* assets.
acto, *s. m.* act; ceremony; *en el* ~ right away.
actor, *s. m.* actor; plaintiff.
actriz, *s. f.* actress.
actual, *adj.* present, current; real, true.
actualidad, *s. f.* present time; *en la* ~ at present.
actualmente, *adv.* at present.
actuar, *v. n.* act.
acuarela, *s. f.* watercolour.
acuario, *s. m.* aquarium.
acuático, *adj.* water-.
acudir, *v. n.* rush; ~ *a la cita* keep an appointment.
acueducto, *s. m.* waterconduit.
acuerdo, *s. m.* agreement; *estar de* ~ be of the same opinion; *de* ~ *con* in accordance with.
acumulador, *s. m.* accumulator.
acumular, *v. a.* accumulate.
acuoso, *adj.* watery; juicy.
acusación, *s. f.* accusation.
acusado, *s. m.* defendant.
acusar, *v. a.* accuse; ~ *recibo* acknowledge receipt.
acusativo, *s. m.* accusative.
adelantado, *adj.* progressive; *por* ~ in advance; *ir* ~ be fast.
adelantar, *v. a.* surpass, take the lead; *nos adelantaron* they passed us; *v. n.* gain time, be fast; improve, advance; ~*se* beat sy to.
adelante, *adv.* forward; ¡~! come in!
adelgazar, *v. a.* make thin; *v. n.* lose weight.
ademán, *s. m.* bearing; gesture.
además, *adv.* moreover, besides; ~ *de* in addition to.
adentro, *adv.* within, inside.
adición, *s. f.* addition.
adicional, *adj.* additional.
adicionar, *v. a.* add.
adiestrar, *v. a.* train; (horse) break in.
adinerado, *adj.* well-to-do.
adiós *s. m.* good-bye; so long!
adivinanza, *s. f.* riddle, puzzle.
adivinar, *v. a.* foresee; guess.
adivino, *s. m.* fortuneteller.
adjetivo, *m.* adjective.
adjudicar, *v. a.* adjudicate.
adjunto, *adv.* & *adj.* enclosed.
administración, *s. f.* administration, manage-

ment.
administrador, *s. m.* manager; superintendent.
administrar, *v. a.* manage, administer.
administrativo, *adj.* administrative..
admirable, *adj.* admirable, excellent, wonderful.
admiración, *s. f.* admiration, wonder.
admirador, *s. m.* admirer.
admirar, *v. a.* admire, amaze.
admisión, *s. f.* admission.
admitir, *v. a.* admit; let, allow; accept.
adobar, *v. a.* prepare, cook.
adolescencia, *s. f.* adolescence, youth.
adolescente, *adj.* & *s. m.* adolescent.
adonde, *conj.* where, to what place; — *pron.* *¿adónde?* where to?
adorable, *adj.* adorable.
adorar, *v. a.* adore, worship.
adormitarse, *v. n.* fall into a slumber.
adornar, *v. a.* decorate, trim.
adorno, *s. m.* ornament, trimming.
adquirir, *v. a.* acquire.
adquisición, *s. f.* acquisition.
adrede, *adv.* deliberately.
aduana, *s. f.* customhouse; customs.
aduanero, *s. m.* customs officer.
adulterar, *v. a.* adulterate.
adulto, *adj.* & *s.* adult.
adunar, *v. a.* unite, join.
adverbio, *s. m.* adverb.
adversario, *s. m.* opponent.
adversidad, *s. f.* adversity, misfortune.
adverso, *adj.* adverse.
advertencia, *s. f.* warning.
advertir, *v. a.* notice, observe; advise, warn.
aeración, *s. f.* airing, ventilation.
aéreo, *adj.* aerial; *correo ~* air mail.
aerodinámico, *adj.* streamlined.
aeródromo, *s. m.* airport.
aeronauta, *s. m.* aeronaut.
aeronáutica, *s. f.* aeronautics.
aeronáutico, *adj.* aeronautic.
aeronave, *s. f.* airship.
aeroplano, *s. m.* airplane.
aeropuerto, *s. m.* air-port.
afabilidad, *s. f.* affability.
afamado, *adj.* famous.
afanoso, *adj.* industrious.
afección, *s. f.* affection.
afectación, *s. f.* affectation.
afectado, *adj.* affected, unnatural.
afectar, *v. a.* affect.
afecto, *s. m.* affection, regard.
afectuoso, *adj.* affectionate.
afeitar, *v. a.* shave; *v. n.* ***~se*** shave (oneself).
afición, *s. f.* fondness, inclination.
aficionado, *adj.* attached, devoted; — *s. m.* fan; amateur.
aficionarse *a*, *v. n.* become fond of.
afilado, *adj.* sharp.
afilalápices, *s. m.* pencil-sharpener.
afilar, *v. a.* sharpen.
afinar, *v. a.* refine; tune.
afinidad, *s. f.* relation-

ship (by marriage).
afirmación, *s. f.* affirmation.
afirmar, *v. a.* affirm, assert, maintain.
afirmativo, *adj.* affirmative.
aflicción, *s. f.* affliction, sorrow, grief.
afligir, *v. a.* grieve sy; *v. n.* *~se* grieve.
afluir, *v. n.* flow into.
aforrar, *v. a.* line, fur.
afortunadamente, *adv.* fortunately.
afortunado, *adj.* fortunate, lucky.
afrenta, *s. f.* affront, insult.
africano, *adj.* & *s.* African.
afuera, *adv.* out, outside; ¡~! get out!
afueras, *pl. f.* suburbs, outskirts.
agencia, *s. f.* agency; *~ de informaciones* inquiry-agency; *~ de viajes, ~ de turismo* tourist office.
agenda, *s. f.* note-book; agenda.
agente, *s. m.* agent, representative; *~ de policia* policeman; *~ de transportes* forwarding agent.
ágil, *adj.* quick, agile.
agilidad, *s. f.* quickness, agility.
agitación, *s. f.* agitation, excitement.
agitar, *v. a.* shake; stir up, excite; *v. n.* *~se* become excited.
agonía, *s. f.* agony.
agonizar, *v. n.* agonize.
agosto, *s. m.* August.
agotar, *v. a.* use up, exhaust; *v. n.* *~se* wear oneself out, give out.
agraciado, *adj.* graceful, charming.
agradable, *adj.* agreeable, pleasant.
agradar, *v. n.* be pleasing.
agradecer, *v. a.* appreciate; *Le agradezco mucho su ayuda* I thank you very much for your help.
agradecido, *adj.* thankful, grateful; *estoy muy ~ a usted* I'm very grateful.
agradecimiento, *s. m.* gratitude.
agrandar, *v. a.* enlarge; let out (garment).
agrario, *adj.* agricultural.
agravar, *v. a.* aggravate, make worse; *v. n.* *~se* get worse.
agregado, *s. m.* attaché.
agregar, *v. a.* add; *v. n.* *se a* join, follow.
agresión, *s. f.* aggression.
agresivo, *adj.* aggressive.
agresor, *s. m.* aggressor.
agrícola, *adj.* agricultural.
agricultor, *s. m.* farmer.
agricultura, *s. f.* agriculture.
agrio, *adj.* sour.
agrupar, *v. a.* group.
agua, *s. f.* water; *~s termales* hot springs.
aguador, *s. m.* water-carrier.
aguafuerte, *s. f.* etching.
aguanieve, *s. f.* sleet.
aguantar, *v. a.* bear, endure, stand; hang on, not give up; *v. n.* *~se* be patient, take it.
aguar, *v. a.* add water to sg.
aguardar, *v. a.* expect, wait for.
aguardiente, *s. m.* brandy,

whisky.
agudeza, *s. f.* sagacity; wit.
agudo, *adj.* sharp, keen; clever; high-pitched; witty; *ángulo* ~ acute angle.
águila, *s. f.* eagle.
aguja, *s. f.* needle; switch (railway); hand (of watch); ~ *de hacer media* knitting-needle.
agujero, *s. m.* hole.
aguzar, *v. a.* sharpen to a point; ~ *el oido* prick up one's ears.
¡ah! *int.* oh!
ahí *adv.* there; *por* ~ that way; around here.
ahogar, *v. a.* choke; — *v. n.* ~*se* drown, be drowned; be suffocated.
ahondar, *v. a.* deepen; *v. n.* plunge.
ahora, *adv.* now; ~ *bien* now then; ~ *mismo* at once, right away, just now; *de* ~ *en adelante* from now on; *hasta* ~ up to now, so far; *por* ~ for the present.
ahorrar, *v. a.* save (money).
ahorro, *s. m.* saving; *caja (s. f.) de* ~*s* savings-bank.
ahumado, *adj.* smoked; — *s. m.* smoked meat.
ahumar, *v. a.* smoke.
aire¹, *s. m.* air; wind; look, appearance; *al* ~ *libre* in the open air; *tomar el* ~ get some fresh air.
aire², *s. m.* melody; time.
airear, *v. a.* air, ventilate; *v. n.* ~*se* get some fresh air; catch cold.
airoso, *adj.* smart; handsome.
aislado, *adj.* isolated.
aislador, *s. m.* insulator.
aislamiento, *s. m.* isolation.
aislar, *v. a.* isolate, cut off.
¡ajá! *int.* so that's it!
ajedrecista, *s. m.* chess-player.
ajedrez, *s. m.* chess; *jugar al* ~ play chess.
ajenjo, *s. m.* absinthe.
ajeno, *adj.* another's, someone else's.
ajo, *s. m.* garlic.
ajustar, *v. a.* settle, agree about, adjust; tighten (screw); *v. n.* fit.
al (a + el); *see* **a.**
ala, *s. f.* wing; brim (of hat).
alabar, *v. a.* praise; *v. n.* ~*se* boast.
alacena, *s. f.* wall-cupboard.
alado, *adj.* winged.
alambicar, *v. a.* distil.
alambique, *s. m.* retort.
alambre, *s. m.* wire.
alameda, *s. f.* alley, public walk (lined with poplars).
álamo, *s. m.* poplar.
alargar, *v. a.* lenghten, extend; hand; ~ *el paso* force one's pace.
alarma, *s. f.* alarm; *freno de* ~ emergency brake.
alarmar, *v. a.* alarm; *v. n.* ~*se* get anxious.
alba, *s. f.* dawn.
albañil, *s. m.* mason, bricklayer.
albaricoque, *s. m.* apricot.
albergar, *v. a.* harbour, lodge.
albergue, *s. m.* lodgings; shelter.
albóndiga, *s. f.* meat ball.
albornoz, *s. m.* bathing-

gown.
alborotar, *v. a. & n.* disturb, make noise.
alboroto, *s. m.* tumult, uproar.
álbum, *s. m.* album.
alcachofa, *s. f.* artichoke.
alcalde, *s. m.* mayor.
alcance, *s. m.* reach.
alcanfor, *s. m.* camphor.
alcantarilla, *s. f.* canal; duct.
alcanzar, *v. a.* cath up with, overtake; reach, attain.
alcázar, *s. m.* fortress; Royal Palace.
alción, *s. m.* kingfisher.
alcoba, *s. f.* bedroom.
alcohol, *s. f.* alcohol.
alcohólico *adj. & s.* alcoholic.
aldaba, *s. f.* knocker.
aldea, *s. f.* village.
aldeana, *s. f.* countrywoman.
aldeano, *s. m.* countryman.
alegrar, *v. a.* cheer up brighten; *v. n. ~se de* rejoice, be glad.
alegre, *adj.* glad, happy; cheerful; bright (colour); drunk, tipsy.
alegría, *s. f.* delight, joy, pleasure.
alejar, *v. a.* remove, send away; *v. n. ~se* withdraw, go away.
alemán, *adj. & s.* German.
alerta, *adj. & adv.* (on the) alert.
aleta, *s. f.* fin.
aletear, *v. n.* flutter.
alfabético, *adj.* alphabetical.
alfabeto, *s. m.* alphabet.
alféizar, *s. m.* window-sill.
alférez, *s. m.* cadet.
alfil, *s. m.* bishop (chess).
alfiler, *s. m.* pin.
alfombra, *s. f.* carpet, rug.
algo, *pron.* something; — *adv.* rather, somewhat; *~ de dinero* some money; *por ~* for some reason; *servir para ~* be good for something.
algodón, *s. m.* cotton; *~ en rama* cotton-wool.
alguacil, *s. m.* usher (in court).
alguien, *pron.* somebody, someone; anybody, anyone.
algún, *adj.* some; *~ día* some day.
alguno, *adj.* some, any; *alguna cosa más* anything else; *alguna vez* now and then, ever; *~s* some people.
alhaja, *s. f.* jewel.
aliado, *adj.* allied; — *s.* ally.
alianza, *s. f.* union, alliance.
aliarse, *v. n.* form an alliance, ally oneself.
alienar, *v. a.* alienate.
aliento, *s. m.* breath.
aligerar, *v. a.* lighten; *v. n.* hasten, hurry.
alimentar, *v. a.* feed, nourish.
alimento, *s. m.* food, nourishment.
alistar, *v. a.* enlist; *v. n. ~se* enlist; get ready.
aliviar, *v. n.* relieve, alleviate; *v. n.* recover.
alivio, *s. m.* relief; recovery.
alma, *s. f.* soul; *lo siento en el ~* I'm terribly sorry; *¡hijo de mi ~!* my dear child!
almacén, *s. m.* warehouse; store(s).

almendra, *s. f.* almond.
almendro, *s. m.* almond-tree.
almíbar, *s. m.* syrup.
almidonar, *v. a.* starch.
alminar, *s. m.* minaret.
almirante, *s. m.* admiral.
almohada, *s. f.* pillow; *consultar con la* ~ sleep on it.
almorzar, *v. n.* lunch, breakfast.
almuerzo, *s. m.* lunch, noon meal; breakfast.
alojamiento, *s. m.* dwelling, lodgings.
alojar, *v. a.* put up, lodge, quarter; *v. n.* ~*se* stay.
alquilar, *v. a.* rent, hire; let.
alquiler, *s. m.* (price of) rent.
alrededor, *adv.* around; — *prep.* ~ *de* around, about; — *s. pl. m.* ~*es* outskirts, surroundings.
altar, *s. m.* altar.
altavoz, *s. m.* loud speaker.
alterar, *v. a.* change, transform; — *v. n.* ~*se* get excited.
alternar, *v. n.* alternate; take turns.
alternativa, *s. f.* alternative.
alternativamente, *adv.* by turns.
alternativo, *adj.* alternate.
alto[1], *adj.* high, tall; *hablar* ~ talk loud; *a altas horas de la noche* very late at night; *pasar por* ~ overlook, forget.
alto[2], *s. m.* stop, halt; *hacer* ~ stop; ¡~! halt! stop!.
altura, *s. f.* height, altitude, elevation.
aludir *a, v. n.* allude to, refer to.
alumbrado, *s. m.* lighting.
alumbrar, *v. a.* give light, light, illuminate.
alumbre, *s. m.* alum.
aluminio, *s. m.* aluminium.
alumno, *s. m.* pupil, student.
alusión, *s. f.* allusion; reference; hint.
aluvión, *s. f.* inundation, flood.
alzar, *v. a.* lift, raise; cut (cards); *v. n.* ~*se* rise; revolt.
allá, *adv.* there; *por* ~ over there.
allegado, *adj.* related, kindred.
allende, *adv.* beyond.
allí, *adv.* there; *de* ~ from there; *por* ~ that way.
ama, *s. f.* mistress of the house; hostess; ~ *de llaves* housekeeper.
amabilidad, *s. f.* kindness.
amable, *adj.* kind, amiable.
amador, *s. m.* lover.
amaestrar, *v. a.* train; instruct.
amanecer, *v. n.* dawn; — *s. m.* daybreak, dawn.
amansar, *v. a.* tame, domesticate.
amante, *adj.* loving; — *s. m.* lover; *s. f.* mistress.
amapola, *s. f.* poppy.
amar, *v. a.* love; *hacerse* ~ win sy's affection.
amargar, *v. n.* be bitter; *v. a.* make bitter, make miserable.
amargo, *adj.* bitter.
amargura, *s. f.* bitterness.
amarillento, *adj.* yellowish.
amarillo, *adj.* yellow.

amarrar, *v. a.* tie, fasten.
amasar, *v. a.* massage; knead.
amatista, *s. f.* amethyst.
ámbar, *s. m.* amber.
ambición, *s. f.* ambition.
ambicionar, *v. a.* strive after.
ambicioso, *adj.* overambitious.
ambiente, *s. m.* atmosphere, environment.
ambigú, *s. m.* bar, buffet.
ambigüedad, *s. f.* ambiguity.
ambiguo, *adj.* ambiguous.
ambos, *adj. pl.* both.
ambulancia, *s. f.* ambulance.
ambulante, *adj.* migrant, wandering.
amén, *s. m.* amen; — *prep.* *~ de* besides.
amenazar, *v. a.* threaten, menace.
ameno, *adj.* lovely, charming.
americana, *s. f.* coat (of a man's suit), jacket.
americano, *adj. & s.* American.
amianto, *s. m.* asbestos.
amiga, *s. f.* (girl)friend.
amígdala, *s. f.* tonsil.
amigdalitis, *s. f.* tonsiilitis.
amigo, *adj.* friendly; — *s. m.* friend.
aminorar, *v. a.* diminish.
amistad, *s. f.* friendship; *hacer ~* become friends; *hacer ~es* get acquainted.
amistoso, *adj.* friendly.
amo, *s. m.* master of the house; host; owner, proprietor; boss.
amontonar, *v. a.* heap, pile up.
amor, *s. m.* love; darling; *~ propio* self-esteem, pride; *por ~ de Dios* for goodness sake.
amortiguar, *v. a.* weaken, diminish.
amortizar, *v. a.* amortize.
amotinarse, *v. n.* mutiny.
amparar, *v. a.* protect, defend.
amparo, *s. m.* protection; aid.
ampliar, *v. a.* enlarge, amplify, extend.
amplio, *adj.* ample, roomy, large.
amputar, *v. a.* amputate.
amueblado, *adj.* furnished.
amueblar, *v. a.* furnish.
ánade, *s. m.* duck.
analfabeto, *adj. & s.* illiterate.
análisis, *s. m.* analysis.
analizar, *v. a.* analyse.
ananá, *s. m.* pineapple.
anaquel, *s. m.* shelf.
anaranjado, *adj.* orange-coloured.
anarquía, *s. f.* anarchy.
anciano, *adj.* aged, very old.
ancla, *s. f.* anchor; *echar ~s* cast anchor; *levar ~s* weigh anchor.
anclaje, *s. m.* berth.
anclar, *v. n.* anchor.
ancho, *adj.* wide, broad.
anchoa, *s. f.* anchovy.
andar, *v. n.* walk, go on foot; run, work (clock).
andén, *s. m.* (railway) platform.
anfiteatro, *s. m.* dress-circle.
ángel, *s. m.* angel.
anglosajón, *adj.* Anglo-Saxon.
angosto, *adj.* narrow.
anguila, *s. f.* eel.
ángulo, *s. m.* angle.
angustia, *s. f.* fear, anxiety.
angustiar, *v. a.* alarm.
anhelar, *v. n.* pant, gasp;

v. a. long for.
anhelo, *s. m.* longing.
anidar, *v. n.* nest.
anillo, *s. m.* ring.
animación, *s. f.* animation, liveliness.
animado, *adj.* animated, lively.
animal, *adj.&s. m.* animal.
animar, *v. a.* cheer, encourage.
ánimo, *s. m.* (state of) mind, spirits; courage; *dar* ~*s* cheer up, encourage.
animosidad, *s. f.* grudge; courage.
animoso, *adj.* courageous.
aniñado, *adj.* childish.
aniquilar, *v. a.* annihilate.
aniversario, *s. m.* anniversary.
anoche, *adv.* last night.
anochecer, *v. n.* grow dark; — *s. m.* dusk, nightfall.
ánodo, *s. m.* anode.
anómalo, *adj.* anomalous.
anónimo, *adj.* anonymous; *sociedad* ~*a* joint-stock company.
ansia, *s. f.* fear, anxiety; desire, eagerness.
ansiar, *v. a.* long for, crave for.
ansiedad, *s. f.* anxiety.
ansioso, *adj.* anxious, eager, impatient.
antaño, *adv.* formerly.
ante, *prep.* in front of; ~ *todo* first of all.
anteanoche, *adv.* night before last.
anteayer, *adv.* day before yesterday.
antecedente, *adj. & s. m.* antecedent; ~*s* past, police-record.
anteceder, *v. n.* precede.
antedatar, *v. a.* date back.
antedicho, *adj.* aforementioned.
anteguerra, *s. f.*; *periodo (s. m.) de* ~ pre-war time.
antemano, *adv.*; *de* ~ in advance, beforehand.
antena, *s. f.* feeler; aerial.
anteojo, *s. f.* field-glass; ~*s* eyeglasses, spectacles.
anterior, *adj.* previous, last.
anterioridad, *s. f.* antecedence; *con* ~ previously.
antes, *adv.* before, formerly; — *prep.* ~ *de,* *conj.* ~ *que* before; *cuanto* ~ as soon as possible; *poco* ~ not long ago; *el dia* ~ the day before.
antesala, *s. f.* waiting-room.
anticipación, *s. f.* anticipation.
anticipar, *v. a.* advance; lend; get ahead of; *v. n.* ~*se* arrive ahead of time.
anticipo, *s. m.* advanced money.
anticuado, *adj.* antiquated.
antigüedad, *s. f.* antiquity.
antiguo, *adj.* former; old, ancient; *a la antigua* in an old-fashioned way.
antipatía, *s. f.* dislike.
antipático, *adj.* disagreeable.
antiséptico, *adj. & s. m.* antiseptic.
antorcha, *s. f.* torch.
antro, *s. m.* cave; den.
anual, *adj.* annual, yearly.
anuario, *s. m.* annual.
anublar, *v. a.* cloud.
anudar, *v. a.* tie.

anular[1], *v. a.* annul.
anular[2], *adj.* annular; *dedo* ~ ring-finger.
anunciar, *v. a.* announce, advertise.
anuncio, *s. m.* advertisement, announcement; notice.
anzuelo, *s. m.* fishing-hook
añadir, *v. a.* add to.
año, *s. m.* year; ~ *bisiesto* leap year; *feliz* ~ *nuevo* Happy New Year; *tengo cuarenta* ~*s* I'm forty years old.
añoso, *adj.* aged.
apagar, *v. a.* put out, extinguish; *v. n.* ~*se* go out (lights).
aparador, *s. m.* sideboard; dresser.
aparato, *s. m.* apparatus; set.
aparecer, *v. n.* show up, appear.
aparentar, *v. a.* pretend.
aparente, *adj.* apparent.
aparición, *s. f.* appearance; apparition.
apariencia, *s. f.* appearance, looks.
apartar, *v. a.* separate, divide.
aparte, *adj.* separate; — *adv.* aside, separately.
apasionado, *adj.* passionate; ~ *por* partial to.
apeadero, *s. m.* halt.
apearse, *v. n.* get off.
apelación, *s. f.* appeal.
apelar, *v. n.* appeal.
apellidar, *v. a.* name, call.
apellido, *s. m.* (family) name.
apenas, *adv.* scarcely, hardly; *conj.* as soon as.
apéndice, *s. m.* appendix.
apendicitis, *s. f.* appendicitis.
aperitivo, *adj.* appetizing; — *s. m.* appetizer; aperient.
apertura, *s. f.* opening.
apestar, *v. a.* infect, poison.
apetecer, *v. a.* desire, crave for.
apetito, *s. m.* appetite.
apilar, *v. a.* pile up, stack.
apio, *s. m.* celery.
aplastar, *v. a.* crush; flatten.
aplaudir, *v. n.* applaud.
aplauso, *s. m.* applause.
aplazar, *v. a.* adjourn.
aplicado, *adj.* studious, industrious.
aplicar, *v. a.* apply.
apoplejía, *s. f.* apoplexy.
aposento, *s. m.* room, apartment.
apostar, *v. n.* bet.
apóstol, *s. m.* apostle.
apoyar, *v. a.* rest, prop; back, support, second; *v. n.* ~*se* support oneself, lean.
apoyo, *s. m.* prop, support.
apreciar, *v. a.* appreciate.
aprender, *v. a.* learn.
aprendiz, *s. m.* apprentice.
aprendizaje, *s. m.* apprenticeship.
aprestar, *v. a.* prepare, dress.
apresurar, *v. a.* hasten, hurry; *v. n.* ~*se* hurry up.
apretar, *v. a.* tighten, press down, compress; grip; clench; *v. n.* be too tight; go faster, sprint.
aprieto, *s. m.* jam, tight spot.
aprisa, *adv.* swiftly, fast, quickly.
aprisionar, *v. a.* arrest.

aprobar, *v. a.* approve of; pass (an examination).
aprovechar, *v. a.* profit by, make use of; – *v. n.* ~*se de* take advantage of.
aprovisionar, *v. a.* supply, provision.
aproximarse, *v. n.* approach, move near.
aptitud, *s. f.* aptitude.
apto, *adj.* apt.
apuesta, *s. f.* bet, wager.
apuesto, *adj.* well-shaped.
apuntar, *v. a.* aim; make a note, jot down; prompt.
apurado, *adj.* difficult, hard.
apurar, *v. a.* drain, drink up, consume; *v. n.* ~*se* worry; hurry.
apuro, *s. m.* jam, tight spot, fix.
aquel, aquella *adj.* that.
aquí, *adv.* here; ~ *dentro* in here; *de* ~ *en adelante* from now on; *por* ~ here, this way.
árabe, *adj.* & *s. m.* Arab(ian).
arado, *s. m.* plough.
arancel, *s. m.* tariff.
araña, *s. f.* spider.
arañar, *v. a.* & *n.* scratch.
arañazo, *s. m.* scratch.
arar, *v. a.* plow.
arbitrar, *v. n.* arbitrate.
arbitrario, *adj.* arbitrary.
árbitro, *s. m.* arbiter, umpire, referee.
arbol, *s. m.* tree.
arbusto, *s. m.* bush, shrub.
arca, *s. f.* trunk, chest; safe.
arcilla, *s. f.* clay.
arco, *s. m.* arch; bow (for arrows); ~ *iris* rainbow.
archiduque, *s. m.* archduke.
archiduquesa, *s. f.* archduchess.
archipiélago, *s. m.* archipelago.
archivo, *s. m.* archives.
arder, *v. n.* burn.
ardid, *s. m.* ruse; trick.
ardiente, *adj.* burning.
ardilla, *s. f.* squirrel.
ardor, *s. m.* heat; ardour.
arena, *s. f.* sand; arena.
arenque, *s. m.* herring.
argentino, *adj.* & *s. m.* Argentine.
argüir, *v. n.* argue.
argumentar, *v. a.* deduce, conclude.
argumento, *s. m.* argument, logic, premises; plot, story.
árido, *adj.* arid, dry, barren.
arma, *s. f.* weapon.
armada, *s. f.* navy.
armadura, *s.* f. armour; framework.
armar, *v.* arm; put together; ~ *jaleo* make a racket; – *v. n.* ~*se de* provide oneself with.
armario, *s. m.* closet, wardrobe.
armonía, *s. f.* harmony.
arpa, *s. f.* harp.
arquitecto, *s. m.* architect.
arquitectura, *s. f.* architecture.
arrancar, *v. a.* root out, pull out; *v. n.* start.
arranque, *s. m.* sudden impulse; starter.
arrastrar, *v. a.* drag along; *v. n.* ~*se* crawl, creep, drag oneself.
arreglar, *v. a.* arrange, adjust, settle; fix; *v. n.* ~*se* tidy up, dress.

arreglo, *s. m.* arrangement, settlement, agreement; *con* ~ according to, in accordance with.
arrendar, *v. a.* rent, let; hire.
arrepentirse, *v. n.* be sorry for, regret.
arrestar, *v. a.* arrest, imprison.
arresto, *s. m.* arrest, imprisonment.
arriba, *adv.* up, above; upstairs.
arribar, *v. n.* land; arrive.
arriero, *s. m.* mule-driver.
arriesgar, *v. a.* risk, hazard; *v. n.* ~*se* take risk.
arrodillarse, *v. n.* kneel down.
arrogante, *adj.* arrogant, haughty, proud.
arrojar, *v. a.* throw, hurl, cast; *v. n.* ~*se* rush, plunge.
arroyo, *s. m.* brook; stream.
arroz, *s. m.* rice.
arruinar, *v. a.* destroy, ruin.
arte, *s. m. (s. pl. f.)* art; skill; craft, cunning.
artefacto, *s.m.* machinery, mechanism.
arteria, *s. f.* artery.
artesano, *s. m.* artisan, craftsman.
articulación, *s. f.* joint; articulation.
articular, *v. a.* articulate.
artículo, *s. m.* joint; article; news article; ~*s* things, goods.
artificial, *adj.* artificial.
artificio, *s. m.* artifice, trick, knack.
artillería, *s. f.* artillery.
artista, *s. m., f.* artist.
artístico, *adj.* artistic.
arzobispo, *s. m.* archbishop.
as, *s. m.* ace, star; ace (cards).
asa, *s. f.* handle.
asado, *s. m.* roast.
asalto, *s. m.* assault, attack.
asamblea, *s. f.* assembly, convention.
asar, *v. a.* roast.
ascender, *v. a.* ascend, go up; be promoted; ~ *a* amount to.
ascensor, *s. m.* lift.
asco, *s. m.* nausea, disgust.
asegurar, *v. a.* secure, fasten; assure, affirm, maintain; insure; *v. n.* ~*se* make sure; get insured.
asenso, *s. n.* consent.
asentir, *v. n.* assent, agree.
aseo, *s. m.* care of the body.
aseverar, *v. a.* affirm.
asfalto, *s. m.* asphalt.
así, *adv.* so, that way; in this manner, this way; therefore, and so; ~ ~ so so; ~ *como* ~ any way; ~ *que* as soon as, after.
asiduidad, *s. f.* assiduity.
asiduo, *adj.* assiduous, industrious.
asiento, *s. m.* seat, chair; *tome usted* ~ take a seat.
asignar, *v. a.* assign.
asilo, *s. m.* orphanage; home (for aged).
asimilar, *v. a.* assimilate.
asimismo, *adv.* likewise, in the same way.
asistencia, *s. f.* attendance, presence; assistance, help.
asistenta, *s. f.* char-

woman.

asistente, *s. m.* assistant, help.

asistir, *v. a. & n.* assist, help, take care of; ~ *a* attend, be present at.

asma, *s. f.* asthma.

asno, *s. m.* ass, donkey.

asociación, *s. f.* association, club.

asociado, *s. m.* associate, partner.

asociar, *v. a. & n.* associate.

asomar, *v. a.* put out (one's head); *v. n.* *~se a* lean out of.

asombrar, *v. a.* astonish, amaze; *v. n.* *~se* wonder at; be astonished by, be amazed at.

asordar, *v. a.* deafen; stun.

aspecto, *s. m.* appearance, look; sight, aspect.

áspero, *adj.* rough, rash.

aspiración, *s. f.* respiration; ambition.

aspirador *(s. m.) de polvo* vacuum cleaner.

aspirante, *s. m.* aspirant.

aspirar, *v. a. & n.* aspire.

aspirina, *s. f.* aspirin.

asqueroso, *adj.* filthy, nasty, mean, low.

asta, *s. f.* shaft; horn (of a bull).

astil, *s. m.* handle, haft; quill.

astilla, *s. f.* chip; splinter.

astillero, *s. m.* dockyard.

astro, *s. m.* star; constellation.

astrología, *s. f.* astrology.

astrólogo, *s. m.* astrologer.

astronomía, *s. f.* astronomy.

astrónomo, *s. m.* astronomer.

astucia, *s. f.* cunning.

astuto, *adj.* astute, crafty.

asunto, *s. m.* subject; affair, business.

asustar, *v. a.* frighten; *v. n.* *~se* be frightened.

atacar, *v. a.* attack.

atajar, *v. a.* take a short cut; overtake, catch up with; interrupt, cut short.

atajo, *s. m.* short cut, shorter road.

atañer, *v. a.* concern; affect.

ataque, *s. m.* attack, assault; fit.

atar, *v. a.* tie, bind, lace; ~ *cabos* put two and two together.

atardecer, *v. n.* night is falling; — *s. m.* evening.

atareado, *adj.* busy.

ataúd, *s. m.* coffin.

atemperar, *v. a.* moderate, mitigate.

atención, *s. f.* attention; kindness; *llamar la ~* attract attention.

atender, *v. a. & n.* attend, wait on; pay attention to; look after, take care of.

atenerse *a, v. n.* depend on.

atentado, *s. m.* attempt (on the life of sy).

atento, *adj* polite, courteous; attentive; *su ~ y seguro servidor* yours faithfully.

aterrar[1], *v. a.* terrify.

aterrar[2], *v. n.* land.

aterrizaje, *s. m.* landing.

aterrizar, *v. n.* land.

aterrorizar, *v. a.* terrorize.

atestación, *s. f.* testimony, statement.

atestado, *adj.* obstinate; overfilled, crammed; — *s. m.* attestation, certificate.

atestiguar, *v. a.* testify.
atlántico, *adj.* Atlantic.
atleta, *s. m., f.* athlete.
atlético, *adj.* athletic.
atmósfera, *s. f.* atmosphere.
atolladero, *s. m.* pool, puddle.
atomico, *adj.* atomic; *bomba∼a* atomic bomb; *energia ∼a* atomic energy; *pila ∼a* atomic pile.
atomo, *s. m.* atom.
atormentar, *v. a.* torment, torture.
atornillar, *v. a. & n.* screw; turn a screw.
atracción, *s. f.* attraction.
atraco, *s. m.* robbery, hold-up.
atractivo, *adj.* attractive, charming; — *s. m.* charm, appeal.
atraer, *v. a.* attract, charm.
atrás, *adv.* back; *dar marcha ∼* go into reverse, back; *hacia ∼* backward; *quedarse ∼* stay behind.
atrasado, *adj. & adv.* backward, behind.
atrasar, *v. a.* delay, detain; put back (watch); *v. n.* go *or* be slow, lose time; *∼se* remain behind; be late.
atraso, *s. m.* backwardness; delay.
atravesar, *v. a.* pierce; cross.
atreverse, *v. n.* dare, venture.
atribuir, *v. a.* attribute.
atrocidad, *s. f.* atrocity, horrible thing.
atropellar, *v. a.* run over, knock down.
atropello, *s. m.* accident; abuse, outrage.
atroz, *adj.* terrible, atrocious.
atún, *s. m.* tunny.
aturdir, *v. a.* rattle; *v. n.* *∼se* be stunned.
audaz, *adj.* bold, daring.
audición, *s. f.* (radio) reception; *∼ musical* radio concert.
audiencia, *s. f.* audience; courtroom.
auditorio, *s. m.* audience, listeners.
aula, *s. f.* auditorium, lecture-room, hall.
aumentar, *v. a.* increase.
aumento, *s. m.* increase.
aun, aún, *adv.* still; even; yet; *∼ cuando* even though, even if.
aunque, *conj.* although, even if.
áureo, *adj.* golden.
auricular, *s. m.* ear-piece.
aurora, *s. f.* dawn.
auscultar, *v. a.* examine by auscultation.
ausencia, *s. f.* absence.
ausente, *adj.* absent.
austral, *adj.* austral.
austriaco, *adj. & s.* Austrian.
auténtico, *adj,* authentic.
auto, *s. m.* auto, car.
autobús, *s. m.* bus.
autocar, *s. m.* sightseeing car.
autogiro, *s. m.* gyroplane, autogiro.
automación, *s. f.* automation.
automático, *adj.* automatic.
automóvil, *s. m.* automobile.
automovilismo, *s. m.* motoring.
automovilista, *s. m., f.* motorist.

autopista, *s. f.* motorway.
autopsia, *s. f.* autopsy.
autor, *s. m.* author.
autora, *s. f.* authoress.
autoridad, *s. f.* authority; ~*es* authorities, government.
autorización, *s. f.* authorization.
autorizar, *v. s.* authorize.
auxilio, *s. m.* aid, help.
avalancha, *s. f.* avalanche.
avance, *s. m.* advance; advance payment.
avanzado, *adj.* advanced, progressive.
avanzar, *v. n.* move forward; advance.
avaricia, *s. f.* avarice.
avaricioso, avariento *adj.* avaricious.
avaro, *adj.* &. *s. m.* miser(ly).
ave, *s. f.* bird, fowl.
avellana, *s. f.* hazel-nut.
avena, *s. f.* oats.
avenida, *s. f.* avenue flood.
aventura, *s. f.* adventure.
aventurar, *v. a.* risk, hazard.
aventurero, *s. m.* adventurer.
avergonzar, *v. a.* shame, make ashamed; *v. n.* ~*se* be ashamed.
avería, *s. f.* average, damage.
averiarse, *v. n.* be damaged, be spoiled.
averiguar, *v. a.* find out.
aversión, *s.. f.* aversion, dislike.
avestruz, *s. m.* ostrich.
aviación, *s. f.* aviation.
aviador, *s. m.* aviator.
ávido, *adj.* eager, anxious.
avión, *s. m.* (air)plane.
avisar, *v. a.* notify, inform; warn, advise, counsel.
aviso, *s. m.* announcement, notice; warning.
¡ay! oh! ouch!
ayer, *adv.* yesterday.
ayuda, *s. f.* help, aid, assistance.
ayudar, *v. a.* help, aid, assist.
ayunar, *v. n.* fast.
ayuntamiento, *s. m.* townhall.
azafata, *s. f.* stewardess, air-hostess.
azar, *s. m.* chance, risk; *al* ~ at random.
azorar, *v. a.* frighten; embarras, confuse; *v. n.* ~*se* be embarrassed.
azúcar, *s. m.* sugar.
azucarar, *v. a.* sugar.
azucarera, *s. f.* sugar-basin.
azufre, *s. m.* sulphur.
azul, *adj.* blue.

B

babucha, *s. f.* slipper.
bacalao, *s. m.* codfish.
bacilo, *s. m.* microbe.
bacteria, *s. f.* bacterium.
bache, *s. m.* pot-hole.
bachiller, *s. m.* graduate.
bagaje, *s. m.* luggage.
bagatela, *s. f.* trifle.
bahía, *s. f.* bay (arm of sea).
bailador, *adj.* dancing; — *s. m.* dancer.
bailar, *v. a.* & *n.* dance.
bailarín, *s. m.* dancer.
bailarina, *s. f.* dancer.
baile, *s. m.* dance, ball.
bailete, *s. m.* ballet.
baja, *s. f.* drop, fall (in price); (military) casualty; *dar de* ~ drop out; *darse de* ~ resign, withdraw.
bajar, *v. n.* go down, descend; fall, drop;

~se bend over; get down, get off; — *v. a.* bring down, take down, lower.
bajo, *adj.* low; short (not tall); soft (voice); bass (instrument); — *s. m.* groundfloor; — *adv.* below; — *prep.* below.
bala[1], *s. f.* bullet.
bala[2], *s. f.* bale.
balance, *s. m.* swaying, wobbling; balance; balance sheet.
balancear, *v. a.* balance; *v. n.* (*~se*) sway, rock, swing.
balanza, *s. f.* scales, balance.
balcánico, *adj.* Balkan.
balcón, *s. m.* balcony.
balde, *s. m.* bucket, pail; *de ~* gratis, free; *en ~* in vain, without success.
balneario, *s. m.* bathing-resort.
balompié, *s. m.* football.
balón, *s. m.* football.
baloncesto, *s. m.* basketball.
balonmano, *s. m.* handball.
balonvolea, *s. m.* volleyball.
balsa, *s. f.* raft; ferry.
baluarte, *s. m.* bulwark.
ballena, *s. f.* whale.
bambú, *s. m.* bamboo (cane).
banal, *adj.* banal, trite, commonplace.
banana, *s. f.* banana.
banca, *s. f.* stand, stall; bank(ing).
banco, *s. m.* bank; bench.
banda[1], *s. f.* sash, band (wide strip); side (of a ship).
banda[2], *s. f.* (music) band; gang.
bandeja, *s. f.* tray.
bandera, *s. f.* flag.
banderola, *s. f.* pennon.
bandido, *s. m.* bandit.
bando, *s. m.* party, sect.
banquero, *s. m.* banker.
banqueta, *s. f.* stool.
banquete, *s. m.* banquet.
banquetear, *v. n.* banquet.
banquillo, *s. m.* dock, prisoner's box.
bañador, *adj.* & *s. m.* bather.
bañar, *v. a.* bathe; *v. n.* *~se* take a bath.
bañera, *s. f.* bathtub; bath attendant.
bañero, *s. m.* swimming master.
bañista, *s. m., f.* visitor at a spa.
baño, *s. m.* bath; bathroom; bathtub; *~s* wateringplace, spa.
bar, *s. m.* bar; taproom.
baraja, *s. f.* pack of cards.
barajar, *v. a.* shuffle (cards).
barato, *adj.* cheap; — *adj.* cheaply; — *s. m.* sale.
barba, *s. f.* beard; chin.
bárbaro, *adj.* & *s. m.* barbarian.
barbero, *s. m.* barber.
barbudo, *adj.* bearded.
barca, *s. f.* (small) boat.
barcaza, *s. f.* barge; launch.
barco, *s. m.* boat, ship; *~ de vapor* steamship; *~ de vela* sailing-vessel.
barómetro, *s. m.* barometer.
barón, *s. m.* baron.
baronesa, *s. f.* baroness.
barquero, *s. m.* boatman.

barra, *s. f.* bar, rod; *~de labios* lipstick.
barraca, *s. f.* hut, peasant-cottage.
barrena, *s. f.* borer, gimlet.
barrer, *v. a.* sweep.
barrera, *s. f.* barrier, gate.
barrica, *s. f.* tun.
barriga, *s. f.* belly, paunch.
barril, *s. m.* barrel, cask.
barrilero, *s. m.* cooper.
barrio, *s. m.* quarter, district.
barro, *s. m.* mud; clay.
barroco, *adj.* & *s. m.* baroque.
bártulos, *s. m. pl.* bag and baggage.
basa, *s. f.* base of a column.
basar, *v. a.* & *n.* base.
báscula, *s. f.* platform-balance.
base, *s. f.* base; basis; *punto de ~* starting-point; *a ~ de* on the basis of.
básico, *adj.* basic; *inglés ~* Basic-English.
¡basta! enough! stop!
bastante, *adj.* & *adv.* enough, sufficient; rather.
bastar, *v. n.* be enough.
bastardilla, *s. f.* italics.
bastidores, *s. m. pl.* scenes; *entre ~* behind the scenes, backstage.
bastión, *s. m.* bastion.
bastón, *s. m.* cane, walking stick.
basura, *s. f.* garbage, refuse.
bata, *s. f.* robe, bathrobe; house coat.
batalla, *s. f.* battle.
batata, *s. f.* sweet potato.
batel, *s. m.* boat.
batería, *s. f.* battery; *~ de cocina* kitchen utensils.
batida, *s. f.* battue; raid.
batir, *v. a.* beat; defeat; *v. n. ~se* fight (a duel).
batuta, *s. f.* baton.
baúl, *s. m.* trunk.
bautismo, *s. m.* baptism.
bautizar, *v. a.* baptize.
baya, *s. f.* berry.
baza, *s. f.* trick (cards).
bazar, *s. m.* bazaar.
beatitud, *s. f.* happiness, bliss.
beato, *adj.* pious, religious.
bebé, *s. m.* baby.
bebedor, *s. m.* drinker, drunkard.
beber, *v. a.* drink.
bebida, *s. f.* drink, beverage.
beca, *s. f.* scholarship.
becerro, *s. m.* calf; calfskin.
beldad, *s. f.* beauty.
belga, *adj.* & *s. m., f.* Belgian.
beligerante, *adj.* & *s. m.* belligerent.
belleza, *s. f.* beauty.
bello, *adj.* beautiful; *el ~ sexo* the fair sex; *las bellas letras* polite letters; *las bellas artes* the fine arts.
bencina, *s. f.* benzine; petrol.
bendecir, *v. a.* bless; *¡que Dios le bendiga!* God bless you!
bendición, *s. f.* blessing.
bendito, *adj.* blessed, holy.
beneficencia, *s. f.* charity.
beneficio, *s. m.* favour; profit.
benéfico, *adj.* beneficent.
benemérito, *adj.* meri-

torious.
benevolencia, *s. f.* kindness, good will.
benévolo, *adj.* benevolent.
benigno, *adj.* good, kind.
bermejo, *adj.* bright red, vermilion.
berza, *s. f.* cabbage.
besar, *v. a.* kiss.
beso, *s. m.* kiss.
bestia, *s. f.* beast; blockhead.
bestial, *adj.* bestial, brutal.
Biblia, *s. f.* Bible.
biblioteca, *s. f.* library.
bibliotecario, *s. m.* librarian.
bicicleta, *s. f.* bicycle; *ir en* ~ ride a bicycle.
bicho, *s. m.* vermin; ~ *raro* funny person.
bidón, *s. m.* can, container.
bien, *adv.* well; very; *muy* ~ very well; *está* ~ all right; *no* ~ scarcely; *si* ~ although; *ahora* ~ now then; — *s. m.* good; welfare; benefit; ~*es* property, estate.
bienal, *adj.* biennial.
bienestar, *s. m.* well-being, comfort.
bienvenida, *s. f.* safe arrival; *dar la* ~ welcome.
bienvenido, *adj.* welcome.
biftec, *s. m.* beefsteak.
bigote, *s. m.* moustache.
bilis, *s. f.* bile.
billar, *s. m.* billiards, pool.
billete, *s. m.* ticket; ~ *de andén* platform ticket; ~ *de banco* banknote; ~ *de ida y vuelta* return ticket; ~ *de correspondencia* transfer ticket.
billón, *s. m.* a million millions.
bimestral, *adj.* bimensal.
biografía, *s. f.* biography.
biología, *s. f.* biology.
biombo, *s. m.* screen.
bis *adv.* once more; — *int.* encore!
bisemanal, *adj.* biweekly.
bisonte, *s. m.* bison.
bistec, *s. m.* beefsteak.
bizarro, *adj.* courageous; noble-minded.
bizcocho, *s. m.* (ship's) biscuit, sponge-cake.
blanco, *adj.* white; *en* ~ blank; — *s. m.* white person; target; *hacer* ~ hit the mark; *tirar al* ~ shoot at the target.
blando, *adj.* soft, tender.
blanquear, *v. a.* bleach; whitewash.
blasón, *s. m.* (coat of) arms; glory, fame.
blindado, *adj.* armoured, iron-clad.
blindaje, *s. m.* armour-plating.
blindar, *v. a.* armour.
bloque, *s. m.* block, piece.
bloquear, *v. a.* block, brake.
blusa, *s. f.* blouse.
bobina, *s. f.* spool, reel.
bobo, *adj.* foolish.
boca, *s. f.* mouth; entrance; ~ *de riego* hydrant, fire-plug.
bocacalle, *s. f.* street-crossing, turning.
bocadillo, *s. m.* sandwich.
bocallave, *s. f.* keyhole.
bocina, *s. f.* horn.
bocha, *s. f.* skittle-ball; ~*s* ninepin, skittles.
bochorno, *s. m.* sultry weather; embarrassment.
bochornoso, *adj.* sultry;

embarrassing; shameful.
boda, *s. f.* wedding.
bodega, *s. f.* (wine) cellar; (ship's) hold.
bofetada, *s. f.* slap.
boina, *s. f.* beret.
bola, *s. f.* ball; round body *or* mass; shoe-polish; false report, hoax.
bolero[1], *s. m.* swindler; liar.
bolero[2], *s. m.* bolero-dancer.
boletín, *s. m.* slip (of paper); ~ *meteorológico* weather report; ~ *oficial* official gazette; ~ *de equipaje* luggage-ticket.
bolsa, *s. f.* purse; bag; stock exchange.
bolsillo, *s. m.* pocket.
bolso, *s. m.* (woman's) handbag.
bollo, *s. m.* (French) roll.
bomba[1], *s. f.* pump; ~ *de incendios* fire engine.
bomba[2], *s. f.* bomb; *a prueba de* ~ shell-proof.
bombardear, *v. a.* bombard, shell.
bombero, *s. m.* fireman.
bombilla, *s. f.* (incandescent) bulb.
bombón, *s. m.* bonbon, sweet.
bonachón, *adj.* good-natured.
bondad, *s. f.* kindness, goodness; *tenga la* ~ please.
bondadoso, *adj.* kind.
bonificación, *s. f.* compensation; amelioration.
bonito, *adj.* pretty.
bono, *s. m.* credit note.
boquilla, *s. f.* cigarette holder.
bordado, *s. m.* embroidery.
borde, *s. m.* edge, border.
bordo, *s. m.* (ship)board; *a* ~ aboard.
boreal, *adj.* northerly; *aurora* ~ northern lights.
borla, *s. f.* tassel; powder-puff.
borracho, *adj.* drunk; — *s. m.* drunkard.
borrador, *s. m.* (rough) sketch.
borrar, *v. a.* rub out, erase.
borrasca, *s. f.* storm; ~ *de nieve* snow-storm.
bosque, *s. m.* forest, woods.
bostezar, *v. n.* yawn.
bota, *s. f.* boot; wine bag.
botánica, *s. f.* botany.
botánico, *adj.* botanic(al).
bote, *s. m.* boat; tin, box; stab; jump.
botella, *s. f.* bottle.
botica, *s. f.* pharmacy.
boticario, *s. m.* chemist.
botín, *s. m.* lace-shoe; booty, prey.
botiquín, *s. m.* portable medicine-case.
botón, *s. m.* button; bud.
botones, *s. m.* (hotel) page-boy.
bóveda, *s. f.* vault.
boxear, *v. n.* box.
boxeo, *s. m.* boxing-match.
boya, *s. f.* buoy.
brasero, *s. m.* brazier, fire-pan.
brasileño, *adj.* & *s. m.* Brasilian.
bravo, *adj.* fierce, wild; angry, mad; courageous; *¡~!* Bravo!

brazalete, *s. m.* bracelet.
brazo, *s. m.* arm (of body); foreleg; branch, bough; manpower; might, strength; force.
brea, *s. f.* pitch, tar.
breve, *adj.* brief, short; *en* ~ in a little while, shortly.
bribón, *s. m.* rascal, rogue.
brillante, *adj.* shiny, bright; – *s.m.* diamond.
brillar, *v. n.* shine.
brillo, *s. m.* shine, gloss.
brindar, *v. n.* drink to a person's health.
brindis, *s. m.* toast.
brío, *s. m.* vigour, energy.
brisa, *s. f.* breeze.
brocha, *s. f.* paint-brush, shaving-brush.
broche, *s. m.* hook; brooch.
broma, *s. f.* joke, jest.
bromear, *v. n.* joke.
bromista, *s. m.* joker, wag.
bronquitis, *s. f.* bronchitis.
brotar, *v. n.* bud, sprout.
brote, *s. m.* bud, sprout.
bruja, *s. f.* witch.
brújula, *s. f.* (mariner's) compass.
brumoso, *adj.* foggy.
brusco, *adj.* abrupt, rough.
brutalidad, *s. f.* brutality.
bruto, *adj.* brutish; stupid.
bucle, *s. m.* curl, ringlet.
budín, *s. m.* pudding.
bueno, *adj.* good; *no estoy muy* ~ I'm not feeling very well; *¡~!* all right!; *~s días* good morning; *por las buenas* willingly.
buey, *s. m.* ox, bullock.
bufanda, *s. f.* muffler, scarf.
bufón, *adj.* foolish; – *s. m.* court-fool.
buho, *s. m.* owl.
buitre, *s. m.* vulture.
bujía, *s. f.* candle; sparking-plug.
bulto, *s. m.* bundle; *sacar el* ~ duck out.
bulla, *s. f.* noise, racket.
buque, *s. m.* ship, steamer; ~ *de guerra* man-of-war; ~ *de vela* sailing-vessel.
burgués, *s. m.* bourgeois; citizen.
burla, *s. f.* mockery, jest; *por* ~ in jest, for fun.
burlador, *s. m.* rogue.
burlesco, *adj.* burlesque.
burocracia, *s. f.* red tape.
burro, *s. m.* donkey, ass; jackass, dope.
busca, *s. f.* search; *en* ~ *de* in search of.
buscar, *v. a.* look for, seek.
busto, *s. m.* bust (body).
butaca, *s. f.* armchair; orchestra stall seat.
buzo, *s. m.* diver.
buzón, *s. m.* letter-box.

C

¡ca!, *int.* oh no! no indeed.
cabal, *adj.* complete.
cábala, *s. f.* cabal, intrigue.
caballa, *s. f.* mackerel.
caballeresco, *adj.* chivalrous.
caballería, *s. f.* cavalry; saddle-horse.
caballeriza, *s. f.* stable.
caballero, *s. m.* knight; nobleman; gentleman; *¡~!* sir!

caballo, *s. m.* horse; (chess) knight; *a ~* on horseback.
cabaña, *s. f.* cabin, hut.
cabaret, *s. m.* cabaret, night-club.
cabecear, *v. n.,* shake (head); doze off; pitch (boat).
cabecera, *s. f.* head (of a bed, table); seat of honour; *médico de ~* family doctor.
cabello, *s. m.* hair (of the head).
caber, *v. n.* fit, be contained in; go through; *no cabe duda* there is no doubt.
cabeza, *s. f.* head; mind, brains; *s. m.* chief, leader, head.
cabezudo, *adj.* stubborn, obstinate.
cabildo, *s. m.* municipal council.
cable, *s. m.* cable; cablegram.
cabo, *s. m.* end; cape; corporal; *al ~* at the end; *al ~ de* after; *de ~ a rabo* from beginning to end; *dar ~ a* end, put an end to; *llevar a ~* carry out.
cabotaje, *s. m.* coasting.
cabra, *s. f.* goat.
cabritilla, *s. f.* kid (glove).
cacahuete, *s. m.* peanut.
cacao, *s. m.* cacao tree, cocoa bean.
cacería, *s. f.* hunting.
cacerola, *s. f.* casserole.
cacharro, *s. m.* old rickety vehicle.
cachear, *v. a.* search sy.
cada, *adj.* every, each; *~ dia* every day; *~ cual, ~ uno* every one; *~ vez que* whenever.
cadáver, *s. m.* corpse.
cadena, *s. f.* chain; range (of mountains).
cadena-oruga, *s. f.* caterpillar tread.
cadera, *s. f.* hip.
cadete, *s. m.* cadet.
caer, *v. n.* fall; *~ enfermo* fall ill; *~ en la cuenta* realize, notice, think of; *dejar ~* drop.
café, *s. m.* coffee; café.
cafetera, *s. f.* coffee-pot.
caida, *s. f.* fall, drop; collapse; *a la ~ del sol* at sunset.
caja, *s. f.* box, case; cash desk; *~ de ahorros* savingsbank; *~ de caudales* safe; *~ registradora* cash register.
cajero, *s. m.* cashier.
cajón, *s. m.* box; drawer.
cajetilla, *s. f.* pack of cigarettes.
cal, *s. f.* lime.
calabaza, *s. f.* pumpkin; *dar ~s* plough (at an examination); refuse, reject (a declaration of love).
calamar, *s. m.* cuttle-fish, squid.
calambre, *s. m.* cramp.
calamidad, *s. f.* calamity disaster, misfortune.
calamitoso, *adj.* disastrous.
calar, *v. a. & n.* pierce, penetrate; *~se* get drenched.
calavera, *s. f.* skull; madcap.
calcañar. *s. m.* heel.

calcetín, *s. m.* sock.
calculación, *s. f.* calculation.
calculadora, *s. f.* calculating machine.
calcular, *v. a.* calculate, figure out.
cálculo, *s. m.* calculation.
calda, *s. f.* heating.
caldear, *v. a.* heat.
caldera, *s. f.* kettle, boiler.
caldo, *s. m.* broth, beef-tea.
calefacción, *s. f.* heating (system).
calendario, *s. m.* calendar.
calentador, *s. m.* boiler.
calentar, *v. a.* & *n.* heat, warm; *~se* get warm.
calentura, *s. f.* fever.
calidad, *s. f.* quality.
cálido, *adj.* warm, hot.
caliente, *adj.* hot; ardent.
calificable, *adj.* qualifiable.
calificación, *s. f.* qualification.
calificar, *v. a.* qualify.
cáliz, *s. m.* cup.
calma, *s. f.* calm, quiet.
calmante, *adj.* & *s. m.* anodyne, analgesic, sedative.
calmar, *v. a.* calm, soothe; *v. n.* *~se* calm down.
calor, *s. m.* heat; *hace ~* it's warm; *tengo ~* I'm warm.
calumnia, *s. f.* slander.
calumniar, *v. a.* slander.
calumnioso, *adj.* slanderous.
caluroso, *adj.* warm, hot.
calva, *s. f.* bald head; baldness.
calvo, *adj.* bald.
calzada, *s. f.* paved highway.
calzado, *s. m.* footwear.
calzador, *s. m.* shoehorn.
calzar, *v. a.* put on *or* wear (shoes).
calzones, *s. m. pl.* breeches; *~ de baño* bathing-drawers.
calzoncillos, *s. m. pl.* drawers, shorts.
callado, *adj.* silent.
callar, *v. a.* conceal; *v. n.* keep quiet; *~se* shut up, stop talking.
calle, *s. f.* street: *echar a la ~* throw out, fire.
callejón, *s. m.* alley, lane.
callo, *s. m.* corn (on the foot).
cama, *s. f.* bed; *guardar ~* be confined to bed.
cámara, *s. f.* camera; *~ de comercio* chamber of commerce.
camarada, *s. m., f.* comrade; pal.
camarera, *s. f.* (chamber)maid; waitress.
camarero, *s. m.* waiter; valet, steward.
camarote, *s. m.* cabin, stateroom.
cambiar, *v. a.* change.
cambio, *s. m.* change; small change, coins; *~ del dia* rate of the day; *a ~ de* in exchange for.
cambista, *s. m.* money changer.
camello, *s. m.* camel.
camilla, *s. f.* stretcher, litter.
caminador, *s. m.* walker.
caminar, *v. n.* walk.
caminata, *s. f.* long walk, hike.

camino, *s. m.* road, way; method; *ponerse en* ~ set out.
camión, *s. m.* (motor) lorry.
camioneta, *s. f.* delivery-van.
camisa, *s. f.* shirt.
camisería, *s. f.* gentlemen's outfitting.
camiseta, *s. c.* under-vest.
camisón, *s. m.* night-dress.
campamento, *s. m.* camp.
campana, *s. f.* bell; ~ *de chimenea* chimney-hood.
campanada, *s. f.* stroke of a bell *or* clock.
campanario, *s. m.* bell-tower, belfry.
campanilla, *s. f.* small bell, hand-bell.
campaña, *s. f.* campaign.
campeón, *s. m.* champion.
campeonato, *s. m.* championship.
campesino, *s. m.* peasant.
campestre, *adj.* rural.
campo, *s. m.* country; field; *en el* ~ in the country.
caña, *s. f.* leg (of a boot); reed, cane; walking stick; ~ *de azúcar* sugar-cane; ~ *de pescar* fishing-rod; ~ *de la pierna* shin-bone.
canal, *s. m.* canal; strait, channel.
canalizar, *v. a.* canalize; sewer.
canalla, *s. f.* mob; scamp.
canalón, *s. m.* eaves.
canapé, *s. m.* sofa.
canario, *s. m.* canary; *¡~!* the deuce!
canasta, *s. f.* wide basket.
cañaveral, *s. m.* reeds; sugar-cane plantation.
cancelar, *v. a.* cancel.
cáncer, *s. m.* cancer.
cancha, *s. f.* sports ground.
canciller, *s. m.* chancellor.
canción, *s. f.* song.
candado, *s* ·padlock.
candela, *s. f.* candle.
candelero, *s. m.* candlestick.
candidato, *s. m.* candidate, applicant.
canela, *s. f.* cinnamon.
cañería, *s. f.* water-pipe, pipeline.
cangrejo, *s. m.* crab (shellfish).
canilla, *s. f.* shin-bone; tap.
canjear, *v. a.* exchange.
canoa, *s. f.* canoe.
canónigo, *s. m.* canon.
canoso, *adj.* grey-haired.
cansado, *adj.* tired; tiresome, boring.
cansancio, *s. m.* tiredness, fatigue.
cansar, *v. a.* tire; *v. n.* ~*se* get tired.
cantante, *s. m., f.* singer.
cantar, *v. a.* sing.
cántara, *s. f.* jug.
cantatriz, *s. f.* singer.
cántico, *s. m.* choral, sacred song.
cantidad, *s. f.* amount, quantity.
cantimplora, *s. f.* canteen, water-bottle.
cantina, *s. f.* canteen; wine-cellar.
canto[1], *s. m.* singing, song.
canto[2], *s. m.* edge.
cantor[1], *adj.* singing; *ave* ~*a* singing bird.
cantor[2], *s. m.* singer.
canturrear, *v. a.* & *n.* hum (a tune).

cañón, *s. m.* barrel (of a gun); cannon, gun; canyon, gorge.
cañonazo, *s. m.* cannon-shot.
caoba, *s. f.* mahogany.
caos, *s. m.* chaos.
caótico, *adj.* chaotic.
capa, *s. f.* cape (clothing); coat (of paint); (social) class, rank.
capacidad, *s. f.* capacity; capability.
capataz, *s. m.* foreman.
capaz, *adj.* capable; able, competent; large.
capilla, *s. f.* chapel; hood.
capital, *adj.* capital; *pena* ~ capital punishment; — *s. m.* capital (money) *s. f.* capital (city).
capitán, *s. m.* captain.
capó, *s. m.* (engine) bonnet.
capote, *s. m.* cloak, overcoat.
capricho, *s. m.* whim, fancy.
caprichoso, *adj.* capricious.
captar, *v. a.* get, pick up (broadcasting station).
captura, *s. f.* capture.
capturar, *v. a.* capture.
cara, *s. f.* face.
carabina, *s. f.* carabine.
caracol, *s. m.* snail; *escalera (s. f.) de* ~ winding staircase.
carácter, *s. m.* character; firmness.
característica, *s. f.* characteristic.
caracterizar, *v. a.* characterize; act, play (a part).
¡caramba! *int.* gosh! heavens!
caramelo, *s. m.* candy, sweet.
carbón, *s. m.* coal.
carbonera, *s. f.* coal-scuttle.
carburador, *s. m.* carburetter.
carcajada, *s. f.* burst of laughter, loud laughter.
cárcel, *s. f.* jail, prison.
carcelero, *s. m.* jailer.
carda, *s. f.* teasel.
cardenal[1], *s. m.* cardinal.
cardenal[2], *s. m.* bruise, contusion.
cardinal, *adj.* cardinal; *los puntos ~es* the cardinal points.
cardiograma, *s. m.* cardiogram.
cardo, *s. m.* thistle.
carecer *de*, *v. n.* lack, not to have.
carestía, *s. f.* famine, starvation; rise in prices.
careta, *s. f.* mask; ~ *antigas* gas-mask.
carga, *s. f.* load, freight.
cargamento, *s. m.* shipload; cargo, freight.
cargar, *v. a.* load; charge.
cargo, *s. m.* load; burden; debit; post, charge; *hacerse* ~ *de* assume.
caricatura, *s. f.* caricature.
caricia, *s. f.* caress.
caridad, *s. f.* charity.
caries, *s. f.* (dental) caries.
cariño, *s. m.* affection, love.
cariñoso, *adj.* affectionate.
carlinga, *s. f.* cockpit.
carnaval, *s. m.* carnival.
carne, *s. f.* meat; ~ *de vaca* beef.
carnero, *s. m.* ram; mutton.
carnicería, *s. f.* butcher's shop.
carnicero, *s. m.* butcher.
caro, *adj.* dear; expen-

sive.
carpa, *s. f.* carp.
carpeta *s. f.* letter-file, folder; writing-case; table-cover.
carpintero, *s. m.* carpenter.
carrera, *s. f.* race; sprint; highway; career.
carreta, *s. f.* cart.
carretera, *s. f.* road, highway.
carro, *s. m.* cart.
carroza, *s. f.* coach.
carruaje, *s. m.* carriage (vehicle).
carta, *s. f.* letter; (play) card; ~ *blanca* full discretionary power; ~ *certificada* registered letter; *jugar a las* ~*s* play cards.
cartel, *s. m.* placard, bill, poster; ~ *de teatro* playbill.
cartera, *s. f.* letter-case, wallet; document-case, brief-case.
cartero, *s. m.* postman.
cartón, *s. m.* cardboard.
cartucho, *s. m.* cartridge.
casa, *s. f.* house; home; *voy a* ~ I go home; *en* ~ at home; ~ *de banco* banking-house; ~ *de comercio* commercial firm; ~ *de empeños* pawnshop; ~ *de huéspedes* boarding house; ~ *de socorro* emergency hospital.
casado, *adj.* married.
casamiento, *s. m.* wedding, marriage.
casar, *v. a.* marry; *v. n.* ~*se* get married; ~*se con* marry sy.
cascabel, *s. m.* little bell.
cascada, *s. f.* cascade, waterfall.
cascar, *v. a.* crack.
cáscara, *s. f.* rind, peel; shell (of nuts, eggs).
casco, *s. m.* helmet; hull (of ship); fragment; ~ *de caballo* horse's hoof.
caserío, *s. m.* small village, settlement.
casero, *adj.* home-made; — *s. m.* landlord.
casi, *adv.* almost, nearly.
casilla, *s. f.* hut; pigeonhole; square.
caso, *s. m.* case; occurrence, event; *en tal* ~ in such a case; *en todo* ~ at all events, anyway; *hacer* ~ *a* pay attention to, heed.
¡cáspita! *int.* good gracious! the deuce!
castaña, *s. f.* chestnut.
castañeta, *s. f.* castanet.
castaño, *adj.* brown; — *s. m.* chestnut-tree.
castillo, *s. m.* castle.
castizo, *adj.* correct, pure; genuine, real.
casto, *adj.* chaste; pure.
casual, *adj.* accidental.
casualidad, *s. f.* coincidence; *por* ~ by chance.
catálogo, *s. m.* catologue, list.
catarro, *s. m.* cold, catarrh.
catástrofe, *s. f.* catastrophe.
cátedra, *s. f.* lecturing desk.
catedral, *s. f.* cathedral.
catedrático, *s. m.* professor.
categoría, *s. f.* category, class; rank; *de* ~ of importance.
católico, *adj.* & *s. m.* Catholic.
catorce, *adj.* & *s. m.* fourteen.
catre, *s. m.* campbed.
caución, *s. f.* guarantee,

bail.
caucho, *s. m.* rubber (material).
caudal, *s. m.* fortune, wealth, means; volume (of water).
caudillo, *s. m.* leader, chief.
causa, *s. f.* cause; case, trial, lawsuit; *a ~ de* because of.
causar, *v. a.* cause, occasion.
cautela, *s. f.* (pre)caution; reserve.
cautivar, *v. a.* capture.
cauto, *adj.* cautious, careful.
cavar, *v. a.* dig.
caverna, *s. f.* cavern, cave.
cavial, caviar, *s. m.* caviar.
caza, *s. f.* hunt, hunting; game; *andar a ~ de* go in search of.
cazador, *s. m.* hunter.
cazar, *v. a. & n.* hunt.
cebada, *s. f.* barley.
cebar, *v. a.* feed; nourish.
cebo, *s. m.* bait.
cebolla, *s. f.* onion; bulb.
ceder, *v. a.* transfer, turn over, cede; *v. n.* yield, give in.
cédula, *s. f.; ~ personal* identity card.
ceja, *s f.* eyebrow.
celda, *s. f.* cell.
celebración, *s. f.* celebration.
celebrar, *v. a.* celebrate, commemorate; praise, applaud, approve; be glad, rejoice; hold (a session).
célebre, *adj.* famous.
celebridad, *s. f.* celebrity.
celeridad, *s. f.* swiftness, speed.
celo, *s. m.* zeal, enthusiasm; *~s pl.* jealousy; *tener ~s* be jealous.
celosía, *s. f.* Venetian blind, jealousy.
celoso, *adj.* jealous; zealous.
celulosa, *s. f.* cellulose.
cementerio, *s. m.* cemetery, graveyard.
cemento, *s. m.* cement, concrete; *~ armado* ferro-concrete.
cena, *s. f.* dinner, supper.
cenar, *v. n.* dine, eat; *v. a.* have for supper.
cenicero, *s. m.* ash-tray.
ceniza, *s. f.* ashes, cinders.
censura, *s. f.* censorship; reproach, criticism.
censurar, *v. a.* blame, criticize.
centavo, *s. m.* a hundredth; centavo (money of South America).
centella, *s. f.* spark.
centenar, *s. m.* a hundred.
centenario, *adj. & s. m.* centenary.
centeno, *s. m.* rye.
centésimo, *adj.* hundredth.
centímetro, *s. m.* centimetre.
céntimo, *s. m.* cent, céntimo (Spanish money).
centinela, *s. m.* sentry, guard; *estar de ~* be on guard.
central, *adj. & s. f.* central; *~ eléctrica* electric power plant.
céntrico, *adj.* central.
centrifugador, *s. m.* separator, centrifuge.
centro, *s. m.* centre; city.
cepillar, *v. a.* brush; plane, make smooth.
cepillo, *s. m.* brush; *~ de cabeza* hairbrush; *~ de carpintero* car-

penter's plane; ~ *de dientes* toothbrush; ~ *de ropa* clothes brush.
cera, *s. f.* wax.
cerámica, *s. f.* ceramics.
cerca[1], *s. f.* fence.
cerca[2], *adv.* near; nearly, about, almost; *por aquí* ~ near here; – *prep.* ~ *de* near (in place).
cercanía, *s. f.* nearness, proximity.
cercano, *adj.* near, close.
cercar, *v. a.* surround, fence in.
cerciorarse, *v. n.*: ~ *de* make sure of sg.
cerdo, *s. m.* pig; pork.
cereal, *adj.* & *s. m.* cereal.
cerebro, *s. m.* brain(s).
ceremonia, *s. f.* ceremony.
ceremonioso, *adj.* formal, ceremonial.
cereza, *s. f.* cherry.
cerilla, *s. f.* match.
cero, *s. m.* zero; nought.
cerradura, *s. f.* lock.
cerrar, *v. a.* close, shut.
cerro, *s. m.* hill.
cerrojo, *s. m.* bolt, latch.
certero, *adj.* well-aimed.
certeza, *s. f.* assurance, certainty.
certificado, *adj.*; *carta* ~*a* registered letter; – *s. m.* certificate.
certificar, *v. a.* attest, certify; register (a letter).
cervecería, *s. f.* brewery; beer-saloon.
cerveza, *s. f.* beer, ale.
cesar, *v. a.* stop, cease; *sin* ~ without interruption.
cesión, *s. f.* cession.
césped, *s. m.* lawn, grass.
cesta, *s. f.* basket.
cesto, *s. m.* large basket.
ciática, *s. f.* sciatica.
cicatriz, *s. f.* scar.
cicatrizar, *v. n.* cicatrize, scar.
ciclismo. *s. m.* cycling.
ciclista, *s. m., f.* cyclist.
ciclón, *s. m.* cyclone.
ciego, *adj.* & *s. m.* blind (person); *a ciegas* in the dark, blindly.
cielo, *s. m.* sky; paradise, heaven; *llovido del* ~ out of a clear sky.
cien, *adj.* & *s. m.* one hundred; ~ *mil* a hundred thousand.
ciencia, *s. f.* science.
científico, *adj.* scientific.
ciento, *adv* & *s. m.* one hundred; *por* ~ per cent.
cierre, *s. m.* closing, closure; ~ *metálico* rolling shutter; ~ *de cremallera* zip fastener.
cierto, *adj.* sure, certain, true; – *adv.* certainly.
ciervo, *s. m.* deer.
cifra, *s. f.* figure, digit; code; *en* ~ in code.
cifrar, *v. a.* figure; code.
cigarrera, *s. f.* woman cigar maker; cigar-box.
cigarrillo, *s. m.* cigarette.
cigarro, *s. m.* cigar.
cigüeña, *s. f.* stork.
cilindro, *s. m.* cylinder.
cima, *s. f.* summit, peak.
cinco, *adj.* & *s. m.* five.
cincuenta, *adj.* & *s. m.* fifty.
cine, *s. m.* cinema, the pictures.
cínico, *adj.* cynic(al).
cinta, *s. f.* ribbon; ~ *(cinematográfica)* film, moving picture; ~ *magnetofónica* recording tape.
cintura, *s. f.* waist.
cinturón, *s. m.* belt.
circo, *s. m.* circus.
circuito, *s. m.* (electric)

circuit; *corto* ~ short circuit.
circulación, *s. f.* circulation; traffic.
circular[1], *v. n.* move about, get around, circulate.
circular[2], *adj.* circular; — *s. f.* circular (letter).
círculo, *s. m.* circle; club.
ciruela, *s. f.* plum.
cirugía, *s. f.* surgery.
cirujano, *s. m.* surgeon.
cisne, *s. m.* swan.
cisterna, *s. f.* cistern.
cita, *s. f.* appointment, date; quotation.
citación, *s. f.* summons; citation; quotation.
ciudad, *s. f.* city; town.
ciudadanía, *s. f.* citizenship.
ciudadano, *s. m.; -a, s. f.* citizen; towns(wo)man.
cívico, *adj.* civic.
civil, *adj.* civil; *guardia* ~ constabulary; *guerra* ~ civil war; *derechos ~es* civil rights.
civilización, *s. f.* civilization, culture.
civilizar, *v. a.* civilize.
clara, *s. f.* white of egg.
claramente, *adv.* clearly, openly, frankly.
clarear, *v. n.* dawn; grow light.
claridad, *s. f.* clearness, distinctness.
clarín, *s. m.* trumpet.
claro, *adj.* clear; plain; transparent; thin (hair); fair, cloudless (day); light (suit).
clase, *s. f.* class, kind, sort; classroom; *dar* ~ give a lesson, teach.
clásico, *adj.* classical; — *s. m.* classic.
clasificar, *v. a.* sort out, classify.
claustro, *s. m.* cloister.
clavar, *v. a.* nail; stick, pin.
clave, *s. f.* key (of a code); key (in music).
clavel, *s. m.* carnation, pink.
clavo, *s. m.* nail; clove; *dar en el* ~ hit the nail on the head.
clérigo, *s. m.* clergyman.
clero, *s. m.* clergy.
cliente, *s. m.* client, customer.
clientela, *s. f.* clientèle.
clima, *s. m.* climate.
clínica, *s. f.* clinic.
cloaca, *s. f.* sewer, sink.
clorosis, *s. f.* greensickness, chlorosis.
clorótico, *adj.* chlorotic.
club, *s. m.* club.
cobarde, *adj.* cowardly; — *s. m., f.* coward.
cobardía, *s. f.* cowardice.
cobertizo, *s. m.* shed.
cobrador, *s. m.* collector (of bills, taxes); conductor (of bus, trolley).
cobrar, *v. a.* collect, receive; cash; *v. n.* charge.
cobre, *s. m.* copper.
cobro, *s. m.* collection (of money due).
cocer, *v. a. & n.* boil; bake.
cocina, *s. f.* kitchen; cuisine, cooking.
cocinar, *v. a. & n.* cook.
cocinera, *s. f.*; **cocinero,** *s. m.* cook.
coche, *s. m.* carriage, coach; car; *~-cama* sleeping-car; *~-comedor* dining-car.
cochero, *s. m.* coachman.
código, *s. m.* code (of laws).

codo, *s. m.* elbow.
cofre, *s. m.* trunk; chest.
coger, *v. a.* catch; pick, gather .
coincidencia, *s. f.* coincidence.
coincidir, *v. n.* coincide, agree.
cojín, *s. m.* pad, cushion.
cojo, *adj.* lame, limping.
col, *s. f.* cabbage.
cola[1], *s. f.* tail; train (of dress); line of people, queue; *hacer* ~ stand in line, queue.
cola[2], *s. f.* glue.
colaboración, *s. f.* collaboration, working together.
colaborador, *s. m.* collaborator, co-worker.
colaborar, *v. n.* collaborate, cooperate; contribute.
colación, *s. f.* snack; comparison.
colador, *s. m.* colander, strainer.
colar, *v. a.* strain.
colcha, *s. f.* bedspread.
colchón, *s. m.* mattress.
colección, *s. f.* collection (of things).
coleccionar, *v. a.* collect (stamps, coins).
colecta, *s. f.* collection (charity).
colectivo, *adj.* collective.
colega, *s. m.* fellow-worker, colleague.
colegio, *s. m.* school; association, college.
cólera[1], *s. f.* anger, rage, fury.
cólera[2], *s. f.* cholera.
colgadero, *s. m.* hook.
colgar, *v. a.* hang.
coliflor, *s. f.* cauliflower.
colina, *s. f.* hill.
colindante, *adj.* adjacent, contiguous.
colisión, *s. f.* collision.
colmena, *s. f.* bee-hive.
colmo, *s. f.* excess; *fig.* top.
colocación, *s. f.* arrangement; job, position.
colocar, *v. a.* put, arrange; take on; ~ *dinero* invest (money); *v. n.* ~*se* take a job.
colonia, *s. f.* colony; settlement; *(agua de) Colonia* eau-de-Cologne.
color, *s. m.* colour; complexion; *de* ~ coloured.
colorar, *v. a.* colour.
colorido, *s. m.* colours, colouring.
columna, *s. f.* column.
columpio, *s. m.* swing.
comadre, *s. f.* godmother; midwife; old woman; gossip.
comadrear, *v. n.* gossip.
comandante, *s. m.* commander; major.
comandita, *s. f.* sociedad *(s. f.) en* ~ limited partnership.
comarca, *s. f.* tract of land, region.
combatir, *v. a.* combat, fight; attack; oppose.
combinar, *v. a.* combine, join, unite.
combustible, *s. m.* fuel.
comedia, *s. f.* comedy; play.
comediante, *s. m.* actor.
comedor, *s. m.* dining-room.
comentar *v. a.* & *n.* comment on.
comentario, *s. m.* remark, comment, commentary.
comenzar, *v. a.* & *n.* begin, commence.
comer, *v. a.* eat; dine; ~*se* eat up.
comercial, *adj.* commercial.
comerciante, *s. m.* mer-

chant.

comerciar, *v. n.* trade, deal.

comercio, *s. m.* commerce, trade, business; store, shop.

comestible, *adj.* edible, good to eat; — **~s** *s. m. pl.* eatables, victuals; *tienda (s. f.) de* **~s** provision stores.

cometa, *s. m.* comet; kite.

cometer, *v. a.* commit.

cómico, *adj.* comic, funny, amusing; — *s. m.* actor.

comida, *s. f.* food; dinner.

comienzo, *s. m.* beginning; start.

comillas, *s. f. pl.* quotation mark, inverted comma.

comisaría, *s. f.* police-station.

comisario, *s. m.*; *~ de policía* chief of police.

comisión, *s. f.* assignment; committee, delegation.

comité, *s. m.* board, committee.

comitiva, *s. f.* suite, retinue.

como, *conj. & adv.* how; as; since; like; if.

¿cómo? *adv. & conj.* how? why?

cómoda, *s. f.* chest of drawers.

comodidad, *s. f.* convenience, ease, comfort.

cómodo, *adj.* convenient, handy; comfortable.

compadecer, *v. a.* pity, sympathize with.

compadre, *s. m.* godfather, gossip.

compañero, *s. m.* companion, pal, schoolmate.

compañía, *s. f.* company; *hacer ~ a* keep company with sy.

comparable, *adj.* comparable.

comparación, *s. f.* comparison.

comparar, *v. a.* compare.

comparecer, *v. n.* appear (in answer to summons).

comparsa, *s. f.* suite; (theatre) extra.

compartimiento, *s. m.* compartment.

compartir, *v. a.* share.

compás, *s. m.* compass; rhythm, time; (music) bar.

compasión, *s. f.* compassion, pity, sympathy.

compasivo, *adj.* pitiful, compassionate.

compatriota, *s. m., f.* (fellow) countryman, fellow citizen.

compendiar, *v. a.* abridge.

compendio, *s. m.* extract, summary; compendium.

compensar, *v. a.* balance, compensate.

competencia, *s. f.* competition, rivalry.

competidor, *s. m.* competitor, rival.

competir, *v. n.* compete.

complacer, *v. a.* please, accommodate; *v. n.* **~se** *en* take pleasure in sg.

completar, *v. a.* complete, finish.

completo, *adj.* complete; full; *por ~* completely.

cómplice, *s. m., f.* accomplice.

componente, *s. m.* component (part).

componer, *v. a.* repair, fix; compose; *v. n.* **~se** *de* be composed of, consist of.

comportar, *v. a.* tolerate; *v. n.* **~se** behave oneself.
composición, *s. f.* composition.
compositor, *s. m.* composer.
compota, *s. f.* stewed fruit.
compotera, *s. f.* compote dish.
compra, *s. f.* purchase, buy; *ir de ~s* go shopping.
comprador, *s. m.* purchaser, buyer.
comprar, *v. a.* purchase, buy.
comprender, *v. a.* understand, comprehend; include, comprise.
comprimir, *v. a.* compress.
comprobar, *v. a.* verify, confirm; check.
comprometer, *v. a.* risk; expose, jeopardize, endanger; *v. n.* **~se** get involved; become engaged.
compromiso, *s. m.* obligation, engagement; predicament, plight, fix.
computar, *v. a.* compute, calculate.
común, *adj.* common, usual, general; *por lo ~* as a rule, in general.
comunicación, *s. f.* communication.
comunicar, *v. a.* communicate, transmit, issue; *v. n.* **~se** tell one another.
con, *prep.* with; *~ tal que* provided that.
concebir, *v. a.* imagine.
conceder, *v. a.* give, grant.
concentrar, *v. a. & n.* concentrate.
concepto, *s. m.* judgement, opinion.
concertar, *v. a.* close, settle; agree.
concesión, *s. f.* concession, grant.
conciencia, *s. f.* conscience; consciousness; scruples; *a ~* conscientiously; painstakingly.
concienzudo, *adj.* conscientious.
concierto, *s. m.* concert; agreement.
conciliar, *v. a.* conciliate, reconcile; *~ el sueño* fall asleep; *v. n.* **~se** be reconciled with sy.
concilio, *s. m.* council.
conciudadano, *s. m.* fellow-citizen.
concluir, *v. a.* conclude, end, close, finish.
concluyente, *adj.* conclusive.
concordar, *v. a. & n.* concord.
concretar, *v. a.* express concretely.
concreto, *adj.* definite, concrete; *en ~* concretely.
concurrencia, *s. f.* concurrence, participants, public.
concurrente, *adj.* concurrent; — *s. m.* competitor.
concurrido, *adj.* much frequented, well-attended.
concurrir, *v. n.* attend.
concurso, *s. m.* competition, contest.
concha, *s. f.* shell; prompter's box.
condado, *s. m.* county.
conde, *s. m.* count (title).
condecoracón, *s. f.* decoration; order, medal.
condecorar, *v. a.* decorate

(with a medal).
condena, *s. f.* sentence, term of imprisonment, penalty.
condenar, *v. a.* sentence; declare guilty; condemn, blame.
condensar, *v. a.* condense.
condición, *s. f.* condition; character; quality, state; *condiciones s. f. pl.* terms; *a ~ de que* on condition that, provided that.
condiscípulo, *s. m.* schoolmate, fellow-student.
condolerse, *v. n.* condole.
condonar, *v. a.* condone.
conducir, *v. a.* lead; drive; take, accompany; *v. n.* *~se* act, behave.
conducta, *s. f.* behaviour; conduct.
conducto, *s. m.* pipe, duct.
conductor, *s. m.* guard; conductor; driver.
conectar, *v. a.* connect.
conejo, *s. m.* rabbit.
conexión, *s. f.* connection.
confección, *s. f.* confection.
confeccionar, *v. a.* make, manufacture.
conferencia, *s. f.* conference, meeting; public lecture; (telephone) trunk call.
conferenciar, *v. n.* confer, consult together.
confesar, *v. a.* admit, confess.
confesión, *s. f.* confession, acknowledgment.
confiado, *adj.* trusting, unsuspecting.
confianza, *s. f.* confidence, faith; *de ~* informal, intimate; *en ~* confidentially; in confidence; *tener ~ con* be on intimate terms with; *tener ~ en* trust sy.
confiar, *v. a. & n.* entrust to; *~ en* rely on, trust in, count on.
confidencial, *adj.* confidential.
confidente, *s. m.* intimate friend.
confirmar, *v. a.* confirm, corroborate.
confitería, *s. f.* confectioner's shop.
confitero, *s. m.* confectioner.
confitura, *s. f.* preserves.
conflicto, *s. m.* conflict, struggle.
confluencia, *s. f.* confluence.
conformar, *v. a.* conform; *v. n.* *~se con* content oneself with.
conforme, *adj.* conformable; *estar ~ con* be resigned to, be in agreement with; — *conj.* as; — *prep.* *~ a* in accordance with; ¡~! agreed!
confortante, *s. m.* restorative, tonic.
confundir, *v. a.* confound, mix up; *v. n.* *~se* make a mistake.
confusión, *s. f.* confusion, disorder; embarrassment.
confuso, *adj.* confusing, not clear; confused, mixed up; hazy, vague.
confutar, *v. a.* confute.
congelación, *s. f.* congelation, freezing.
congelarse, *v. n.* congeal.
congestionado, *adj.* congested (traffic).
congraciarse *con,* *v. n.* get into one's good graces.

congratulación, *s. f.* congratulation, good wishes.
congratular, *v. a.* congratulate.
congregar, *v. a.* congregate, assemble; *v. n.* ~*se* gather, assemble.
congreso, *s. m.* congress, convention; *Congreso de los Diputados* House of Representatives.
cónico, *adj.* cone-shaped.
conjeturar, *v. a.* conjecture.
conjunto, *adj.* joint, unified; — *s. m.* whole, entirety; *en* ~ as a whole.
conmemoración, *s. f.* commemoration.
conmemorativo, *adj.* commemorative.
conmigo, *prep.* & *pron.* with me.
conmover, *v. a* move, shock.
conmutador, *s. m.* switch.
conmutar, *v. a.* switch over; commute.
cono, *s. m.* cone.
conocer, *v. a.* know, understand; be acquainted with; *v. n.* ~*se* meet, become acquainted; know each other.
conocido, *adj.* prominent, well-known; — *s. m.* acquaintance.
conocimiento, *s. m.* knowl edge, understanding; consciousness.
conque, *conj.* thus; well then.
conquista, *s. f.* conquest.
conquistador, *s. m.* conqueror; lady-killer.
conquistar, *v. a.* conquer, subdue; win.
consciente, *adj.* conscious.
consecuencia, *s. f.* consequence.
consecuente, *adj* consequential.
consecutivo, *adj.* consecutive.
conseguir, *v. a.* attain, obtain, get; succeed in.
consejero, *s. m.* councillor.
consejo, *s. m.* advice, counsel; council; ~ *de ministros* Cabinet Meeting.
consentir, *v. a.* allow, permit, tolerate; spoil, coddle.
conserje, *s. m.* porter, janitor; care-taker.
conserva, *s. f.* preserves.
conservador, *s. m.* conservative.
conservar, *v. a.* conserve, preserve, keep; *v. n.* ~*se* be well preserved.
consideración, *s. f.* consideration, account; respect; *tomar en* ~ take into consideration.
considerar, *v. a.* consider, think over; esteem highly.
consigna, *s. f.* password; slogan.
consignar, *v. a.* consign.
consigo, *prep.* & *pron.* with himself, (herself, yourself, themselves); *hablar* ~ *mismo* talk to himself.
consiguiente, *adj.* consistent, logical; *por* ~ consequently, therefore.
consistir *en, v. n.* consist of.
consolación, *s. f.* comfort, consolation.
consolar, *v. a.* comfort, console.

consolidar, *v. a.* consolidate, strengthen.
consorcio, *s. m.* syndicate.
consorte, *s. m., f.* partner.
constancia, *s. f.* perseverance.
constante, *adj.* firm, faithful, constant.
constar, *v. n.* be evident, be clear, be certain; be recorded, be registered; ~ *de* consist of, be composed of.
constipado, *s. m.* cold (in the head); catarrh.
constiparse, *v. n.* catch cold.
constitución, *s. f.* constitution.
constituir, *v. a.* constitute; establish, organize.
construcción, *s. f.* construction; structure, building.
constructor, *s. m.* builder.
construir, *v. a.* build, construct.
consuelo, *s. m.* consolation, comfort.
cónsul, *s. m.* consul.
consulado, *s.m.* consulate.
consulta, *s. f.* consultation, conference; office hours.
consultar, *v. a.* consult.
consumado, *adj.* complete, perfect, accomplished.
consumar, *v. a.* carry out, commit.
consumidor, *s. m.* consumer.
consumir, *v. a.* consume, use up.
consumo, *s. m.* consumption.
contabilidad, *s. f.* bookkeeping, accounting.
contable, *s. m.* bookkeeper, accountant.
contacto, *s. m.* contact, touch; ignition.
contado; *al* ~ (for) cash.
contador, *s. m.* accountant, book-keeper; meter (for gas, water etc.).
contaduría, *s. f.* bookkeeping department; *en* ~ booking in advance.
contagiar, *v. a.* infect.
contagio, *s. m.* contagion.
contagioso, *adj.* contagious.
contante, *adj.* cash (money).
contar, *v. a.* count; relate, tell; ~ *con* depend upon, count on.
contemporáneo, *adj.* & *s. m.* contemporary.
contener, *v. n.* contain; check; control; *v. n;* ~*se* contain oneself.
contenido, *s. m.* contents.
contentar, *v. a.* satisfy, please; *v. n.* ~*se con* be satisfied with.
contento, *adj.* happy, glad.
contestación, *s. f.* reply, answer.
contestar, *v. a.* & *n.* reply, answer.
contigo, *prep.* & *pron.* with you.
contiguo, *adj.* adjacent, next.
continental, *adj.* continental.
continente, *s. m.* continent.
continuación, *s. f.* continuation; sequence; *a* ~ immediately, right away.
continuar, *v. a.* & *n.* continue, carry on; go on, keep on; remain.

continuo, *adj.* continuous, uninterrupted.
contorno, *s. m.* contour, outline; neighbourhood.
contra, *prep.* against; *llevar la ~* oppose.
contrabando, *s. m.* contraband, smuggling.
contraer, *v. a.* contract (illness); incur, run into (debt); *~ matrimonio* marry, get married.
contrariar, *v. a.* annoy.
contrariedad, *s. f.* disappointment.
contrario, *adj.* contrary; *al ~, por el ~* on the contrary; *de lo ~* otherwise, if not; *todo lo ~* just the opposite.
contrasentido, *s. m.* nonsense.
contraseña, *s. f.* countersign; check (for readmittance).
contrastar, *v. n.* contrast, be opposed; *~ bien* harmonize; *~ mal* clash.
contraste, *s. m.* contrast.
contratar, *v. a.* engage, hire.
contrato, *s. m* contract.
contravención, *s. f.* transgression, infringement.
contribución, *s. f.* contribution; tax.
contribuir, *v. n.* contribute.
contribuyente, *s. m.* taxpayer.
control, *s. m.* control.
controlar, *v. á.* control.
contusión, *s. f.* contusion.
convalecer, *v. n.* convalesce.
convencer, *v. a.* convince.
convención, *s. f.* agreement, arrangement.
convencional, *adj.* conventional.
conveniencia, *s. f.* decency; self-interest, advantage.
conveniente, *adj.* convenient, suitable; desirable, advisable.
convenir, *v. n.* agree; be advisable; suit.
convento, *s. m.* convent.
conversación, *s. f.* conversation, talk.
conversar, *v. n.* converse, talk.
convertir, *v. a.* convert, turn.
convicción, *s. f.* conviction, belief.
convidado, *s. m.* invited guest.
convidar, *v. a.* invite.
convite, *s. m.* treat, invitation.
convocar, *v. a.* convoke, call.
cooperación, *s. f.* co-operation.
cooperar, *v. n.* co-operate.
copa, *s. f.* (stem)glass, goblet; drink; treetop; crown (of hat); hearts(of playing cards); *sombrero (s. m.) de ~* tophat.
copia, *s. f.* copy.
copiar, *v. a.* copy, make a copy of.
copioso, *adj.* copious.
copla, *s. f.* popular song.
copo, *s. m.* flake (of snow).
coque, *s. m.* coke.
corazón, *s. m.* heart; core (of fruits); *de buen ~* kind-hearted; *de (todo) ~* heartily, sincerely.
corbata, *s. f.* necktie.
corcho, *s. m.* cork.
cordel, *s. m.* thin rope,

cord.
cordero, *s. m.* lamb.
cordial, *adj.* cordial, hearty; — *s. m.* cordial.
cordillera, *s. f.* mountain range.
cordón, *s. m.* cord, lace; cordon (of police).
corneja, *s. f.* crow.
corneta, *s. f.* bugle; cornet.
coro, *s. m.* chorus, choir.
corona, *s. f.* crown; wreath.
coronar, *v. a.* crown.
coronel, *s. m.* colonel.
corral, *s. m.* corral; *aves (s. f. pl.) de* ~ domestic fowls.
correa, *s. f.* strap, belt.
corrección, *s. f.* correction; blame, censure; *casa de* ~ penitentiary.
correcto, *adj.* correct, right; irreproachable.
corredor, *s. m.* runner, racer; corridor.
corregir, *v. a.* correct.
correo, *s. m.* mail; post-office; *echar al* ~ mail; *lista (s. f.) de* ~*s* general delivery.
correr, *v. n.* run, race; flow (river); *v. a.* move, push; draw (the curtain); go over, travel over.
correspondencia, *s. f.* correspondence; mail.
corresponder, *v. a.* return; *v. n.* correspond, match; concern, be up to; ~*se* carry on correspondence.
corresponsal, *s. m.* correspondent.
corrida *(s. f.) de toros* bullfight.
corriente, *adj.* current, common; ordinary; running, flowing (water); instant, present (month, year); — *s. f.* current (of electricity, air, river); *al* ~ informed; *contra* ~ upstream, against the tide.
corromper *v. a.* corrupt.
corrupto, *adj.* corrupt.
cortaplumas, *s. m.* pocket-knife.
cortar, *v. a.* cut; cut short, interrupt; cut off; cut out.
cortauñas, *s. m.* nail-scissors.
corte[1], *s. m.* cut.
corte[2], *s. f.* court; *hacer la* ~ court sy; *las* ~*s* the Spanish parliament.
cortés, *adj.* polite, courteous.
cortesía, *s. f.* courtesy.
corteza, *s. f.* bark (of tree) crust (of bread).
cortina, *s. f.* curtain.
corto, *adj.* short; ~ *de vista* near-sighted.
corzo, *s. m.* roe, doe.
cosa, *s. f.* thing.
cosecha, *s. f.* crop, harvest.
cosechar, *v. a.* reap, harvest.
coser, *v. a. & n.* sew; *máquina (s. f.) de* ~ sewing-machine.
cosmético, *s. m.* cosmetics.
costa[1], *s. f.* expenses, cost; *a* ~ *de* at the expense of; *a poca* ~ with little effort; *a toda* ~ at any cost.
costa[2], *s. f.* coast.
costado, *s. m.* side, flank.
costar, *v. n.* cost.
coste, *s. m.* cost, price.
costilla, *s. f.* rib.

costo, *s. m.* cost, price.
costoso, *adj.* costly, expensive.
costumbre, *s. f.* custom; habit.
costura, *s. f.* sewing; seam.
costurera, *s. f.* seamstress.
cotidiano, *adj.* daily.
cráneo, *s. m.* skull.
creación, *s. f.* creation.
creador, *s. m.* creator.
crear, *v. a.* create.
crecer, *v. n.* increase, grow.
crédito, *s. m.* credit; *dar ~ a* believe.
creencia, *s. f.* belief.
creer, *v. a.* believe; think.
crema, *s. f.* cream (of milk); (cosmetic) cream.
cremallera, *s. f.* cog; zip-fastener.
crepúsculo, *s. m.* nightfall, dusk.
crespo, *adj.* curly.
cría, *s. f.* breeding; the young (of animals).
criada, *s. f.* maid, servant.
criado, *s. m.* man-servant.
criar, *v. a.* raise, bring up.
criatura, *s. f.* baby, infant.
crimen, *s. m.* crime.
criminal, *adj.* & *s. m.* criminal.
crisis, *s. f.* crisis.
cristal, *s. m.* crystal, glass; window-pane; lens.
cristianismo, *s. m.* Christianity.
cristiano, *adj.* & *s. m.* Christian.
criterio, *s. m.* criterion, judgment.
crítica, *s. f.* criticism.
criticar, *v. a.* criticize.
crítico, *adj.* critical; — *s. m.* critic.
cruce, *s. m.* crossing, crossroads.
crudo, *adj.* raw; crude.
cruel, *adj.* cruel.
cruz, *s. f.* cross.
cruzar, *v. a.* cross, go across.
cuaderno, *s. m.* exercise-book, notebook.
cuadra, *s. f.* stable.
cuadro, *s. m.* painting; scene; *a ~s* checked.
cual, *pron.* which; *~ si* as if; *por lo ~* for that reason; that's why.
¿cuál? *pron.* which? which one? what?
cualidad, *s. f.* quality.
cualquier(a), *pron.* any, whatever; anyone.
cuando, *conj.* when; if; *~ más* at most; *~ quiera* when you please; *de ~ en ~* from time to time.
¿cuándo? *adv.* when?
cuanto, *conj.* & *pron.* as much as, all that; *~ antes* as soon as possible.
¿cuánto? *pron.* how much?; *¿~s?* how many?; *¡cuánto me alegro!* how glad I am!
cuarenta, *adj.* & *s. m.* forty.
cuaresma, *s. f.* Lent.
cuartel, *s. m.* barracks.
cuarto, *adj.* fourth; — *s. m.* quarter; room; *son las dos y ~* it's a quarter past two; *~ de baño* bathroom.
cuatro, *adj.* & *s. m.* four.
cuba, *s. f.* barrel, cask.
cubierta, *s. f.* wrapping; cover (of book); deck (of ship).

cubierto, *adj.* covered; cloudy; – *s. m.* place (at table); *~s pl.* set of silver.
cubo, *s. m.* die; cube; bucket, pail.
cubrir, *v. a.* cover; *v. n.* *~se* put on one's hat.
cucaracha, *s. f.* cockroach.
cucurucho, *s. m.* (paper-) bag.
cuchara, *s. f.* spoon.
cucharada, *s. f.* spoonful.
cucharadita, *s. f.* teaspoonful.
cucharita, *s. f.* teaspoon.
cucharón, *s. m.* ladle.
cuchillo, *s. m.* knife.
cuello, *s. m.* neck; collar.
cuenca, *s. f.* deep valley.
cuenta, *s. f.* account; bill.
cuento, *s. m.* story, tale.
cuerda, *s. f.* cord; string; spring (of a watch); *dar ~ a* wind up (a clock).
cuerdo, *adj.* wise, sensible.
cuerno, *s. m.* horn; bugle.
cuero, *s. m.* skin; leather.
cuerpo, *s. m.* body; corps.
cuervo, *s. m.* crow.
cuesta, *s. f.* slope, hill.
cuestión, *s. f.* question, problem; argument.
cuestionario, *s. m.* questionnaire.
cueva, *s. f.* cave; cellar.
cuidado, *s. m.* care; *tener ~* be careful; *¡~!* look out!
cuidadoso, *adj.* careful.
cuidar, *v. a.* take care of, mind; *v. n.* *~se de* take care of.
culpa, *s. m.* fault, blame; sin; *tener la ~* be to blame.
culpable, *adj.* guilty.
culpar, *v. a.* blame, accuse.
cultivar, *v. a.* cultivate.
cultivo, *s. m.* cultivation, cultivated field.
culto, *adj.* cultured, educated; – *s. m.* worship.
cultura, *s. f.* culture (of the mind).
cumbre, *s. f.* top, summit.
cumpleaños, *s. m.* birthday.
cumplido, *adj.* polite.
cumplimiento, *s. m.* performance, fulfilment; compliment.
cumplir, *v. a.* carry out, execute; *~ los veinte años* reach one's twentieth birthday.
cuna, *s. f.* cradle.
cuneta, *s. f.* ditch, gutter (along highway).
cuña, *s. f.* wedge.
cuñada, *s. f.* sister-in-law.
cuñado, *s. m.* brother-in-law.
cuota, *s. f.* share; quota.
cúpula, *s. f.* dome.
cura,[1] *s. m.* priest, minister.
cura,[2] *s. f.* cure, treatment; *~ de urgencia* first aid.
curación, *s. f.* healing, recovery.
curar, *v. a.* cure, treat; *v. n.* *~se* recover.
curiosidad, *s. f.* curiosity.
curioso, *adj.* curious, inquisitive; odd, strange, quaint, rare.
cursar, *v. a. & n.* study.
curso, *s. m.* course.
curva, *s. f.* curve.
curvo, *adj.* curved, bent.
custodia, *s. f.* custody.
custodiar, *v. a.* guard, watch.

cutaneo, *adj.* cutaneous.
cúter, *s. m.* cutter.
cutis, *s. m.* complexion, skin.
cuyo, *pron.* whose.

Ch

chacal, *s. m.* jackal.
chal, *s. m.* shawl.
chaleco, *s. m.* waistcoat.
chalupa, *s. f.* sloop.
champaña, *s. m.* champagne.
champú, *s. m.* shampoo.
chamuscar, *v. a.* singe.
chancleta, *s. f.* slipper.
chanclo, *s. m.* rubbershoe, galosh.
chantaje, *s. m.* blackmail.
chanza, *s. f.* joke, jest.
chapa, *s. f.* plate, sheet (of metal).
chaparrón, *s. m.* heavy shower, downpour.
chapurrear, *v. a.* speak (a language) brokenly.
chaqueta, *s. f.* jacket, coat.
charco, *s. m.* puddle, pond.
charla, *s. f.* chat.
chelín, *s. m.* shilling
cheque, *s. m.* check (money); *talonario (s. m.) de ~s* cheque-book.
chica, *s. f.* little girl.
chico, *adj.* little, small; — *s. m.* little boy, kid.
chicle, *s. m.* chewing gum.
chiflado, *adj.* eccentric, stupid.
chillar, *v. n.* screech, scream.
chimenea, *s. f.* chimney; fire-place; (ship) funnel.
china, *s. f.* pebble, small stone.
chinche, *s. f.* bedbug; drawing-pin.
chino, *adj.* & *s. m.* Chinese.
chiquillo, *s. m.* small child.
chisme, *s. m.* gossip, malicious remark.
chispa, *s. f.* spark; *echar ~s* rage, be furious.
chiste, *s. m.* joke.
chistoso, *adj.* funny, witty.
chivo, *s. m.* kid.
chocante, *adj.* surprising, witty; annoying.
chocar, *v. n.* collide, crash.
chocolate, *s. m.* chocolate.
chófer, *s. m.* chauffeur, driver.
choque, *s. m.* collision, crash.
chorizo, *s. m.* Spanish sausage.
chorro, *s. m.* jet; spurt; *a ~s* abundantly; *llover a ~s* pour (rain).
choza, *s. f.* hut, cabin.
chuleta, *s. f.* chop, cutlet.
chulo, *adj.* good-loking; pretty, handsome; — *s. m.* a tough (in Madrid).
chupar, *v. a.* suck.
churro, *s. m.* a kind of doughnut.
chuzo, *s. m.* spear, pike; spit.

D

dado, *s. m.* die; *jugar a los ~s* play at dice.
dama, *s. f.* lady.
danza, *s. f.* dance.
danzar, *v. n.* dance (as a performance).
dañar, *v. a.* damage; *v. n.*

~*se* go wrong; break down.
daño, *s. m.* damage; *hacerse* ~ get hurt, hurt oneself.
dar, *v. a.* give; *la ventana da a la calle* the window faces the street; ~ *las gracias* thank; ~ *parte* report; ~ *por cierto* feel sure; ~ *recuerdos* give regards; ~*se la mano* shake hands; ~*se prisa* hurry.
datar, *v. a.* date.
dátil, *s. m.* date (fruit).
datos, *s. m. pl.* data.
de, *prep.* of, 's; from; about; *la casa* ~ *mi padre* my father's house; *él es* ~ *Madrid* he is from Madrid; *he llegado* ~ *París* I've come from Paris; *adv.* ~ *memoria* by heart; ~ *niño* as a child; ~ *noche* at night.
debajo, *adv.* below; downstairs; — *prep.* ~ *de* beneath, under.
debate, *s. m.* debate.
deber[1], *v. a. & n.* owe; to have to; *debemos irnos* we have to go; *debe de hacer frío* it must be cold.
deber[2], *s. m.* duty, obligation; homework.
débil, *adj.* weak.
década, *s. f.* decade.
decano, *s. m.* dean.
decena, *s. f.* ten (pieces of sg).
decenio, *s. m.* decennium.
decente, *adj.* decent, nice; honest.
decepcionar, *v. a.* disappoint.
decidido, *adj.* determined.
decidir, *v. a.* decide; *v. n.* ~*se* make up one's mind.
décima, *s. f.* tenth (part).
décimo, *adj.* tenth.
decir, *v. a.* tell, say; *es* ~ that is to say; *decir para sí* say to oneself; *¿qué quiere* ~ *eso?* what does that mean?
decisión, *s. f.* decision; determination.
declamar, *v. a.* declaim.
declaración, *s. f.* declaration, statement; ~ *de aduana* customs declaration.
declarar, *v. a.* declare; testify; *v. n.* ~*se* declare one's love.
declinar, *v. a.* decline.
declive, *s. m.* declivity.
decoración, *s. f.* decoration; (stage) setting.
decorar, *v. a.* decorate.
decoro, *s. m.* dignity, decorum.
decretar, *v. a.* decree.
decreto, *s. m.* decree.
dedicar, *v. a.* dedicate; devote; inscribe, autograph.
dedillo, *s. m.* little finger; *saber al* ~ know perfectly.
dedo, *s. m.* finger; toe.
deducir, *v. a.* deduce, imagine; subtract.
defectivo, *adj.* defective.
defecto, *s. m.* defect, imperfection, shortcoming.
defender, *v. a.* defend; protect.
defensa, *s. f.* defence; protection; — *s. m.* (football) back.
defensor, *s. m.* defender; legal adviser.
deficiencia, *s. f.* deficiency.
deficiente, *adj.* deficient.
definitivo, *adj.* final,

definite.
defuera, *adv.* outside.
defunción, *s. f.* death, decease.
degenerar, *v. n.* degenerate.
dejar, *v. a.* let; leave, abandon; permit, allow; ~ *caer* drop; ~ *dicho* leave word; *déjeme en paz* leave me alone; *dejó de comer* he stopped eating.
del *(de + el), see* **de.**
delantal, *s. m.* apron.
delante, *adv.* in front; — *prep.* ~ *de* before, in front of; in the presence of.
delantera, *s. f.* start, lead; *tomar la* ~ take the lead; front row (of seats); front (of building).
delantero, *s. m.* (football) forward.
delegación, *s. f.* delegation; substitution, proxy.
delegado, *adj.* delegated; — *s. m.* delegate.
delegar, *v. a.* delegate.
deleitar, *v. a.* delight.
deletrear, *v. a.* spell.
delfín, *s. m.* dolphin.
delgado, *adj.* thin, slim; light (coat).
deliberar, *v. a. & n.* deliberate.
delicadeza, *s. f.* delicacy.
delicado, *adj.* delicate.
delicia, *s. f.* delight.
delicioso, *adj.* delightful; delicious.
delineante, *s. m.* draftsman.
delito, *s. m.* crime.
demanda, *s. f.* claim, request; demand, call; legal proceeding, court action; *oferta y* ~ supply and demand.
demandado, *s. m.* defendant.
demandante, *s. m.* plaintiff, claimant.
demandar, *v. a.* claim, demand, request.
demás, *pron. lo* ~ the rest; *los* ~ the others.
demasiado, *adv.* too much; — *adj.* too many.
democracia, *s. f.* democracy.
demócrata, *s. m., f.* democrat.
democrático, *adj.* democratic.
demoler, *v. a.* demolish.
demonio, *s. m.* devil; *¡~!* damn it!
demostración, *s. f.* demonstration; proof.
demostrar, *v. a.* show; prove.
denegar, *v. a.* deny, refuse.
densidad, *s. f.* density.
denso, *adj.* dense, thick.
dentadura, *s. f.* set of teeth.
dentífrico, *s. m.* dentifrice.
dentista, *s. m.* dentist.
dentro, *adv.* inside, within; *por* ~ on the inside; — *prep.* ~ *de* inside (of); ~ *de poco* soon, in a little while.
denunciar, *v. a.* denounce.
departamento, *s. m.* section, department; compartment.
depender *de, v. n.* depend on, be dependent; *depende* it depends.
dependiente, *s. m.* subordinate; shop-assistant.
deplorar, *v. a.* deplore, regret, lament.
deponer, *v. a.* depose.
deportar, *v. a.* deport.

exile.
deporte, *s. m.* sport.
deportista, *s. m., f.* sports(wo)man.
deportivo, *adj.* sport, athletic.
depositar, *v. a.* deposit, put.
depósito, *s. m.* deposit, bond; warehouse; *~ de equipajes* cloak-room.
depresión, *s. f.* depression.
deprimir, *v. a.* depress.
derecha, *s. f.* right hand, right side; *a ~s* right, well; *a la ~* to the right.
derecho[1], *adj.* right (opposed to left); straight; — *adv. siga usted todo ~* go straight ahead.
derecho[2], *s. m.* right; law; tax, duty; *~s de aduana* customs duties; *~s de autor* copyright.
derivar, *v. a.* divert; derive.
derramar, *v. a.* spill.
derretir, *v. a. & n. (~se)* melt.
derribar, *v. a.* demolish, tear down; knock down; overthrow; shoot down (a plane).
derrota, *s. f.* defeat.
derrotar, *v. a.* defeat.
derrumbar, *v. a.* throw down, fell; *v. n. ~se* collapse, tumble down.
desabotonar, *v. a.* unbutton.
desabrigarse, *v. n.* take off the outer clothing.
desacostumbrar *de, v. a.* disaccustom to sg.
desacreditar, *v. a.* discredit.
desacuerdo, *s. m.* disagreement.
desafiar, *v. a.* challenge, defy.
desafío, *s. m.* duel; challenge.
desafortunado, *adj.* unlucky.
desagradable, *adj.* disagreeable, unpleasant.
desagradar, *v. n.* displease.
desaguar, *v. a.* drain.
desagüe, *s. m.* drainage.
desairar, *v. a.* scorn, disregard.
desalentar, *v. a.* discourage.
desaliento, *s. m.* discouragement.
desalojar, *v. a.* expel, evict, eject; *v. n.* move (from dwelling).
desalquilado, *adj.* unrented, vacant.
desalquilarse, *v. n.* become vacant.
desamueblado, *adj.* unfurnished.
desanimado, *adj.* low-spirited, dull, flat.
desanimar, *v. a.* discourage, dishearten; *v. n. ~se* become discouraged.
desanudar, *v. a.* untie.
desapacible, *adv.* grim, raw; dismal.
desaparecer, *v. n.* disappear.
desaparición, *s. f.* disappearance.
desapercibido, *adj.* unprepared.
despreciar, *v. a.* despise.
desaprobar, *v. a.* disapprove.
desarmar, *v. a.* disarm; take to pieces.
desarme, *s. m.* disarmament.
desarraigar, *v. a.* uproot; eradicate.
desarreglar, *v. a.* disar-

range.
desarreglo, *s. m.* disorder.
desarrollar, *v. a. & n.* (*~se*) develop.
desarrollo, *s. m.* development.
desaseado, *adj.* slovenly, not clean.
desastre, *s. m.* disaster, catastrophe.
desastroso, *adj.* disastrous, unfortunate.
desatar, *v. a.* untie.
desatento, *adj.* inattentive; discourteous.
desaviar, *v. a.* mislead.
desayunar, *v. n.* have breakfast.
desayuno, *s. m.* breakfast.
desbaratar, *v. a.* destroy, ruin; *v. n.* *~se* fall to pieces.
desbordar(se), *v. a. & n.* overflow.
descalificar, *v. a.* disqualify.
descalzarse, *v. n.* take off one's shoes.
descalzo, *adj.* barefoot.
descansar, *v. n.* rest.
descanso, *s. m.* rest; interval; landing (of staircase).
descargar, *v. a.* unload; free (from obligation or debt).
descargo, *s. m.* unloading.
descartar, *v. a.* discard, eliminate.
descendencia, *s. f.* descendants.
descender, *v. n.* descend, go down, come down; drop, decrease.
descendiente, *s. m., f.* descendant.
descenso, *s. m.* descent, going down; fall, decrease.
descifrar, *v. a.* decipher, make out.
descolgar, *v. a.* take down.
descolorido, *adj.* faded, pale.
descomponer, *v. a.* decompose, take to pieces; upset (plans); *v. n.* *~se* get out of order; dislocate; spoil; get angry.
descompuesto, *adj.* out of order; spoiled.
desconcertar, *v. a.* disturb, confuse.
desconectar, *v. a.* switch off, disconnect.
desconfiar *de*, *v. n.* distrust, suspect.
desconocer, *v. a.* disregard, ignore.
desconocido, *adj.* unknown, strange; — *s. m.* stranger.
desconsolado, *adj.* disconsolate.
descontar, *v. a.* discount, deduct.
descontento, *adj.* dissatisfied, displeased; — *s. m.* dissatisfaction.
descorchar, *v. a.* uncork.
descortés, *adj.* discourteous, rude.
describir, *v. a.* describe.
descubrimiento, *s. m.* discovery.
descubrir, *v. a.* discover; disclose, show; *v. n.* *~se* take off one's hat.
descuento, *s. m.* discount; deduction.
descuidado, *adj.* slovenly, unclean; careless, negligent; unaware.
descuidar, *v. a.* neglect; *v. n.* *descuide* don't worry.

descuido, *s. m.* carelessness, negligence; *al ~* carelessly; *por ~* through carelessness.
desde, *prep.* from; since; *~ ahora* from now on; *~ entonces* since then.
desdeñoso, *adj.* contemptuous.
desdicha, *s. f.* misfortune.
desdichado, *adj.* unhappy, unfortunate.
desdoblar, *v. a.* unfold.
desear, *v. a.* desire, want, like.
desecar, *v. a.* dry up.
desembalar, *v. a.* unpack.
desembarcar, *v. a.* unload, put ashore; *v. n.* land, disembark.
desembarco, *s. m.* landing, disembarkation.
desembocar, *v. n.* flow into (river); end, lead (street).
desembolsar, *v. a. & n.* pay out.
desembragar, *v. a.* disconnect, uncouple; declutch.
desempeñar, *v. a.* redeem (pawn); carry out (duty, office).
desencantar, *v. a.* disenchant, dissappoint.
desengañar, *v. a.* undeceive, set right; *v. n.* *~se* be disillusioned.
desengaño, *s. m.* disillusion, disappointment.
desenvuelto, *adj.* forward; free and easy.
deseo, *s. m.* desire, wish; *tengo ~ de* I'm eager to.
deseoso *de*, *adj.* desirous, eager.
desertar, *v. n.* desert.
desertor, *s. m.* deserter.
desesperación, *s. f.* desperation.
desesperar, *v. n.* despair, lose hope.
desfavorable, *adj.* unfavourable.
desfilar, *v. n.* march past, parade.
desfile, *s. m.* parade.
desgana, *s. f.* dislike; lack of appetite.
desgarrar, *v. a.* tear, rip.
desgracia, *s. f.* misfortune; sorrow, grief; *por ~* unfortunately.
desgraciado, *adj.* unfortunate.
deshabitado, *adj.* uninhabited.
deshacer, *v. a.* undo; untie, unwrap; dissolve; solve, upset; *v. n.* *~se* wear oneself out; *~se de* dispose of, get rid of.
deshecho, *adj.* undone, not made; worn out, exhausted.
deshielo, *s. m.* thaw.
deshonesto, *adj.* dishonest.
desierto, *adj.* deserted; uninhabited; — *s. m.* desert.
designar, *v. a.* name, appoint.
desigual, *adj.* unequal; uneven.
desilusión, *s. f.* disillusionment.
desinfectante, *s. m. & adj.* disinfectant.
desinfectar, *v. a.* disinfect.
desinteresado, *adj.* disinterested; impartial.
desistir *de*, *v. n.* give up; call off.
desleal, *adj.* disloyal.
deslizarse, *v. n.* slip, slide, glide.
deslumbrar, *v. a.* dazzle.

desmayarse, *v. n.* faint.
desmayo, *s. m.* swoon.
desmentir, *v. a.* disprove; *v. n.* ~*se* take back, retract.
desnudar, *v. a.* undress; *v. n.* ~*se* take off one's clothes, get undressed.
desnudo, *adj. & s. m.* naked, bare, nude.
desobedecer, *v. a.* disobey.
desocupación, *s. f.* unemployment.
desocupado, *adj.* unoccupied, vacant; not occupied.
desocupar, *v. a.* vacate, empty.
desolación, *s. f.* desolation.
desolado, *adj.* desolate, disconsolate; disappointed.
desorden, *s. m.* disorder, confusion, mess.
desordenado, *adj.* disorderly.
desordenar, *v. a.* upset.
desorientar, *v. a.* confuse; *v. n.* ~*se* get confused.
despacio, *adv* slowly.
despachar, *v. a.* ship, send out; attend to, take care of; wait on; dismiss, fire.
despacho, *s. m.* dispatch; office; ~ *de billetes* booking-office.
despedida, *s. f.* farewell.
despedir, *v. a.* see sy off; dismiss, discharge; *v. n.* ~*se* take leave, say good-bye.
despegar, *v. a.* unglue; take off; *v. n.* rise, start (plane).
despejado, *adj.* bright (boy); cloudless (sky).
despejar, *v. a.* clear.
despensa, *s. f.* pantry, larder.
desperdiciar, *v. a.* waste.
desperdicio, *s. m.* waste; ~*s pl.* refuse, garbage.
desperezarse, *v. n.* stretch oneself.
despertador, *s. m.* alarm-clock.
despertar, *v. a.* wake up; arouse, excite; *v. n.* ~*se* wake up.
despierto, *adj.* awake; smart.
despojar, *v. a.* strip, despoil; *v. n.* ~*se de* take off (clothing).
despreciar, *v. a.* despise; scorn, reject.
desprecio, *s. m.* contempt.
después, *adv.* later, then, afterwards; — *prep.* ~ *de* after; ~ *de todo* after all.
desquitarse, *v. n.* get even.
destacado, *adj.* distinguished, famous.
destapar, *v. a.* open (bottle); take off (lid, cover).
destinar, *v. a.* appoint, assign.
destinatario, *s. m.* addressee.
destino, *s. m.* destiny, fate; destination; job; *con ~ a* bound for, going to.
destornillador, *s. m.* screwdriver.
destornillar, *v. a.* unscrew.
destreza, *s. f.* skill.
destrucción, *s. f.* destruction.
destruir, *v. a.* destroy.
desván, *s. m.* attic.
desventaja, *s. f.* disadvantage; handicap.
desventura, *s. f.* misfortune, mishap.
desvergonzado, *adj.* im-

pudent, insolent.
detallar, *v. a.* detail, tell in detail.
detalle, *s. m.* detail.
detener, *v. a.* detain, stop; arrest; *v. n.* *~se* stop.
determinar, *v. a.* determine, fix; decide; *v. n.* *~se* make up one's mind.
detrás, *adv.* behind; — *prep.* *~ de* behind, at the back of.
deuda, *s. f.* debt; *estar en ~* be indebted.
deudor, *s. m.* debtor.
devolver, *v. a.* return, give back; pay back; restore.
día, *s. m.* day; *al ~* a day, per day; *ocho ~s* a week; *quince ~s* two weeks; *todos los ~s* daily, every day.
diablo, *s. m.* devil.
diálogo, *s. m.* dialogue.
diamante, *s. m.* diamond.
¡diantre! *int.* the deuce! the devil!
diario, *adj.* daily; — *s. m.* diary, journal; newspaper.
dibujar, *v.a.* draw, sketch.
dibujo, *s. m.* drawing.
diccionario, *s. m.* dictionary.
diciembre, *s.m.* December.
dictar, *v. a.* dictate; issue (by decree).
dicha, *s. f.* happiness.
dicho, *s. m.* saying; witty remark.
diente, *s. m.* tooth cog.
diez, *adj.* & *s. m.* ten.
diferencia, *s. f.* difference.
diferenciar, *v. a.* distinguish.
diferente, *adj.* different.
diferir, *v. a.* postpone, differ.
difícil, *adj.* difficult, hard.
dificultad, *s. f.* difficulty.
difunto, *adj.* dead, decesased.
difusora, *s. f.* broadcasting station.
digerir, *v. a.* digest.
digestión, *s. f.* digestion.
dignidad, *s. f.* dignity; high rank.
digno, *adj.* dignified; worthy.
diligencia, *s. f.* diligence.
diligente, *adj.* industrious.
diluvio, *s. m.* flood, deluge.
dinamarqués, *adj.* Danish; — *s. m.* Dane.
dineral, *s. m.* large sum of money.
dinero, *s. m.* money.
Dios, *s. m.* God; *¡a ~!* goodbye!; *gracias a ~* thank God.
dique, *s. m.* dam; dock.
dirección, *s. f.* direction; address; board of directors; management; *calle (s. f.) de ~ única* one-way street.
directo, *adj.* direct.
director, *s. m.* director; manager; *~ de escena* stage manager; *~ de escuela* headmaster; *~ de orquesta* conductor.
dirigible, *s. m.* dirigible.
dirigir, *v. a.* direct; address; lead; steer; manage; *v. n.* *~se a* to go to.
discípulo, *s. m.* student, pupil.
disco, *s. m.* disk; (gramophone) record.
discreto, *adj.* discreet; fair.
disculpa, *s. f.* excuse.
disculpar, *v. a.* excuse, pardon; *v. n.* *~se* apologize.
discurso, *s. m.* speech.
discusión, *s. f.* discussion.

discutir, *v. a.* discuss; argue.
disgustar, *v. a.* grieve, displease; *v. n.* *~se* be hurt *or* displeased.
disgusto, *s. m.* quarrel; grief, sorrow.
disimular, *v. a.* conceal, dissimulate.
disminuir, *v. a.* decrease; *v. n.* decline, lessen, diminish.
disolver, *v. a.* dissolve.
disparar, *v. n.* shoot, fire.
disparate, *s. m.* nonsense; mistake.
dispensar, *v. a.* excuse; *dispénseme* excuse me.
disponer, *v. a.* place; arrange; order, decree; *v. n.* *~se a* get ready to.
disponible, *adj.* availal
disposición, *s. f.* dispos..., service; order; arrangement.
dispuesto, *adj.* disposed, ready.
distancia, *s. f.* distance.
distante, *adj.* far, distant.
distar, *v. n.* be distant, be far.
distinción, *s. f.* distinction, difference.
distinguir, *v. a.* distinguish; esteem, show regard for.
distintivo, *s. m.* badge.
distinto, *adj.* different.
distracción, *s. f.* absentmindedness; diversion, pastime, amusement.
distraer, *v. a.* distract; entertain, divert; *v. n.* *~se* be distracted; amuse oneself.
distribución, *s. f.* distribution.
distribuir, *v. a.* distribute.
distrito, *s. m.* district.
disturbar, *v. a.* disturb.
diurno, *adj.* daily.
divagar, *v. n.* digress.
diván, *s. m.* couch.
diverso, *adj.* different.
divertir, *v. a.* amuse. entertain, divert; *v. n.* *~se* be entertained, have a good time.
dividir, *v. a.* divide.
divino, *adj.* divine.
división, *s. f.* division.
divorciarse, *v. n.* get a divorce.
divulgar, *v. a.* reveal, let out; popularize.
doblar, *v. a.* fold; double.
doble, *adj.* double; thick, heavy; deceitful.
doce, *adj.* & *s. m.* twelve.
docena, *s. f.* dozen.
dócil, *adj.* docile, obedient.
doctor, *s. m.* doctor.
documento, *s. m.* document, paper.
dólar, *s. m.* dollar.
doler, *v. n.* hurt, pain.
dolor, *s. m.* pain, ache; sorrow, grief.
domar, *v. a.* tame; subdue.
doméstico, *adj.* domestic; — *s. m.* domestic, servant.
domicilio, *s. m.* residence.
dominar, *v. a.* & *n.* dominate, predominate; overlook, command a view; *v. n.* *~se* control oneself.
domingo, s. m. Sunday.
doncella, *s. f.* maid, servant; girl.
donde, *conj.* & *adv.* where.
¿dónde? *adv.* where?; *¿a ~?* where to?; *¿de ~?* where from ?; *¿por ~?* which way?
dondequiera, *pron.* wher-

ever, anywhere.
dorado, *adj.* gold, gilded.
dormilón, *s. m.* lie-abed.
dormir, *v. n.* sleep; *v. n. ~se* fall asleep.
dormitorio, *s. m.* bedroom.
dos, *adj.* & *s. m.* two; *el ~ de enero* the second of January; *de ~ en ~* in pairs, by twos.
doscientos, *pl.* two hundred.
dote, *a. f.* dowry; talent.
drama, *s. m.* play, drama.
droga, *s. f.* drug.
droguería, *s. f.* druggist's shop.
ducha, *s. f.* shower (bath).
duda, *s. f.* doubt; *sin ~* certainly, without doubt.
dudar, *v. a.* doubt; hesitate.
duelo[1], *s. m.* mourning; sorrow.
duelo[2], *s. m.* duel.
dueño, *s. m.* owner, landlord; master.
dulce, *adj.* sweet; — *s. m.* (a piece of) candy.
duodécimo, *adj.* twelfth.
duplicado, *s. m.* duplicate.
duplicar, *v. a.* double, duplicate, repeat.
duque, *s. m.* duke.
duquesa, *s. f.* duchess.
duradero, *adj.* lasting, durable.
durante, *prep.* during.
durar, *v. n.* last.
duro, *adj.* hard; rough; stubborn; — *adv. trabaja muy ~* he works very hard; *a duras penas* with difficulty; hardly.

E

e *conj.* and (before *i* or *hi*); *padre e hijo* father and son.
ebanista, *s. m.* cabinetmaker.
ébano, *s. m.* ebony.
eco, *s. m.* echo.
economía, *s. m.* economy; *~ política* economics; *~s pl.* savings.
económico, *adj.* economical.
economizar, *v. a.* save.
ecuador, *s. m.* equator.
echar, *v. a.* throw; discharge, dismiss, fire; pour; *~ a correr* begin to run; *~ a perder* spoil, ruin; *~ de menos* miss; *~ la llave* lock the door; *v. n. ~se* lie down; *~se a perder* spoil.
edad, *s. f.* age.
edificar, *v. a.* build.
edificio, *s. m.* building.
editor, *s. m.* publisher.
educación, *s. f.* education, breeding, upbringing.
educar, *v. a.* educate; train.
efecto, *s. m.* effect; impression; *en ~* in fact; *~s pl.* securities; commodities.
efectuar, *v. a.* carry out, put into effect.
eficaz, *adj.* efficient, effective.
egipcio, *adj.* & *s. m.* Egyptian.
egoísta, *adj.* selfish.
eje, *s. m.* axle, axis.
ejecución, *s. f.* execution; performance.
ejecutar, *v. a.* execute, carry out.
ejemplar, *adj.* exemplary; — *s. m.* copy.
ejemplo, *s. m.* example; *por ~* for instance.

ejercer, *v. a.* practise; handle, hold.
ejercicio, *s. m.* exercise, drill.
ejército, *s. m.* army.
el, *m.* (definite article) the.
él, *m. pron.* he.
elástico, *s. m.* & *adj.* elastic.
elección, *s. f.* election; choice.
electricidad, *s. f.* electricity.
electricista, *s. m.* electrician.
eléctrico, *adj.* electric.
elefante, *s. m.* elephant.
elegancia, *s. f.* elegance.
elegante, *adj.* elegant, stylish, smart.
elegir, *v. a.* choose, select, elect.
elemento, *s. m.* element, factor.
elevar, *v. a.* erect; *v. n.* *~se* climb, ascend.
eliminar, *v. a.* eliminate.
elogiar, *v. a.* praise.
elogio, *s. m.* praise.
ella, *f. pron.* she.
ellas, *f. pl. pron.* they.
ello, *pron.* it, that.
ellos, *pl. m. pron.* they.
embajada, *s. f.* embassy; delegation.
embajador, *s. m.* ambassador.
embarcación, *s. f.* shipment; ship.
embarcar, *v. a.* ship, send by boat; *v. n.* *(~se)* embark.
embargo, *s. m.* seizure, confiscation; *sin ~* however, nevertheless.
embellecer, *v. a.* embellish.
emblema, *s. m.* emblem; insignia.
embolsar, *v. a.* put in, pocket.
embragar, *v. a.* couple, put clutch in.
embrague, *s. m.* clutch (car).
embromar, *v. a.* make jokes on.
embuchado, *s. m.* sausage.
embuste, *s. m.* lie.
embustero, *s. m.* liar.
emergencia, *s. f.* emergency.
emigración, *s. f.* emigration.
emigrante, *adj.* & *s. m., f.* emigrant.
emigrar, *v. n.* emigrate.
eminente, *adj.* eminent, famous.
emisión, *s. f.* emission; issue; transmission.
emisora, *s. f.* broadcasting station.
emitir, *v. a.* emit; transmit, broadcast.
emocionarse, *v. n.* be moved.
empacar, *v. a.* pack.
empalmar, *v. n.* make connexions with a train.
empalme, *s. m.* junction; connexion.
empanada, *s. f.* pie.
empapar, *v. a.* soak; *v. n.* *~se* be soaked, be drenched.
emparedado, *s. m.* sandwich.
empastar, *v. a.* stop, fill (tooth).
empate, *s. m.* draw.
empeñar, *v. a.* pledge, give; pawn; *v. n.* *~se* be bent on.
empeño, *s. m.* determination, firmness; pawn, pawning; *con ~* emphatically.
empeorarse, *v. n.* grow worse.
emperador, *s. m.* emper-

or.
empezar, *v. a. & n.* begin.
empleado, *s. m.* employee.
emplear, *v. a.* employ, use; hire; invest.
empleo, *s. m.* employment, use.
empolvarse, *v. n.* powder oneself; get dusty.
emprender, *v. a.* undertake.
empresa, *s. f.* undertaking; enterprise; project; company,
empresario, *s. m.* (theatrical) manager; promoter.
empujar, *v. a.* push.
empujón, *s. m.* push.
en, *prep.* in; on; at; *~ vano* in vain.
enamorado, *adj. & s. m.* in love; sweetheart.
enamorar, *v. a.* make love to, flirt with: *v. n. ~se de* fall in love with.
enano, *s. m.* dwarf.
encadenar, *v. a.* chain.
encajar, *v. n.* fit (in).
encaje, *s. m.* lace.
encaminar, *v. a.* direct; *v. n. ~se* make one's way, go.
encanecer, *v. n.* become gray.
encantador, *adj.* charming.
encantar, *v. a.* charm, delight.
encanto, *s. m.* charm.
encargado, *adj.* in charge; — *s. m.* person in charge, manager.
encargar, *v. a.* entrust; urge, ask; *v. n. ~se* take charge of sg.
encargo, *s. m.* errand; job, assignment.
encarnado, *adj.* red.
encendedor, *s. m.* lighter.
encender, *v. a.* light, put on; *v. n. ~se* light up, go on.
encendido, *adj.* bright-coloured; *ponerse ~* blush.
encerado, *s. m.* oilcloth; blackboard.
encerrar, *v. a.* lock up; include, contain.
encima, *adv.* above; *por ~* superficially; — *prep. ~ de* above.
encinta, *adj. f.* pregnant.
encoger, *v. n.* shrink; *v. n. ~se de hombros* shrug one's shoulders.
encogido, *adj.* bashful.
encolerizar, *v. a.* anger; *v. n. ~se* become angry.
encomendar, *v. a.* entrust to, charge with.
encontrar, *v. a.* find; meet; *v. n. ~se* meet; collide; be (somewhere); feel.
encrucijada, *s. f.* street intersection.
encuadernar, *v. a.* bind (book).
encubridor, *s. m.* receiver (of stolen goods).
encuentro, *s. m.* meeting; match; *salir al ~ de* go to meet sy.
enchufar, *v. a.* join, link up, plug in.
enderezar, *v. a.* straighten; *v. n. ~se* straighten up, sit up.
endosar, *v. a.* endorse.
endulzar, *v. a.* sweeten.
enemigo, *s. m.* enemy.
enemistad, *s. f.* enmity.
energía, *s. f.* energy;

~ eléctrica electric power.
enérgico, *adj.* energetic.
enero, *s. m.* January.
enfadar, *v. a.* anger, annoy; *v. n.* *~se* get angry.
énfasis, *s. m.* emphasis.
enfermar(se), *v. a.* & *n.* fall ill, get sick.
enfermedad, *s. f.* illness, sickness, disease.
enfermera, *s. f.* nurse.
enfermería, *s. f.* sickroom, infirmary.
enfermero, *s. m.* hospital attendant.
enfermo, *adj.* sick; — *s. m.* patient.
enfocar, *v. a.* focus.
enfrenar, *v. a.* rein, check; brake.
enfrente, *adv.* opposite, across; — *prep.* *~ de* opposite.
enfriar, *v. a.* cool; *v. n.* *~se* cool off, become cold; get chilled.
enfurecerse, *v. n.* rage.
enganchar, *v. a.* hook on.
engañar, *v. a.* deceive; *v. n.* *~se* make a mistake, be wrong.
engaño, *s. m.* deceit.
engordar, *v. a.* fatten; *v. n.* get fat.
engrandecer, *v. a.* enlarge, magnify.
engrasar, *v. a.* grease.
enhorabuena, *s f.* congratulations.
enigma, *s. m.* riddle, enigma, puzzle.
enjabonar, *v. a.* soap; lather.
enjuagar, *v. a.* rinse.
enlace, *s. m.* connection; marriage.
enlazar, *v. a.* & *n.* connect.
enojar, *v. a.* anger; *v. n.* *~se* get angry.
enojo, *s. m.* anger, trouble.
enorme, *adj.* enormous.
enrabiar, *v. a.* enrage.
enriquecer, *v. a.* & *n.* enrich; get rich.
enrojecerse, *v. n.* blush.
enrollar, *v. a.* roll up.
enronquecer, *v. n.* get hoarse.
ensalada, *s. f.* salad.
ensanchar, *v. a.* widen; let out, enlarge.
ensayar, *v. a.* try, test; rehearse.
enseñanza, *s. f.* instruction, teaching.
enseñar, *v. a.* teach; show, point out.
ensillar, *v. a.* saddle.
ensordecer, *v. a.* deafen.
ensuciar, *v. a.* soil, dirty.
ensueño, *s. m.* dream.
entablar, *v. a.* board up; begin, start.
ente, *s. m.* being.
entender, *v. a.* understand; be good at, be familiar with, *a mi ~* in my opinion.
entendido, *adj.* informed; skilled; *está ~* it is understood.
entendimiento, *s. m.* understanding; mind.
enteramente, *adv.* entirely, wholly.
enterar, *v. a.* inform, report; *v. n.* *~se* pay attention; find out, inquire; learn.
entero, *adj.* entire, whole.
enterrar, *v. a.* bury.
entierro, *s. m.* burial.
entonces, *adv.* then, at the time; *desde ~* since that time.
entrada, *s. f.* entrance;

admission; attendance; ticket, seat; beginning.
entrar, *v. n.* enter, come in, go in; fit; join.
entre, *prep.* between; among.
entreabierto, *adj.* & *adv.* ajar, half-open.
entreacto, *s. m.* interval.
entrega, *s. f.* delivery.
entregar, *v. a.* deliver; hand (over); give up, surrender; *v. n.* *~se* give in, yield; surrender.
entrenador, *s. m.* trainer, coach.
entrenamiento, *s. m.* training, coaching.
entrenar *v. a.* train.
entresuelo, *s. m.* intermediate storey.
entretanto, *adv.* meanwhile.
entretener, *v. a.* entertain, amuse; delay; *v. n.* *~se* amuse oneself; be delayed.
entretenido, *adj.* entertaining, amusing.
entretenimiento, *s. m.* pastime.
entrevista, *s. f.* interview.
entusiasmo, *s. m.* enthusiasm.
envenenar, *v. a.* poison.
enviado, *s. m.* envoy.
enviar, *v. a.* send.
envidia, *s. f.* envy.
envidiar, *v. a.* envy.
envidioso, *adj.* envious, invidious.
envío, *s. m.* s nding; consignment.
envolver, *v. a.* wrap.
episodio, *s. m.* episode.
época, *s. f.* epoch; period, time.
equilibrio, *s. m.* balance.
equipaje, *s. m.* luggage.
equipo, *s. m.* team; equipment.
equivocación, *s. f.* mistake.
equivocar, *v. a.* mistake, confuse; *v. n.* *~se* make a mistake, be wrong.
equívoco, *adj.* ambiguous.
era, *s. f.* age; threshing-floor.
erario, *s. m.* treasury.
errar, *v. a.* miss.
error, *s. m.* mistake.
esbelto, *adj.* slender, slim.
esbozo, *s. m.* sketch.
escala, *s. f.* ladder; scale; *hacer ~* make a stop, (ship) call at.
escalera, *s. f.* ladder· staircase, stairs.
escalofrío, *s. m.* shivering fit.
escalopa, *s. f.* veal scallop.
escama, *s. f.* scale (of fish).
escandalizar, *v. a.* shock, scandalize.
escándalo, *s. m.* scandal.
escapar(se), *v. n.* escape; run away; slip out.
escaparate, *s. m.* shop-window.
escape, *s. m.* escape, exhaust (car).
escarlata, *s. f.* scarlet.
escasear, *v. n.* be scarce.
escasez, *s. f.* shortage.
escaso, *adj.* scarce, short.
escena, *s. f.* scene; stage.
escenario, *s. m.* stage (of a theatre).
esclavo, *s. m.* slave.
escocés, *adj.* Scotch; — *s. m.* Scotchman.
escoger, *v. a.* choose, select.
esconder, *v. a.* hide.

escopeta, *s. f.* shotgun.
escorpión, *s. m.* scorpion.
escribir, *v. a.* write; ~ *a máquina* type, typewrite.
escrito, *adj.* written; — *s. m.* writing; *por* ~ in writing.
escritor, *s. m.* writer, author.
escritorio, *s. m.* office; desk.
escuadra, *s. f.* (naval) fleet; carpenter's square.
escuchar, *v. a.* listen to.
escudo, *s. m.* shield.
escuela, *s. f.* school.
escultura, *s. f.* sculpture.
ese, *m.*; esa, *f. adj.* that; *esos, esas pl.* those.
ése, *m.*; **ésa,** *f. pron.* that one; *ésos, ésas pl.* those.
esencia, *s. f.* essence.
esencial, *adj.* essential.
esfera, *s. f.* sphere.
esfuerzo, *s. m.* effort.
esmeralda, *s. f.* emerald.
espacio, *s. m.* space; blank; line.
espada, *s. f.* sword; spade (cards); *s. m.* bullfighter.
espalda, *s. f.* back (of the body); *a ~s de* behind one's back.
espantar, *v. a.* scare, frighten.
espanto, *s. m.* fear, fright.
español, *adj.* & *s. m.* Spanish; Spaniard.
espárrago, *s. m.* asparagus.
especial, *adj.* special.
especialista, *s. m., f.* expert, specialist.
espectáculo, *s. m.* spectacle, show; scene.
espejo, *s. m.* mirror.
espera, *s. f.* wait; *sala de* ~ waiting-room.
esperanza, *s. f.* hope.
esperar, *v. a.* hope, expect; wait for.
espeso, *adj.* thick.
espía, *s. m., f.* spy.
espina, *s. f.* thorn; (fish) bone.
espinacas, *s. f. pl.* spinach.
espinazo, *s. m.* spine.
espíritu, *s. m.* spirit, soul.
espléndido, *adj.* splendid, wonderful; generous.
esponja, *s. f.* sponge.
esposa, *s. f.* wife.
esposo, *s. m.* husband.
espuma, *s. f.* foam; lather.
esqueleto, *s. m.* skeleton.
esquema, *s. m.* scheme.
esquí, *s. m.* ski.
esquiar, *v. n.* ski.
esquina, *s. f.* corner (outer).
establecer, *v. a.* establish; *v. n.* *~se* settle.
establecimiento, *s. m.* establishment.
establo, *s. m.* stable.
estación[1], *s. f.* season.
estación[2], *s. f.* station; stop.
estacionar, *v. a.* park (car).
estadio, *s. m.* stadium.
estado, *s. m.* condition; status; state; government.
estanco, *s. m.* tobacconist's shop.
estanque, *s. m.* pond.
estante, *s. m.* shelf.
estar, *v. n.* be (in a place); look, seem; *¿a cuántos estamos? estamos a 2 de mayo* what's the date? it's the second of May; ~ *de*

acuerdo agree; ~ *de viaje* be travelling; *estoy para salir* I'm about to leave: *estoy leyendo* I'm reading; *está bien* all right.
estatua, *s. f.* statue.
estatura, *s. f.* stature; height.
este[1], *s. m.* east.
este[2], *m.*, **esta** *f. adj.* this.
estos, *m. pl.*, **estas,** *f. pl. adj.* these.
éste, *m.*, **ésta,** *f. pron.* this one.
estéril, *adj.* sterile.
esterlina; *libra (s. f.)* ~ pound sterling.
estilo, *s. m.* style.
estilográfica, *s. m.* fountain-pen.
estimar, *v. a.* value, respect.
estimular, *v. a.* stimulate.
estirar, *v. a.* stretch, pull.
esto, *pron.* this.
estofado, *s. m.* stew.
estómago, *s. m.* stomach.
estornudar, *v. n.* sneeze.
estrechar, *v. a.* make narrower, take in; ~ *la mano a* shake hands with.
estrecho, *adj.* narrow; tight; close; – *s. m.* strait.
estrella, *s. f.* star.
estrenar, *v. a.* open, represent for the first time (a play).
estropear, *v. a.* ruin, damage; spoil.
estruendo, *s. m.* noise, din.
estuche *s. m.* case, box.
estudiante, *s. m.* student.
estudio, *s. m.* study.
estufa, *s. f.* stove.
estupendo, *adj.* wonderful.
estúpido, *adj.* stupid.
etapa, *s. f.* stage.
etcétera, and so on.
éter, *s. m.* ether.
etiqueta, *s. f.* label; *de* ~ formal.
europeo, *adj.* & *s. m.* European.
evangelio, *s. m.* gospel.
evento, *s. m.* event.
evitar, *v. a.* avoid; prevent.
exactitud, *s. f.* accuracy; punctuality.
exacto, *adj.* exact, correct; accurate.
exagerar, *v. a.* exaggerate.
examen, *s. m.* examination, test.
examinar, *v. a.* examine; inspect; observe,
excelente, *adj.* excellent; fine.
excepción, *s. f.* exception.
exceso, *s. m.* excess.
excursión, *s. f.* excursion.
excusa, *s. f.* excuse.
excusado, *s. m.* lavatory.
excusar, *v. a.* excuse, pardon; decline; *v. n.* ~*se* apologize.
exhibir, *v. a.* exhibit, show.
exigir, *v. a.* require; demand.
existencia, *s. f.* existence, life; stock.
éxito, *s. m.* success.
expedir, *v. a.* dispatch.
experiencia, *s. f.* experience, experiment.
experto, *adj.* expert, skilled.
expirar, *v. n.* expire.
explicar, *v. a.* explain.
explorador, *s. m.* explorer; boy scout.
explosión, *s. f.* explosion, blast.
explotar, *v. a.* exploit, work; use.

exponer, *v. a.* expose; explain.
exportación, *s. f.* export.
exportar, *v. a.* export.
exposición, *s. f.* exhibition.
expresar, *v. a.* express; *v. n.* *~se* express oneself, speak.
expresión, *s. f.* expression.
expresivo, *adj.* expressive; affectionate.
expreso, *adj.* express, explicit; *tren ~* fast train, express.
exprimir, *v. a.* squeeze out.
expuesto, *adj.* exhibited; in danger.
expulsar, *v. a.* expel.
exquisito, *adj.* delicious; exquisite.
externo, *adj.* external.
extracto, *s. m.* extract.
extranjero, *adj.* foreign; — *s. m.* foreigner; *en el ~* abroad.
extraño, *adj.* strange; — *s. m.* stranger.
extraordinario, *adj.* extraordinary.
extraviarse, *v. n.* lose one's way.
extremo, *adj.* extreme; — *s. m.* end.

F

fábrica, *s. f.* factory
fabricación, *s. f.* manufacture.
fabricante, *s. m.* manufacturer, maker.
fabricar, *v. a.* manufacture, make.
fábula, *s. f.* fable.
fabuloso, *adj.* fabulous.
facción, *s. f.* faction; *facciones pl.* features (of the face).
fácil, *adj.* easy.
facilidad, *s. f.* facility, ease; aptitude.
facilitar, *v. a.* facilitate, make easier; supply.
factura, *s. f.* bill, invoice.
facultad, *s. f.* faculty.
fachada, *s. f.* front (of a building).
faja, *s. f.* sash; girdle; (postal) wrapper.
falda, *s. f.* skirt; lap; slope, (mountain) side.
falsedad, *s. f.* falsehood, lie.
falsificar, *v. a.* forge, counterfeit.
falso, *adj.* false, untrue; forged; — *s. m.* padding, wadding.
falta, *s. f.* error, mistake; fault; misdemeanour; *a ~ de* for lack of; *hacer ~* be necessary, be needed; miss; *me hace falta un tenedor* I need a fork; *sin ~* without fail.
faltar, *v. n.* lack, be missing, be needed; *faltan tres minutos para las seis* it's three minutes to six; *~ a la clase* be absent from class; *¡no faltaba más!* of course! by all means!
fallecer, *v. n.* die.
fama, *s. f.* fame; reputation.
familia, *s. f.* family.
familiar, *adj.* familiar; — *s. m.* relative.
famoso, *adj.* famous.
fanático, *adj. & s. m.* fanatic.
fanfarronear, *v. n.* brag, exaggerate.
fango, *s. m.* mud.

fantasía, *s. f.* imagination; whim; fantasy.
fantasma, *s. m.* ghost.
fantástico, *adj.* fantastic, unbelievable; extravagant.
fardo, *s. m.* big bundle, bale.
faringe, *s. f.* throat, gullet.
farmacéutico, *s. m.* chemist.
farmacia, *s. f.* chemist's shop.
faro, *s. m.* beacon, lighthouse; headlight.
farol, *s. m.* lantern; street-lamp.
farsa, *s. f.* farce.
fase, *s. f.* phase.
fastidiar, *v. a.* annoy, bother.
fastidioso, *adj.* annoying, tiresome.
fatal, *adj.* fatal.
fatalidad, *s. f.* fate.
fatigar, *v. a.* tire; *v. n.* *~se* get tired.
favor, *s. m.* favour; *a ~ de* with, aided by; in favour of; *¿me hace el ~ de pasarme la sal?* will you please pass me the salt?; *por ~* please.
favorable, *adj.* favourable.
fe, *s. f.* faith; *de buena ~* in good faith.
fealdad, *s. f.* ugliness.
febrero, *s. m.* February.
febril, *adj.* feverish.
fecundo, *adj.* prolific, fruitful.
fecha, *s. f.* date.
federación, *s. f.* federation.
felicidad, *s. f.* happiness.
felicitación, *s. f.* congratulations.
felicitar, *v. a.* congratulate.
feliz, *adj.* happy.
femenino, *adj.* feminine.
fenómeno, *s. m.* phenomenon; prodigy.
feo, *adj.* ugly.
feraz, *adj.* fertile.
féretro, *s. m.* coffin.
feria, *s. f.* country-market; fair.
ferretería, *s. f.* ironmonger's shop.
ferrocarril, *s. m.* railway.
fértil, *adj.* fertile.
festivo, *adj.* humorous; gay; *dia ~* holiday.
fiambres, *s. m. pl.* cold meat, cold cuts.
fidelidad, *s. f.* fidelity; faithfulness; exactness.
fideos, *s. m. pl.* vermicelli.
fiebre, *s. f.* fever.
fiel, *adj.* faithful; accurate.
fieltro, *s. m.* felt (material).
fiera, *s. f.* wild animal, beast.
fiesta, *s. f.* holiday; party.
figura, *s. f.* figure, build.
figurar, *v. n.* figure; be conspicuous; *~se* imagine, think.
fijar, *v. a.* fix, set; post; establish; *~ los ojos en* stare at; *v. n.* *~se* imagine; *~se en* pay attention to.
fijo, *adj.* permanent; fixed, set; fast; *de ~* surely.
fila, *s. f.* row; line, rank; *en ~* in line.
filete, *s. m.* steak.
film, *s. m.* film.
filtrar, *v. a.* filter.
fin, *s. m.* end; aim, purpose; *a ~ de que* so that; *a ~es de* toward

the end of; *al* ~ at last, finally; *al* ~ *y al cabo* after all; *por* ~ at last.

final, *adj.* final; — *s. m.* end, conclusion.

finca, *s. f.* piece of land, estate, farm.

fineza, *s. f.* politeness, kindness, courtesy.

fino, *adj.* fine; delicate; refined; thin, sharp; courteous.

firma, *s.f.* signature; firm, commercial house.

firmar, *v. a.* sign.

firme, *adj.* firm, steady.

firmeza, *s. f.* firmness.

fiscal, *adj.* fiscal; — *s. m.* Attorney General.

física, *s. f.* physics.

físico, *adj.* physical; — *s. m.* physicist.

flaco, *adj.* thin, lean; weak.

flan, *s. m.* caramel custard.

flaqueza, *s. f.* weakness.

flauta, *s. f.* flute.

flecha, *s. f.* arrow.

flexible, *adj.* flexible; — *s. m.* electric cord.

flirtear, *v. n.* flirt.

flojo, *adj.* loose; slack; lazy.

flor, *s. f.* flower.

florecer, *v. n.* bloom.

florero, *s. m.* florist; flower-vase.

florido, *adj.* florid, flowery; in bloom.

flota, *s. f.* fleet (of ships).

flotar, *v. n.* float.

flúido, *adj.* & *s. m.* fluid.

foco, *s. m.* focus.

fogón, *s. m.* cooking-stove, range.

follaje, *s. m.* foliage.

folleto, *s. m.* booklet, pamphlet.

fonda, *s. f.* inn.

fondo, *s. m.* bottom; back, background; ~*s pl.* funds; *a* ~ thoroughly; *artículo (s. m.) de* ~ editorial; *en el* ~ at heart, at bottom.

forma, *s. f.* shape, form; way, manner.

formal, *adj.* reliable; serious, settled.

formalidad, *s. f.* red tape; earnestness, seriousness.

formalizar, *v. a.* arrange, legalize.

formar, *v. a.* form, make

fórmula, *s. f.* formula; solution.

formular, *v. a.* draw up, formulate.

foro, *s. m.* law-court; background (stage).

forraje, *s. m.* feed.

forro, *s. m.* lining (in clothing).

fortaleza, *s. f.* fortress; fortitude, strength.

fortuna, *s. f.* fortune; luck; *por* ~ fortunately.

forzar, *v. a.* force, compel.

forzoso, *adj.* compulsory; unavoidable; *paro* ~ unemployment.

fosa, *s. f.* grave.

foso, *s. m.* pit; trap-door.

fósforo, *s. m.* match.

fotografía, *s. f.* photography.

fotografiar, *v. a.* photograph.

fotógrafo, *s. m.* photographer.

fractura, *s. f.* fracture.

fragancia, *s. f.* fragrance.

frágil, *adj.* fragile.

fragmento, *s. m.* fragment.

fraile, *s. m.* monk, friar.

francés, *adj.* French; — *s. m.* Frenchman.

franco, *adj.* frank; free; exempt; ~ *de porte* prepaid.
franela, *s. f.* flannel.
franja, *s. f.* fringe.
franquear *v. a.* prepay, stamp.
franqueo, *s. m.* postage, amount of postage.
franqueza, *s. f.* frankness; *con* ~ frankly.
frasco, *s. m.* bottle, flask.
frase, *s. f.* phrase.
fraternidad, *s. f.* brotherliness, fraternity.
fray, *s. m.* monk, friar.
frecuentar, *v. a.* frequent.
frecuente, *adj.* frequent.
fregadero, *s. m.* kitchensink.
freir, *v. a.* fry.
frenar, *v. a.* (put on the) brake; restrain.
frenesí, *s. m.* madness; frenzy.
frenético, *adj.* very angry; frenzied.
freno, *s. m.* brake; bit (for horses).
frente, *s. f.* forehead; *s. m.* front, battle-field.
fresa, *s. f.* strawberry.
fresco, *adj.* cool; fresh; cheeky; — *s. m.* fresco (painting); *tomar el* ~ get some fresh air.
frescura, *s. f.* coolness; nerve, cheek.
frialdad, *s. f.* coldness; coolness, unconcern.
frigorífico, *s. m.* coldstorage plant, fridge.
frío, *adj.* cold; *hace* ~ it's cold; *tengo* ~ I'm cold.
frito, *adj.* fried; *estar* ~ be annoyed.
fritura, *s. f.* fritter.
frontera, *s. f.* frontier, boundary.
frotar, *v. a.* rub.
fructuoso, *adj.* useful, profitable, fruitful.
fruta, *s. f.* (edible) fruit.
frutal: *adj. árbol (s. m.)* ~ fruit-tree.
frutero, *s. m.* fruiterer.
fruto, *s. m.* fruit; reward; profit.
fuego, *s. m.* fire; *hacer* ~ fire (a weapon).
fuente, *s. f.* fountain; source; dish.
fuera, *adv.* out, outside; *desde* ~ from the outside; *por* ~ on the outside; — *prep.* ~ *de* out of; ~ *de sí* beside oneself; ~ *de eso* besides, moreover; *¡~!* get out!
fuerte, *adj.* strong; intense (cold); heavy (rain); — *adv. hablar* ~ speak loud; — *s. m.* fort; strong point.
fuerza, *s. f.* power; *a la* ~ forcibly.
fuga, *s. f.* flight, escape.
fulano, *s. m.* Mr. so-and-so.
fulminar, *v. n.* flash.
fumador, *s. m.* smoker.
fumar, *v. a.* & *n.* smoke.
función, *s. f.* function, duty, position; show, performance.
funcionamiento, *s. m.* working, functioning.
funcionar, *v. n.* work, function, run.
funcionario, *s. m.* official; functionary.
funda, *s. f.* case, pillowcase.
fundación, *s. f.* foundation, founding.
fundador, *s. m.* founder.
fundamento, *s. m.* basis.
fundar, *v. a.* found, es-

tablish; *v. n.* **~se** base oneself.
funeral *adj.* funeral; – *s. m.* funeral service.
funicular, *s. m.* cable railway.
furgón, *s. m.* luggage-van.
furia, *s. f.* fury.
furioso, *adj.* furious.
furor, *s. m.* fury, anger; rage, fashion.
fusible, *adj.* fusible; – *s. m.* fuse, cut-out.
fusil, *s. m.* (shot)gun.
fusión, *s. f.* fusion.
fútbol, *s. m.* soccer, football (game).
futuro, *adj.* & *s. m.* future; *en lo* ~ in the future, hereafter.

G

gabán, *s. m.* overcoat.
gabinete, *s. m.* cabinet; study, small living-room.
gafas, *s. f. pl.* eye-glasses, spectacles.
gala, *s. f.* gala; *función (s. f.) de* ~ gala performance; *traje (s. m.) de* ~ dress-suit.
galante, *adj.* attentive.
galantería, *s. f.* compliment; courtesy.
galera, *s. f.* galley; tophat.
galería, *s. f.* (art) gallery; (theatre) gallery; passageway (underground).
galgo, *s. m.* greyhound.
galopar, *v. n.* gallop.
galope, *s. m.* gallop, canter.
galleta, *s. f.* ship's biscuit; slap.
gallina, *s. f.* hen; coward.
gallinero, *s. m.* hen-house; (theatre) top-gallery.
gallo, *s. m.* cock; bully.
gamuza, *s. f.* chamois; yellow duster.
gana, *s. f.* desire, mind; *de buena* ~ willingly; *de mala* ~ unwillingly; *tener* ~*s de* feel like.
ganado, *s. m.* cattle.
ganador, *s. m.* winner.
ganar, *v. a.* win; gain; earn; ~ *tiempo* save time; *v. n.* **~se la vida** earn a living.
gancho, *s. m.* hook.
ganso, *s. m.* & *f.* goose, gander.
garaje, *s. m.* garage.
garantía, *s. f.* security.
garantizar, *v. a.* guarantee, vouch for.
garbanzo, *s. m.* chick-pea.
garbo, *s. m.* grace.
garganta, *s. f.* throat.
gárgara, *s. f.* gargle; *hacer* ~*s* gargle.
garrafa, *s. f.* decanter.
gas, *s. m.* gas.
gasa, *s. f.* gauze.
gaseosa, *s. f.* soda-water.
gasolina, *s. f.* petrol.
gasolinera, *s. f.* motor-boat.
gastar, *v. a.* spend; waste; wear, use; ~ *bromas* joke, jest.
gasto, *s. m.* expense; wear and tear; *pagar los* ~*s* foot the bill.
gata, *s. f.* (she-)cat.
gato, *s. m.* cat, tom-cat; jack (car).
gemelo, *s. m.* twin; ~*s pl.* cuff-links; binoculars, opera-glasses.
gemir, *v. n.* moan, whine, groan.
general, *adj.* general; *en* ~, *por lo* ~ usually,

generally; *por regla* ~ as a general rule; — *s. m.* general.
generalizar, *v. a.* generalize; *v. n.* *~se* become general.
género, *s. m.* kind; gender; ~ *humano* mankind.
generosidad, *s. f.* generosity.
generoso, *adj.* generous.
genial, *adj.* brilliant.
genio, *s. m.* genius; temper, nature; *buen* ~ good nature; *mal* ~ bad temper.
gente, *s. f.* people; folks.
gentil, *adj.* gracious, kind.
gentileza, *s. f.* graciousness, kindness.
geografía, *s. f.* geography.
geográfico, *adj.* geographical.
gerente, *s. m.* manager.
gesticular, *v. n.* gesticulate.
gesto, *s. m.* gesture; *hacer* *~s* make gestures, signal.
gigante, *s. m.* giant.
gimnasia, *s. f.* gymnastics; *hacer* ~ practise gymnastics.
ginebra, *s. f.* gin.
girar, *v. n.* revolve, turn; draw (of money).
giro, *s. m.* turn; draft; ~ *postal* money-order.
gitana, *s. f.*, **gitano,** *s. m.* gipsy.
glacial, *adj.* icy.
glándula, *s. f.* gland.
globo, *s. m.* globe; sphere; balloon.
gloria, *s. f.* glory; heaven.
gloriarse, *v. n.* boast.
glorificar, *v. a.* glorify.
glorioso, *adj.* glorious.
glotón, *s. m.* glutton.
gobernación, *s. f.* government; *Ministerio de la Gobernación* Ministry of the Interior; Home Office.
gobernador, *s. m.* governor.
gobernar, *v. a.* govern.
gobierno, *s. m.* government; cabinet (of ministers); control.
golfo, *s. m.* gulf.
golondrina, *s. f.* swallow.
golosina, *s. f.* dainty, delicacy.
golpe, *s. m.* blow; *de* ~ suddenly; ~ *de Estado* coup d'état; *dar* *~s* knock, pound.
golpear, *v. n.* pound.
goma, *s. f.* glue; rubber, eraser.
gordo, *adj.* fat; *premio* ~ first prize in lottery.
gorra, *s. f.* cap.
gorrión, *s. m.* sparrow.
gorro, *s. m* cap.
gota, *s. f.* drop; gout.
gotear, *v. n.* drizzle; leak.
gótico, *adj.* Gothic.
gozar, *v. a. & n.* enjoy; enjoy oneself, have a good time.
grabado, *s. m.* engraving, etching; picture (illustration).
grabar, *v. a.* engrave; cut (a record).
gracia, *s. f.* charm, grace; mercy; wit, joke; name; *tiene* ~ it's funny; *gracias pl.* thanks.
grado, *s. m.* degree; *de mal* ~ unwillingly, reluctantly.
graduar, *v. a.* gauge; *v. n.* *~se* graduate.
gráfica, *s. f.* graph, diagram.
gráfico, *adj.* graphic.

gramática, *s. f.* grammar.
gramo, *s. m.* gram(me) (weight).
gramófono, *s. m.* gramophone.
gran, grande, *adj.* large; tall; great; *en* ~ on a large scale.
grandeza, *s. f.* greatness.
grandioso, *adj.* grandiose, magnificent.
granero, *s. m.* granary.
granizar, *v. n.* hail.
granizo, *s. m.* hail.
granja, *s. m.* farm.
grano, *s. m.* grain; ~*s pl.* cereals; *ir al* ~ get to the point.
grasa, *s. f.* fat; grease.
grasiento, *adj.* greasy, oily.
gratificación, *s. f.* gratification, tip.
gratificar, *v. a.* reward.
gratis, *adv.* gratis, free.
gratitud, *s. f.* gratitude.
grato, *adj.* pleasant.
gratuito, *adj.* free.
gratulación, *s. f.* congratulation. good wishes.
gratular, *v. a.* congratulate.
grave, *adj.* grave, serious; deep (voice).
griego, *adj.* & *s. m.* Greek.
grieta, *s. f.* crack.
grifo, *s. m.* water-tap.
grillo, *s. m.* cricket (insect).
gripe, *s. f.* grippe, influenza.
gris, *adj.* gray.
gritar, *v. n.* shout, scream.
grito, scream, shout.
grosero *adj.* rude, coarse.
grúa, *s. f.* crane.
gruesa, *s. f.* gross (twelve dozen).
grueso, *adj.* stout, thick; – *s. m.* main body (of troops).
gruñido, *s.m.* growl, grunt.
grupo, *s. m.* group; clump.
guante, *s. m.* glove.
guapo, *adj.* handsome, pretty.
guarda, *s. m.* guard.
guardabarrera, *s. m.* gatekeeper.
guardabosque, *s. m.* forest ranger.
guardacostas, *s. m.* coastguard.
guardar, *v. a.* keep, guard; ~ *silencio* keep quiet; *v. n.* ~*se de* avoid.
guardarropa, *s. m.* wardrobe; cloakroom.
guardia, *s. f.* guard; *en* ~ on guard; *estar de* ~ be on (guard) duty; *s. m.* policeman; ~ *civil* member of the civil guard.
guardián, *s. m.* watchman.
guarnición, *s. f.* trimming, edging; garrison.
guerra, *s. f.* war; *Gran Guerra* World War.
guerrero, *s. m.* warrior.
guía, *s. m., f.* guide; *s. f.* guide-book, directory; ~ *de ferrocarriles* railway guide; ~ *telefónica* telephone directory.
guiar, *v. a.* guide; drive (a car); *v. n.* ~*se por* follow.
guisante, *s. m.* pea.
guisar, *v. a.* & *n.* cook.
guitarra, *s. f.* guitar.
gusano, *s. m.* worm; ~ *de luz* glow-worm; ~ *de seda* silkworm.
gustar, *v. a.* please; *n e gusta eer* I like read-

ing; *nos gustan los deportes* we like sports.
gusto, *s. m.* taste; liking; *a* ~ comfortable; *con mucho* ~ with much pleasure, gladly, willingly; *dar* ~ *a* please; *tengo mucho* ~ *en conocerle* I'm very glad to meet you.
gustoso, *aoj.* savoury.

H

haba, *s. f.* broad bean.
haber, *(auxiliary verb) he leido que* I have read that; *he de hacerlo* I have to do it; *hay* there is, there are; *hay que comer* it's necessary to eat; *no hay de que* don't mention it; you're welcome; — *s. m.* credit; ~*es, pl.* incomings, revenues.
hábil, *adj.* skilful, clever.
habilidad, *s. f.* ability.
habitación, *s. f.* dwelling; room.
habitante, *s. m., f.* inhabitant.
habitar, *v. a.* & *n.* inhabit.
habitual, *adj.* habitual; — *s. m.* customer.
habituar, *v. a.* accustom; *v. n.* ~*se* get accustomed.
habitud, *s. f.* habit, custom.
habla, *s. f.* speech; language.
hablador, *adj.* talkative.
hablar, *v. a.* & *n.* speak, talk.
hacer, *v. a.* make; do; *hace frio* it's cold; *hace calor* it's hot; ~ *caso a* pay attention to; ~ *el favor* please; ~ *el honor de* do the honour of; ~ *los honores* act as host(ess); ~ *furor* make a hit; ~ *el sueco* pretend not to understand; ~*se* become; *hace una semana* a week ago.
hacia, *prep.* toward; ~ *adelante* forward; ~ *allá* that way; ~ *atrás* backwards.
hacienda, *s. f.* country seat, estate; fortune; *Ministro de Hacienda* Minister of Finance.
hacha, *s. f.* axe.
hallar, *v. a.* find; *v. n.* ~*se* be.
hamaca, *s. f.* hammock.
hambre, *s. f.* hunger; *tengo mucha* ~ I'm very hungry.
hambriento, *adj.* hungry, starved.
harina, *s. f.* flour, meal.
harinoso, *adj.* mealy.
hartar, *v. a.* satiate, satisfy, *v. n.* ~*se* gorge, stuff oneself.
harto, *adj.* full, stuffed; fed up.
hasta, *prep.* until; ~ *aquí* so far; ~ *la vista,* ~ *luego* so long; ~ *las seis* till six o'clock; — *adv.* even.
hay, *see* **haber.**
hazaña, *s. f.* feat, exploit, deed
hectárea, *s. f.* hectare.
hectolitro, *s. m.* hectolitre.
hecho, *adj.* done; ready-made; — *s. m.* deed; fact.
heder, *v. n.* stink.
helada, *s. f.* white frost.

helado, *adj.* frozen; – *s. m.* ice-cream.
helar, *v. a.* freeze; *v. n.* ~*se* freeze up.
hélice, *s. f.* propeller (of ship).
hembra, *s. f.* female.
hemisferio, *s. m.* hemisphere.
hemorragia, *s. f.* haemorrhage.
hemorroide, *s. f.* haemorrhoids, piles.
heno, *s. m.* hay.
heredar, *v. a.* inherit.
heredero, *s. m.* heir.
hereditario, *adj.* hereditary.
herencia, *s. f.* inheritance
herida, *s. f.* wound.
herido, *s. m.* wounded man.
herir, *v. a.* wound, hurt.
hermana, *s. f.* sister; nun.
hermano, *s. m.* brother.
hermoso, *adj.* beautiful, handsome.
héroe, *s. m.* hero.
heroína, *s. f.* heroine.
herradura, *s. f.* horseshoe.
herramienta, *s. f.* tool; set of tools.
herrería, *s. f.* forge, smithy; blacksmith's shop; ironworks.
herrero, *s. m.* blacksmith.
herrumbre, *s. m.* rust.
hervir, *v. n.* boil.
hidráulica, *s. f.* hydraulics.
hidroavión, *s. m.* hydroplane.
hidrógeno, *s. m.* hydrogen.
hiel, *s. f.* gall; bitterness.
hielo, *s. m.* ice.
hierba, *s. f.* grass; *mala* ~ weed.
hierro, *s. m.* iron.
hígado, *s. m.* liver.
higiene, *s. f.* hygiene.
higiénico, *adj.* hygienic.
higo, *s. m.* fig.
higuera, *s. f.* fig-tree.
hija, *s. f.* daughter.
hijastra, *s. f.* stepdaughter.
hijastro, *s. m.* stepson.
hijo, *s. m.* son.
hila, *s. f.* row, line
hilar, *v. a.* spin.
hilera, *s. f.* row, line.
hilo, *s. m.* thread; wire.
himno, *s. m.* hymn.
hincha, *s. f.* fan.
hinchado, *adj.* swollen; haughty.
hinchar, *v. n.* swell.
hipocresía, *s. f.* hypocrisy.
hipócrita, *adj.* hypocritical; – *s. m.* hypocrite.
hipódromo, *s. m.* racecourse, racetrack.
hipoteca, *s. f.* mortgage.
hipotecar, *v. a.* mortgage.
hipótesis, *s. f.* hypothesis.
historia, *s. f.* history, story, tale.
histórico, *adj.* historic.
historieta, *s. f.* short story; comics.
hogar, *s. m.* fireplace; home, hearth.
hoguera, *s. f.* bonfire.
hoja, *s. f.* leaf, page; blade; ~ *de lata* tinplate; *doblar la* ~ charge the subject.
hojalata, *s. f.* tin.
hojalatero, *s. m.* tinsmith; plumber.

hojear, *v. a.* thumb through, glance through (a book).
¡hola! *int.* hello!
holgazán, *adj.* lazy.
hollín, *s. m.* soot.
hombre, *s. m.* man; ~ *de Estado* statesman.
hombrecillo, *s. m.* little man.
hombro, *s. m.* shoulder.
homenaje, *s. m.* homage.
hondo, *adj.* deep.
honesto, *adj.* decent, honest.
hongo, *s. m.* fungus; mushroom.
honor, *s. m.* honour.
honra, *s. f.* honour; ~*s pl.* obsequies.
honradez, *s. f.* honesty, integrity.
honrado, *adj.* honest.
honrar, *v. a.* honour.
hora, *s. f.* hour; time; *¿qué ~ es?* what time is it?; *a última ~* at the last moment.
horario, *adj.* hourly; — *s. m.* time-table.
horizontal, *adj.* horizontal.
horizonte, *s. m.* horizon.
hormiga, *s. f.* ant.
hormigón, *s. m.* concrete; ~ *armado* reinforced concrete.
hormiguero, *s. m.* ant-hill; crowd, throng.
hornillo, *s. m.* cooking-range.
horno, *s. m.* baking-oven; *alto ~* blast-furnace.
horquilla, *s. f.* hairpin.
horrible, *adj.* horrible, horrid.
horror, *s. m.* horror.
hortaliza, *s. f.* vegetable.
hospedar, *v. a.* lodge, accommodate, shelter.
hospicio, *s. m.* hospice.
hospital, *s. m.* hospital.
hospitalario, *adj.* hospitable.
hospitalidad, *s. f.* hospitality.
hostil, *adj.* hostile.
hotel, *s. m.* hotel.
hoy, *adv.* today; *por ~* for the present.
hoyo, *s. m.* hole; ditch.
hueco, *adj.* hollow, empty; — *s. m.* hole.
huelga, *s. f.* strike (of workers).
huelguista, *s. m.* striker.
huella, *s. f.* track; footprint, fingerprint; trace, sign.
huérfano, *adj.* & *s. m.* orphan.
huerta, *s. f.* large vegetable garden.
huerto. *s. m.* orchard.
hueso, *s. m.* bone; stone (of fruit).
huésped, *s. m.* guest; *casa de ~es* boarding-house.
huevera, *s. f.* egg-cup.
huevo, *s. m.* egg.
huir, *v. n.* flee.
hule, *s. m.* oilcloth.
hulla, *s. f.* pit-coal.
humanidad, *s. f.* humanity; humaneness.
humear, *v. n.* smoke.
humedad, *s. f.* dampness, humidity, moisture.
humedecer, *v. a.* moisten.
húmedo, *adj.* damp, humid.
humilde, *adj.* humble.
humillar, *v. a.* humiliate.
humo, *s. m.* smoke;

~*s* *pl*. airs, affected manner.
humor, *s. m.* humour, mood; wit.
humorismo, *s. m.* humour.
humorista, *s. m.* humorist.
hundir, *v. a.* sink; destroy; *v. n.* ~*se* sink; fall off, diminish.
huracán, *s. m.* hurricane.
hurtar, *v. a.* steal, pilfer.
hurto, *s. m.* theft, larceny.
huso, *s. m.* spindle.

I

iberoamericano, *adj.* & *s. m.* Latin American.
ida, *s. f.* leaving, going; *billete (s. m.) de ~ y vuelta* return ticket.
idea, *s. f.* idea.
ideal, *adj.* ideal, perfect; — *s. m.* ideal, principle.
idear, *v. a.* plan, invent.
identidad, *s. f.* identity.
idioma, *s. m.* language.
ídolo, *s. m.* idol.
iglesia, *s. f.* church; clergy.
ignición, *s. f.* ignition.
ignorante, *adj.* ignorant.
ignorar, *v. a.* not to know, lack knowledge; ignore.
ignoto, *adj.* unknown.
igual, *adj.* same; similar; ~ *a* equal to; *pienso ~ que usted* I think the same as you.
igualar, *v. a.* equal; level (road); *v. n.* ~*se* be equal, be tied (score).
igualdad, *s. f.* equality; evenness, smoothness.
ilegalidad, *s. f.* illegality.
ilegible, *adj.* illegible.
ilimitado, *adj.* boundless, unlimited.
iluminación, *s. f.* illumination.
iluminar, *v. a.* light, illuminate.
ilusión, *s. f.* illusion, delusion; *hacerse ilusiones* chase after rainbows.
ilusionar, *v. a.* thrill; *v. n.* ~*se* get thrilled *or* excited.
ilusorio, *adj.* illusory.
ilustración, *s. f.* illustration, picture; learning.
ilustrado, *adj.* illustrated, with pictures; learned.
ilustrar, *v. a.* illustrate.
ilustre, *adj.* illustrious, distinguished.
imagen, *s. f.* image.
imaginación, *s. f.* imagination.
imaginar, *v. a.* think of, devise, figure out; *v. n.* ~*se* imagine, suspect.
imán, *s. m.* magnet.
imitar, *v. a.* imitate.
impaciencia, *s. f.* impatience.
impacientarse, *v. n.* be impatient.
impaciente, *adj.* impatient.
impacto, *s. m.* impact.
impar, *adj.* unlike; odd.
impecable, *adj.* blameless.
impedir, *v. a.* prevent; ~ *el paso* block the way.
imperativo, *adj.* imperative.
imperdible, *s. m.* safety-

pin.
imperdonable, *adj.* unpardonable.
imperfecto, *adj.* imperfect.
imperio, *s. m.* empire; command; spell.
impermeable, *adj.* waterproof; — *s. m.* raincoat.
impertinente, *adj.* impertinent.
impertinentes, *s. m. pl.* lorgnette.
ímpetu, *s. m.* impetus, impulse.
impetuoso, *adj.* impetuous.
implicar, *v. a.* involve, implicate.
implorar, *v. a.* beg, implore.
imponente, *adj.* imposing.
imponer, *v. a.* impose, levy; *v. n.* *~se* assert oneself; dominate; get one's way.
importación, *s. f.* import, importation.
importador, *s. m.* importer.
importancia, *s. f.* importance.
importante, *adj.* important.
importar, *v. a.* import; *v. n.* *¿cuánto importa?* what does it amount to?; *no importa* it doesn't matter, never mind.
importe, *s. m.* amount.
importuno, *adj.* importunate, annoying.
imposibilidad, *s. f.* impossibility.
imposible, *adj.* impossible.
impotencia, *s. f.* impotence, weakness.
impotente, *adj.* impotent.
impregnar, *v. a.* impregnate.
imprenta, *s. f.* press; print; *error (s. m.) de ~* printer's error.
impresión, *s. f.* impression; imprint; printing.
impresionar, *v. a.* impress; expose (photo); make *or* cut (a record); *v. n.* *~se* be moved.
impreso, *s. m.* printed matter; blank (to be filled).
imprevisto, *adj.* unforeseen, unexpected.
imprimir, *v.a.* print.
improductivo, *adj.* unfruitful.
improperio, *s. m.* abuse, invective.
impropio, *adj.* inappropriate, unfitting.
improvisado, *adj.* makeshift.
improvisar, *v. a.* improvise.
improviso, *adj.* unforeseen.
imprudente, *adj.* imprudent, unwise.
impuesto, *s. m.* tax.
inaceptable, *adj.* unacceptable.
inadvertido, *adj.* inattentive, careless.
inagotable, *adj.* inexhaustible.
inaudito, *adj.* unheard of, strange, unexpected.
inauguración, *s. f.* inauguration, opening (ceremony).
inaugurar, *v. a.* inaugurate, open.
incansable, *adj.* untiring.

incapaz, *adj.* incompetent, incapable.
incendiar, *v. a.* set on fire.
incendio, *s. m.* fire (conflagration).
incidente, *s. m.* incident, disturbance.
incierto, *adj.* uncertain, doubtful.
inclinación, *s. f.* inclination; bent; slope.
inclinar, *v. a.* bend, bow; *v. n.* *~se* bow; yield, give in; *~se a* be inclined to.
incluir, *v. a.* include; enclose.
inclusión, *s. f.* inclusion.
inclusivo, *adj.* inclusive.
incomodar, *v. a.* disturb, inconvenience, bother; *v. n.* *~se* become angry, be upset.
incomodidad, *s. f.* inconvenience.
incómodo, *adj.* uncomfortable.
incompleto, *adj.* incom plete.
inconsciente, *adj.* unconscious.
inconsecuente, *adj.* contradictory, inconsequential.
inconveniente, *adj.* unbecoming, improper; — *s. m.* disadvantage; objection.
incorporar, *v. a.* incorporate, unite; add; *v. n.* *~se* sit up (in bed); join (a military unit).
increíble, *adj.* incredible, unbelievable.
incubadora, *s. f.* incubator.
inculpar, *v. a.* inculpate.
inculto, *adj.* uncultivated.
incumplido, *adj.* unfulfilled.
incurrir, *v. n.* incur.
indagar, *v. a.* investigate.
indecente, *adj.* indecent, obscene.
indeciso, *adj.* vacillating, hesitant; indefinite.
indefenso, *adj.* defenceless.
indefinido, *adj.* indefinite.
indemnización, *s. f.* indemnity, compensation.
indemnizar, *v. a.* indemnify.
independencia, *s. f.* independence.
indescriptible, *adj.* indescribable.
indeterminado, *adj.* indeterminate, indefinite.
indicación, *s. f.* hint, suggestion; instruction.
indicar, *v. a.* indicate, hint, show.
indicativo, *s. m.* & *adj.* indicative.
índice, *s. m.* index; table of contents; forefinger.
indicio, *s. m.* indication, clue; evidence.
indiferente, *adj.* indifferent.
indígena, *adj.* native, aboriginal; — *s. m.* native, aborigine.
indigestión, *s. f.* indigestion.
indignar, *v. a.* fill with indignation; *v. n.* *~se* become indignant.
indigno, *adj.* despicable, unworthy.
indio, *adj.* & *s. m.* Indian; Hindu.
indirecta, *s. f.* insinuation, hint; *echar ~s* make insinuations.

indisciplinado, *adj.* undisciplined.
indiscreto, *adj.* indiscreet.
indiscutible, *adj.* unquestionable.
indisoluble, *adj.* indissoluble.
indisponer, *v. a.* prejudice, set against; *v. n.* *~se* become ill.
indispuesto, *adj.* indisposed, ill.
individual, *adj.* individual, separate; — *s. m.* single (tennis).
individuo, *s. m.* individual, person.
índole, *s. f.* nature, character; class, kind.
indomable, *adj.* indomitable.
indudable, *adj.* indubitable, certain, evident.
indulto, *s. m.* pardon; amnesty.
industria, *s. f.* industry.
industrial, *adj.* industrial; — *s. m.* manufacturer.
ineficaz, *adj.* inefficient.
inesperado, *adj.* unexpected.
inestimable, *adj.* invaluable.
inexperto, *adj.* inexperienced.
infame, *adj.* infamous; — *s. m.* scoundrel.
infancia, *s. f.* infancy, childhood.
infantería, *s. f.* infantry.
infantil, *adj.* infantile, childlike.
infatigable, *adj.* untiring.
infección, *s. f.* infection.
infeccioso, *adj.* infectious.
infeliz, *adj.* unhappy; poor.
inferior, *adj.* inferior, lower; — *s. m.* inferior.
inferioridad, *s. f.* inferiority.
infiel, *adj.* unfaithful.
infierno, *s. m.* hell; pain.
ínfimo, *adj.* lowest.
infinidad, *s. f.* endless number, a lot.
infinito, *adj.* infinite; — *s. m.* infinity.
inflación, *s. f.* inflation.
inflamar, *v. a.* set on fire; *v. n.* *~se* catch fire.
influencia, *s. f.* influence.
influir *en, v. n.* (have) influence on sy.
influyente, *adj.* influential.
información, *s. f.* information.
informar, *v. a.* inform, tell; *v. n.* *~se* get information; find out.
informativo, *adj.* informative.
informe, *s. m.* report; information.
infortunio, *s. m.* great misfortune; ill-luck.
ingeniero, *s. m.* engineer.
ingenio, *s. m.* talent, genius; wit.
ingenioso, *adj.* ingenious.
ingenuo, *adj.* ingenuous; candid, innocent.
inglés, *adj.* English; — *s. m.* Englishman.
ingrato, *adj.* ungrateful, thankless.
ingrediente, *s. m.* ingredient.
ingresar, *v. a.* deposit; *v. n.* enter, join.
ingreso, *s. m.* entrance (joining); *~s pl.* income, earnings.
inhalar, *v. a.* inhale.
inhibir, *v. a.* inhibit.
inhumanidad, *s. f.* inhumanity.
inicial, *adj.* & *s. f.* initial.

iniciar, *v. a.* initiate, begin.
iniciativa, *s. f.* initiative.
injuria, *s. f.* insult.
injuriar, *v. a.* injure, insult.
injusticia, *s. f.* injustice.
inmediato, *adj.* immediate; adjoining, next.
inmenso, *adj.* immense.
inmigración, *s. f.* immigration.
inmigrante, *s. m. f.* immigrant.
inmigrar, *v. n.* immigrate.
inmóvil, *adj.* motionless.
inmueble, *s. m.* real estate.
innecesario, *adj.* unnecessary, needless.
inocente, *adj.* innocent; not guilty; simple.
inocular, *v. a.* inoculate.
inodoro, *adj.* inodorous.
inolvidable, *adj.* unforgettable.
inquietar, *v. a.* worry, trouble; *v. n.* **~se** become restless *or* worried.
inquilino, *s. m.* tenant.
inquirir, *v. n.* inquire, investigate.
insaciable, *adj.* insatiable, greedy.
insano, *adj.* insane; unhealthy, unsanitary.
inscribir, *v. a.* register, enroll.
inscripción, *s. f.* inscription; registration.
insecto, *s. m.* insect.
inseguro, *adj.* insecure, unsafe, unsteady.
insensato, *adj.* senseless, stupid, foolish.
insensible, *adj.* insensitive; heartless.
inserción, *s. f.* insertion.
insertar, *v. a.* insert.
insípido, *adj.* insipid, tasteless.
insistir *en, v. n.* insist on.
insolencia, *s. f.* insolence.
insolente, *adj.* insolent.
inspección, *s. f.* inspection, examination.
inspeccionar, *v. a.* inspect, examine.
inspector, *s. m.* inspector.
inspirar, *v. a.* inspire.
instalar, *v. a.* install, set up; *v. n.* **~se** establish oneself; take quarters.
instancia, *s. f.* petition, application; *a* **~** *de* at the request of.
instantánea, *s. f.* snapshot.
instante, *s. m.* instant, moment; *al* **~** instantly, at once.
instinto, *s. m.* instinct.
institución, *s. f.* institution.
instituto, *s. m.* institute; school.
instrucción, *s. f.* instruction, direction; education.
instructivo, *adj.* instructive.
instructor, *s. m.* instructor; *juez* **~** examining magistrate.
instruir, *v. a.* teach, instruct.
instrumento, *s. m.* instrument.
insurrección, *s. f.* insurrection; rebellion.
insurrecto, *adj.* & *s. m.* insurgent.
integridad, *s. f.* integrity; entirety.
íntegro, *adj.* complete, whole; honest, righteous.
intelectual, *adj.* & *s. m.*

intellectual.
inteligente, *adj.* intelligent.
intención, *s. f.* intention, purpose.
intensidad, *s. f.* intensity.
intenso, *adj.* intense.
intentar, *v. a.* attempt, try.
intento, *s. m.* intent.
interés, *s. m.* interest; rate of interest.
interesado, *adj.* interested; selfish.
interesante, *adj.* interesting.
interesar, *v. a.* interest; *v. n.* *~se* be interested.
interino, *adj.* temporary.
interior, *adj.* interior; domestic; — *s. m.* inside.
intermediario, *s. n.* mediator.
intermedio, *adj.* intermediate; — *s. m.* interval; *en el ~* in the meantime; *por ~ de* through (the intervention of).
interminable, *adj.* endless.
internacional, *adj.* inter national.
interno, *adj.* internal; — *s. m.* boarding student.
interpretar, *v. a.* inter pret.
intérprete, *s m.* interpreter.
interrogación, *s. f.* interrogation; question-mark.
interrogar, *v. a.* question, interrogate.
intervalo, *s. m.* interval.
intervención, *s. f.* intervention; mediation.
intervenir, *v. n.* intervene.
intestino, *adj.* intestinal; — *s. m.* intestine.
intimar, *v. n.* become an intimate friend.
intimidad, *s. f.* intimity.
intimidar, *v. a.* frighten, intimidate.
íntimo, *adj.* & *s. m.* intimate (friend).
intoxicar, *v. a.* poison; drug.
intranquilo, *adj.* restless, worried.
intransitable, *adj.* impassable.
intratable, *adj.* unsociable.
intrépido, *adj.* brave, fearless.
introducir, *v. a.* put in, insert; present (a person).
intuición, *s. f.* intuition.
inundación, *s. f.* flood, inundation.
inun ar, *v. a.* flood.
inútil, *adj.* useless.
inválido, *adj.* &. *s. m.* invalid; useless.
invasión, *s. f.* invasion.
invencible, *adj.* invincible, unconquerable.
invención, *s. f.* inv n-tion.
inventar, *v. a.* invent.
inventario, *s. m.* inventory.
invento, *s. m.* invention; lie.
inventor, *s. m.* inventor.
invernadero, *s. m.* hothouse.
invernal, *adj.* wintry.
inverosímil, *adj.* unlikely, improbable.
invertir, *v. a.* reverse, turn upside down; invest; spend (time).
investigación, *s. f.* investigation, inquiry; research.

investigar, *v. a.* investigate; do research work.
invierno, *s. m.* winter.
invitación, *s. f.* invitation.
invitado, *s. m.* guest.
invitar, *v. a.* invite.
involuntario, *adj.* involuntary.
inyectar, *v. a.* inject.
ir, *v. n.* go; lead (road); *¿cómo le va?* how are you? *ese color le va muy bien* that colour is very becoming to you; **~** *a caballo* ride on horseback; **~** *a pie* walk, go on foot; **~** *del brazo* walk arm in arm; **~** *de paseo* go for a walk; **~***se* leave, go away.
ira, *s. f.* anger.
iris, *s. m.* iris; *arco* **~** rainbow.
irónico, *adj.* ironical, sarcastic.
irregularidad, *s. f.* irregularity.
irremediable, *adj.* irreparable, hopeless.
irritar, *v. a.* irritate.
isla, *s. f.* island, isle.
isleño, *s. m.* islander.
istmo, *s. m.* isthmus.
itinerario, *s. m.* itinerary.
izar, *v. a.* hoist (up).
izquierda, *s. f.* left hand; *a la* **~** on the left.
izquierdo, *adj.* left.

J

jabón, *s. m.* soap.
jabonar, *v. a.* soap; lather.
jabonera, *s. f.* soap-dish.
jadear, *v. n.* pant, gasp.
jalea, *s. f.* jelly.
jaleo. *s. m.* revels, uproar.
jamás, *adv.* never, ever.
jamón, *s. m.* ham.
jaque, *s. m.* check; *dar* **~** (give) check; *tener en* **~** keep in check.
jaquear, *v. a.* (give) check.
jaqueca, *s. f.* headache, migraine.
jarabe, *s. m.* syrup.
jardín, *s. m.* garden.
jardinero, *s. m.* gardener.
jarra, *s. f.* water-jug, pitcher.
jarro, *s. m.* jug, pitcher.
jaula, *s. f.* cage, prison.
jefatura, *s. f.* chief's office; headquarters.
jefe, *s. m.* chief, leader, head; boss; **~** *de tren* guard.
jerga, *s. f.* slang.
jeringa, *s. f.* syringe.
jícara, *s. f.* small cup.
jinete, *s. m.* horseman.
jofaina, *s. f.* wash-basin.
jornada, *s. f.* journey; day's work; day's walk.
jornal, *s. m.* day's wages.
jornalero, *s. m.* day-labourer.
jota, *s. f.* the letter „j"; Aragonese folk-dance.
joven, *adj.* young; — *s. m., f.* young person.
jovial, *adj.* jovial; merry, gay.
joya, *s. f.* gem.
joyería, *s. f.* jeweller's shop.
jubilar, *v. a.* pension off.
jubileo, *s. m.* jubilee.
júbilo, *s. m.* jubilation; glee.
judía, *s. f.* bean; **~***s verdes* French beans.
judío, *adj.* Jewish; — *s. m.* Jew.
juego, *s. m.* game; play,

playing; gambling; *un* ~ *de mesa* table-service; ~ *de palabras* play on words, pun; *hacer* ~ match.
jueves, *s. m.* Thursday.
juez, *s. m.* judge.
jugada, *s. f.* move (chess); trick, prank.
jugador, *s. m.* player; gambler.
jugar, *v. a.* & *n.* play; gamble.
jugo, *s. m.* juice.
jugoso, *adj.* juicy, succulent.
juguete, *s. m.* toy.
juguetería, *s. f.* toy-shop.
juicio, *s. m.* judgment; trial (law).
juicioso, *adj.* judicious.
julio, *s. m.* July.
junio, *s. m.* June.
junta, *s. f.* meeting; board; joint, joining (carpentry).
juntar, *v. a.* join, connect; *v. n.* ~*se* meet, gather.
junto, *adj.* & *adv.* together; *vamos* ~*s* let's go together; — *prep.* ~ *a* next to, beside; ~ *con* with.
juntura, *s. f.* hinge; joint.
jurado, *s. m.* juryman; jury.
juramento, *s. m.* oath; swearing.
jurar, *v. n.* swear; curse.
jurídico, *adj.* juridical.
jurisconsulto, *s. m.* counsel, legal adviser.
justicia, *s. f.* justice.
justificar, *v. a.* justify.
justo, *adj.* right, just; correct, exact; tight (clothes).
juvenil, *adj.* juvenile.
juventud, *s. f.* youth; youthfulness.
juzgado, *s. m.* law-court; district court.
juzgar, *v. a.* judge; try.

K

kermesse, *s. f.* kermess.
kilo, *s. m.* kilogram.
kilociclo, *s. m.* kilocycle.
kilogramo, *s. m.* kilogram.
kilómetro, *s. m.* kilometre.
kilovatio, *s. m.* kilowatt.
kiosco, *see* **quiosco.**
kirsch, *s. m.* cherry-brandy.
kodak, *s. m.* camera.
kummel, *s. m.* cumin brandy.

L

la, *f.* *(definite article)* ~ *mesa* the table; — *pron.* her, it; *las, pl.* them.
labio, *s. m.* lip.
labor, *s. f.* work, task.
laborable, *adj.*; *dia (s. m.)* ~ workday.
laboratorio, *s. m.* laboratory.
labrador, *s. m.* countryman, farmer.
lacrar, *v. a.* seal (up).
lacre, *s. m.* sealing-wax.
lado, *s. m.* side; edge, margin; *al* ~ *de* by the side of, next door to; *de* ~ sideways, on its side.
ladrillo, *s. m.* brick.
ladrón, *s. m.* thief, robber.
lagarto, *s. m.* lizard.
lago, *s. m.* lake.
lágrima, *s. f.* tear.
laguna, *s. f.* lagoon.
lamentar, *v. n.* be sorry;

~*se* lament, wail, moan.
lamento, *s. m.* moan.
lamer, *v. a.* lick, lap.
lámina, *s. f.* sheet, plate.
lámpara, *s. f.* lamp; bulb.
lana, *s. f.* wool.
lance, *s. m.* throwing; occurrence; *de* ~ secondhand.
lanceta, *s. f.* lancet.
lancha, *s. f.* (small) boat.
langosta, *s. f.* lobster; locust (insect).
lanzar, *v. a.* throw, hurl; *v. n.* ~*se* throw oneself, rush.
lápida, *s. f.* commemorative tablet; headstone.
lápiz, *s. m.* pencil.
largar, *v. a.* let loose; *v. n.* ~*se* leave, go away.
largo, *adj.* long; – *s. m.* length; *a lo* ~ *de* along.
laringe, *s. f.* larynx.
lástima, *s. f.* pity; *¡qué* ~*!* what a pity!; *dar* ~ inspire pity.
lastimarse, *v. n.* hurt oneself.
lata, *s. f.* tin (plate); tin box; *hoja (s. f.) de* ~ sheet metal; *dar la* ~ annoy, bother, pester.
latín, *s. m.* Latin (language).
latino, *adj. & s. m.* Latin.
latón, *s. m.* brass.
lavabo, *s. m.* washstand; washroom.
lavadero, *s. m.* washtub.
lavamanos, *s. m.* washbasin.
lavandera, *s. f.* laundress.
lavandería, *s. f.* laundry.
lavar, *v. a.* wash; *v. n.* ~*se* wash.
laxante, *adj. & s. m.* laxative.
le, *pron.* him; to him, to her, to you; *les, pl.* them, to them, to you.
leal, *adj.* loyal.
lección, *s. f.* lesson.
lectura, *s. f.* reading; *salón (s. m.) de* ~ reading-room.
leche, *s. f.* milk.
lechera, *s. f.* milk-woman.
lechería, *s. f.* dairy.
lechero, *s. m.* milk-man.
lecho, *s. m.* bed, couch.
lechuga, *s. f.* lettuce.
leer, *v. a.* read.
legación, *s. f.* legation.
legal, *adj.* legal, lawful.
legalidad, *s. f.* legality.
legalizar, *v. a.* legalize.
legendario, *adj.* legendary.
legible, *adj.* legible, readable.
legitimar, *v. a.* legitimate; *v. n.* ~*se* prove one's identity.
legítimo, *adj.* lawful, legitimate.
legua, *s. f.* league (measure of length).
legumbre, *s. f.* vegetable.
lejano, *adj.* distant, far.
lejos, *adv.* far; *a lo* ~ in the distance: *desde* ~ from a distance; – *prep.* ~ *de* far from.
lengua, *s. f.* tongue; language.
lenguado, *s. m.* sole, flounder (fish).
lenguaje, *s. m.* language, speech.
lenitivo, *adj. & s. m.* lenitive.
lente, *s. m.* (optical) lens; ~*s, pl.* eyeglasses; ~ *de aumento* magnifying glass.
lenteja, *s. f.* lentil.
lento, *adj.* slow.
leña, *s. f.* firewood.

leñador, *s. m.* woodcutter.
león, *s. m.* lion.
les, *pron., see* **le.**
lesión, *s. f.* lesion.
lesionar, *v. a.* hurt, injure.
letra, *s. f.* letter (of alphabet); handwriting; *~ de cambio* draft; *~ de imprenta* type; *escribir cuatro ~s* write a few lines.
letrero, *s. m.* sign (-board), signpost.
levadura, *s. f.* yeast.
levantar, *v. a.* raise, lift; pick up; rise up; build; *v. n. ~se* get up.
levante, *s. m.* East.
levantino, *adj.* Eastern; Oriental.
leve, *adj.* light, slight.
ley, *s. f.* law.
leyenda, *s. f.* legend.
liar, *v. a.* bind; wind, roll.
liberación, *s. f.* libera-
liberar, *v. a.* liberate, free.
libertad, *s. f.* liberty, freedom.
libertador, *s. m.* liberator.
libertar, *v. a.* free.
libra, *s. f.* pound (weight).
librar, *v. a.* free, deliver; *v. n. ~se de* get rid of.
libre, *adj.* free; disengaged.
librería, *s. f.* bookshop.
librero, *s. m.* bookseller.
libreta, *s. f.* savings book; notebook.
libro, *s. m.* book; *~ de apuntes* notebook; *~ de cuentas* account book.
licencia, *s. f.* licence; permit; furlough.
licenciado, *s. m.* *;~ del ejército* veteran; *~ en filosofía* Master of Arts.
licenciar, *v. a.* discharge; *v. n. ~se* get a degree.
licitar, *v. a.* bid (auction).
licor, *s. m.* liqueur; cordial.
liebre, *s. f.* hare.
lienzo, *s. m.* canvas, picture.
liga, *s. f.* union, league; garter.
ligar, *v. a.* tie, bind, join.
ligero, *adj.* light, thin (coat); fast; unimportant; *a la ligera* quickly, superficially.
lima, *s. f.* file.
limar, *v. a.* file.
limitado, *adj.* limited.
limitar, *v. a.* restrict, limit.
límite, *s. m.* limit, boundary.
limón, *s. m.* lemon.
limonada, *s. f.* lemonade.
limosna, *s. f.* alms.
limpiabotas, *s. m.* bootblack.
limpiar, *v. a.* clean.
limpieza, *s. f.* cleanliness.
limpio, *adj.* clean; clear (sky); *poner en ~* make a fair copy.
lindar *con, v. n.* border on.
lindo, *adj.* lovely, pretty; *de lo ~* very much.
línea, *s. f.* line; figure; *en ~* in a row; *entre ~s* between the lines.
lino, *s. m.* flax; linen.
linterna, *s. f.* lantern; flashlight.
lío, *s. m.* bundle; trouble, mess, jam.
liquidación, *s. f.* liquidation, clearance sale.
liquidar, *v. a.* liquidate; sell out; pay up.

líquido, *adj.* liquid; just; net (balance); — *s. m.* liquid.
lirio, *s. m.* lily.
lisiado, *s. m.;* ~ *de guerra* war-disabled.
liso, *adj.* smooth; plain.
lista, *s. f.* stripe; list; ~ *de platos* bill of fare.
listo, *adj.* ready; clever.
literario, *adj.* literary.
literato, *s. m.* author, writer.
literatura, *s. f.* literature.
litro, *s. m.* litre.
lo, *(neuter article) lo mejor* the best; — *pron.* him, it.
lobo, *s. m.* wolf; ~ *marino* seal.
local, *adj.* local; — *s. m.* place (indoors).
localidad, *s. f.* locality, place; seat (in a theatre).
localizar, *v. a.* locate; localize; find out.
loco, *adj.* insane, crazy; — *s. m.* madman, lunatic.
locomotora, *s. f.* locomotive.
locura, *s. f.* insanity, madness; folly.
locutor, *s. m.;* **-a,** *s. f.* announcer.
locutorio, *s. m.* telephone box.
lodo, *s. m.* mud.
lógica, *s. f.* logic.
lógico, *adj.* logical.
lograr, *v. a.* get, obtain; succeed in.
lomo, *s. m.* loin.
lona, *s. f.* canvas.
lonja, *s. f.* cut, slice.
loro, *s. m.* parrot.
los, *pron. m. pl.* them.
lote, *s. m.* share.
lotería, *s. f.* lottery.
lubrificar, *v. a.* lubricate.
lucido, *adj.* magnificent.
luciente, *adj.* shining, brilliant.
lucir, *v. n.* shine, glitter, sparkle; ~ *un traje nuevo* wear a new dress; ~ *bien* look well; ~*se* do splendidly.
lucha, *s. f.* struggle, fight.
luchar, *v. n.* struggle, fight.
luego, *adv.* afterwards; next; then; immediately, right away; *desde* ~ naturally, of course; *¡hasta* ~*!* so long!
lugar, *s. m.* place; room, space; position, office; *en* ~ *de* instead of; *en primer* ~ in the first place; *dar* ~ cause; *tener* ~ take place.
lujo, *s. m.* luxury.
lujoso, *adj.* luxurious.
lujuria, *s. f.* luxuriance.
lumbre, *s. f.* fire (in stove); *¿quiere usted darme* ~*?* will you give me a light?
luna, *s. f.* moon; ~ *de miel* honeymoon.
lunes, *s. m* Monday.
lustrar, *v. a.* polish, shine.
luto, *s. m.* mourning; grief; *estar de* ~ be in mourning.
luz, *s. f.* light; *luces* intelligence; *a todas luces* any way you look at it; *entre dos luces* in the twilight; *dar a* ~ give birth (to a child); *dar a la* ~ publish.

Ll

llaga, *s. f.* open sore.
llama, *s. f.* flame.
llamada, *s. f.* call.
llamar, *v. a.* call; knock; ring (a bell); ~ *a* call upon, summon; ~ *por teléfono* phone; *v. n.* ~*se* be called *or* named; *¿cómo se llama usted?* what's your name?; *¿cómo se llama esto?* what's the name of this?
llamativo, *adj.* striking, conspicuous.
llano, *adj.* level, even; simple, plain; frank, unaffected; — *s. m.* plain.
llanta, *s. f.* tire.
llanura, *s. f.* plain.
llave, *s. f.* key; switch; tap; ~ *inglesa* monkey-wrench; *echar la* ~ lock the door.
llavero. *s. m.* key-ring.
llegada, *s. f.* arrival.
llegar, *v. n.* arrive; come; reach; extend, go as far as; amount; ~ *a* succeed in; ~ *a ser* get to be, become; ~ *a saber* come to know.
llenar, *v. a.* fill (up); fill out; satisfy.
lleno, *adj.* full; *de* ~ fully; ~ *de* full of, — *s. m.* full house (theatre).
llevar, *v. a.* take, carry; wear (dress); take, guide, lead; conduct; *¿adónde lleva este camino?* where does this road lead?; *¿cuánto tiempo lleva usted en España?* how long have you been in Spain?; *llevo mucho tiempo esperando* I have been waiting for a long time; ~ *a cabo* carry through; accomplish; ~ *la delantera* be ahead; ~ *mala vida* lead a bad life; *v. n.* ~*se* carry away, take; ~*se bien* get along well; ~*se el premio* win the prize; ~*se un chasco* be disappointed.
llorar, *v. n.* weep, cry.
llover, *v. n.* rain; ~ *a cántaros* pour (rain); *como llovido del cielo* like manna from heaven.
lloviznar, *v. n.* drizzle.
lluvia, *s. f.* rain.
lluvioso, *adj.* rainy.

M

macarrones, *m. pl.* macaroni.
maceta, *s. f.* flowerpot.
macizo, *adj.* solid; — *s. m.* masonry.
mácula, *s. f.* spot, blemish.
machete, *s. m.* long and broad knife.
macho, *adj. & s. m.* male (animal).
madeja, *s. f.* clue, ball.
madera, *s. f.* wood; lumber, timber; talent, qualities.
madero, *s. m.* beam; timber.
madrastra, *s. f.* stepmother.
madre, *s. f.* mother; origin, source; ~ *política* mother-in-law; *salirse de* ~ overflow (river).
madreperla. *s. f.* mother-of-pearl, nacre.

madrileño, *adj.* & *s. m.* from *or* of Madrid.
madrina, *s. f.* godmother.
madrugada, *s. f.* dawn; *de* ~ at dawn.
madrugar, *v. n.* rise early;
madurar, *v. n.* ripen. think out, develop (an idea); mature.
maduro, *adj.* ripe; mature.
maestra, *s. f.* teacher.
maestral, *adj.* masterly.
maestría, *s. f.* mastery.
maestro, *s. m.* teacher; master, craftsman; composer.
mágico, *adj.* magical.
magistrado, *s. m.* magistrate; judge.
magnético, *adj.* magnetic.
magnífico, *adj.* magnificent; excellent, grand.
mago, *s. m.* wizard.
magro, *adj.* meagre, lean.
maíz, *s. m.* maize, Indian corn.
maizal, *s. m.* maize-field.
majestad, *s. f.* majesty.
majestuoso, *adj.* grand, majestic.
mal, *adj.* bad; — *adv.* badly; — *s. m.* illness; harm; wrong; *de* ~ *en peor* from bad to worse.
malacostumbrado, *adj.* ill-bred.
malandante, *adj.* unlucky.
malaventura, *s. f.* misfortune.
malcomido, *adj.* undernourished.
malcontento, *adj.* dissatisfied.
malcriado, *adj.* ill-bred, spoiled.
maldad, *s. f.* wickedness.
maldecir, *v. a.* & *n.* damn, curse.
maldiciente, *adj.* slanderous.
maldición, *s. f.* curse.
maldispuesto, *adj.* reluctant.
maldito, *adj.* cursed, damned.
maleante, *adj.* malicious.
malecón, *s.m.* dike, dam; promenade.
maléfico, *adj.* maleficent.
malestar, *s. m.* indisposition; discontent.
maleta, *s. f.* suitcase.
maletín, *s. m.* small case.
maleza, *s. f.* underwood, scrub.
malgastar, *v. a.* waste, lavish.
malhadado, *adj.* unhappy.
malhechor, *s. m.* evildoer.
malhumorado, *adj.* ill-humoured.
malicia, *s. f.* malice; *tener* ~ be malicious.
malintencionado, *adj.* wicked.
malo, *adj.* bad, unpleasant; difficult, hard; ill.
malograr, *v. a.* miss, fail; *v. n.* ~*se* fail.
malquerer, *v. a.* wish ill to sy.
malsano, *adj.* unhealthy, unwholesome.
maltratar, *v. a.* mistreat, abuse.
maltrato, *s. m.* mistreat, abuse.
maltrecho, *adj.* maltreated.
malucho, *adj.* sickly.
malvado, *adj.* wicked; — *s. m.* wicked person, villain.
malla, *s. f.* mesh; stitch.
mamá, *s. f.* mamma, mummy.
mamar, *v. a.* & *n.* suck; *dar de* ~ suckle, nurse.

mamífero, *s. m.* mammal.
manantial, *s. m.* spring, source of stream.
manco, *adj.* one-armed.
mancha, *s. f.* spot, stain; patch.
manchado, *adj.* spotted, mottled.
manchar, *v. a.* stain, soil.
mandadero, *s. m.* messenger; errand-boy.
mandado, *s. m.* errand; message.
mandamiento, *s m.* order, command(ment).
mandar, *v. a.* send, transmit; order, direct.
mandatario, *s. m.* proxy; deputy.
mandato, *s. m.* order, command; mandate.
mandíbula, *s. f.* jaw.
mando, *s. m.* order; leadership; control; *cuadro de ~* dashboard, control panel.
manejar, *v. a.* manage, handle; drive; *v. n.* *~se* manage, succeed in.
manejo, *s. m.* handling; management, control; intrigue.
manera, *s. f.* way, manner; *de esta ~* in this manner; *de mala ~* rudely; *de ~ que* so, as a result; *de ninguna ~* by no means; *de otra ~* in another way, otherwise; *de todas ~s* at any rate.
manga, *s. f.* sleeve; hose; *en ~s de camisa* in shirt-sleeves.
mango, *s. m.* handle.
manía, *s. f.* madness; mania; hobby.
manicomio, *s. m.* lunatic asylum.
manifestación, *s. f.* demonstration.
manifestante, *s. m., f.* demonstrator.
manifestar, *v. a.* express, show.
manifiesto, *adj.* manifest, plain, obvious; — *s. m.* manifesto.
manija, *s. f.* handle.
maniobra, *s. f.* handling; manoeuvre; trick, knack.
maniobrar, *v. n.* manoeuvre.
manipular, *v. a.* manipulate.
manivela, *s. f.* crank, winch.
mano, *s. f.* hand; coat (of paint); first player (next to dealer).
manojo, *s. m.* bunch (of flowers, vegetables).
mansión, *s. f.* stay; residence.
manso, *adj.* tame; meek; calm.
manta, *s. f.* blanket.
manteca, *s. f.* lard, fat.
mantel, *s. m.* table-cloth.
mantener, *v. a.* support, provide for; hold; maintain, defend (an opinion); keep up (a conversation); *v. n.* *~se* support oneself.
mantequilla, *s. f.* butter.
mantilla, *s. f.* mantilla; — *pl.* baby-clothes.
manto, *s. m.* overcoat.
manual, *adj.* manual, physical; *trabajo ~* manual labour, handwork; — *s. m.* manual, handbook.
manubrio, *s. m.* handle, crank.
manufactura, *s. f.* manufacture.
manufacturar, *v. a.* manufacture.

manuscrito, *adj.* handwritten: — *s. m.* manuscript.
manzana, *s. f.* apple; block (of houses).
manzano, *s. m.* apple-tree.
mañana, *s. f.* morning; *s. m.* future; — *adv.* tomorrow: ~ *por la* ~ tomorrow morning; *de* ~ early in the morning; *¡hasta* ~*!* see you tomorrow.
mapa, *s. m.* map.
mapamundi, *s. m.* map of the world.
máquina, *s. f.* machine; ~ *de escribir* typewriter; *a toda* ~ at full speed.
maquinaria, *s. f.* machinery.
maquinista, *s. m.* engine-driver.
mar, *s. m., f.* sea; *alta* ~ high sea, open sea; *la* ~ *de gente* a lot of people.
maravilla, *s. f.* wonder, marvel.
maravillar, *v. a.* amaze; *v. n.* ~*se* be astonished.
maravilloso, *adj.* wonderful.
marca, *s. f.* mark; characteristic; ~ *de fábrica* trademark, brand.
marcar, *v. a.* mark.
marco, *s. m.* frame (of door, picture); mark (German money).
marcha, *s. f.* march; speed; *apresurar la* ~ hurry; speed up.
marchar, *v. n.* run; progress, go along; go (watch); ~*se* leave, go away.
marchito, *adj.* faded, withered.
marea, *s. f.* tide.
marear, *v. a.* bother; *v. n.* ~*se* get seasick; get dizzy.
mareo, *s. m.* seasickness; dizziness.
marfil, *s. m.* ivory.
margarita, *s. f.* daisy.
margen, *s. m., f.* margin; edge, border.
marido, *s. m.* husband.
marina, *s. f.* seascape, marine painting; navy; ~ *de guerra* navy; ~ *mercante* merchant marine.
marinero, *s. m.* sailor, seaman.
marino, *adj.* marine, of the sea, maritime; — *s. m.* seaman.
mariposa, *s. f.* butterfly.
mariscal, *s. m.* marshal.
marítimo, *adj.* maritime.
mármol, *s. m.* marble.
marquesina, *s. f.* sunshine roof; lean-to.
marrón, *adj.* brown.
marta, *s. f.* marten.
martes, *s. m.* Tuesday.
martillar, *v. a.* & *n.* hammer.
martillo, *s. m.* hammer.
mártir, *s. m., f.* martyr.
martirio, *s. m.* martyrdom; torture.
marzo, *s. m.* March.
más, *adv.* more; longer; plus; *a lo* ~ at most; *a* ~ *tardar* at the latest; *de* ~ too much, too many; *estar de* ~ be unnecessary; ~ *adelante* later on; ~ *allá* farther on; ~ *bien* rather; ~ *que* more than; *no* ~ *que* only.
mas, *adv.* but.
masa, *s. f.* dough; mass

(of people); *con las manos en la ~* red-handed.
masaje, *s. m.* massage.
mascar, *v. a.* chew.
máscara, *s. f.* mask; *baile (s. m.) de ~s* masquerade ball; *~ contra gases* gas-mask; *vestido de ~* in costume.
masculino, *adj.* masculine.
masticar, *v. a.* chew.
mástil, *s. m.* mast, pole, post.
mata, *s. f.* plant, bush; shrub.
matadero, *s. m.* slaughter-house.
matafuego, *s. m.* fire-extinguisher.
matar, *v. a.* kill; trump; *~ la sed* quench one's thirst; *~ de aburrimiento* bore to death; *~ el tiempo* kill time; *v. n. ~se* kill oneself, get killed.
matasellos, *s. m.* post-mark.
mate, *s. m.* maté (South American tea); mate (chess); – *adj.* mat, dim, dull.
matemáticas, *s. f.* mathematics.
materia, *s. f.* material, substance; matter, topic, subject; *~ prima* raw material; *entrar en ~* come to the point.
material, *adj.* material; – *s. m.* material; equipment.
maternidad, *s. f.* maternity.
matinal, *adj.* morning.
matiz, *s. m.* shade, tint.
matizar, *v. a.* shade, tint.
matorral, *s. m.* thicket, bush.
matrícula, *s. f.* register; registration number.
matricular, *v. a.* matriculate.
matrimonio, *s. m.* matrimony, marriage; married couple.
matriz, *s. f.* matrix.
máxima, *s. f.* maxim; proverb.
máxime, *adv.* chiefly, mainly.
máximo, *adj.* & *s. m.* maximum.
mayo, *s. m.* May.
mayonesa, *s. f.* mayonnaise.
mayor[1], *adj.* larger, largest; bigger, biggest; older, oldest; *calle ~* main street; *Estado ~* General Staff; *al por ~* wholesale; *ser ~ de edad* be of age.
mayor[2], *s. m.* major.
mayordomo, *s. m.* butler; administrator.
mayoría, *s. f.* majority, greater part.
mayúscula, *s. f.* large letter; bold type.
maza, *s. f.* club.
mazapán, *s. m.* marzipan.
mazo, *s. m.* mallet.
me, *pron.* me, to me.
mecánica, *s. f.* mechanics.
mecánico, *adj.* mechanical; – *s. m.* mechanic.
mecanismo, *s. m.* mechanism.
mecanógrafa, *s. f.* typist.
mecanografiar, *v. a.* typewrite.
mecer, *v. a.* rock.
medalla, *s. f.* medal.
media, *s. f.* stocking.
mediación, *s. f.* mediation.
mediado, *adj.* half-filled,

half-full; *a ~s de mayo* in the middle of May.
mediador, *s. m.* mediator.
mediano, *adj.* medium; mediocre.
medianoche, *s. f.* midnight.
mediante, *prep.* through, by means of.
mediar, *v. a. & n.* mediate.
medicina, *s. f.* medicine.
médico, *adj.* medical; — *s. m.* physician.
medida, *s. f.* measure; rule; number, size; *a la ~* (made) to measure; *tomar ~s* take measures *or* steps.
medio, *adj.* half; middle of; *a ~ camino* halfway to a place; *a ~ hacer* half-done; — *s. m.* middle; means; *por ~ de* by means of.
mediodía, *s. m.* noon, midday.
medir, *v. a.* measure.
médula, *s. f.* marrow.
mejilla, *s. f.* cheek.
mejor, *adj. & adv.* better, best; *a lo ~* perhaps; maybe; *~ dicho* or rather, or better; *tanto ~* so much the better.
mejorar, *v. a.* improve.
melocotón, *s. m.* peach.
melodía, *s. f.* melody.
melón, *s. m.* melon.
meloso, *adj.* honeylike, very sweet.
mellizo, *adj. & s. m.* twin.
memoria *s. f.* memory; memorandum, report; *de ~* by heart.
mención, *s. f.* mention.
mencionar, *v. a.* mention.
mendigo, *s. m.* beggar.
menester, *s. m.* necessity; *es ~* it's necessary.
menor, *adj.* smaller, smallest; younger, youngest; less, least; slightest; *al por ~* at retail; minutely; *~ de edad,* under age, minor.
menos, *adv.* less, least; — *prep.* except; but; *al ~* at least, *a ~ que* unless; *echar de ~* miss; *~ de* less than; *por lo ~* at least.
mensaje, *s. m.* dispatch.
mensajero, *s. m.* courier.
mensual, *adj.* monthly.
menta, *s. f.* mint, peppermint.
mente, *s. f.* mind.
mentir, *v. n.* lie, tell lies.
mentira, *s. f.* lie.
menudo, *adj.* tiny, very small; *a ~* often.
meñique, *s. m.* little finger.
mercado, *s. m.* market.
mercancía, *s. f.* merchandise, goods.
mercantil, *adj.* commercial, mercantile.
merced, *s. f.* favour; mercy.
mercería, *s. f.* haberdashery.
mercurio, *s. m.* mercury.
merecer, *v. a.* deserve; *no merece la pena* it isn't worth while.
merendar, *v. n.* have a snack in the afternoon; picnic.
meridional, *adj.* southern.
merienda, *s. f.* afternoon snack, picnic.
mérito, *s. m.* merit, worth.
mermelada, *s. f.* jam; marmalade.
mes, *s. m.* month.
mesa, *s. f.* table; *poner la ~* set the table.
meseta, *s. f.* plateau.
meta, *s. f.* aim, goal.
metal, *s. m.* metal; brass.

metálico, *adj.* metallic; — *s. m.* coin(s).
meteorología, *s. f.* meteorology.
meter, *v. a.* put; ~ *miedo* frighten; ~ *ruido* make noise; *v. n.* ~*se en* get into; be nosy.
metódico, *adj.* systematic, methodical.
método, *s. m.* method.
metro, *s. m.* metre; underground railway.
mezclar, *v. a.* mix; blend; *v. n.* ~*se* get mixed up.
mezquita, *s. f.* mosque.
mi, *adj.* my; ~ *sombrero* my hat; *mis hijos* my sons.
mí, *pron.* me; *¿hay cartas para ~?* are there letters for me?
microbio, *s. m.* microbe.
micrófono, *s. m.* microphone.
microscopio, *s. m.* microscope.
miedo, *s. m.* fear; *tener ~* be afraid.
miel, *s. f.* honey.
miembro, *s. m.* limb; member.
mientras, *conj.* while; ~ *tanto* meanwhile.
miércoles, *s. m.* Wednesday.
miga, *s. f.* crumb.
mil, *adj. & s. m.* thousand.
milagro, *s. m.* miracle, marvel.
militar, *adj.* military; — *s. m.* military man.
milla, *s. f.* mile.
millar, *s. m.* one thousand.
millón, *s. m.* million.
millonario, *s. m.* millionaire.
mimar, *v. a.* spoil (a child).
mina, *s. f.* mine (excavation and explosive).
mineral, *adj. & s. m.* mineral.
minero, *s. m.* miner.
mínimo, *adj. & s. m.* minimum.
ministerio, *s. m.* ministry.
ministro, *s. m.* minister.
minoría, *s. f.* minority.
minúscula, *s. f.* small letter.
minuta, *s. f.* draft; memorandum.
minuto, *adj.* minute; — *s. m.* minute.
mío, *adj. & pron.* (of) mine; *estos lápices son míos* these pencils are mine.
miope, *adj.* short-sighted.
mirada, *s. f.* look, glance.
mirar, *v. a.* look at; glance; regard; consider, think; watch, be careful; ~ *alrededor* look around; ~*se* look at each other.
misa, *s. f.* Mass.
miseria, *s. f.* poverty, trifle, pittance.
misericordia, *s. f.* mercy, compassion.
misión, *s. f.* mission.
misionero, *s. m.* missionary.
mismo, *adj. & pron.* same, identical; *yo ~* I myself; *aquí mismo* right here; *me da lo ~* it's all the same to me.
misterio, *s. m.* mistery.
mitad, *s. f.* half; *a ~ de camino* half-way.
mitin, *s. m.* meeting, rally.
mixto, *adj.* mixed.
mobiliario, *s. m.* furniture.
mochila, *s. f.* knapsack.
moda, *s. f.* fashion, style; *a la ~* fashionable; *pasado de ~* out of style.
modelo, *adj.* model, per-

fect; — *s. m.* model; pattern.
moderar, *v. a.* restrain, moderate; *v. n.* **~se** control oneself.
moderno, *adj.* modern.
modestia, *s. f.* modesty, humbleness.
modesto, *adj.* simple.
modificar, *v. a.* modify.
modista, *s. m., f.* dressmaker.
modo, *s. m.* method, way; *de este ~* in this way; *de ~ que* so, therefore; *de ningún ~* by no means; *de todos ~s* anyhow.
mojar, *v. a.* wet, moisten; drench.
moler, *v. a.* grind, mill.
molestar, *v. a.* disturb; annoy; bother, inconvenience; hurt; *v. n.* **~se** be ennoyed; bother.
molestia, *s. f.* trouble, discomfort.
molesto, *adj.* uncomfortable; annoyed.
molinero, *s. m.* miller.
molinillo, *s. m.* coffee-mill.
molino, *s. m.* mill.
momento, *s. m.* moment; *al ~* immediately.
momia, *s. f.* mummy.
mona, *s. f.* female monkey; drunkenness; — *adj.* pretty.
monarquía, *s. f.* monarchy.
mondar, *v. a.* peel, clean.
moneda, *s. f.* coin; currency.
monja, *s. f.* nun.
monje, *s. m.* monk.
mono, *adj.* cute; — *s. m.* monkey; overalls.
monstruoso, *adj.* monstrous.
montador, *s. m.* fitter, assembler (of machinery).
montaje, *s. m.* assembling.
montaña, *s. f.* mountain.
montañoso, *adj.* mountainous.
montar, *v. a.* ride (horseback); set up, assemble, install; *v. n.* *~ a* amount to (in money); *~ en cólera* get furious.
monte, *s. m.* mountain; woods, forest.
montón, *s. m.* heap; pile.
montuoso, *adj.* mountainous.
monumento, *s. m.* monument.
mora, *s. f.* blackberry.
morada, *s. f.* dwelling, stay.
moral, *adj.* moral; — *s. m.* morale; black mulberry tree.
morder, *v. a. & n.* bite.
moreno, *adj.* dark-skinned, brunette.
morir, *v. n.* die; *v. n.* *~se de hambre* starve to death.
moro, *adj.* Moorish; — *s. m.* Moor.
mortal, *adj.* deadly, terrible, mortal; — *s. m.* mortal being.
mosaico, *s. m.* mosaic.
mosca, *s. f.* fly.
mosquito, *s. m.* mosquito.
mostaza, *s. f.* mustard.
mosto, *s. m.* must.
mostrador, *s. m.* counter (in a shop).
mostrar, *v. a.* show, display; *v. n.* **~se** appear, show oneself.
motivar, *v. a.* cause.
motivo, *s. m.* motive, reason; *con ~ de* on the occasion of.
motocicleta, *s. f.* motor-

cycle.
motolancha, *s. f.* motor boat.
motor, *s. m.* motor.
mover, *v. a.* move; stir; *v. n.* *~se* move.
móvil, *adj.* mobile; – *s. m.* motive.
movilizar, *v. a.* mobilize.
movimiento, *s. m.* movement, move; traffic; animation.
mozo, *s. m.* waiter; porter; lad, young man.
muchacha, *s. f.* young girl; maid.
muchacho, *s. m.* boy.
muchedumbre, *s. f.* crowd (of people); multitude.
mucho, *adj.* much; *~s pl.* many; – *adv.* much, a lot; long; *sentir ~* be very sorry.
mudanza, *s. f.* change of residence.
mudar, *v. a.* change; *v. n.* *~se* change (clothes); *~se de casa* change residence.
mudo, *adj.* dumb, mute.
mueble, *adj.* movable; *s. m.* piece of furniture.
muela, *s. f.* molar (tooth); millstone; *dolor (s. m.) de ~s* toothache.
muelle, *adj.* soft; – *s. m.* spring (wire); pier.
muerte, *s. f.* death.
muerto, *adj.* & *s. m.* dead; dummy (bridge).
muestra, *s. f.* sample.
mujer, *s. f.* woman; wife.
mula, *s. f.* female mule.
mulato, *adj.* & *s. m.* mulatto.
muleta, *s. f.* crutch.
mulo, *s. m.* mule.
multa, *s. f.* fine (punishment).
multicolor. *adj.* coloured.
múltiple, *adj.* manifold.
multiplicar, *v. a.* multiply.
multitud, *s. f* crowd, masses.
mundano, *adj.* worldly.
mundial, *adj.* universal; *guerra ~* World War.
mundo, *s. m.* world; *gran ~* high society; *todo el ~* everybody.
munición, *s. f.* ammunition.
municipal, *adj.* municipal; – *s. m.* constable.
municipalidad, *s. f.* citizens, municipality.
municipio, *s. m.* municipal council.
munífico, *adj.* liberal, generous.
muñeca, *s. f.* wrist; doll.
muralla, *s. f.* wall (of a city).
murciélago, *s. m.* bat.
muro, *s. m.* outside wall.
músculo, *s. m.* muscle.
musculoso, *adj.* muscular.
museo, *s. m.* museum.
musgo, *s. m.* moss.
música, *s. f.* music; band (of musicians).
musical, *adj.* musical.
músico, *adj.* musical; – *s. m.* musician.
muslo, *s. m.* thigh.
mustio, *adj.* withered; depressed.
mutilar, *v. a.* mutilate.
mutis, *s. m.* (theatre) exit.
mutuo, *adj.* mutual, reciprocal.
muy, *adv.* very.

N

nabo, *s. m.* turnip.
nacer, *v. n.* be born; rise, spring, have its

source; sprout.
nación, *s. f.* nation.
nacional, *adj.* national.
nacionalidad, *s. f.* nationality.
nada, *s. f.* nothing; — *adv.* not at all; ~ *más* nothing else; *de* ~ don't mention it.
nadador, *s. m.* swimmer.
nadar, *v. n.* swim.
nadie, *pron.* nobody, no one, not anybody.
naipe, *s. m.* (playing) card.
naranja, *s. f.* orange.
naranjada, *s. f.* orangeade.
naranjero, *s. m.* orange-seller.
naranjo, *s. m.* orange tree.
narcótico, *adj.* narcotic; — *s. m.* narcotic, dope.
nariz, *s. f.* nose.
narrar, *v. a.* narrate.
nata, *s. f.* cream; ~ *batida* whipped cream.
natación, *s. f.* (art of) swimming.
natal, *adj.* native; *país* ~ native country.
natalicio, *s. m.* birthday.
natural, *adj.* natural; — *s. m.* native; nature, disposition.
naturaleza, *s. f.* nature, constitution; temperament.
naturalidad, *s. f.* naturalness.
naturalizar, *v. a.* naturalize.
naufragar, *v. n.* be shipwrecked; fail, fall through.
naufragio, *s. m.* shipwreck.
náusea, *s. f.* nausea.
náutica, *s. f.* navigation.
náutico, *adj.* nautical; *deporte* ~ aquatic sports.
navaja, *s. f.* penknife; razor.
nave, *s. f.* ship; nave.
navegación, *s. f.* navigation; voyage.
navegar, *v. n.* navigate, sail.
Navidad, *s. f.* Christmas.
neblina, *s. f.* mist, fog.
necesario, *adj.* necessary.
necesidad, *s. f.* need, necessity.
necesitar, *v. a.* need.
negación, *s. f.* negation.
negar, *v. a.* deny; refuse; *v. n.* ~*se a* refuse to do sg.
negativa, *s. f.* negative.
negativo, *adj.* negative.
negligente, *adj.* negligent.
negociación, *s. f.* negotiation.
negociante, *s. m.* business man.
negociar, *v. a.* & *n.* negotiate; do business.
negocio, *s. m.* business; interest.
negro, *adj.* black; dark; — *s. m.* Negro; black colour.
nena, *s. f.*, **nene,** *s. m.* baby.
neoyorquino, *adj.* & *s. m.* New Yorker.
nervio, *s. m.* nerve.
nervioso, *adj.* nervous.
neto, *adj.* net.
neumático, *adj.* pneumatic; — *s. m.* tire.
neumonía, *s. f.* pneumonia.
neuralgia, *s. f.* neuralgia.
neutralidad, *s. f.* neutrality.
nevada, *s. f.* snowfall.
nevar, *v. n.* snow.
nevera, *s. f.* refrigerator.
ni, *conj.* neither, nor.
nido, *s. m.* nest.
niebla, *s. f.* fog, mist, haze.
nieta, *s. f.* granddaughter.

nieto, *s. m.* grandson
nieve, *s. f.* snow.
ningun, *adj.* not a, not one.
ninguno, *adj.* not any, none; *de ninguna manera* by no means.
niña, *s. f.* girl; *~ del ojo* pupil (of the eye); apple of the eye.
niñera, *s. f.* nurse(-maid).
niñez, *s. f.* childhood.
niño, *adj.* young; childish; — *s. m.* boy; *~s pl.* children.
nivel, *s. m.* level; *a ~* horizontal, level.
nivelar, *v. a.* level; balance.
no, no, not; *~ más* only, no more.
noche, *s. f.* evening; night; *esta ~* tonight
Nochebuena, *s. f.* Christmas Eve.
nogal, *s. m.* walnut-tree.
nombramiento, *s. m.* nomination; appointment.
nombrar, *v. a.* name, mention; appoint.
nombre, *s. m.* name; fame, reputation; noun; *~ de familia* familyname, surname; *~ de pila* first *or* Christian name.
nordeste, *s. m.* northeast.
norma, *s. f.* norm.
normal, *adj.* normal; standard.
noroeste, *s. m.* northwest.
norte, *s. m.* north.
norteamericano, *adj.* & *s. m.* North American.
noruego, *adj.* & *s. m.* Norwegian.
nos, *pron.* us, to us.
nosotros, *pron.* we.
nota, *s. f.* note; (school) mark; footnote, marginal note.
notar, *v. a.* notice, note.
notario, *s. m.* notary public.
noticia, *s. f.* news; notice.
notificar, *v. a.* notify, inform.
novedad, *s. f.* novelty: news; surprise; *sin ~* as usual; nothing new.
novela, *s. f.* novel.
noveno, *adj.* ninth.
noventa, *adj.* & *s. m.* ninety.
novia, *s. f.* fiancée; bride.
noviembre, *s. m.* November.
novio, *s. m.* fiancé; bridegroom.
nube, *s. f.* cloud.
nublado, *adj.* cloudy, overcast.
nuca, *s. f.* (nape of the) neck.
nudo, *s. m.* knot.
nuera, *s. f.* daughter-in-law.
nuestro, *adj.* & *pron.* our, of ours.
nueve, *adj.* & *s. m.* nine.
nuevo, *adj.* new; *de ~* again.
nuez, *s. f.* walnut.
numerar, *v. a.* number.
número, *s. m.* number; size; edition.
numeroso, *adj.* numerous.
nunca, *adv.* never, not ever; *~ jamás* nevermore.
nutrir, *v. a.* nourish.

Ñ

ñandú, *s. m.* (South American) ostrich.
ñato, *adj.* pug-nosed.
ñoñería, *s. f.* silliness.
ñoño, *adj.* silly.
ñu, *s. m.* gnu.

O

o, *conj.* or; *o...o* either...or; *o sea* that is.
obedecer, *v. a.* obey.
obediente, *adj.* obedient.
obispo, *s. m.* bishop.
objetivo, *adj.* & *s. m.* objective.
objeto, *s. m.* object; purpose.
oblea, *s. f.* wafer.
oblicuo, *adj.* oblique.
obligación, *s. f.* obligation, responsibility; duty.
obligar, *v. a.* oblige, compel, force.
obligatorio, *adj.* obligatory, compulsory.
obra, *s. f.* work, books, works; show, performance; *~ maestra* masterpiece.
obrar, *v. n.* do, act; behave.
obrero, *s. m.* worker, labourer.
obsequiar, *v. a.* present with; be very kind.
obsequio, *s. m.* gift, present.
observar, *v. a.* watch, observe; notice; *~ buena conducta* behave well.
observatorio, *s. m.* observatory.
obstáculo, *s. m.* obstacle, hindrance.
obstante, *adv.*; *no ~* notwithstanding.
obstinado, *adj.* stubborn.
obstinarse *en*, *v. n.* insist on.
obtener, *v. a.* get, obtain.
ocasión, *s. f.* occasion, time; chance, opportunity; *de ~* second-hand.
ocasionar, *v. a.* cause.
occidental, *adj.* western, Occidental.
occidente, *s. m.* west; occident.
océano, *s. m.* ocean.
octavo, *adj.* eighth.
octubre, *s. m.* October.
oculista, *s. m., f.* oculist.
ocultar, *v. a.* hide.
ocupación, *s. f.* occupation; business.
ocupado, *adj.* occupied, taken; busy.
ocupar, *v. a.* occupy, take possession of; *v. n.* *~se de* take care of, pay attention to.
ocurrencia, *s. f.* incident, witticism.
ocurrir, *v. n.* occur, happen; *se me ocurre* it comes to my mind.
ochenta, *adj.* & *s. m.* eighty.
ocho, *adj.* & *s. m.* eight.
odiar, *v. a.* hate.
odio, *s. m.* hatred.
oeste, *s. m.* west.
ofender, *v. a.* offend; *v. n.* *~se* take offense.
ofensa, *s. f.* insult, offence.
ofensiva, *s. f.* offensive.
oferta, *s. f.* offer.
oficial, *adj.* official; — *s. m.* officer, clerk.
oficina, *s. f.* office (room).
oficio, *s. m.* manual work, occupation, trade; *~ divino* church service.
ofrecer, *v. a.* offer.
ofrecimiento, *s. m.* offer, offering.
oída, *s. f.* hearing; *de ~s, por ~s* by hearsay.
oído, *s. m.* (inner) ear; hearing; *dar ~s* listen, lend an ear.
oír, *v. a.* hear; listen; *¡oiga!* hello! (telephone).
ojal, *s. m.* buttonhole.
ojalá! *int.*; *¡~ fuera possible!* if only it were

possible!
ojeada, *s. f.* glance; *echar una ~* cast a glance.
ojear, *v. a.* glance through.
ojo, *s. m.* eye; *~ de la llave* keyhole; *cuesta un ~ de la cara* it costs plenty.
ola, *s. f.* wave (of water).
¡olé! *int.* bravo!; well done!
óleo, *s. m.* oil (-colour).
oler, *v. a. & n.* smell.
olfato, *s. m.* sense of smell.
olímpico, *adj.* Olympic.
oliva, *s. f.* olive.
olivo, *s. m.* olive tree.
olmo, *s. m.* elm.
olor, *s. m.* smell, odour.
oloroso, *adj.* fragrant.
olvidar, *v. a.* forget.
olla, *s. f.* pot.
omisión, *s. f.* omission.
omitir, *v. a.* omit.
once, *adj. & s. m.* eleven.
onda, *s. f.* wave; ripple (of water); *~ corta* short wave; *~ larga* long wave (radio).
ondulación, *s. f.* wave; *~ permanente* permanent wave.
ondulado, *adj.* wavy; — *s. m.* wave, waving.
ondular, *v. a. & n.* wave; ripple.
onza, *s. f.* ounce.
opera, *s. f.* opera.
operación, *s. f.* operation.
operador, *s. m.* operator.
operar, *v. a.* operate on.
operario, *s. m.* skilled worker.
opereta, *s. f.* operetta; musical (comedy).
opinión, *s. f.* opinion.
oponer, *v. a.* set up; — *v. n. ~se a* oppose.
oportunidad, *s. f.* opportunity.
oportuno, *adj.* opportune, appropriate, fitting.
oprimir, *v. a.* oppress.
óptica, *s. f.* optics.
óptico, *s. m.* optician.
optimista, *adj. & s. m. f.* optimist(ic).
óptimo, *adj.* excellent.
opuesto, *adj.* opposite.
oración, *s. f.* sentence; prayer.
orador, *s. m.* orator.
orden, *s. m.* order; — *s. f.* command, instruction; (commercial) order; (religious) order; *a sus órdenes* at your service; *en ~* in order; *~ del día* agenda, order of the day.
ordenar, *v. a.* put in order; order.
ordeñar, *v. a.* milk.
ordinario, *adj.* usual; ordinary, vulgar; *de ~* usually.
oreja, *s. f.* ear.
orfanato, *s. m.* orphanage.
orgánico, *adj.* organic.
organillo, *s. m.* barrel-organ.
organismo, *s. m.* organism.
organización, *s. f.* organization.
organizador, *s. m.* organizer.
organizar, *v. a.* organize; arrange.
órgano, *s. m.* organ.
orgullo, *s. m.* pride.
orgulloso, *adj.* proud, haughty.
oriental, *adj.* eastern; Oriental; — *s. m.* Oriental.

orientar, *v. a.* orientate; *v n.* **~se** orient oneself.
oriente, *s. m.* east; Orient.
origen, *s. m.* origin; descent, extraction.
original, *adj.* original; eccentric, odd; — *s. m.* original.
originalidad, *s. f.* originality; eccentricity, oddity.
originar, *v. a.* start.
orilla, *s. f.* bank; edge, rim; *~ del mar* seashore; *a ~s de* on the shore of.
orla, *s. f.* seam, hem.
orlar, *v. a.* hem, border.
oro, *s. m.* gold.
orquesta, *s. f.* orchestra.
ortiga, *s. f.* stinging nettle.
ortografía. *s. f.* orthography.
oruga, *s. f.* caterpillar; *cadena-~* caterpillar track.
os, *pron.* you, to you.
oscurecer, *v. n.* get dark.
oscuridad, *s. f.* obscurity, darkness.
oscuro, *adj.* dark; obscure.
oso, *s. m.* bear.
ostra, *s. f.* oyster.
otoñal, *adj.* autumnal.
otoño, *s. m.* autumn.
otorgar, *v. a.* grant, allow; issue.
otro, *adj.* another, other; *alguna otra cosa* something else; *uno a ~* each other; *otra vez* again; *por otra parte* on the other hand; *el ~ dia* lately, of late; *~ tanto* just as much; *¡otra!* da capo! encore!
ovación, *s. f.* ovation, cheering.
oveja, *s. f.* sheep.
ovillo, *s. m.* clue, ball.
oxidar, *v. a.* oxidize.
óxido, *s. m.* oxide.
oxígeno, *s. m.* oxygen.
oyente, *s. m., f.* hearer, listener.

P

pabellón, *s. m.* pavilion.
paciencia, *s f.* patience; forbearance.
paciente, *adj. & s. m., f.* patient.
pacífico, *adj.* pacific.
pacto, *s. m.* agreement, pact.
padecer, *v. n.* suffer from.
padrastro, *s. m.* stepfather.
padre, *s. m.* father; priest; *~s pl.* parents.
padrino, *s. m.* godfather; patron, sponsor.
paella, *s. f.* dish of rice with meat or chicken.
paga, *s. f.* wages, pay.
pagar, *v. a.* pay.
página, *s. f.* page (of a book).
pago, *s. m.* payment.
país, *s. m.* country; *del ~* domestic, local.
paisaje, *s. m.* landscape, scenery.
paisano, *s. m.* person from the same country or city; civilian.
paja, *s. f.* straw.
pájaro, *s. m.* bird.
pala, *s. f.* spade, shovel.
palabra, *s. f.* word; *¡~!* honestly! no fooling!
palacio, *s. m.* palace.
paladar, *s. m.* palate.
palanca, *s. f.* lever.
palangana, *s. f.* washbasin.
palco, *s. m.* (theatre) box.

paliativo, *adj.* & *s. m.* palliative.
palidecer, *v. n.* turn pale.
palidez, *s. f.* pallor.
pálido, *adj.* pale.
paliza, *s. f.* beating, spanking.
palma, *s. f.* palm (leaf, tree, hand); *llevar la* ~ win the prize.
palmada, *s. f.* clapping; pat (on the back); *dar* ~*s* clap; applaud.
palmera, *s. f.* palmtree.
palmo, *s. m.* span.
palmotear, *v. n.* applaud.
palo, *s. m.* stick; pole; wood; suit (in cards); *dar de* ~*s* club, beat.
paloma, *s. f.* pigeon, dove.
palomar, *s. m.* dovecot.
palpar, *v. a.* touch, finger.
pan, *s. m.* bread; ~ *integral* whole-wheat bread; ~ *tierno* fresh bread.
pana, *s. f.* plush.
panadería, *s. f.* bakery.
panadero, *s. m.* baker.
panecillo, *s. m.* roll (bread).
pantalones, *s. m. pl.* trousers, pants.
pantalla, *s. f.* lampshade; screen; film.
pantano, *s. m.* swamp, marsh, bog.
pantorrilla, *s. f.* calf (of the leg).
panza, *s. f.* belly, paunch.
paño, *s. m.* cloth.
pañuelo, *s. m.* handkerchief.
Papa, *s. m.* Pope.
papa, *s. f.* potato.
papá, *s. m.* papa, dad.
papagayo, *s. m.* parrot.
papel, *s. m.* paper; document; role, part; ~ *pintado* wallpaper; ~ *secante* blotting-paper; ~ *de cartas* stationery; ~ *de seda* tissue paper; ~ *moneda* paper money, bills.
papelería, *s. f.* stationer's shop.
paquete, *s. m.* parcel; package.
par, *adj.* even (of numbers); — *s. m.* pair; couple; equal; *sin* ~ incomparable.
para, *prep.* & *conj.* *¿~ qué?* why?; what for?; ~ *(que)* to, in order to; so that; *¿~ dónde?* where to?; *salgo ~ Barcelona* I leave for Barcelona; *taza ~ té* tea-cup.
parabrisas, *s. m.* windscreen.
paracaídas, *s. m.* parachute.
parada, *s. f.* stop; (military) parade.
paradero, *s. m.* whereabouts.
parado, *adj.* shut down; unemployed; standing.
parador, *s. m.* inn, hostelry.
paraguas, *s. m.* umbrella.
paraíso, *s. m.* paradise, heaven; (theatre) gallery.
parar, *v. n.* stop; stay (in a hotel); end up, turn out; ~*se* stop.
parcial, *adj.* partial.
parche, *s. m.* plaster, patch.
pardo, *adj.* brown; dark-gray.
parecer, *v. n.* look, appear; seem; *según parece* as it seems, apparently;

~se be alike; — *s. m.* opinion; *al ~* apparently.
parecido, *adj.* like, similar; — *s. m.* resemblance; *bien ~* good-looking.
pared, *s. f.* wall.
pareja, *s. f.* pair, couple; team; dancing partner.
parejo, *adj.* equal, the same.
parentela, *s. f.* relations.
parentesco, *s. m.* relationship.
paréntesis, *s. m.* bracket, parenthesis.
paridad, *s. f.* parity.
pariente, *s. m., f.* relative.
parlamento, *s. m.* parliament.
paro, *s m.* stoppage; unemployment; strike.
párpado, *s. m.* eyelid.
parque, *s. m.* park.
párrafo, *s. m.* paragraph.
parrilla, *s. f.* grate; grill.
parroquiano, *s. m.* parishioner, customer.
parte, *s. m.* report; — *s. f.* part; share; (legal) party; *dar ~* inform, notify; *de mi ~* on my behalf; *en todas ~s* everywhere; *tomar ~* take part.
participante, *s. m., f.* participant.
participar, *v. a.* announce; *v. n. ~ en* take part in.
particular, *adj.* special, particular; private; odd, peculiar.
partida, *s. f.* departure; item (in an account); game; certificate.
partidario, *s. m.* follower.
partido, *s. m.* party, faction; match, game; *sacar ~ de* profit by.
partir, *v. a.* split; cut; divide; *v. n.* leave for; *~se* break.
parto, *s. m.* birth.
pasa, *s. f* raisin.
pasado, *adj.* last; *la semana ~a* last week; *~ mañana* day after tomorrow; — *s. m.* past.
pasaje, *s. m.* crossing; journey, voyage; fare; arcade; passage (from book).
pasajero, *adj.* passing, transitory; — *s. m.* passenger.
pasaporte, *s. m.* passport.
pasar, *v. a.* pass, overtake; hand; go through; cross; move, transfer; spend (time); tolerate, overlook; *v. n.* happen; come in; get along, make out; pass (at cards); stop (of rain); *~ de moda* go out of style; *~ el rato* kill time; *~ lista* call the roll; *~ por alto* skip, overlook; *~se sin* do without.
pasarela, *s. f.* gangway.
pasatiempo, *s. m.* pastime, amusement.
Pascua, *s. f.*; *~ de Navidad* Christmas; *~ florida, ~ de Resurrección* Easter; *¡ Felices Pascuas!* Merry Christmas!
pase, *s. m.* pass, permit.
pasear, *v. n.* stroll, take a walk.
paseo, *s. m.* walk; *dar un ~* take a walk.
pasillo, *s. m.* passage,

corridor.
pasión, *s. f.* emotion, passion.
paso, *s. m.* step; gait; (mountain) pass; progress; *de ~* in passing; *~ a nivel* railway crossing.
pasta, *s. f.* paste; binding, cover; tea-cake; plastic; dough (money); *de buena ~* good-natured; *~ de dientes* toothpaste; *sopa de ~* noodle-soup.
pastel, *s. m.* pie; cake; pastel.
pastelería, *s. f.* confectioner's shop.
pastilla, *s. f.* tablet; drop.
pastor, *s. m.* shepherd.
pata, *s. f.* foot, leg (of an animal).
patata, *s. f.* potato.
patente, *adj.* evident; — *s. f.* patent.
patín, *s. m.* skate; *~ de ruedas* roller-skate.
patinar, *v. n.* skate; skid, slip.
patio, *s. m.* patio, courtyard; *~ de butacas* (theatre) orchestra-stalls.
pato, *s. m.* duck.
patria, *s. f.* fatherland, native land.
patrimonio, *s. m.* patrimony.
patriota, *s. m., f.* patriot.
patriótico, *adj.* patriotic.
patrón, *s. m.* patron saint; employer, boss; pattern.
pausa, *s. f.* rest; brake.
pausar, *v. n.* pause; hesitate.
pava, *s. f.* turkey-hen.
pavimento, *s. m.* pavement.
pavo, *s. m.* turkey-cock; *~ real* peacock.
pavaso, *s. m.* clown.
paz, *s. f.* peace; *hacer las paces* become reconciled.
peatón, *s. m.* pedestrian.
pecado, *s. m.* sin.
pecar, *v. n.* sin.
pecho, *s. m.* chest; bosom.
pedazo, *s. m.* piece, bit.
pedicura, *s. f.* pedicure.
pedido, *s. m.* order, commission.
pedir, *v. a.* ask, request; order; *~ limosna* beg for alms; *a ~ de boca* according to desire.
pegar, *v. a.* stick; glue; sew on; hit, beat, strike; infect with; *~ fuego* set fire; *v. n.* *~se* adhere, stick.
peinado, *s. m.* hair-style.
peinar, *v. a.* comb.
peine, *s. m.* comb.
pelar, *v. a.* pick, pluck (fowl); skin.
peldaño, *s. m.* stair, step.
pelea, *s. f.* fight, quarrel.
pelear, *v. n.* fight, quarrel.
peletería, *s. f.* furrier's shop.
película, *s. f.* film; picture.
peligro, *s. m.* danger; *correr ~* run a risk.
peligroso, *adj.* dangerous.
pelo, *s. m.* hair; *tomar el ~* pull one's leg.
pelota, *s. f.* ball (for games).
peluca, *s. f.* wig.
peludo, *adj.* hairy.
peluquería, *s. f.* hairdresser's shop.
peluquero, *s. m.* hair-

dresser.
pellizcar, *v. a.* pinch.
pena, *s. f.* penalty; pain, sorrow; trouble; *a duras* ~*s* with great difficulty; *vale la* ~ it's worth while.
pendiente, *adj.* pending; — *s. m.* earring; — *s. f.* slope.
penetrar, *v. a.* penetrate; determine, make out.
península, *s. f.* peninsula.
pensamiento, *s. m.* thought, idea; pansy (flower).
pensar, *v. n.* think; intend; ~ *en* think of *or* about.
pensión, *s. f.* pension; boarding-house.
Pentecostés, *s. m.* Whitsuntide.
peón, *s. m.* workman; (chess) pawn.
peor, *adj.* & *adv.* worse, worst.
pepino, *s. m.* cucumber.
pequeño, *adj.* small, little.
pera, *s. f.* pear.
peral, *s. m.* pear-tree.
percha, *s. f.* rack (for clothes); hanger.
perder, *v. a.* lose; miss (the train); ruin; ~ *de vista* lose sight of; *echar a* ~ ruin, spoil; *v. n.* ~*se* get lost; become spoiled.
pérdida, *s. f.* loss.
perdiz, *s. f.* partridge.
perdón, *s. m.* forgiveness; pardon.
perdonar, *v. a.* pardon; forgive; excuse.
perecer, *v. n.* perish.
peregrino, *adj.* exotic, strange; — *s. m.* pilgrim.
perejil, *s. m.* parsley.
pereza, *s. f.* laziness.
perezoso, *adj.* lazy.
perfecto, *adj.* perfect.
perfil, *s. m.* profile; outline.
perfumar, *v. a.* perfume
perfume, *s. m.* perfume.
periódico, *adj.* periodical; — *s. m.* newspaper.
periodista, *s. m. f.* journalist.
perito, *adj.* & *s. m.* expert.
perjudicar, *v. a.* damage, hurt, injure.
perjuicio, *s. m.* prejudice; damage, injury, harm.
perla, *s. f.* pearl.
permanecer, *v. n.* stay, remain.
permanente, *adj.* & *s. f.* permanent (wave).
permiso, *s. m.* permission, licence; permit; *con* ~ excuse me.
permitir, *v. a.* permit, allow.
pero, *conj.* but.
perra, *s. f.* bitch.
perro, *s. m.* dog.
persiana, *s. f.* Venetian blind.
persona, *s. f.* person.
personaje, *s. m.* personage; character.
personal, *adj.* personal; — *s. m.* personnel.
persuadir, *v. a.* persuade, convince.
pertenecer, *v. n.* belong to; pertain to, concern.
pesadilla, *s. f.* nightmare.
pesado, *adj.* heavy; boring, dull, tiresome; sultry (weather); sound (sleep); stuffy.
pesadumbre, *s. f.* grief.
pésame, *s. m.* condolence.
pesar,[1] *v. a.* & *n.* weigh; be important, count:

me pesa I regret it.
pesar², *s. m.* sorrow; remorse; *a ~ de* in spite of.
pesca, *s. f.* fishing; *ir de ~* go fishing.
pescado, *s. m.* (caught) fish.
pescador, *s. m.* fisherman.
pescar, *v. a. & n.* fish; catch, get.
peseta, *s. f.* peseta (monetary unit of Spain).
pésimo, *adj.* the very worst
peso, *s. m.* weight; load; burden; peso (monetary unit); *de ~* weighty, important.
petición, *s. f.* petition, request.
petróleo, *s. m.* mineral oil, petroleum.
pez, *s. m.* fish (in the water); — *s. f.* tar.
picadillo, *s. m.* minced meat, hash.
picadura, *s. f.* sting; smoking tobacco.
picante, *adj.* spiced.
picar, *v. a.* sting, bite, (of insects); chop (meat); nibble; *v. n.* itch; burn.
pícaro, *adj.* mischievous; — *s. m.* rascal, rogue.
pico, *s. m.* beak; sharp point, corner; pickaxe; summit, peak.
pie, *s. m.* foot; base; *a ~* on foot; *de ~* standing.
piedad, *s. f.* piety; pity.
piedra, *s. f.* stone.
piel, *s. f.* skin; leather; fur; peel; *abrigo de ~es* fur coat.
pierna, *s. f.* leg.
pieza, *s. f.* part (of a machine); play; piece (of music); piece in games; room.
pila, *s. f.* basin; sink; electrical battery; pile; *~ de bautismo* baptismal font.
píldora, *s. f.* pill, pellet.
piloto, *s. m.* pilot.
pimentón, *s. m.* red pepper, paprika.
pimienta, *s. f.* pepper (spice).
pimiento, *s. m.* pepper (vegetable).
pino, *s. m.* pine (tree).
pintar, *v. a.* paint; *v. n. ~se* make up.
pintor, *s. m.* painter.
pintoresco, *adj.* picturesque.
pintura, *s. f.* painting; picture; paint.
piña, *s. f.* pineapple.
piojo, *s. m.* louse.
pipa, *s. f.* (smoking) pipe.
pique, *s. m.* resentment.
piropo, *s. m.* compliment, flattery.
pisar, *v. a.* step on, tread on.
piscina, *s. f.* swimming pool.
piso, *s. m.* floor; storey; *~ bajo* ground-floor.
pista, *s. f.* trace, track; manoeuvring area.
pistola, *s. f.* pistol.
pitar, *v. n.* whistle.
pitillo, *s. m.* cigarette.
pito, *s. m.* whistle.
pizarra, *s. f.* slate; blackboard.
placa, *s. f.* plaque.
placer, *s. m.* pleasure.
plaga, *s. f.* plague, epidemic.
plan, *s. m.* plan.
plancha, *s. f.* plate; flatiron; *hacer una ~*

make a fool of oneself.
planchar, *v. a.* iron, press.
plano, *adj.* flat; — *s. m.* plan, drawing.
planta, *s. f.* sole; plant; floor, storey.
plantar, *v. a.* plant.
plástico, *adj.* plastic, pliable.
plata, *s. f.* silver.
plataforma, *s. f.* platform.
plátano, *s. m.* banana.
platea, *s. f.* orchestra (in the theatre).
platillo, *s. m.* saucer.
plato, *s. m.* plate; dish; course.
playa, *s. f.* beach, shore.
plaza, *s. f.* square; market; job, position; seat (taxi); ~ *de toros* bull ring.
plazo, *s. m.* (space of) time, term; instalment.
plegar, *v. a.* fold.
pleito, *s. m.* lawsuit; dispute.
pleno, *adj.* full, complete.
pliego, *s. m.* sheet (of folded paper).
plomero, *s. m.* plumber.
plomo, *s. m.* lead (metal); fuse.
pluma, *s. f.* feather; pen; ~ *fuente* fountain-pen.
población, *s. f.* population; town; village.
pobre, *adj.* poor; humble; — *s. m.* poor person; beggar.
pobreza, *s. f.* poverty.
poco, *adj. & adv.* little; *dentro de* ~ soon, in a short time; ~ *a* ~ little by little, gradually; *por* ~ almost nearly; *un* ~ *de* a small amount of.
poder[1], *v. n.* be able; *a más no* ~ to the utmost: *no* ~ *más* be exhausted; *no* ~ *menos de* not to be able to help.
poder[2], *s. m.* power; influence.
poema, *s. m.* poem.
poesía, *s. f.* poetry.
poeta, *s. m.* poet.
policía, *s. f.* police; — *s. m.* policeman.
político, *adj.* political; in-law; — *s. m.* politician.
polo, *s. m.* pole; polo.
polvo, *s. m.* dust; *-s pl.* powder.
pólvora, *s. f.* gunpowder.
polvoriento, *adj* dusty.
pollo, *s. m.* chicken.
pompa, *s. f.* pomp, display.
poner, *v. a.* put, place, lay; suppose, assume; put on, wear; *v. n.* ~*se* get, become; ~*se a* begin, start; ~*se, en camino* set out; ~*se en pie* get up, rise.
poniente, *s. m.* west.
popular, *adj.* popular.
poquito, *adj.* little.
por, *prep.* by; through; for; in order to; across, over; ~ *escrito* in writing; ~ *eso* therefore; ¿~ *qué?* why?; ~ *supuesto* of course.
porcelana, *s. f.* china; porcelain.
porción, *s. f.* portion, part.
porque, *conj.* because, for, as.
porqué, *s. m.* reason.
porquería, *s. f.* dirty trick.
portaaviones, *s. m.* aircraft carrier.

portamonedas, *s. m.* purse.
portarse, *v. n.* behave oneself.
porte, *s. m.* postage; bearing (of a person).
portero, *s. m.* goal-keeper; porter.
portugués, *adj.* & *s. m.* Portuguese.
porvenir, *s. m.* future.
posada, *s. f.* lodging-house, inn.
poseer, *v. a.* possess, own.
posesión, *s. f.* possession, property.
posibilidad, *s. f.* possibility.
posible, *adj.* possible.
posición, *s. f.* position; place.
postal, *adj.* postal; — *s. f.* postcard.
posterior, *adj.* rear, back; later.
postizo, *adj.* artificial, false.
postre, *s. m.* dessert, pudding.
potable, *adj.* drinkable.
pote, *s. m.* pot, jar.
potente, *adj.* powerful, strong, potent.
pozo, *s. m.* well (for water).
práctica, *s. f.* practice.
practicar, *v. a.* practise; carry out.
práctico, *adj.* practical; — *s. m.* harbour pilot.
prado, *s. m.* lawn, field, meadow.
precio, *s. m.* price; *~s fijos* fixed prices.
precioso, *adj.* beautiful; precious.
precisar, *v. a.* fix, set; make clear; *v. n.* be necessary, must.
preciso, *adj.* accurate, exact; *es ~* it's necessary.
preferible, *adj.* preferable.
preferir, *v. a.* prefer.
pregunta, *s. f.* question.
preguntar, *v. a.* ask; inquire.
premiar, *v. a.* reward, give a prize.
premio, *s. m.* prize, reward.
prenda, *s. f.* security; *~ de vestir* garment.
prender, *v. a.* fix, pin, catch; *~ fuego a* set on fire.
prensa, *s. f.* press; newspapers.
preocupar, *v. a.* preoccupy, worry; *v. n. ~se de* care for.
preparar, *v. a.* prepare; arrange.
preparativos, *s. m. pl.* preparations.
presa, *s. f.* prey; dam (for water).
prescribir, *v. a.* prescribe.
presencia, *s. f.* presence; appearance.
presenciar, *v. a.* see, witness.
presentar, *v. a.* present, introduce; put on (programme); *v. n. ~se* present oneself.
presente, *adj.* present; *al ~* at present; *tener ~* bear in mind.
presidente, *s. m.* president, chairman.
presión, *s. f.* pressure.
préstamo, *s. m.* loan.
prestar, *v. a.* lend, loan; *~ atención* pay attention; *~ ayuda* help.
pretender, *v. a.* pretend; intend, try.
pretensión, *s. f.* pretension; claim.
pretexto, *s. m.* pretext; excuse.

prevenir, *v. a.* prevent, avoid; prepare; forewarn.
previo, *adj.* previous.
prima, *s. f.* female cousin.
primavera, *s. f.* spring (season).
primero, *adj.* first.
primo, *s. m.* male cousin.
princesa, *s. f.* princess.
principal, *adj.* main, principal; – *s. m.* principal.
príncipe, *s. m.* prince.
principiante, *s. m., f.* beginner.
principiar, *v. a. & n.* begin, start.
principio, *s. m.* beginning; main dish; principle.
prisa, *s. f.* hurry; *a toda* ~ at full speed; *de* ~ quickly.
prisión, *s. f.* prison.
prisionero, *s. m.* prisoner.
privar, *v. a.* deprive.
probable, *adj.* probable.
probar, *v. a.* try, test; taste; prove; *v. n.* ~*se* try on.
problema, *s. m.* problem.
proceder, *v. n.* proceed; come, be the result; act; behave; – *s. m.* conduct, behaviour.
procedimiento, *s. m.* method, procedure.
proceso, *s. m.* process; trial (court).
procurar, *v. a.* try; *v. n.* ~*se* get, obtain.
producir, *v. a.* produce, give.
producto, *s. m.* product.
profesión, *s. f.* profession.
profesional, *adj.* professional.
profesor, *s. m.* teacher, professor.
profeta, *s. m.* prophet.
profundo, *adj.* deep, profound.
programa, *s. m.* programme.
progresar, *v. n.* (make) progress, advance.
progreso, *s. m.* progress.
prohibir, *v. a.* forbid; *se prohibe fumar* no smoking.
promesa, *s. f.* promise.
prometer, *v. a.* promise.
prometido, *adj.* engaged.
pronto, *adj.* ready; *de* ~ suddenly; *tan* ~ *como* as soon as; – *adv.* quickly; soon.
pronunciar, *v. a.* pronounce.
propiedad, *s. f.* property.
propietario, *s. m.* owner, proprietor.
propina, *s. f.* tip; gratuity.
propio, *adj.* own; proper, right.
proponer, *v. a.* propose; *v. n.* ~*se* plan, intend.
proposición, *s. f.* proposition.
propósito, *s. m.* purpose, intention; *a* ~ on purpose; *a* ~ *de* in connection with.
propuesta, *s. f.* proposal.
prosperar, *v. n.* prosper.
proteger, *v. a.* protect.
protesta, *s. f.* protest.
protestar, *v. n.* protest.
provecho, *s. m.* profit; *de* ~ useful; *buen* ~ enjoy your meal.
provechoso, *adj.* profitable.
provincia, *s. f.* province.
provocar, *v. a.* provoke.
proximidad, *s. f.* vicinity.
próximo, *adj.* next; close.
proyectar, *v. a.* plan; pro-

ject, show.
proyecto, *s. m.* project, plan.
prudente, *adj.* prudent, wise.
prueba, *s. f.* proof, evidence; test.
pua, *s. f.* prick, sting, barb.
publicar, *v. a.* publish.
publicidad, *s. f.* publicity.
público, *adj.* public; — *s. m.* public, audience.
puchero, *s. m.* cooking-pot, stew.
pudín, *s. m.* pudding.
pueblo, *s. m.* town, village; people.
puente, *s. m.* bridge.
puerco, *s. m.* pig; pork.
puerta, *s. f.* door; gate.
puerto, *s. m.* port, pass (mountain).
pues, *adv. & conj.* because, as, since; anyhow; well; ~ *bien* all right then.
puesta, *s. f.* stake.
puesto, *s. m.* place; position, job; stall, stand, booth.
púgil, *s. m.* boxer.
pulga, *s. f.* flea.
pulgada, *s. f.* inch.
pulgar, *s. m.* thumb.
pulmón, *s. m.* lung.
pulmonía, *s. f.* pneumonia.
pulsera, *s. f.* bracelet; *reloj (s. m.) de* ~ wrist watch.
pulso, *s. m.* pulse.
punta, *s. f.* point; end, tip; top.
punto, *s. m.* point, dot; place, spot; *al* ~ instantly; *a tal* ~ that far; *coche (s. m.) de* ~ taxi, car for hire; *dar en el* ~ hit the nail; *estar a* ~ *de* be about to; ~ *de vista* point of view; ~ *y coma* semicolon; *géneros (s. m. pl.) de* ~ knitted goods.
puntual, *adj.* punctual.
puntualidad, *s. f.* punctuality.
puñado, *s. m.* handful.
puñal, *s. m.* dagger.
puño, *s. m.* fist; handle; cuff.
pupila, *s. f.* pupil (of eye).
pupitre, *s. m.* (school) desk.
pureza, *s. f.* purity.
purgante, *adj. & s. m.* purgative.
puro, *adj.* pure; clear; — *s. m.* cigar.
puya, *s. f.* lance.

Q

que, *pron.* that, wich; who, whom; what; — *conj.* that; *de manera* ~ so that; *esta habitación es mejor* ~ *la otra* this room is better than the other.
¿qué? *pron.* which? *¿por* ~ *?* why?; *para* ~*?* what for?; *¡*~*!* what!; *¿*~ *más da?* what's the difference?; *!* ~ *va!* go on! come on? how come?; *un no sé* ~ a certain something.
quebrado, *adj.* rough, rugged; broken; *número* ~ fraction.
quebrar, *v. a.* break; fail; *v. n.* ~*se* break.
quedar(se), *v. a. & n.* remain, be left; ~ *bien con* get along well

with; ~ *en* agree, have an understanding; ~*se atrás* stay behind; *me quedo con esto* I'll take this.
quehaceres, *s. m. pl.;* ~ *de casa* household chores.
queja, *s. f.* complaint.
quejarse, *v. n.* complain.
quemado, *adj.* burnt; ~ *por el sol* sunburned.
quemadura, *s. f.* burn, scald.
quemar, *v. a.* burn; *v. n.* ~*se* burn oneself.
querer, *v. a.* want, wish; love; *quisiera* I should like.
querido, *adj.* dear, beloved.
queso, *s. m.* cheese.
quien, *pron.* who; whoever, anyone.
¿quién? *pron.* who?; *¿a* ~*?* whom?; *con* ~ *(es)?* with whom?
quienquiera, *pron.* whoever.
quieto, *adj.* still; calm; quiet.
química, *s. f.* chemistry.
químico, *adj.* chemical: — *s. m.* chemist.
quince, *adj. & s. m.* fifteen.
quincena, *s. f.* two weeks.
quinientos, *adj. & s. m. pl.* five hundred.
quinina, *s. f.* quinine.
quinta, *s. f.* country house.
quintal, *s. m.* a hundred pounds (weight).
quinto, *adj.* fifth.
quiosco, *s. m.* newsstall.
quitar, *v. a.* take away, substract; *v. n.* ~*se* take off (clothing).
quizá(s), *adv.* perhaps, maybe.

R

rábano, *s. m.* radish.
rabia, *s. f.* rage, fury; rabies.
rabiar, *v. n.* be mad, rage.
rabioso, *adj.* furious, enraged; rabid.
rabo, *s. m.* tail.
racimo, *s. m.* cluster, bunch.
ración, *s. f.* ration.
racionar, *v. a.* ration.
radiador, *s. m.* radiator.
radiar, *v. a.* radiate.
radio, *s. m.* radius; radium; ~ *de acción* range; — *s. f.* radio, wireless.
radioactivo, *adj.* radioactive.
redioescucha, *s., m., f.* listener (of radio).
radiografía, *s. f.* radiography.
radiorreceptor, *s. m.* receiver.
rad otransmisor, *s. m.* transmitter, broadcasting station.
radioyente, *s. m., f.* listener (of radio).
raíz, *s. f.* root.
rama, *s. f.* branch, twig, bough.
ramillete, *s. m.* bunch of flowers.
ramo, *s. m.* bough (cut off tree); bouquet, bunch; branch, line of business.
rana, *s. f.* frog.
rancio, *adj.* rancid; oldfashioned, antiquated.
rancho, *s. m.* mess (dining-room); hut (South

America).
rápido, *adj.* rapid, quick; — *s. m.* express (train).
raro, *adj.* rare, unusual; odd, strange.
rascacielos, *s. m.* skyscraper.
rascar, *v. a.* scratch.
rasgar, *v. a.* tear.
rasgo, *s. m.* stroke; flourish; **~s** *pl.* features; characteristics.
raspar, *v. a.* scrape, scratch.
rata, *s. f.* rat.
ratero, *s. m.* pickpocket.
ratificar, *v. a.* ratify.
rato, *s. m.* while; *al poco* **~** very soon; *a* **~***s perdidos* in one's spare time; *pasar el* **~** pass the time away; *pasar un buen* **~** have a good time.
ratón, *s. m.* mouse.
ratonera, *s. f.* mousetrap.
raya, *s. f.* dash, line; parting (in hair); ray fish.
rayado, *adj.* striped.
rayo, *s. m.* ray; flash of lightning.
raza, *s. f.* (anthropological) race.
razón, *s. f.* reason; cause; explanation; **~** *social* commercial house, firm; *a* **~** *de* at the rate of; *tengo* **~** I'm right; *n tiene* **~** he's wrong.
razonable, *adj.* reasonable.
real, *adj.* real, actual; royal.
realidad, *s. f.* reality, fact.
realizar, *v. a.* accomplish; carry out; sell out.
rebaja, *s. f.* reduction.
rebajar, *v. a.* reduce, lower.
rebanada, *s. f.* slice of bread.
rebaño, *s. m.* herd, flock.
recado, *s. m.* message; errand.
recaída, *s. f.* relapse.
recambio, *s. m.* exchange; *pieza (s. f.) de* **~** spare (part).
recelo, *s. m.* suspicion.
recepción, *s. f.* reception; formal gathering.
receta, *s. f.* prescription (medicine); **~** *de cocina* recipe.
recibir, *v. a.* receive.
recibo, *s. m.* receipt.
recién, *adv.* recently, newly; just; **~** *llegado* newcomer.
reciente, *adj.* new, fresh; recent.
recipiente, *s. m.* container; bin; tank.
reclamación, *s. f.* reclamation, complaint; claim.
reclamar, *v. a.* claim.
recobrar, *v. a.* recover, regain.
recoger, *v. a.* get; collect; gather up, pick up; take in, shelter.
recomendar, *v. a.* recommend; advise.
reconocer, *v. a.* inspect, examine; recognize; acknowledge, admit; *estoy reconocido* I'm grateful.
reconquista, *s. f.* reconquest.
reconstruir, *v. a.* rebuild, reconstruct.
recordar, *v. a.* remember; remind.
recorrer, *v. a. & n.* cover (distance); travel.
recorrido, *s. m.* route, course, run.
recreo, *s. m.* recreation.
recto, *adj.* straight; just, fair.
recuerdo, *s. m.* remembrance, memory; sou-

venir, memento.
recurso, *s. m.* argument; *~s pl.* means, resources.
red, *s. f.* net; trap, snare.
redactar, *v. a.* compose.
redondo, *adj.* round; *a la redonda* around.
reducción, *s. f.* reduction, decrease.
reducir, *v. a.* reduce.
reembolso, *s. m.* repayment; cash on delivery.
reemplazar, *v. a.* replace.
referencia, *s. f.* reference; *dar ~s* inform.
referir, *v. a.* relate; *v. n.* *~se* refer to.
reflujo, *s. m.* ebb, low tide.
reforma, *s. f.* alteration.
refran, *s. m.* proverb, saying.
refrescar, *v. a.* cool, refresh; *v. n.* *~se* cool off.
refresco, *s. m.* refreshment; cold drink.
refrigerador, *s. m.* refrigerator.
refugio, *s. m.* refuge; shelter.
regalar, *v. a.* present, give (gift).
regalo, *s. m.* present, gift.
regar, *v. a.* water, irrigate.
regata, *s. f.* regatta.
regateo, *s. m.* bargaining, haggling.
régimen, *s. m.* regime, political system; diet.
región, *s. f.* region.
registrar, *v. a.* search; examine (luggage); record, keep a record.
regla, *s. f.* rule, regulation; ruler (for drawing lines); *en ~* in order.
regresar, *v. n.* return.
regreso, *s. m.* return, coming *or* going back.
regular, *adj.* regular, orderly; moderate; so-so.
reina, *s. f.* queen.
reinar, *v. n.* reign.
reino, *s. m.* kingdom.
reir(se), *v. n.* laugh.
relación, *s. f.* story, account; *relaciones pl.* relations, connections.
relacionar, *v. a.* relate, connect.
relámpago, *s. m.* lightning.
relampaguear, *v. n.* lighten.
relatar, *v. a.* relate, tell.
religión, *s. f.* religion.
religioso, *adj.* religious.
reloj, *s. m.* clock, watch.
relojería, *s. f.* watchmaker's shop.
relojero, *s. m.* watchmaker.
relleno, *adj.* stuffed, filled; — *s. m.* stuffing.
remar, *v. n.* row (a boat).
remedio, *s. m.* remedy, medicine.
remendar, *v. a.* mend, patch, repair.
remitente, *s. m., f.* sender.
remitir, *v. a.* remit, send.
remo, *s. m.* oar.
remolacha, *s. f.* beet.
remolcador, *s. m.* tugboat.
remolcar, *v. a.* tow.
remordimiento, *s. m.* remorse.
remoto, *adj.* remote, distant, out-of-the-way.
remover, *v. a.* dig up; stir; shake; dismiss (from a post).
remunerar, *v. a.* remunerate.
rendido, *adj.* exhausted.
rendir, *v. a.* surrender; yield, produce; *v. n.* *~se* surrender, yield, give in.
renglón, *s. m.* line; row.

renombrado, *adj.* famous, renowned.
renovar, *v. a.* renovate.
renta, *s. f.* rent; income.
renunciar, *v. a.* renounce, give up; resign; refuse, reject.
reo, *s. m.* accused.
reparar, *v. a.* repair; *~ en* consider; notice.
reparo, *s. m.* objection, help.
repartir, *v. a.* distribute.
repasar, *v. a.* check (account); revise (lesson); mend (clothes).
repaso, *s. m.* revision; mending.
repente, *s. n.* sudden impulse; *de ~* suddenly, unexpectedly.
repentino, *adj.* sudden.
repetición, *s. f.* repetition.
repetir, *v. a.* repeat.
replicar, *v. n.* reply, answer back; argue.
repollo, *s. m.* (head of) cabbage.
reponer, *v. a.* replace; repair; *v. n. ~se* recover (health).
reposar, *v. n.* rest.
reposo, *s. m.* rest.
representación, *s. f.* performance.
representante, *adj.* representing; *— s. m.* travelling salesman, agent.
representar, *v. a.* represent, perform.
reproducir, *v. a.* reproduce.
reptil, *s. m.* reptile.
república, *s. f.* republic.
republicano, *adj. & s. m.* republican.
repuesto, *s. m.* store, stock; supply; *de ~* extra, spare.
reputación, *s. f.* reputation, repute.
resbaladizo, *adj.* slippery.
resbalar(se), *v. n.* slip.
reserva, *s. f.* reserve; secrecy, discretion; *guardar ~* use discretion.
reservar, *v. a.* reserve; *~se* keep for oneself.
resfriado, *s. m.* cold (illness).
resfriarse, *v. n.* catch cold.
resignarse, *v. n.* be resigned.
resistente, *adj.* strong, resistant.
resistir, *v. n.* resist; *v. n. ~se* refuse to.
resolución, *s. f.* decision, resolution; resoluteness.
resolver, *v. a.* decide; solve; *v. n. ~se* decide, make up one's mind to.
resorte, *s. m.* (elastic) spring.
respecto, *s. m.* respect; *con ~ a* with regard to.
respetable, *adj.* respectable: considerable.
respeto, *s. m.* respect.
respiración, *s. f.* respiration.
respirar, *v. n.* breathe.
responder, *v. a. & n.* answer, respond; react.
responsable, *adj.* responsible.
respuesta, *s. f.* answer, reply.
restablecerse, *v. n.* recover.
restaurante, *s. m.* restaurant.
resto, *s. m.* rest, remainder.
resultado, *s. m.* result.
resumen, *s. m.* summary.
retardar, *v. a.* retard.
retener, *v. a.* withhold; remember, retain; hold, keep.
retirar, *v. a.* withdraw;

retire; pull back, put aside; — *v. n.* ~*se* withdraw, retire.
retiro, *s. m.* retirement.
retrasar, *v. a.* postpone; delay; set back; *v. n.* ~*se* be late; run slow.
retraso, *s. m.* delay; lateness.
retratar, *v. a.* portray.
retrato, *s. m.* portrait, painting, photograph.
retrete, *s. m.* lavatory.
reunión, *s. f.* meeting, assembly, party.
reunir, *v. a.* unite, bring together; collect; *v. n.* ~*se* meet, unite.
revelar, *v. a.* reveal, show; develop.
reventa, *s. f.* retail, resale.
reventar, *v. n.* burst.
revés, *s. m.* wrong side, reverse side.
revisar, *v. a.* revise; review; examine.
revisor, *s. m.* guard (on train).
revista, *s. f.* review; magazine.
revocar, *v. a.* revoke.
revolución, *s. f.* revolution; revolt; turn.
revolucionario, *adj.* & *s m.* revolutionary.
revólver, *s.m.* revolver.
revolver, *v. a.* revolve; stir; turn upside down.
rey, *s. m.* king.
rezar, *v. a.* & *n.* pray, say (prayers).
rezo, *s. m.* praying.
riachuelo, *s. m.* rivulet.
ribera, *s. f.* coast; beach.
rico, *adj.* rich, wealthy; delicious; cute.
ridículo, *adj.* ridiculous.
riego, *s. m.* watering; irrigation.
riel, *s. m.* rail.
riesgo, *s. m.* danger, risk.
rígido, *adj.* stiff, rigid; severe, stern.
riguroso, *adj.* rigorous.
rincón, *s. m.* (inside) corner.
riña, *s. f.* quarrel.
riñón, *s. m.* kidney.
río, *s. m.* river.
riqueza, *s. f.* wealth; abundance.
risa, *s. f.* laugh, laughter.
rizar, *v. a.* curl.
rizo, *s. m.* curl.
robar, *v. a.* rob; steal.
roble, *s. m.* oak.
robo, *s. m.* robbery, theft.
robusto, *adj.* robust.
roca, *s. f.* rock; cliff.
rodar, *v. n.* roll; *v. a.* ~ *una película* shoot a film.
rodear, *v. a.* surround, encircle.
rodeo, *s. m.* turn winding.
rodilla, *s. f.* knee.
rogar, *v. a.* request, beg.
rojo, *adj.* red.
rollo, *s. m.* roll.
romper, *v. a.* break.
roncar, *v. n.* snore.
ronco, *adj.* hoarse.
ropa, *s. f.* clothes; ~ *blanca* linen; ~ *de cama* bedding.
ropero, *s. m.* wardrobe.
rosa, *s. f.* rose; *color de* ~ pink.
rosario, *s. m.* rosary.
rosbif, *s. m.* roast beef.
rosca, *s. f.* thread (screw); spiral; ring (bread or cake).
rostro, *s. m.* face.
roto, *adj.* broken; — *s. m.* tear.
rótulo, *s. m.* sign; label.
rozar, *v. a.* clear; graze, rub.

rubia, *s. f.* blonde.
rubio, *adj.* blond(e), fair.
rudo, *adj.* rude, rough.
rueda, *s. f.* wheel.
ruego, *s. m.* request, plea.
ruido, *s. m.* noise; comment, discussion.
ruidoso, *adj.* noisy.
ruina, *s. f.* ruin, decline.
ruiseñor, *s. m.* nightingale.
rumano, *adj.* & *s. m.* Rumanian.
rumbo, *s. m.* direction.
rumor, *s. m.* murmur; rumour.
rural, *adj.* rustic, rural.
ruso, *adj.* & *s. m.* Russian.
ruta, *s. f.* route, way.
rutina, *s. f.* routine.

S

sábado, *s. m.* Saturday.
sábana, *s. f.* sheet.
saber, *v. a.* know; taste; *¿sabe usted español?* do you know Spanish?; *esto sabe mal* this tastes bad; *a ~* namely; — *s. m.* knowledge.
sabio, *adj.* wise; — *s. m.* learned *or* wise person.
sabor, *s. m.* taste, flavour.
saborear, *v. a.* taste, relish.
sabroso, *adj.* savoury, tasty.
sacacorchos, *s. m.* corkscrew.
sacar, *v. a.* draw (out), take out, put out; get, win; *~ copia* make a copy; *~ una fotografía* take a picture.
sacerdote, *s. m.* priest.
saco, *s. m.* sack, bag; jacket.
sacudir, *v. a.* shake; jolt.
sagrado, *adj.* sacred, holy.
sainete, *s. m.* one-act farce.
sal, *s. f.* salt.
sala, *s. f.* living room, parlour; *~ de espera* waiting-room.
salario, *s. m.* salary, wages.
salchicha, *s. f.* sausage.
salchichón, *s. m.* (large) sausage.
saldo, *s. m.* balance; sale.
salero, *s. m.* salt-cellar.
salida, *s. f.* departure; exit; expenditure; *callejón (s. m.) sin ~* blind alley, cul-de-sac.
salir, *v. n.* go out, leave; come off, disappear (spots); rise (sun); grow, come up; come out, be published; stick out; *~ de compras* go shopping.
salmón, *s. m.* salmon.
salón, *s. m.* living-room, hall.
salsa, *s. f.* gravy, sauce.
saltar, *v. n.* jump, spring; bounce.
salto, *s. m.* jump.
salud, *s. f.* health; *¡a su ~!* to your health!
saludar, *v. a.* greet; salute.
saludo, *s. m.* greeting, salute.
salvaje, *adj.* savage, wild.
salvar, *v. a.* save, rescue.
salvo, *adj.* sound, unhurt.
san, *adj.* saint.
sanar, *v. a.* heal, cure.
sangre, *s. f.* blood; *~ fría* composure, coolness of mind.
sangriento, *adj.* bloody.
sano, *adj.* healthy.
santidad, *s. f.* holiness, sanctity.

santo, *adj.* & *s. m.* holy; saint.
sardina, *s. f.* sardine.
sastre, *s. m.* tailor.
satisfecho, *adj.* satisfied.
sazón, *s. f.* ripeness, maturity.
sazonar, *v. a.* season; ripen.
se, *pron.* oneself; (to) himself, herself, itself; (to) themselves, yourselves; (to) each other; ~ *dice* they say, it's said; *se habla español* Spanish spoken.
secante, *s. m.* blotter.
secar, *v. a.* dry; wither.
sección, *s. f.* section.
seco, *adj.* dry; dried.
secretaría, *s. f.* secretary's office.
secretaria, *s. f.* secretary.
secretario, *s. m.* secretary.
secreto, *s. m.* secret.
sed, *s. f.* thirst; *tengo mucha* ~ I'm very thirsty.
seda, *s. f.* silk.
seguida; *en* ~ *adv.* immediately, right away.
seguir, *v. a.* follow; continue; *siga a la derecha* keep to the right.
según, *prep.* according to; as; it depends.
segundo, *s. m.* second; — *adj.* second.
seguridad, *s. f.* security.
seguro, *adj.* sure, certain: safe, secure; steady; — *s. m.* insurance.
seis, *adj.* & *s. m.* six.
selección, *s. f.* selection, choice.
selva, *s. f.* woods, forest.
sellar, *v. a.* stamp; seal.
sello, *s. m.* stamp; seal.
semana, *s. f.* week.
semanal, *adj.* weekly.
sembrar, *v. a.* sow; spread.
semejante, *adj.* similar; such; — *s. m.* fellowman.
semejanza, *s. f.* resemblance, similarity.
semilla, *s. f.* seed.
sencillez, *s. f.* simplicity.
sencillo, *adj.* simple, plain; unaffected.
senda *s. f.* path.
sendero, *s. m.* footpath.
sensación, *s. f.* sensation.
sensato, *adj.* sensible, wise.
sensible, *adj.* sensitive, keen.
sentar, *v. a.* & *n.* seat; fit; ~*se* sit down; *siéntese usted* sit down.
sentencia, *s. f.* sentence.
sentido, *adj.* sincere; moving; — *s. m.* sense; meaning; direction.
sentimiento, *s. m.* sentiment, feeling; sorrow, grief.
sentir, *v. a.* feel; hear; regret; be sorry; *lo siento mucho* I'm very sorry; *v. n.* ~*se* feel; *me siento mal* I feel ill.
seña, *s. f.* sign; mark; ~*s pl.* address.
señal, *s. f.* signal; mark; ~*es de tráfico* traffic signs.
señalar, *v. a.* point out, mark.
señor, *s. m.* sir; *¿está el* ~ *Pérez?* is Mr. Pérez in?; man, gentleman.
señora, *s. f.* madam; *quisiera hablar con la* ~ *González* I'd like to speak to Mrs. González; lady.
señorita, *s. f.* Miss; young lady.
señorito, *s. m.* young gentleman; master of

the house.
separar, *v. a.* separate; divide; move away; lay aside; *v. n.* *~se* separate.
septiembre, *s. m.* September.
séptimo, *adj.* seventh.
sepultar, *v. a.* bury, inter.
sepultura, *s. f.* grave.
sequedad, *s. f.* aridity, dryness.
ser, *v. n.* be; *soy médico* I'm a doctor; *él es de Madrid* he is from Madrid.
serenata, *s. f.* serenade.
sereno, *adj.* clear, fair; calm, serene; — *s. m.* night-watchman; dew.
serie, *s. f.* series.
serio, *adj.* serious, solemn; *en ~* seriously.
servicio, *s. m.* service; set.
servidor, *s. m.* man-servant.
servidora, *s. f.* servant.
servidumbre, *s. f.* (staff of) servants; servitude.
servilleta, *s. f.* table napkin.
servir, *v. a. & n.* serve; wait on; *~ para* be good for; *~se* help oneself.
sesenta, *adj. & s. m.* sixty.
sesión, *s. f.* session; meeting.
setenta, *adj. & s. m.* seventy.
severo, *adj.* severe, rigorous.
sexo, *s. m.* sex.
sexto, *adj.* sixth.
sexual, *adj.* sexual.
si, *conj.* if, whether.
sí[1], yes; *~ que* certainly.
sí[2], *pron.* oneself.
sidra, *s. f.* cider.
siempre, *adv.* always; *~ que* whenever; *para ~* forever.
sien, *s. f.* temple (anatomy).
sierra, *s. f.* saw; mountain range.
siesta, *s f.* afternoon nap.
siete, *adj. & s. m.* seven.
siglo, *s. m.* century.
significado, *s. m.* meaning.
significar, *v. a.* mean.
significativo, *adj.* significant.
signo, *s. m.* sign, mark, symbol.
siguiente, *adj.* following, next.
sílaba, *s. f.* syllable.
silbar, *v. n.* whistle.
silencio, *s. m.* silence; *guardar ~* keep quiet.
silencioso, *adj.* silent.
silla, *s. f.* chair; *~ de montar* saddle.
sillón, *s. m.* armchair.
simpatía, *s. f.* sympathy.
simpático, *adj.* congenial, nice, pleasant.
simple, *adj.* simple, easy.
simular, *v. a. & n.* simulate.
sin, *prep.* without; *~ embargo* however, nevertheless.
sincero, *adj.* sincere.
sindicato, *s. m.* trade-union.
singular, *adj. & s. m.* singular.
siniestro, *adj.* sinister.
sino, *conj.* but; except; *no . . . ~* not . . . but.
síntoma, *s. m.* symptom.
siquiera, *adv.* at least; *ni ~* not even.
sirvienta, *s. f.* maid, servant.
sistema, *s. m.* system.
sitio, *s. m.* spot, site;

place, seat; room, space; siege.
situación, *s. f.* situation; location, site.
smoking, *s. m.* dinner jacket.
sobornar, *v. a.* bribe.
sobra, *s. f.* excess, surplus; *de* ~ more than enough; *estar de* ~ be superfluous, be in the way.
sobrar, *v. n.* be in excess; be superfluous.
sobre, *prep.* over; on, upon; about, concerning; — *s. m.* envelope.
sobrina, *s. f.* niece.
sobrino, *s. m.* nephew.
sobrio, *adj.* sober, temperate.
social, *adj.* social.
socialismo, *s. m.* socialism.
sociedad, *s. f.* society; ~ *anónima* joint-stock company.
socio, *s. m.* partner (in business); member (of club).
socorrer, *v. a.* help.
socorro, *s. m.* help, aid.
sofá, *s. m.* sofa.
sofocar, *v. a.* suffocate; stifle; choke.
soga, *s. f.* rope.
sol, *s. m.* sun; sunlight.
soldado, *s. m.* soldier.
soldar, *v. a.* solder, weld.
soledad, *s. f.* solitude.
solemne, *adj.* solemn.
soler, *v. n.* be in the habit of, have the custom of; *suelo levantarme a las seis* I usually get up at six o'clock.
solicitar, *v. a.* request, apply for.
solicitud, *s. f.* solicitude; application, request.
sólido, *adj.* solid, firm.
solo, *adv.* alone; — *adj.* lonely; — *s. m.* solo.
sólo, *adv.* only.
soltar, *v. a.* loosen; let out, let go.
soltero, *s. m.* bachelor.
solución, *s. f.* solution; result.
solucionar, *v. a.* solve
sollozar, *v. n.* sob.
sombra, *s. f.* shade; shadow; dark, darkness.
sombrero, *s. m.* hat.
sombrilla, *s. f.* parasol.
sombrío, *adj.* gloomy, sombre.
son, *s. m.* sound.
sonar, *v. n.* sound, ring; strike (clock); ~*se* blow one's nose.
sonido, *s. m.* sound.
sonoro, *adj.* sonorous.
sonreír, *v. n.* smile.
sonrisa, *s. f.* smile.
soñar, *v. n.* dream.
sopa, *s. f.* soup.
sopera, *s. f.* tureen.
soplar, *v. n.* blow.
soplo, *s. m.* blow(ing), puff, gust (of air); breath; tip, hint.
soportar, *v. a.* bear; suffer.
sorber, *v. a.* sip.
sorbo, *s. m.* sip.
sordo, *adj.* deaf; muffled; dull.
sordomudo, *adj.* & *s. m* deaf and dumb; deaf-mute.
sorprendente, *adj.* surprising.
sorprender, *v. a.* surprise.
sorpresa, *s. f.* surprise.
sortear, *v. n.* draw lots.
sortija, *s. f.* ring.
soso, *adj.* tasteless; insipid.
sospecha, *s. f.* suspicion.
sospechar, *v. a.* suspect.

sospechoso, *adj.* suspicious.
sostén, *s. m.* bra.
sostener, *v. a.* hold; support; maintain.
sótano, *s. m.* basement.
su, *pron.* your, his, her, its, their; *sus pl.*
suave, *adj.* delicate, soft, gentle, light; smooth; mellow, mild; meek, docile.
subasta, *s. f.* auction.
súbdito, *s. m.* subject.
subir, *v. a.* bring up; put on, set on; lift up, raise; *v. n.* go up; amount; rise, increase; ascend.
súbito, *adj.* sudden.
subrayar, *v. a.* underline.
su(b)scribirse, *v. n.* subscribe.
su(b)scripción, *s. f.* subscription.
su(b)stituir, *v. a.* replace.
su(b)stituto, *s. m.* substitute.
subterráneo, *adj. & s. m.* underground (railway).
suburbio, *s. m.* suburb.
suceder, *v. n.* succeed; happen.
suceso, *s. m.* event.
sucio, *adj.* dirty; unfair.
sudamericano, *adj. & s. m.* South American.
sudar, *v. n.* sweat.
sudeste, *s. m.* southeast.
sudoeste, *s. m.* southwest.
sudor, *s. m.* sweat.
sueco, *adj.* Swedish; – *s. m.* Swede.
suegra, *s. f.* mother-in-law.
suegro, *s. m.* father-in-law.
suela, *s. f.* sole.
suelo, *s. m.* floor; soil; ground.
suelto, *adj.* loose; free; – *s. m.* (loose) change.
sueño, *s. m.* sleep; dream; *echar un* ~ take a nap.
suerte, *s. f.* fate, luck; *por* ~ fortunately.
suéter, *s. m.* sweater.
suficiente, *adj.* sufficient.
sufrir, *v. a. & n.* suffer; endure, put up with; undergo (operation).
sugerir, *v. a.* suggest.
sugestionar, *v. a.* influence.
suicida, *s. m. f.* suicide (person).
suicidarse, *v. n.* commit suicide.
suicidio, *s. m.,* suicide (act).
suizo, *adj. & s. m.* Swiss.
sujetar, *v. a.* hold; fasten.
sujeto, *adj.* fastened; – *s. m.* subject; fellow, guy.
suma, *s. f.* amount, sum; *en* ~ in short.
sumar, *v. a.* amount to.
sumo, *adj.* great; *a lo* ~ at most.
suntuoso, *adj.* sumptuous.
superficie, *s. f.* surface
superior, *adj.* superior, better; higher; – *s. m.* superior.
superioridad, *s. f.* superiority.
supersticioso, *adj.* superstitious.
suplente, *s. m.* deputy; substitute.
súplica, *s. f.* request; supplication.
suplicante, *s. m.* petitioner.
suplicar, *v. a.* request; entreat, implore.

suponer, *v. a.* suppose, assume; imagine.
suprimir, *v. a.* suppress; abolish; omit.
supuesto, *adj.* assumed, supposed; *por* ~ of course.
sur, *s. m.* south.
surtido, *s. m.* assortment, collection.
surtidor, *s. m.* fountain; ~ *(de gasolina)* petrol station.
surtir, *v. a.* supply.
suspender, *v. a.* suspend, stop; hang.
suspirar, *v. n.* sigh.
suspiro, *s. m.* sigh.
sustituir, *v. a.* substitute, replace.
sustituto, *s. m.* substitute.
susto, *s. m.* fright, scare; *dar un* ~ frighte
sustraer, *v. a.* subtract.
susurrar, *v. n.* murmur.
sutil, *adj.* thin; shrewd.
suyo, *adj.* (of) his, hers, theirs; *los* ~*s pl.* his (her, your, their) folks.

T

tabaco, *s. m.* tobacco.
tabaquero, *s. m.* tobacconist.
taberna, *s. f.* tavern.
tabla, *s. f.* board, plank; list, table (of contents, prices); ~*s pl.* stage (theatre); draw (in a game).
tablero, *s. m.* (chess) board.
taburete, *s. m.* stool.
tacón, *s. m.* heel (of shoe).
tacto, *s. m.* touch; tact.
tajada, *s. f.* slice.
tajo, *s. m.* cut.
tal, *adj. & pron.* such (a); *con* ~ *que* provided that; ~ *como* just as; ~ *cual es* as it is; — *s. m., f.* such a thing *or* person; *un* ~ *Alvarez* a certain Alvarez.
talco, *s. m.* talc.
talento, *s. m.* talent, brains.
talón, *s. m.* heel (of foot); stub (of check).
talonario, *s. m.* cheque-book.
talle, *s. m.* waist, figure.
taller, *s. m.* workshop; factory, mill.
tamaño, *adj.* so great, such a big; — *s. m.* size.
también, *adv. & conj.* also, too.
tambor, *s. m.* drum.
tampoco, *adv.* neither, not either.
tan, *adv.* so; ~ *tarde* so late.
tanque, *s. m.* tank (military and for liquid).
tanto, *adj.* so much, so many; — *adv.* so long; so often; — *s. m.* point (in games); *entre* ~ meanwhile; *por lo* ~ so, therefore.
tapa, *s. f.* lid, cover.
tapar, *v. a.* cover; cover up; obstruct; *v. n.* ~*se* wrap (oneself); cover oneself.
tapete, *s. m.* small rug; table-cover.
tapia, *s. f.* wall, mud fence.
tapiz, *s. m.* tapestry; carpet.
tapizar, *v. a.* paper.
tapón, *s. m.* cork, stopper.
taquigrafía, *s. f.* shorthand.
taquígrafo, *s. m.* stenographer.

taquilla, *s. f.* ticket-office, ticket-window.
taquimecanógrafa, *s. f.* shorthand typist.
tardar, *v. n.* delay, be long.
tarde, *adv.* late; — *s. f.* afternoon, early evening; *buenas ~s* good afternoon, good evening.
tarea, *s. f.* task.
tarifa, *s. f.* rates, tariff; list of prices.
tarjeta, *s. f.* (post)card, visiting card.
tarta, *s. f.* cake, tart.
tasa, *s. f.* rate, tax; fee.
tasar, *v. a.* rate, tax; estimate.
tauromaquia, *s. f.* art of fighting with bulls.
taza, *s. f.* cup.
te, *pron.* (to) you; yourself.
té, *s. m.* tea (beverage).
teatro, *s. m.* theatre.
técnica, *s. f.* technique.
técnico, *adj.* technic(al); — *s. m.* technician.
techado, *s. m.* roof; cover.
techo, *s. m.* ceiling; roof.
tejado, *s. m.* roof.
tejer, *v. a.* weave.
tejido, *s. m.* fabric, textile.
tela, *s. f.* cloth, material.
telaraña, *s. f.* cobweb.
telefonear, *v. n.* telephone.
telefonema, *s. m.* telephone message.
telefonista, *s. m., f.* telephone operator.
teléfono, *s. m.* telephone.
telegrafiar, *v. a. & n.* send a telegram.
telégrafo, *s. m.* telegraph.
telegrama, *s. m.* telegram.
televisión, *s. f.* television.
televisor, *s. m.* T. V. set.
telón, *s. m.* theatre curtain.
tema, *s. m.* subject, topic, theme; translation.
temblar, *v. n.* tremble, shiver.
temer, *v. n.* fear,be afraid.
temerario, *adj.* rash; unwise.
temor, *s. m.* fear.
temperamento, *s. m.* temperament.
temperatura, *s. f.* temperature.
tempestad, *s. f.* storm, tempest.
tempestuoso, *adj.* stormy.
templado, *adj.* temperate, mild; tuned; tepid.
templar, *v. a.* tune.
templo, *s. m.* temple, church.
temporada, *s. f.* period of time, season.
temporal, *adj.* temporary; — *s. m.* storm.
temprano, *adj. & adv.* early.
tenazas, *s. f. pl.* tongs.
tender, *v. a.* stretch; spread out; hang (clothes); extend, offer (one's hand); *v. n. ~se* stretch out, lie at full length.
tendero, *s. m.* shopkeeper.
tenedor, *s. m.* fork; holder, keeper; *~ de libros* book-keeper.
tener, *v. a.* have, possess; hold; contain; *tengo treinta años* I'm thirty years old; *~ cuidado* be careful; *tengo frio* I'm cold; *tenemos hambre* we are hungry; *~ que* have to, be obliged to; *tengo que irme* I must go.

teniente, *s. m.* lieutenant.
tenis, *s. m.* tennis.
tentar, *v. a.* touch, feel; tempt.
tentativa, *s. f.* attempt.
teñir, *v. a.* dye.
teoría, *s. f.* theory.
tercero, *adj.* third.
tercio, *s. m.* one third.
terciopelo, *s. m.* velvet.
terminar, *v. a.* end, finish.
término, *s. m.* end.
termómetro, *s. m.* thermometer.
ternera, *s. f.* female calf; veal.
ternero, *s. m.* male calf.
terrateniente, *s. m.* landed proprietor.
terraza, *s. f.* terrace, drive.
terremoto, *s. m.* earthquake.
terreno, *adj.* earthly; worldly; — *s. m.* piece of ground, lot; soil.
territorio, *s. m.* territory.
terrón, *s. m.* lump (of sugar); clod (of earth).
tertulia, *s. f.* gathering, party, conversation.
tesorería, *s. f.* treasury.
tesorero, *s. m.* treasurer.
tesoro, *s. m.* treasure.
testamento, *s. m.* will (document).
testificar, *v. a.* testify.
testigo, *s. m., f.* witness.
testimonio, *s. m.* testimony.
tetera, *s. f.* teapot.
textil, *adj.* textile.
texto, *s. m.* text; textbook.
tez, *s. f.* complexion.
ti, *pron.*; *a* ~ (to) you; *para* ~ for you.
tía, *s. f.* aunt; old woman.
tibio, *adj.* tepid, lukewarm.
tiburón, *s. m.* shark.
tiempo, *s. m.* time; period, epoch; weather; *a* ~ on time; *ganar* ~ save time; *hace* ~ long ago; *hace mal* ~ it's bad weather.
tienda, *s. f.* shop, store; tent.
tierno, *adj.* tender, soft.
tierra, *s. f.* earth; ground; land; soil; native land, country.
tifus, *s. m.* typhoid fever.
tigre, *s. m.* tiger.
tijeras, *s. f. pl.* scissors, shears.
timbre, *s. m.* electric bell; seal, tax stamp.
tímido, *adj.* shy, timid.
timón, *s. m.* helm; rudder.
tinta, *s. f.* ink.
tinte, *s. m.* shade, tint.
tintero, *s. m.* inkpot.
tinto, *adj.* coloured; *vino* ~ red wine.
tío, *s. m.* uncle; fellow, guy.
típico, *adj.* typical, characteristic.
tiple, *s. f.* soprano.
tipo, *s. m.* type; pattern; fellow.
tirante, *adj.* tight, taut; tense; — *~s, s. m. pl.* pair of braces.
tirar, *v. a. & n.* throw; throw away, discard; shoot, fire; draw (a line); print; ~ *coces* kick; ~ *de* pull.
tiritar, *v. n.* shiver.
tiro, *s. m.* shot; drive; team of horses; *errar el* ~ miss the mark.
tirón, *s. m.* jerk; jolt.
tisis, *s. f.* consumption.
títere, *s. m.* marionette, puppet; dwarf.
titubear, *v. n.* hesitate.
título, *s. m.* title, name;

headline (newspaper); diploma, degree; security.
tiza, *s. f.* chalk.
toalla, *s. f.* towel.
tobillo, *s. m.* ankle.
tocado, *s. m.* hair-style.
tocador, *s. m.* dressing-table.
tocar, *v. a.* touch; play (an instrument); knock; call (at a port); *por lo que a mi toca* as far as I am concerned.
tocino, *s. m.* bacon.
todavía, *adv.* still; yet; even; *~ no* not yet.
todo, *adj. & pron.* all; the whole; *~ el mundo* everybody; *~s pl.* all of them; *~s los días* every day.
toldo, *s. m.* awning; tarpaulin.
tolerar, *v. a.* tolerate; overlook.
tomar, *v. a.* take; drink, eat, have; hire; adopt; capture; *~ por la derecha* go to the right.
tomate, *s. m.* tomato.
tomo, *s. m.* volume.
tonel, *s. m.* cask, barrel.
tonelada, *s. f.* ton.
tonelaje, *s. m.* tonnage.
tono, *s. m.* tone; note; manner; shade; *darse ~* put on airs.
tontería, *s. f.* foolishness, nonsense.
tonto, *adj.* silly, foolish; stupid, dumb; – *s. m.* fool; *hacerse el ~* play the fool.
topo, *s. m.* mole.
torbellino, *s. m.* whirlwind.
torcer, *v. a.* twist, turn.
torero, *s. m.* bullfighter.
tormenta, *s. f.* storm.
tormento, *s. m.* torment, pain.
tornarse, *v. n.* turn, become.
tornasol, *s. m.* sunflower.
tornillo, *s. m.* screw.
toro, *s. m.* bull.
torpe, *adj.* slow; stupid.
torre, *s. f.* tower.
torrente, *s. m.* torrent.
torta, *s. f.* cake.
tortilla, *s. f.* omelet.
tórtola, *s. f.* turtle-dove.
tortuga, *s. f.* tortoise; turtle.
tos, *s. f.* cough.
toser, *v. n.* cough.
tostada, *s. f.* toast.
tostado, *adj.* tanned (by the sun).
tostar, *v. a.* toast.
total, *adj. & s. m.* total.
trabajador, *adj.* industrious; – *s. m.* worker.
trabajar, *v. n.* work.
trabajo, *s. m.* work; labour.
trabar, *v. a.* entangle; *~ amistad* get acquainted with sy.
tradición, *s. f.* tradition.
tradicional, *adj.* traditional.
traducción, *s. f.* translation.
traducir, *v. a.* translate.
traer, *v. a.* bring; fetch; carry.
tráfico, *s. m.* traffic.
tragar, *v. a.* swallow.
tragedia, *s. f.* tragedy.
trágico, *adj.* tragic.
trago, *s. m.* swallow; drink; *echar un ~* take a drink.
traje, *s. m.* dress; *~ de baño* bathing-costume; *~ de etiqueta* evening dress.
tramontana, *s. f.* north wind.

trampa, *s. f.* trap.
trance, *s. m.* critical moment; *a todo ~* at any cost.
tranquilizar, *v. a.* calm, tranquilize; *v. n.* *~se* calm oneself.
tranquilo, *adj.* quiet.
transatlántico, *s. m.* transoceanic steamer, liner.
transcurrir, *v. n.* pass, elapse.
transcurso, *s. m.* lapse, course.
transeúnte, *adj.* transient; — *s. m.* passer-by.
transferir, *v. a.* transfer.
transigir, *v. n.* settle, compromise; agree.
tránsito, *s. m.* passage; thoroughfare.
transmisión, *s. f.* transmission; broadcasting.
transmisora, *s. f.* broadcasting station.
transmitir, *v. a.* transmit, broadcast.
transportar, *v. a.* transport, carry.
transporte, *s. m.* transport, transportation.
tranvía, *s. m.* tram.
trapo, *s. m.* piece of cloth; rag.
tráquea, *s. f.* trachea.
tras, *prep.* behind.
trasero, *adj.* rear, back; — *s. m.* rear, hind part.
trasladar, *v. a.* transfer; *v n.* *~se* move, change place of residence.
traslado, *s. m.* removal, transfer.
trasnochar, *v. n.* be up *or* spend all night.
traspasar, *v.a.* go through, pierce; transfer, trespass.
trasto, *s. m.* household furniture; *~s pl.* implements.
tratado, *s. m.* treaty; treatise.
tratamiento, *s. m.* medical treatment; form of address.
tratar, *v. a.* treat; handle.
trato, *s. m.* treatment; behaviour, manners; pact, agreement; close friendship.
través, *prep.*; *a ~ de* through, across; *de ~* *adv.* sideways.
travesía, *s. f.* voyage, crossing.
trayecto, *s. m.* distance; stretch; line.
trazar, *v. a.* draw, outline.
trébol, *s. m.* clover.
trece, *adj.* & *s. m.* thirteen.
treinta, *adj.* & *s. m.* thirty.
tremendo, *adj.* terrible, dreadful; huge, tremendous.
tren, *s. m.* train.
trepar, *v. n.* climb.
tres, *adj.* & *s. m.* three.
tribu, *s. f.* tribe.
tribuna, *s. f.* tribune.
tribunal, *s. m.* law-court.
trigo, *s. m.* wheat.
trillar, *v. a.* thresh.
trimestre, *s. m.* quarter (of a year); term.
trinchar, *v. a.* carve (meat).
trinchera, *s. f.* trench.
trineo, *s. m.* sledge.
tripa, *s. f.* tripe; intestines.
tripulación, *s. f.* crew.
triste, *adj.* sad; gloomy.
tristeza, *s. f.* sadness.

triunfar, *v. n.* triumph, succeed; win.
triunfo, *s. m.* triumph, victory.
trompeta, *s. f.* trumpet, bugle; — *s. m.* bugler.
tronar, *v. n.* thunder.
tronco, *s. m.* trunk, stalk, stem.
trono, *s. m.* throne.
tropa, *s. f.* troop.
tropezar, *v. n.* stumble; ~ *con* run into, come upon.
tropical, *adj.* tropical.
trópico, *adj.* tropic(al); — *s. m.* tropics.
tropiezo, *s. m.* obstacle, hitch.
trotar, *v. n.* trot.
trote, *s. m.* trot.
trozo, *s. m.* piece; part, fragment; selection, passage (of books).
truco, *s. m.* trick.
trucha, *s. f.* trout.
trueno, *s. m.* thunder.
tu, *adj. tus pl.* your.
tú, *pron.* you.
tubería, *s. f.* pipeline.
tubo, *s. m.* tubo, pipe.
tuerca, *s. f.* nut (hardware).
tuerto, *adj.* one-eyed.
tumba, *s. f.* tomb.
tumbar, *v. a.* knock down; *v. n.* ~*se* tumble.
tumbo, *s. m.* tumble, somersault.
tumor, *s. m.* tumour.
tumulto, *s. m.* mob; noisy crowd.
tunante, *s. m.* idler, ras. cal, rogue.
túnel, *s. m.* tunnel.
turbar, *v. a.* disturb, upset; confuse.
turbina, *s. f.* turbine.
turco, *adj.* Turkish; — *s. m.* Turk.
turismo, *s. m.* tourist traffic.
turista, *s. m., f.* tourist.
turno, *s. m.* turn; *de* ~ on duty.
tutear, *v. a.* use the familiar *tú* in addressing a person.
tutor, *s. m.* guardian.
tuyo, *adj.* (of) yours.

U

u, *conj.* (for *o*, before *o* or *ho) siete u ocho* seven or eight.
úlcera, *s. f.* ulcer, abscess.
ultimar, *v. a.* finish, end.
último, *adj.* last; final; latest.
ultramar, *s. m.* overseas.
ultramarinos, *s. m. pl.* colonial produce, groceries.
un, *m.;* **una,** *f.* a, an; one.
undécimo, *adj.* eleventh.
ungüento, *s. m.* ointment.
unico, *adj.* only, only one.
unidad, *s. f.* unity; unit.
unido, *adj.* united.
unificar, *v. a.* unite.
uniforme, *adj.* & *s. m.* uniform.
unión, *s. f.* union; unity; joining, joint; matrimony.
unir, *v. a.* tie together; link, attach; *v. n.* ~*se* unite, join.
universal, *adj.* universal.
universidad, *s. f.* university.
universo, *s. m.* universe, world.
uno, *adj.* & *s. m.* one;

somebody; ~s *pl.* some, a few.

untar, *v. a.* spread (butter); bribe; ~ *con grasa* grease; *v. n.* ~*se la cara* use cream on one's face.

uña, *s. f.* nail, fingernail, toenail; claw; *ser* ~ *y carne* be fast friends.

urbanidad, *s. f.* good manners.

urbano, *adj.* urban; urbane.

urgencia, *s. f.* urgency, hurry.

urgente, *adj.* pressing, urgent.

usado, *adj.* used, second-hand.

usanza, *s. f.* usage, custom.

usar, *v. a.* use; wear; *v. n* ~*se* be in use.

uso, *s. m.* use.

usted, *pron.* you.

usual, *adj.* usual, customary.

usura, *s. f.* usury.

utensilio, *s. m.* utensil; ~*s pl.* tools, implements.

útil, *adj.* useful; profitable.

utilidad, *s. f.* utility, usefulness.

utilizar, *v. a.* utilize.

uva, *s. f.* grape.

V

vaca, *s. f.* cow; beef.

vacación, *s. f.* vacation, time of rest; *ir de vacaciones* take a holiday.

vacante, *adj.* vacant; — *s. f.* vacancy.

vaciar, *v. a.* empty; drain.

vacío, *adj.* void, empty; unoccupied, vacant; — *s. m.* empty space, vacuum.

vagabundo, *s. f.* tramp.

vagar, *v. n.* rove, wander.

vago, *s. f.* loafer, tramp; — *adj.* vague, hazy.

vagón, *s. m.* railway carriage, goods-van, wagon.

vagoneta, *s. f.* lorry.

vainilla, *s. f.* vanilla.

vajilla, *s. f.* set of dishes.

vale, *s. m.* note; sales slip; coupon.

valentía, *s. f.* courage.

valer, *v. n.* cost; cause, result; be of value; be worth; — *s. m.* worth, merit.

valiente, *adj.* valiant, brave, courageous.

valioso, *adj.* valuable.

valor, *s. m.* value; price; courage; ~*es pl.* stocks, bonds, securities.

vals, *s. m.* waltz.

válvula, *s. f.* valve.

valle, *s. m.* valley.

vanidad, *s. f.* vanity.

vano, *adj.* vain; shallow; *en* ~ in vain.

vapor, *s. m.* steam; steamship.

vaquero, *s. m.* cowboy.

vara, *s. f.* twig; yardstick; rod, shaft.

varar, *v. n.* run aground.

variación, *s. f.* variation, change.

variado, *adj.* various, manifold.

variedad, *s. f.* variety, diversity.

vario, *adj.* various, varied; several.

varonil, *adj.* virile, manly.

vasija, *s. f.* container, receptacle.

vaso, *s. m.* (drinking) glass.
vatio, *s. m.* watt.
vaya! *int.* *¡~ una idea!* what an idea!
vecindad, *s. f.* vicinity, neighbourhood.
vecindario, *s. m.* population of a district.
vecino, *adj.* neighbouring, near-by; — *s. m.* neighbour; tenant.
vegetal, *adj.* & *s. m.* vegetable.
vehículo, *s. m.* vehicle.
veinte, *adj.* & *s. m.* twenty.
vejez, *s. f.* old age.
vejiga, *s. f.* bladder; vesicle.
vela, *s. f.* candle; sail.
velada, *s. f.* evening party.
velar, *v. n.* stay up, stay awake.
velo, *s. m.* veil; film (thin coat).
velocidad, *s. f.* velocity, speed.
veloz, *adj.* swift, fast.
vena, *s. f.* vein.
venado, *s. m.* deer.
vencer, *v. a.* vanquish, defeat; overcome; prevail; win; *v. n.* *~se* control (one's feelings).
venda, *s. f.* bandage.
vendar, *v. a.* bandage, dress.
vendedor, *s. m.* vendor, seller.
vender, *v. a.* sell.
veneno, *s. m.* poison, venom.
venenoso, *adj.* poisonous, venomous.
venganza. *s. f.* revenge, vengeance.
vengar, *v. a.* avenge; *v. n.* *~se* take revenge.
venir, *v. n.* come; *la semana que viene* next week; *~ bien* suit; *~ mal* be inconvenient.
venta, *s. f.* sale, selling.
ventaja, *s. f.* advantage, profit; lead.
ventajoso, *adj.* advantageous.
ventana, *s. f.* window.
ventanilla, *s. f.* ticket *or* car window.
ventilación, *s. f.* ventilation.
ventilador, *s. m.* electric fan, ventilator.
ventilar, *v. a.* air, ventilate.
ventoso, *adj.* windy.
ventura, *s. f.* happiness; luck.
ver, *v. a.* see; *¡a ver!* let's see!; *hasta más ~* see you again; *v. n.* *~se* meet, see each other.
veraneante, *s. m.*, *f.* holiday maker.
veranear, *v. n.* spend the summer.
veraneo, *s. m.* vacation, summer holiday.
verano, *s. m.* summer.
veras, *s. f. pl.* reality, truth; *de ~* in truth, really.
verdad, *s. f.* truth; *¿~?* isn't it so?
verdadero, *adj.* true; real.
verde, *adj.* green.
verdura, *s. f.* vegetables.
vereda, *s. f.* path.
vergüenza, *s. f.* shame; shyness; *me da ~* I'm ashamed.
verificar, *v. a.* verify.
versión, *s. f.* version; translation.
verso, *s. m.* line of poetry; poem.

vestíbulo, *s. m.* vestibule; lobby.
vestido, *s. m.* dress; garments, clothing.
vestir, *v. a. & n.* dress; wear; *~se* dress, clothe oneself.
veterinario, *s. m.* veterinary (surgeon).
vez, *s. f.* turn (in line); time; *una ~* once; *dos veces* twice; *muchas veces* many times, often; *a la ~* at once, simultaneously; *alguna ~, algunas veces* sometimes; *a veces* occasionally; *cada ~* each time; *en ~ de* instead of; *otra ~* again; *tal ~* perhaps.
vía, *s. f.* track; route; — *adv.* via, by way of.
viaducto, *s. m.* viaduct.
viajar, *v. n.* travel.
viaje, *s. m.* travel; trip; *¡buen ~!* have a good trip!
viajero, *s. m.* traveller; passenger.
víbora, *s. f.* viper.
vibrar, *v. n.* vibrate.
vicio, *s. m.* vice, defect.
vicioso, *adj.* defective, given to vice.
víctima, *s. f.* victim.
victoria, *s. f.* victory.
victorioso, *adj.* victorious, triumphant.
vid, *s. f.* vine.
vida, *s. f.* life; way of living; liveliness.
vidrio, *s. m.* glass (material); pane of glass.
viejo, *adj.* old; — *s. m.* old man.
viento, *s. m.* wind.
vientre, *s. m.* belly.
viernes, *s. m.* Friday; *Viernes Santo* Good Friday.
vigilar, *v. a.* watch, guard.
vigor, *s. m.* vigour, strength; *en ~* in effect, in force.
vil, *adj.* vile, mean.
villa, *s. f.* town; country house, villa.
vinagre, *s. f.* vinegar.
vino, *s. m.* wine.
viña, *s. f.* vineyard.
viola, *s. f.* viola.
violento, *adj.* violent, impulsive; *sentirse ~* be embarrassed; feel out of place.
violeta, *s. f.* violet; lilac (colour).
violín, *s. m.* violin.
violinista, *s. m., f.* violinist.
violoncelo, *s. m.* violoncello.
viraje, *s. m.* curve, bend; cornering, turning.
virar, *v. n.* turn. curve.
virgen, *adj. & s. f.* virgin.
viril, *adj.* male, virile.
virtud, *s. f.* virtue, good quality; efficacy.
virtuoso, *adj.* virtuous; — *s. m.* virtuoso.
viruela, *s. f.* smallpox.
visar, *v. a.* visa.
visible, *adj.* visible.
visión, *s. f.* vision; view, opinion.
visita, *s. f.* visit; *hacer una ~* pay a visit.
visitar, *v. a.* visit, call on; make a call; inspect.
víspera, *s. f.* eve, day before.
vista[1], *s. f.* eyesight; sight; view; *corto de ~* nearsighted; *de ~* by sight; *en ~ de* in view of; *¡hasta la ~!* so long!
vista[2], *s. m.* customs

officer.

visto, *pp.*; *por lo ~* apparently; *está ~* it's evident; — *s. m.* approval.

vistoso, *adj.* showy; good-looking.

viuda, *s. f.* widow.

viudo, *s. m.* widower.

¡viva! *int.* long live!

víveres, *s. m. pl.* provisions.

vivienda, *s. f.* dwelling.

vivir, *v. n.* live, exist; dwell.

vivo, *adj.* alive; vivid; intense; *a lo ~* vividly.

vocablo, *s. m.* word.

vocabulario, *s. m.* vocabulary.

volante, *s. m.* steering wheel.

volar, *v. n.* fly; blow up.

volcán, *s. m.* volcano.

volcar, *v. a.* overturn; *v. n.* turn over.

voltio, *s. m.* volt.

voluntad, *s. f.* will; *buena ~* good will.

voluntario, *adj.* voluntary; — *s. m.* volunteer.

volver, *v. a.* turn (pages); return, give back; *v. n.* return, go back; turn (road); *~ en sí* recover consciousness; *volveré a escribirle* I'll write him again; *~se loco* become crazy.

vomitar, *v. n.* vomit.

vómito, *s. m.* vomiting, vomit.

vosotros, *pron. m. pl.* you.

voto, *s. m.* vote.

voz, *s. f.* voice.

vuelo, *s. m.* flight.

vuelta, *s. f.* turn, revolution; curve; change; *a la ~* upon returning; *a la ~ de correo* by return of post; *dar una ~* go for a walk.

vuestro, *adj.& pron.* yours

vulgar, *adj.* vulgar, coarse; common.

vulgo, *s. m.* mob, populace.

X

xenofobia, *s. f.* xenophobia.

xilografía, *s. f.* xylography.

Y

y, *conj.* and.

ya, *adv.* already; *~ no* no longer; *~ que* since; *~ lo creo* of course; *¡ya, ya!* sure!; *~ voy* I'm coming!

yacimiento, *s. m.* layer; stratum.

yanki, *s. m.* yankee.

yegua, *s. f.* mare.

yema, *s. f.* bud; yolk.

yerba, *s. f.* herb; grass.

yerno, *s. m.* son-in-law.

yerro, *s. m.* error, mistake.

yeso, *s. m.* plaster.

yo, *pron.* I; *~ mismo* I myself.

yodo, *s. m.* iodine.

yugo, *s m.* yoke.

yunque *m.* anvil.

yute, *s.* jute.

Z

zafiro, *s. m.* sapphire.

zagal, *s. m.* shepherd boy.
zaguán, *s. m.* entrance, hall, vestibule.
zalamería, *s. f.* flattery.
zambo, *s. m.* half-breed (Negro and Indian).
zambullida, *s. f.* dive, plunge.
zambullir, *v. a.* plunge; *v. n.* *~se* dive.
zanahoria, *s. f.* carrot.
zanco, *s. m.* stilt.
zanja, *s. f.* ditch, trench.
zapatería, *s. f.* shoemaker's shop.
zapatero, *s. m.* shoemaker.
zapatilla, *s. f.* slipper.
zapato, *s. m.* shoe.
zarpa, *s. f.* paw, claw.
zarpar, *v. n.* weigh anchor; sail.
zarza, *s. f.* bramble.
zarzuela, *s. f.* musical comedy.
zona, *s. f.* district, zone.
zoológico, *adj.* zoological; *jardín ~* zoological gardens.
zorra, *s. f.* vixen.
zorro, *adj.* cunning, crafty; — *s. m.* fox.
zozobrar, *v. n.* capsize, founder, sink.
zurcir, *v. a.* darn, mend.
zurdo, *adj.* left-handed.
zurrir, *v. n.* whizz, buzz.

zagal, s. m. shepherd boy
zaguán, s. m. entrance hall, vestibule
zalamería, s. f. flattery
zambo, s. m. half-breed (Negro and Indian)
zambullida, s. f. dive, plunge
zambullir, v. t. plunge, submerge
zanahoria, s. f. carrot
zanco, s. m. stilt
zanja, s. f. ditch, trench
zapatería, s. f. shoemaker's shop
zapatero, s. m. shoemaker
zapatilla, s. f. slipper
zapato, s. m. shoe
zarpa, s. f. paw, claw
zarpar, v. i. weigh anchor, sail
zarza, s. f. bramble
zarzuela, s. f. musical comedy
zona, s. f. district, zone
zoológico, adj. zoological; jardín [illegible], zoological gardens
zorra, s. f. vixen
zorro, adj. cunning; s. f. [illegible], s. m. fox
zozobrar, v. i. capsize, founder, sink
zurdo, adj. left-handed
zurrar, v. t. whip, beat